Spontaneous Shrines and the Public
Memorialization of Death

Spontaneous Shrines and the Public Memorialization of Death

EDITED BY

Jack Santino

First published in 2006 by
PALGRAVE MACMILLAN™
175 Fifth Avenue, New York, N.Y. 10010 and
Houndmills, Basingstoke, Hampshire, England RG21 6XS
Companies and representatives throughout the world.

PALGRAVE MACMILLAN is the global academic imprint of the Palgrave Macmillan division of St. Martin's Press, LLC and of Palgrave Macmillan Ltd. Macmillan® is a registered trademark in the United States, United Kingdom and other countries. Palgrave is a registered trademark in the European Union and other countries.

ISBN 1–4039–6888–8

Library of Congress Cataloging-in-Publication Data is available from the Library of Congress.

A catalogue record for this book is available from the British Library.

Design by Newgen Imaging Systems (P) Ltd., Chennai, India.

First edition: April 2006

10 9 8 7 6 5 4 3 2 1

Printed in the United States of America.

Contents

List of Illustrations   vii

Introduction   1
Jack Santino

1 Performative Commemoratives: Spontaneous
   Shrines and the Public Memorialization of Death   5
   Jack Santino

2 Communicative Commemoration and Graveside Shrines:
   Princess Diana, Jim Morrison, My "Bro" Max, and
   Boogs the Cat   17
   Jeannie Banks Thomas

3 Mourning in Protest: Spontaneous Memorials
   and the Sacralization of Public Space   41
   Harriet F. Senie

4 "We'll Watch Out for Liza and The Kids": Spontaneous
   Memorials and Personal Response at the Pentagon, 2001   57
   Margaret R. Yocom

5 Oh Did You See the Ashes Come Thickly
   Falling Down? Poems Posted in the Wake of
   September 11   99
   Steve Zeitlin

6 Louisiana Roadside Memorials: Negotiating an
   Emerging Tradition   119
   Maida Owens

7 "Like a Trace": The Spontaneous Shrine as a Cultural
   Expression of Grief   147
   Hege Westgaard

8   A Memorial Wall in Philadelphia   177
    Jonathan Lohman

9   Twelve Aggie Angels: Content Analysis of the Spontaneous
    Shrines Following the 1999 Bonfire Collapse
    at Texas A&M University   215
    Sylvia Grider

10 "The Call of the Ice": Tragedy and Vernacular
    Responses of Resistance, Heroic Reconstruction,
    and Reclamation   233
    Diane E. Goldstein and Diane Tye

11 The Missing and Photography: The Uses and Misuses
    of Globalization   255
    Ariel Dorfman

12 *El Dia de los Muertos* in the USA: Cultural Ritual
    as Political Communication   261
    Regina Marchi

13 Signifying Places of Atrocity   285
    Ralph Hartley

14 Forty Years of Conflict: State, Church, and Spontaneous
    Representation of Massacres and Murder in Guatemala   305
    Matthew J. Taylor and Michael K. Steinberg

15 Trains of Workers, Trains of Death: Some Reflections
    after the March 11 Attacks in Madrid   333
    Cristina Sánchez-Carretero

Contributors   349

Index   355

List of Illustrations

2.1 Jim Morrison's graveside shrine, Paris   20
2.2 Photos left at Jim Morrison's graveside shrine, Paris   21
2.3 Greeting card left at graveside shrine, Salt Lake City, Utah   29
2.4 Graveside shrine for a deceased pet, Ogden, Utah   35
4.1 At the memorial, Capt. H.T. Helmkamp promises his
     fallen friend, "We'll watch out for Liza & the kids"   58
4.2 St. Bartholomew's School poster features the hands
     of their students. Damaged wall of the Pentagon
     appears in background   59
4.3 At the Pentagon memorial, a boy gives tribute to
     firefighters at the World Trade Center   63
4.4 With a foam-core poster of their faces, Native Americans
     from Marysville, Washington, tell visitors to the memorial
     that "TULALIP BINGO- CASINO EMPLOYEES
     WILL NEVER FORGET SEPTEMBER 11 2001"   72
5.1 The Twin Towers personified   102
5.2 Posting Poems on Canal Street   103
5.3 "Goin' Home"—Union Square   104
5.4 "Dear Steven, I Never Met You"   113
6.1 Memorial to Jerry and Todd maintained by the
     family members   122
6.2 A cross outside Jennings on the Cajun prairie with a
     Cajun Mardi Gras mask   126
6.3 An elaborate cross in the median of I-49 near Opelousas   128
8.1 The mural on 50th and Wood lawn   179
8.2 Slain child, grieving mother   179
8.3 (a) "Paul Robeson" 4502 Chestnut Street. Artist: Peter
     Pagast.; (b)"Dr. J" Ridge Avenue and Green Street.
     Artist: Kent Twitchell   182
8.4 "Tribute to Atiya," 17th and North Street. MAP photo   189
8.5 "Sunrise—hope for a better tomorrow"   192
8.6 Decorated portrait   198

9.1   Aggie Bonfire   218
9.2   Large plain cross   225
9.3   Shadow cross   226
9.4   Set of twelve angels   228
10.1 Memorial's placement on the bridge overlooking
      the beach. The shrine was constructed of stuffed
      animals and bouquets of flowers   235
10.2 Flowers and stuffed animals tucked into the chain links   236
10.3 Gravesite of Jessie Elliot and Adam Wall   240
12.1 Pan de Muerto offered in memory of a dead migrant   274
12.2 Commemorating unidentified migrants   275
13.1 Sidewalk shrine in the business district of Zagreb   291
13.2 Mothers and wives of the missing mourn with bricks
      in front of the United Nations compound, Zagreb   292
14.1 Inside the Catholic Church in San Juan Cotzal, Quiché   310
14.2 This 15-meter-wide mural is painted on the
      perimeter wall of the Catholic Church in Cantabal,
      Ixcán. This full-color mural was painted in January
      2001, a full four years after signing the peace treaty
      in December 1996   311
14.3 Small wooden crosses on the inside wall of the
      Catholic Church in Nebaj, Quiché record the
      name and date of death of victims   316
14.4 The large monument in Cuarto Pueblo, Ixcán. Built
      by local residents, this white and blue monument
      records the names of over 470 residents murdered
      in Cuarto Pueblo, Xalbal, Zunil, Los Angeles, and
      Ixtahuacan Chiquito by the Guatemalan military in
      March in April 1982   317
14.5 Monument of an indigenous women in the plaza of
      Chimaltenango. An indigenous woman breaks an
      M-16 rifle symbolizing the end of 40 years of civil war.
      This monument occupies a prominent place in the
      plaza of Chimaltenango   318
15.1 A family lighting candles at the shrines in Atocha
      next to a banner used in the demonstration on
      Friday, March 12   335
15.2 Shrines at Atocha train station   337
15.3 Shrines at El Pozo train station   337
15.4 "Colombia cries for the 11M victims"   339
15.5 White palms in Atocha   342
15.6 Black ribbon: "Sergio, 17 year old, why?"   342
15.7 Child's drawing   344

Introduction

Jack Santino

The articles in this volume focus on a wide range of materials: roadside crosses in Louisiana; the responses to September 11 in New York and Washington, DC, and the Texas A&M bonfire collapse among other. While certain well-known tragedies such as the Oklahoma City bombing, the death of Princess Diana, and the September 11 attacks have brought a great deal of mass media attention to the contemporary mourning ritual of spontaneous shrines, this volume does not attempt to be universally inclusive of every such tragedy. That is impossible. Instead, this book will deal directly with certain instances such as 9/11 in New York and at the Pentagon, the Texas A&M Bonfire collapse, as well as traffic fatalities, gang-related violence, and drowning. Many articles analyze the spontaneous shrine tradition with reference to such widely known events as the death of Princess Diana and the Oklahoma City bombing. These articles provide an analytical framework for discussing spontaneous, vernacular responses to untimely death.

An important point of the book is that all of these examples share the qualities of simultaneously commemorating deceased individuals, both celebrities (e.g. Princess Diana, or JFK Jr.) and noncelebrities; at the same time they suggest an attitude toward or a position on a public social issue. I term these two qualities commemoration and performativity. The commemorative aspect is self-evident. I am using the term "performativity," after the linguist J. L. Austin, to refer to the fact that in each case of spontaneous shrine there is a component of addressing a social issue, of trying to convince people, of trying to make something happen. Commemoration can be and often is private. The public aspects of the shrines are due to the social conditions that caused the deaths and the political issues they reference.

Not every public death memorialization shares these two poles of a continuum equally. Some, such as the AIDS quilt, the actions of the Madres de la Plaza, and the Bloody Sunday commemorations in Northern Ireland, clearly emphasize the performative. The people involved are "mourning in protest," to use the title of Harriet Senie's article in this volume; they want to draw attention to a social issue and convince a broad public of the accuracy of their position on it. On the other hand, many roadside crosses emphasize the deaths of the individuals more than the conditions involved in the tragedy. Still, elements of commemoration and performativity are present in each of these cases to a greater or lesser extent.

This volume establishes the spontaneous shrine as a genre of mourning ritual. It examines the dynamics involved in these shrines and memorials, through case studies based on ethnographic fieldwork, and it theorizes this phenomenon generally. The chapters of the book include specific studies by Grider, Zeitlin, Yocom, Lohman, Owens, Westgaard, Sánchez-Carretero and Goldstein and Tye; more widely ranging and theoretical works by Santino, Thomas, and Senie; and examples of more overtly political uses by Marchi, Dorfman Hartley, and Taylor and Steinberg. The articles reflect work done in Philadelphia, Louisiana, California, Washington DC, Paris, Newfoundland, Spain, New York, Texas, Northern Ireland, Norway, Guatemala, Rwanda, and the former Yugoslavia.

The first three articles, by Santino, Thomas, and Senie, take stock of the nature of these public displays of grief and mourning. Jeannie B. Thomas and Harriet Senie both provide overviews of several such phenomena, suggest terminologies for dealing with them, and identify relationships among them. My article analyzes the dynamics and nature of the spontaneous shrine phenomenon with respect to the ways they are related to public issues, and the ways they construct and display relationships. Thomas' article includes the examination of objects left at actual gravesites. Senie suggests that the responses in New York to 9/11 are qualitatively different from those that preceded them, in that the World Trade Center towers themselves were memorialized because it was not immediately known who had lived and who had died. Steve Zeitlin examines the poetry inspired by the devastation, including those notes written as if in the voice of the deceased. Margaret Yocom writes of the often overlooked 9/11 shrines at the Pentagon, which she has documented.

From 9/11 we move to roadside memorials. Not all traffic fatalities result in a memorial that is maintained over time. The focus of Maida Owens' article is on the factors that determine whether a memorial is built and whether it is maintained, and the negotiations involved therein. Hege Westgaard provides a case study from Norway. A young boy killed on a moped in a small village spawned a number of sometimes competing ritual events, including church-sponsored services and roadside shrines and commemorations by his friends. The author examines the ritual nature of the shrines and the different constructions of death in these constructions.

Having dealt with 9/11 and roadside shrines we move to other kinds of events and spontaneous memorializations. Jonathan Lohman examines the mural of a young murder victim in Philadelphia, its reception by the neighborhood, and some of the ritual activities that take place at that site. Sylvia Grider, a professor at Texas A&M, directs the Bonfire Memorial Project there, which she initiated after 12 students were killed in the collapse of the bonfire materials in November, 1999. In her article she examines the artifacts left at the site as archeological evidence that expresses religious and relational attitudes and beliefs. In the next chapter, Diane E. Goldstein and Diane Tye examine grief and memory that is resistant to the official attempts to deal with the deaths of three boys who drowned in a small Newfoundland fishing village. The authors place the memorial materials within a larger web—that of the village's identity as fishing community, its relationship with the government bureaucracy, ghost belief, as well as other expressions of mourning.

The final articles present materials that are more overtly political and performative (as I use the term). Regina Marchi discusses the historical relationship between political protest and death rituals in Latin America noting recent examples of politicized Day of the Dead altars and activities by community activists there (e.g. altars publicly displayed for destroyed rainforests and murdered street children. Similarly, in the United States, altars and processions are used not only to honor the dead but also to challenge American policies. Every November 1, for example, a religious service is held and wooden crosses are placed along the border wall, naming those immigrants who were killed. Ariel Dorfman examines the use of photography in publicizing the identities of disappeared men, women and children in Argentina, Chile, and other countries of North America. Marking the sites of genocidal conflict in war-ravaged areas can be dangerous if the regime in power desires these memories be erased. Ralph Hartley examines such sites and memorials in both Rwanda and the former Yugoslavia (Bosnia, Serbia, and Croatia). Matthew J. Taylor and Michael K. Steinberg examine the memories and memorials deriving from different sources—the church, the state, and the people—that refer to the 200,000 murdered and disappeared Guatemalans, both indigenous and Ladino, of that county's "hidden war." Finally, Cristina Sánchez-Carretero examines the relationships of spontaneous shrine construction to popular political protest in Madrid, following the March 11, 2004 terrorist bombings there.

The authors and the editor hope that the chapters both illuminate each other and add up to a larger understanding of the phenomena, and, perhaps, to draw attention to the ways people commemorate death publicly to address social ills, thereby serving the cause of life.

Chapter 1

Performative Commemoratives: Spontaneous Shrines and the Public Memorialization of Death

Jack Santino

Spontaneous shrines have emerged, both in the United States and internationally, as a primary way to mourn those who have died a sudden or shocking death, and to acknowledge the circumstances of the deaths. The Mourning Wall at the site of the Oklahoma City bombing; the so-called flower revolution in Great Britain after the death of Princess Diana; "Ground Zero" in New York after the terrorist attacks of September 11, 2001, as well as roadside crosses that mark the site of automobile fatalities and memorial walls painted for victims of urban violence are all dramatic examples of public mourning.

As a relatively recent and growing international phenomenon, spontaneous shrines need to be theorized. To do so it is productive to see them in the context of other and in certain key ways similar public and political memorializations of death, such as the AIDS quilt, the demonstrations of the Madres de la Plaza that call attention to the "disappeared" children in Argentina and Chile, or the Bloody Sunday commemorations in Northern Ireland. Also, gang memorial walls, roadside crosses, along with all the other spontaneous shrines (as I term them) that are continuously created and remain visible within the culturescape are of importance here. Central to all of these is the conjunction of the memorializing of personal deaths within the framework of the social conditions that caused those deaths, the performative with the commemorative (or celebratory). To commemorate something or someone is, in a sense, to celebrate something or someone. I am using the terms equivalently, but not interchangeably.

A good example of the type of event I am thinking of is called the "Transformation Project," devoted to victims of domestic violence. I attended an Operation Transformation ceremony at Bowling Green State University (BGSU) in October 2003. The event was sponsored by the BGSU Women's Center, and was held inside a Christian chapel on campus. In front of the prominent cross were 22 votive candles, in purple glass. Purple is the color of mourning; 22 victims were being remembered.

October 1 was the unveiling event of a month-long public display of 22 two-dimensional silhouettes, each shrouded in black cloth. As each effigy was unveiled, a different woman narrated the life story as if it were her own: "My name is ————. I am ———— years old and have ———— children. On ———— I was shot to death in front of my children by my estranged husband. My name was ————; remember my name." Audience members included families of the victims as well as BGSU students. Some of the women reading the brief biographies had trouble maintaining their composure. The victims and the audience members were both younger and older; Black, white, and Latino. All were from the surrounding area.

This ritualesque event, the unveiling, simultaneously memorialized deceased individuals and drew attention to and tried to mobilize action regarding a social problem; that is, domestic violence, the cause of their deaths. Both aspects—the personal identity of the victims and the social malignancy that led to their deaths—were emphatically manifest in the presentation. The readers called attention to the life stories and personal relationships the victims had enjoyed, and the entire event was presented in the context of domestic violence as a gendered crime. Moreover, the ceremony borrowed heavily from traditional Christian ritual.

In a sense, death has always been publicly memorialized. Think of the funeral procession of hearse and cars down the street; the rituals held in houses of worship and in cemeteries. In these and other cases, though, participation in the ritual activities is restricted to a particular group—family and friends, for instance. In this article I am referring to the tendency to commemorate a deceased individual in front of an undifferentiated public that can then become participatory if it so chooses.

First, then, I will explore the concept of the public, beginning with rituals generally, not just rituals concerned with death and mourning.

Rituals in Public

Historian Samuel Kinser cites the slaughtering of "steers and other animals before the Pope and other Roman notables after a parade through the city" as reported in a document circa AD 1140 as the earliest report of festive customs held prior to Lent, that is, Mardi Gras or carnival (Kinser 1990: 3). This is clearly an expressive public event in that it is a festive or ritual act. Public places can be either indoors or outdoors—a church or a plaza for instance. In many ritual events audiences are present but are restricted to, for example, women only, or men, or friends and relatives. In a sense all rituals are public, in that an audience of some kind is necessary to witness and validate the changes wrought by the ritual or at least proclaimed by it. Here we think of ritual as dramatic social enactments that are thought by the participants to have some transformational or confirmatory agency and to derive this power from an overarching parahuman authority, such as a deity, the state, an institution such as a university, and so on; rather than ritual in the sense of custom or even more broadly, routine. The movement in scholarship (e.g., performance studies) toward ritual as public display—that is, applying theories derived from the study of ritual to contemporary public display events—parallels the social development of performative actions intended to produce change that will be seen by a broad and undifferentiated public. Most official rituals do not have general audiences—you have to be invited to attend or be a member of the group involved. However, in events such as the Transformation Project we see public ritualistic events that invite participation from a broad audience.

Clearly the concept of public display is a broad one. Abrahams suggested it with reference to events such as "the parade, the pageant, or the ball game . . . expositions and meets, games and carnivals and auctions" (1981: 303–304). He uses the term to refer to "planned-for public occasions" in which "accumulated feelings may be channeled into contest, drama, or some other form of display," and which also includes "actions and objects [which] are invested with meaning and values are put on display" (1981: 303). Handelman has suggested that we deal with the problem of imprecise terminologies such as ritual, festival, spectacle, rite, and so forth, by developing taxonomies and analytical methodologies based on the events' designs; that is, according to what the particular event is intended to accomplish socially (Handelman 1990). Ronald L. Grimes suggests the term "public ritual" as an inclusive category "capable of including most examples of civil and secular ritual" (Grimes 1982). In a study of a series of "living celebrations" that I curated for the Smithsonian Institution in the early 1980s, I called the staged presentations of traditional cultures, designed in part by the participants who were themselves members of the community whose traditions were being represented, "rites of public presentation" (Santino 1988), a concept related both to the ideas of public display and also to Barbara Myerhoff's concept of "definitional ceremonies"

(Myerhoff 1978: 185–186). I made the point that while the nature of celebratory and ritualistic events were necessarily transformed when staged in a museum setting for an audience that would not otherwise participate in them or be familiar with them in their own lives, the events in question became ritualistic in a different way. Not simply because they were theatrical, but because while they were presented to the public as a kind of entertainment (however edifying), in practice they turned out to be something else, a hybrid form during which audiences actually participated in rites which previously had been foreign to them. The role of the audience members was transformed from passive observer, as at the theatre, to active participant, as at a ritual. Cristina Sánchez-Carretero has examined this phenomenon of public (and private) events being transformed by institutional presentation for the edification of a broad audience of people outside the tradition (2003). One important aspect of public display is the domain in which groups choose certain events of their own culture to publicly present themselves as a group to outsiders: museum, university, street festival, and so on.

Problematizing the "Public"

I have referred above to at least three senses of the term "public": (1) done before an audience; (2) performed in institutionalized contexts such as universities or museums for people unfamiliar with the tradition, and (3) set out before a spectatorship whose make-up is fluid and unpredictable. Still, the concept of "public" needs to be further problematized. For instance, on June 2, 1995, I visited a rag well, that is, a holy well with healing properties, in Dungiven, County Derry, Northern Ireland. This one was surrounded, indeed, almost obscured, by trees and bushes on which were tied rags, strings, ropes, and other pieces of cloth left by previous visitors as votive offerings. The well is located close to the ruins of the medieval priory of St. Mary, overlooking a spectacular view of the valley below, but is easily missed as one walks onto the grounds. Once seen, however, it is unforgettable. The outer branches are unadorned. Only inside the copse, the thicket, the "scrubbery" as they say in Ulster, surrounding the well itself, are the thick, twisted, gnarled, and dense branches covered by rags and materials of all sorts and colors. It is both a wall made of rags and branches, and an environment, a space into which one must enter to get to the small rock basin with its holy water. Most of the rags are faded and in various stages of disintegration. Perhaps people leave these in the belief that as the rags disintegrate the illness to which they correspond will also fade. However, people have to know where it is in order to see it. My friend and I each left a token of our presence—I tore my handkerchief in two and we tied them to branches. Broadly speaking, as tokens of our having visited, the rags are at least in part, memorials. Clearly the motivations that lead to such public acts of memorialization are many and complex, having to do with sickness, belief, personal devotion, attempts to influence that which is beyond human control, and also a need to demonstrate to an audience one does not know that one participated, that one contributed to this monument, that one was here, albeit anonymously. Ironically this rag well is strikingly visual, yet you cannot see it under usual circumstances. Memorialization or commemoration of one's visit is one aspect of the display of cloth here. Performativity—the intent to effect a cure, to make something happen—is another. Both aspects may be present simultaneously in the actions of any one individual who leaves such a token at this place.

The linguist J. L. Austin assigned the term "performative utterances" to those statements that accomplish a social change, statements such as "I do," "I now pronounce you husband and wife," or " I christen this ship . . ." and so on (1962). These statements, often found in rites of passage, cause the effect they declare. Here I am extending the term from utterances to events that attempt to cause social change.

Public decorating for and ritual marking of special times and places is of course a well-known phenomenon internationally. Beyond the obvious examples of domestic and institutional decoration for important religious and calendrical occasions should be added the tendencies to ritualize present absences such as the use of yellow ribbons to denote concern for hostages, or green willows to denote awareness of absent lovers. Likewise, the deceased have been ritualized in most societies for which we have evidence. When death is sudden, untimely, or unexpected, as in for instance automobile accidents, some cultures have found it appropriate to mark the place where the death occurred (see Gillis 1994 for a general discussion of commemorations). Roadside crosses are found throughout the American Southwest and Latin America for instance, as well as in many European countries. In the last decades of the twentieth century this custom has been adapted internationally. No longer a regional tradition, the marking of the place of a shocking death with a spontaneous shrine consisting of flowers and personal memorabilia has become part of the global expressive repertoire, seen most dramatically at the site of the Oklahoma City bombing, in London and Paris after the death of Princess Diana, and in New York after September 11, 2001, Madrid after March 11, 2004, and London after July 7, 2005. In all these examples, the ribbons, flowers, and so forth reference a person or a group who are in a remarkable or significant condition of absence: hostage, distant lover, soldier sent to war, murdered celebrity, martyred leader. Just as importantly, they express an attitude toward that condition and the larger contexts in which it exists: support for the soldier's cause, faithfulness toward the lover, and condemnation of violence. The attitudes expressed are also intended to be shared by those who view the artifacts, to convince, and to have an effect on the aggregate spectatorship. Thus these displays can be said to be performative and are frequently done in conjunction with public events, such as silent witness gatherings. It is their performative aspects that necessitate that they be displayed in public. With most deaths, private mourning and flowers at the grave are sufficient. When the site of an untimely death or its metaphorical analogue is so adorned the element of performativity is being exercised through these spontaneous shrines. We can see a duality in the yellow ribbon displays and the rag wells, but in spontaneous shrines the duality is expressly that they both commemorate deceased individuals and suggest an attitude toward a related public issue.

The examples of such "performative commemoratives" are legion in the contemporary world, as I've already indicated. From the Mourning Wall in Oklahoma City in response to a bombing of a federal building, to memorial walls commemorating gang-member deaths, or the school shootings in Littleton, Colorado in 1999, spontaneous shrines and the public marking of the places where death has occurred have become a primary response. They are no longer emergent. They have clearly emerged as a contemporary mourning ritual or tradition, under certain circumstances—that of untimely death. Concomitantly, newspapers and other media frequently (ritualistically?) feature these shrines as part of their coverage of these events. Here, the media helps spread the tradition, much as David Waldstreicher, following Benedict Anderson (1983), argues that American Independence Day customs were nationalized and standardized by print journalism (1995). Moreover, televised "watches" of the life-cycle events and funerals of public figures such as Princess Diana or John F. Kennedy, Jr., have become part of the rituals themselves (Dayan and Katz 1992). How these traditions have coalesced and spread at this point in history is an important question (see Santino 1992b; 1999), but we should also remember that the actual instances of ritual commemoration are specific to particular times, places, cultures, societies, and people. Here we can see personal, popular actions—the laying on of flowers and wreaths—melded with international media coverage in an interesting conjunction of the intensely personal with the global.

On the other hand, actions such as leaving a piece of rag at a holy well, while it may imply the presence of a deity or a supernatural being as a witness, may simply be thought of as a direct (magical) act in which the rag corresponds to the affliction. The presence of the rag implies a potential audience of future visitors to the well. This points to the fact that ritual in the stricter sense of the term is instrumental: it is believed to be able to effect change. Healing rituals may or may not be successful, but they are thought to be potentially efficacious, regardless of the outcome. Rites of passage are generally accepted among scholars as a social mechanism of status change, although we have all probably had the experience of undergoing some life-cycle event—a birthday, perhaps, or a confirmation—that we felt meant nothing. I would suggest that the materials we analytically call rituals are emically efficacious. Thus they appear to outsiders as largely, even primarily, metaphorical, symbolic, and expressive, regardless of how functional they are thought to be among participants. For devout Roman Catholics, for instance, the bread and wine of the mass is truly, literally, transformed into the body and blood of Christ. For Pentecostals, the Holy Spirit is genuinely present during their services. The problem arises precisely in the kinds of literature we have been referring to, in which other cultural performances are generally categorized along with, or as, ritual. Analytically they share symbolic ceremonialism, cultural patterning, and framing; but for the participants a ritual is a conscious means to a desired end and less a doing for its own sake (Schieffelin 1998). Further, as was mentioned with the case of the rag well, there are multiple intentions involved.

The rag well described above is a prime example of a custom that involves public display, but the well itself is hidden and hard to find. One must know where it is or seek it out. Thus the clientele for this healing well is self-selected. On the other hand, a parade in a city or town will be witnessed by many people who do not set out to watch it. Similarly, a display of festive decoration on the facade of a building, a yellow ribbon, or a spontaneous shrine will be seen by an indiscriminate audience of passers-by. The term "public" here has to do with spectatorship, witness, participation, and social transformation as well as a Habermasian sense of shared civic interest (Habermas 1995).

Performative commemoratives—the concept includes but is not restricted to spontaneous shrines—invite participation, unlike the funeral procession one happens to run across. They also invite interpretation. Once set out before an undifferentiated public, the polysemy inherent in these assemblages allow for a broad range of readings and associations by passersby, regardless of the initial intentions of the originators (Santino 1986; 1992b).

In Northern Ireland in 1992, I was asked to write a catalogue article for a photographic exhibit focusing on sites of political murders, and the flowers, notes, and memorabilia people leave at such places. I deliberately set out to develop an appropriate term and vocabulary for the phenomenon. I decided on "spontaneous shrines" for several reasons (Santino 1992a).

At that time, to my knowledge, the press had not yet begun to use the condescending and inaccurate term "makeshift memorials." I use the word "spontaneous" to indicate the unofficial nature of these; the fact that, for example, a 14-year-old girl decided to place a note and a rose at the site of her father's unexpected murder by a paramilitary gunman in Belfast. No one told her to. These are not instigated by either church or state. They are truly "popular," that is, of the people, or in that sense, "folk."

And I use the word "shrine" because these are more than memorials. They are places of communion between the dead and the living (thus the notes; see Zeitlin, chapter 5). They are sites of pilgrimage, as Grider has noted (2001). They commemorate and memorialize, but they do far more than that. They invite participation even from strangers. They are "open" to the public.

This moves us to another point—the political nature of spontaneous shrines. I suggest that the shrines personalize public and political issues, and in personalizing them, are political themselves, even in the absence of overt political sloganeering, as in Northern Ireland. Spontaneous shrines are silent witnesses. Further, they reflect and comment on public and social issues. The Malice Green site in Detroit, where an African American man was killed while in police custody, is a comment on police brutality. Roadside crosses reflect road conditions and drunk driving issues. The shrines of 9/11 reflect on terrorism or political violence. In Northern Ireland, they reflect and implicitly comment on paramilitary violence by forcing a recognition of the havoc it wreaks on ordinary people. The question of intentionality versus spectator interpretation is important here, as observers' readings and associations will vary from those of the creators. Moreover, the relative degree of performativity versus commemoration varies from assemblage to assemblage and among different types of public memorializations as well. A roadside cross may be primarily commemorative in intent, though it might be viewed as a warning by passing motorists; the performances of the Bloody Sunday protesters in Northern Ireland or the Mothers of the Plaza in South America are intentionally political, but involve the commemoration of the lives of specific, victimized individuals. All these examples involve both performativity and commemoration to a greater or lesser degree. One can view these dimensions as the two ends of a continuum, along which any particular instance of public death memorialization and spontaneous shrine might be placed, according to its emphasis

It is said that in war a combatant is trained to depersonalize the enemy, to demonize the enemy in order to be able to kill that enemy with little or no remorse. Spontaneous shrines act in the opposite way. They perform the opposite task. They insist on the personal nature of the individuals involved in these issues and the ramifications of the actions of those addressed by the shrines. You don't think drunk driving is a problem? My daughter was killed—here, at this spot—because of it. Teenage drinking? Responsible for the deaths of a carload of kids—right here. The county doesn't want to spend money on road improvement? Look at all the crosses along this stretch of road. You are carrying out a holy war? You killed my father. Paramilitaries are killing people in the name of freedom? The IRA killed my wife. That's not a Taig or a Prod—that's my husband; my father; my brother. You are conducting wars against terrorism? You killed my mother; my sister; my daughter.

Now. Defend your actions, your politics, in the light of that. We who build shrines and construct public altars or parade with photographs of the deceased will not allow you to write off victims as mere regrettable statistics. We insist—the shrines insist—by their disruption of the mundane environment, their calling attention to themselves—they insist on us acknowledging the real people, the real lives lost, the devastation to the commonwealth that these politics hold. By translating social issues and political actions into personal terms, the shrines are themselves political statements. Much of their communicative power is derived from their personalization of the public (i.e., performativity) just as a great deal is drawn from the language of mortuary ritual, of death and dying (i.e., of commemoration.) They are, I believe, the voice of the people.

The shrines insert and insist upon the presence of absent people. They display death in the heart of social life. These are not graves awaiting occasional visitors and sanctioned decoration. Instead of a family visiting a grave, the "grave" comes to the "family"—that is, the public. All of us. We are all family, mutually connected and interdependent. Spontaneous shrines both construct the relationship between the deceased and those who leave notes and memorabilia, and present that relationship to visitors. This is manifested in the notes and in the nature of the gifts which are brought, left, and publicly displayed: a high school jacket, a dog tag, an old report card, indicate fellow student, comrade soldier, and bereaved parent respectively. The gifts have personal meaning, and this is indicative of—that is, they index—the nature of the relationship, real or (as with Princess Diana and other celebrities) imagined. Imagined, but no less felt.

Spontaneous shrines place deceased individuals back into the fabric of society, into the middle of areas of commerce and travel, into everyday life as it is being lived. Traditional societies have always done this, as in the Latino Day of the Dead rituals and celebrations, at traditional Irish wakes, New Orleans jazz funerals, or at rural and regional homecomings and Decoration Day traditions. It seems as if people are reacting to the mass industrialization of death and the alienation of contemporary society with new folk traditions, rituals, and celebrations.

There is much more to be investigated, of course. Family members and friends usually create them. Roadside crosses appear largely Christian, in that they frequently feature a cross as the dominant symbol (though not always). Is shrine too narrow a word? Does it exclude non-Christians? Do members of other faiths, or no religion at all, create these as well? They certainly did in New York after 9/11. Would "spontaneous sacralization" be more accurate? It is more unwieldy, and "performative commemoratives" is a larger conceptual categorization.

What about race and gender? How and when do these factor in? Spontaneous shrines seem to be created by women and men of various races and backgrounds. Still, these are questions that need to be examined. Here, I have focused on the dynamics of spontaneous shrines, their combining of memorialization of deceased individuals with their topicality regarding social issues, and their use of funerary tradition to address pervasive, social problems.

References Cited

Abrahams, Roger D. 1981. "Shouting Match at the Border: The Folklore of Display Events." In *"And Other Neighborly Names:" Social Process and Cultural Image in Texas Folklore*, ed. Richard Bauman and Roger D. Abrahams. Austin, TX: University of Texas Press, 303–321.

Anderson, Benedict R. 1983. *Imagined Communities: Reflections on the Origin and Spread of Nationalism*. London: Verso Editions/NLB.

Austin, J. L. 1962. *How to Do Things With Words*. Cambridge: Harvard University Press.

Dayan, Daniel and Elihu Katz. 1992. "Defining Media Events: High Holidays of Mass Communication." In *Media Events: The Live Broadcasting of History*, ed. Dayan, Daniel and Elihu Katz. Cambridge, MA: Harvard University Press, 1–24.

Gillis, John R. (ed.) 1994. *Commemorations: The Politics of National Identity*. Princeton, NJ: Princeton University Press.

Grider, Sylvia. 2001. "Spontaneous Shrines: Preliminary Observations Regarding the Spontaneous Shrines Following the Terrorist Attacks of September 11, 2001." New Directions in Folklore 4.2. <http://www.temple.edu/isllc/newfolk/shrines.html>

Grimes, Ronald D. 1982. "The Lifeblood of Public Ritual: Fiestas and Public Exploration Projects." In *Celebration: Studies in Festivity and Ritual*, ed. Victor Turner. Washington, DC: Smithsonian Institution Press, 272–283.

Habermas, Jurgen. 1995. "Citizenship and National Identity: Some Reflections on the Future of Europe." In *The Nationalism Reader*, ed. Omar Dahbour and Micheline R. Ishay. Atlantic Highlands, NJ: Humanities Press, 333–342.

Handelman, Don. 1990. *Models and Mirrors: Towards an Anthropology of Public Events*. Cambridge: Cambridge University Press.

Kinser, Samuel. 1990. *Carnival American Style: Mardi Gras at New Orleans and Mobile*. Chicago: University of Chicago Press.

Myerhoff, Barbara. 1978. *Number Our Days*. New York: Simon and Schuster.

Sánchez-Carretero, Cristina. 2003. "Day of the Dead: Dying Days in Toledo, Ohio?" In *Holidays, Ritual, Festival, Celebration, and Public Display*, ed. Cristina Sánchez-Carretero and Jack Santino. Alcalá, Spain: University of Alcalá Press.

Santino, Jack. 1986. "The Folk Assemblage of Autumn: Tradition and Creativity in Halloween Folk Art." In *Folk Art and Art Worlds*, ed. John Michael Vlach and Simon Bronner. Ann Arbor, MI: UMI Research Press, 151–169.

————. 1988. "The Tendency to Ritualize: The Living Celebrations Series as a Model for Cultural Presentation and Validation." In *The Conservation of Culture: Folklorists and the Public Sector*, ed. Burt Feintuch. Lexington, KY: The University Press of Kentucky.

————. 1992a. " 'Not An Unimportant Failure': Rituals of Death and Politics in Northern Ireland." In *Displayed in Mortal Light*, ed. Michael McCaughan. Antrim, Northern Ireland: Antrim Arts Council.

————. 1992b. "Yellow Ribbons and Seasonal Flags: The Folk Assemblage of War." *Journal of American Folklore* 103: 19–33.

————. 1999. "Public Protest and Popular Style: Resistance From the Right in Northern Ireland and South Boston." *American Anthropologist* 101:3, 515–528.

————. 2001. *Signs of War and Peace: Social Conflict and the Public Use of Symbols in Northern Ireland*. New York: Palgrave.

Schieffelin, Edward L. 1998. "Problematizing Performance." In *Ritual, Performance, Media*, ed. Felicia Hughes-Freeland. London: Routledge, 194–207.

Waldstreicher, David. 1995. *In the Midst of Perpetual Fetes: The Making of American Nationalism, 1776–1820*. Chapel Hill, NC: University of North Carolina Press.

Chapter 2

Communicative Commemoration and Graveside Shrines: Princess Diana, Jim Morrison, My "Bro" Max, and Boogs the Cat

Jeannie Banks Thomas

Shrines mark hallowed spots; they are composed of culturally or personally significant relics. We travel to shrines to express our devotion and pain, to ask for help, to reach toward other worlds, to remember, and to heal. In this article, I discuss several types of contemporary shrines and detail some of the behaviors surrounding them. While I do not attempt to be exhaustive; I do present specific examples of some common kinds of secular folk shrines, which are part of a material process of communicative commemoration. The shrines I examine include spontaneous shrines, official shrines, roadside shrines, and especially graveside shrines. I delineate the manner in which these shrines are related to each other and also their differing and distinctive features. Finally, I consider spontaneous shrines as a manifestation of consumer culture.

Metro Tickets for Jim Morrison

It was a cool July morning in Paris, and Jim Morrison's grave in Père Lachaise Cemetery was cloaked in shade. The atmosphere was made even chillier by the presence of a Scottish girl, around 16 years old, with long dark hair. She had come to leave an offering for the famed rock star—a poem she had written and encased in a plastic sheet, which she reverently removed from her "Doors" knapsack and left on his grave. But she did not take such care with her friends; she was angrily and loudly telling them how they had ruined her moment with Jim. When she was not berating them, she was casting angry, jealous glances around at any other pilgrims who materialized at the site.

Morrison's marker is neither imposing nor easily located. For the first-time visitor it requires puzzling over cemetery maps and finally following the graffiti on the other tombs toward Morrison's unassuming marker mixed in with a jumble of graves. Some of the graffiti is helpful, such as the arrows with Morrison's name on them or hints like "Jim 6th division." Other graffiti is less directionally oriented: "Jim 'This is the End'," "Jim will come back," "Jim is son," "Jim + drugs," "I see Jim alive," and immediately following that, "Michael saw you still dead."

On that July day, a few blonde teenagers staggered toward the site, red-eyed, stoned, and dragging their uncooperative luggage on wheels, apparently making one last stop before catching a train or a plane elsewhere. Despite the labor of finding the grave, the blonde group was cowed by the glares of the 16-year-old: Jim was *hers*, so they backed off and dragged their recalcitrant luggage down the uneven cobblestones that had brought them to the deep shade at Morrison's grave. Even though everyone recognized the public nature of the site, many of the visitors—like the Scottish girl— looked for a few quiet moments alone with Morrison, although most lacked the teen's ferocity. I stayed long enough to watch the drama and photograph the site; then I too wandered off, eventually ending up at Oscar Wilde's monument, which was covered in red and pink lipstick kisses. The offerings there were elegant: a short, well-crafted note, other missives of thanks penned in French and English, and a few beautifully sensual plums, just ripe, had been left.

Later that same morning, I wound my way back to Jim's grave. The teenager was gone, but her poem was there alongside other leavings: inexpensive flowers, identity cards, the key to a Marriott hotel room, a picture of a purple guitar, a seashell, playing cards, a blue bandana, and a metallic lizard. Part of the Scottish girl's missive, which was written with "all" her love, reads: "You are my destiny / You are an angel sent from heaven above / I ask you / When I leave my life behind me / Will you open your door to me . . . Can I fly with the angels in the sky." Other notes were left for Morrison as well, "For a dead rock star / Rotting in his coffin, IMMACULATE . . . I guess you're FUCKED UP . . . are you? / You would go where? . . . . MR. MOJO RISIN' MR MOJO RISIN' RISE! RISE!

RISE! See all the freaks hauling on your groove?"[1] These notes and items are fairly typical of the offerings left for Jim. However, the grave is cleaned regularly, so the offerings do not accumulate, and different thematic patterns develop. For instance, during another visit to the grave, I noticed that photographs were a much more popular offering. When a visitor sees what others have left at the graveside and realizes that she or he has that item as well, such as a used Metro ticket, this discovery can prompt the visitor to spontaneously decide to leave the object (figure 2.1). Sometimes the offering is directly and personally meant for Jim, as was the teenaged girl's note; at other times, an object is left so that the visitor can momentarily intersect with the famous or historical. For example, during one of my visits to Morrison's grave, I observed a woman leave an empty wine bottle on the grave, and as she was leaving the site, her friend laughingly said to her, "Well, now, you've left your mark."

During a journey to the grave in the off-season when fewer tourists were around, I found leavings similar to those at the height of tourist season; for example, more notes: "I am here to say thank you for the great tunes. You rock," "Death makes angels of us all and gives us wings were we had shoulders smooth as ravens claws," and the more formal, "Nice to meet you." These words were left in amongst packets of sugar, soap, cigarette butts, a wine cork, straws, a necklace, French francs (made obsolete by the Euro), a lit tea candle, an empty wine bottle, origami birds, a plastic clothespin, a Hard Rock Café matchbook, a potted plant with condoms in it, Juicy Fruit gum wrappers, loads of used Metro tickets, and numerous pictures of teenagers, probably taken at the instant photo booths in various Metro stations in Paris (figure 2.2). Not surprisingly, the leavings often bore a notable theme of sex, drugs, adolescent attitude, and rock and roll.

Morrison's gravesite with its ever-morphing offerings shares many of the characteristics of what are often called "spontaneous shrines." Folklorist Jack Santino originated this term in 1992 when writing about street shrines that commemorate the loss of life due to the violence in Northern Ireland (see Santino 1992b). Since Santino's early use, the term is widely employed to describe "temporary monuments to the deceased" that are "created without instigation or coaxing from any church or municipal government" (Santino 2001: 76). Spontaneous shrines articulate pain, make the rest of us take notice of the death, consecrate a site of loss, and mark untimely deaths. They are sites where both God and humanity are addressed. While they are simultaneously personal and communal, their public nature is an important component of their construction (Santino 2001: 76–77, 79, 13). They can serve as public comment on social issues, and some participants in shrine creation "hope to have an effect on the situation" (Santino 2001: 14). Due to their ephemeral and sometimes oppositional nature, they share similarities

Figure 2.1   Jim Morrison's graveside shrine, Paris.
Photo by: Jeannie Banks Thomas.

Figure 2.2   Homemade Jill doll at the grave.
Photo by: Jeannie Banks Thomas.

with fine art "countermonuments." This term refers to late twentieth-century German monuments that reflect a "deep distrust of monumental forms in light of their systematic exploitation by the Nazis" (Young 1993: 27). Spontaneous shrines, like countermonuments, stimulate memory by foregrounding their own changing compositions. Thus they are symbolic of the evolution of memory over time and the "changing of all meaning and memory" (1993: 48).

I would classify the type of spontaneous shrine that Santino describes as a *public* spontaneous shrine. Unless I designate them as "official shrines," all of the shrines I discuss herein could be typed as spontaneous shrines, in general. My point is that there are distinctive types of spontaneous shrines. The basic factors I evaluate when differentiating types of shrines include whether a shrine's construction is official or unofficial, where it is located, its public and private components, and its various functions.

Morrison's grave could be referred to as a spontaneous graveside shrine. Throughout this article, I will refer to Morrison's grave and those like it as *graveside* shrines, both for the sake of brevity and also to signal that there are subtle differences between graveside shrines and the public spontaneous shrines that emerge in response to events such as the Oklahoma bombing, the Columbine shooting, Princess Diana's death, and the September 11 terrorist attacks. However, I don't want to overstate these differences; the graveside shrines share much with public spontaneous shrines. For example, like the spontaneous shrines in Northern Ireland that Santino studies, Morrison's graveside shrine is a temporary monument to the dead, which is constructed by ordinary people without the behest of church or state. It also commemorates an untimely death as do public spontaneous shrines. Graveside shrines also serve as a means of communication with the deceased, as do some public spontaneous shrines (Santino 2001: 90). However, unlike many public spontaneous shrines, graveside ones often do not call attention to the manner in which the life was lost, nor do they usually need to consecrate the place (see Chandler 1999: 154; see also Santino 2001: 76–77); their location in a cemetery is usually sanctified through some sort of official ritual.

In contrast to many public spontaneous shrines, graveside shrines rarely comment on social issues, nor do they routinely seek to affect those issues. Like public spontaneous shrines, graveside shrines make passersby take notice (see Santino 2001: 76), but often graveside shrines are much more concerned with a private relationship with the dead rather than a public statement about the death. Because of his fame, the graveside shrine at Morrison's grave is similar to public spontaneous shrines; however, his shrine and the behaviors that surround it exhibit characteristics of the graveside shrine, even the leaning toward private communion that is so much a part of this type of shrine. In general, graveside shrines are more likely than public spontaneous shrines to demonstrate a higher and consistent level of intimate connection to the deceased. The grave is also the most private spot for a shrine of the locales I discuss. Graveside shrines tend to be less political and less likely to call attention to how the life was lost, characteristics that fit Morrison's shrine. Often—although not always, as Morrison's case demonstrates—a smaller group of people create them, and they also frequently have a more limited audience, as opposed to other types of spontaneous shrines.

A Memorial for Princess Diana, S. V. P.

Far from Morrison's grave, in another part of Paris, is a public spontaneous shrine. Above the *Pont de L'Alma* underpass where Princess Diana was killed in an auto accident on August 31, 1997, stands a monument to French resistance to the Nazis during World War II. It is a large, shiny, gold copy of the flame that the Statue of Liberty holds in her hand. People have chosen to create a public spontaneous shrine to Princess Diana at this monument. I photographed the site in March of 2002, and I found it remarkable both for what was not there—the statue of the flame itself had been removed for "refurbishing"—and what was still there: the spontaneous shrine. Even though it was constructed of more ephemeral materials, the people's shrine remained when the state's disappeared. The spontaneous shrine merely shifted to the temporary barricade placed around the official monument's vacated locale. The graffiti dialogue that marks the overpass by the shrine continued unabated; it also spread to the official sign posted by the city. Unlike the numerous floral tributes at Kensington Palace that appeared soon after Diana's death, which were described as being like "waves break-ing against a sea wall" (Rowbottom 1999: 158),[2] the Paris shrine was spare and subdued but still heartfelt. It consisted of photos, flowers, and notes addressed to Diana, all displayed in a way that indicated that they were meant to be read by the public, too: "Di, We will always miss you loads! Peebles and Dorothy"; "*Ces fleurs (en photo) étaient envoyées ici par les Princes William et Harry en homage à la mémoire de leur Mère, qui a trouvé la mort sous ce tunnel* ("The flowers in the photo are here for the Princes William and Harry in tribute to the memory of their mother, who died in this tunnel"). A news photograph of the Princess in a minefield was posted: "*En Bosnie La Princesse Diana de Galles, Présidente de la Croix Rouge Brittanique, dans un campagne contre le massacre provoqué par les Mines Antipersonel*" (In Bosnia, Princess Diana of Wales, president of the British Red Cross, on a campaign against the massacre caused by antipersonnel mines). Heart stickers with a phone number on them—an advertisement for a sex hotline—surround these tributes. In comparison to the behaviors that indicated visitors wished for some private time "alone" with the subject of the graveside shrines, such as that demonstrated by the girl at Morrison's grave, at this public spontaneous shrine that concern was not paramount.

The commemorative graffiti for Diana left at the site was more political than that left in Morrison's name in Père Lachaise. For example, near these informal tributes was the official sign declaring "*La Mairie de Paris Restaure Flamme de la Liberté*," under which someone had written "*Mémorial Diana*," which was followed by a heart that said "Angel [heart] Elena," more official information about the *Flamme de la Liberté*, another sticker for the sex hotline, and more graffiti such as, "*Ici Il Y/ Avait Une Photo De La Princesse Diana De Galles En Angola Dans Sa Campagne Contre Les Mines Antipersonnel/ À Sa Mémoire A Été Dédié Le Prix Nobel De La Paix 1997*" (Here there used to be a photo of Princess Diana of Wales in Angola on her campaign against antipersonnel mines / The 1997 Nobel Peace Prize was dedicated to her memory). At the bottom of the sign was an official logo,

"*Mairie De Paris,*" above which had been written "*S. V.P Une Plaque Pour La Princesse Diana*" (A plaque for Princess Diana please). The graffiti on the tunnel bore similar messages, "*Au Maire De Paris: S. V.P. Une Plaque Pour La Princesse Diana!*" and "*La Princesse Diana = Héroine De L'Humanité/ A Été Assassinée À Cause De Sa Campagne Contre Le Massacre Provoqué Par Les Mines Antipersonnel*" (Princess Diana—Heroine of Humanity—was assassinated because of her campaign against the massacre caused by antipersonnel mines). And nearby, "*Police Nationale Services Secrets France = Gouvernement Jospin Allié Du Trafic Des Mines*" (National Police/French Secret Service = Jospin government is an ally of mine trafficking). And, again, "*Princesse Diana Assassinée à cause de sa campagne contre les Mines antipersonnel.*"

Santino argues that spontaneous shrines can be performative as well as commemorative, as is the case with some of the flowers left for Diana at Buckingham Palace: "While the flowers commemorated a lost life, and expressed individuals' felt (if imagined) sense of relationship with the former princess, they also contested the style of royalty manifested by the Windsors and, in fact, altered it" (Santino 2001: 14). He describes these public mourning traditions as a form of "cultural–political contestation" (Santino 2001: 103). Specifically, Queen Elizabeth's reaction to Diana's death was viewed by the public as unnecessarily cold. The royal family was in Scotland after Diana's death. Since she was not in Buckingham Palace, following proper royal protocol, Queen Elizabeth did not have the flag there flown at half-mast to mark Diana's death.[3] People read this as a snub of the Princess. The lack of the flag on high contrasted with the "multitude of flowers below"; the flowers represented "popular sentiment from the bottom up" (2001: 103). Santino maintains that the mourning traditions reveal a clash between the elite and the popular (2001: 110), so his argument also indicates the ways in which the marking of death is itself marked by class.

A similar kind of unofficial versus official, the people versus those-in-power response is demonstrated by the public spontaneous shrine and commemorative graffiti for Diana in Paris. Both communicative forms challenge the government. People signal their desire for a monument through the creation of the public spontaneous shrine and the accompanying graffiti. They directly approach the government through the graffiti, asking the city to create an official memorial. The conspiracy legends about Diana's death relayed in the United State and England had the royal family engaged in nefarious activities, but in the graffiti at the Paris shrine, the French government is critiqued, and Diana's death is termed an "assassination," which is linked to her campaign against land mines. This type of political contestation and commentary is more routinely found at the site of spontaneous shrines than at graveside shrines, which are *less* public and *more* private—therefore, not an appropriate venue for commentary meant to be accessible to large audiences.

Graffiti has a relationship with public shrines; it tends to appear at shrines dedicated to famous people or well-known events instead of at the graveside shrines of private citizens. It is part of the process of commemorative communication. Graffiti and the material components of public spontaneous shrines convey why and how those who lost their lives should be remembered—and how their lives and deaths should be interpreted. At the *Pont de L'Alma* site, graffiti tells visitors how to contextualize Diana's death.

In addition to its political nature, the Parisian spontaneous shrine to Diana also fits the previously mentioned characteristics of the public spontaneous shrine: it's a temporary monument to the deceased; it calls attention to how or why the life was lost; it consecrates a site of tragedy, it articulates pain; it marks an untimely death; it is both personal and communal; and it issues political commentary. Like the shrines C. Allen Haney and Dell Davis describe, in the case of Diana's shrine: "no one is automatically included or excluded in the culturally prescribed mourners," and the leavings are often personally meaningful to the mourner (1999: 238).

Morrison's graveside shrine differs from Diana's Paris shrine in that there is less emphasis on the political or physical performative. Most graveside shrines do not work overtly to affect the physical actions of people; instead the shrines attempt to connect the living with inner peace, memories, and the dead; thus, they are *metaphysically performative*. In addition, the notes at spontaneous shrines are commonly displayed in a such manner that the public can read them; people did read the notes that were left in London for Diana after her death (Francis, Neophytou, and Kellaher 1999: 116, 119). Many of the notes left on Morrison's grave were often folded or left in a way that made reading them difficult. When I observed the grave, not one of the many visitors to the site made a concerted effort to read the notes. They were, in fact, surprised and sometimes disturbed when I began unfolding the notes, reading them, and photographing them—although, when I started doing this, some people did read the notes over my shoulder. Reading the notes at Morrison's gravesite felt more like an invasion of privacy than it did at Diana's public spontaneous shrine.

In summary, while public spontaneous shrines can be simultaneously both private and public (Francis, Neophytou, and Kellaher 1999: 118; Santino 2001: 76), they are typically more directed toward the public than the private. They are also more likely to be political than graveside shrines. As opposed to graveside shrines, public spontaneous shrines are usually created by a larger and more diverse body of mourners, who can be unknown to each other and the decedent.

Remembering the Guardians of Peace

Elsewhere in Paris, the buildings mourn—officially. Posted on buildings throughout the city (and in other French towns as well) are plaques commemorating the deaths of resistors at the hands of the Nazis during World War II. The plaques say things such as, *"Ici Est Tombé pour la Libération Montauron Jean / Gardien de la Paix/ 24 Août 1944"* (Here, fallen for the Liberation, Jean Montauron, Guardian of the Peace, 24 August 1944), and *"À La Mémoire De Henri Fançois Paquin / 33 Ans Adjudant Chef du char Rabt / Raymond Berth / 20 ans 1ère Classe de Choisy Le Roi / Escadron de Protection du Général Leclerc Tués sure leur Char le 25 Août 1944/ Jour de L'entree Triomphale des Amees Liberatrices"* (To the memory of Henri François Paquin, 33, Warrant Officer of the tank Rabat, and Raymond Berth, 20, Private First Class of the Choisy le Rio, protective squadron for General Leclerc, killed in their tank the 25th of August 1944, the day of the triumphal entry of the liberating armies). Finally, *"Ici fut tué par les S. S./ Le 19 Août 1944/ le gardien de la Paix/ Perrin André* (Here, killed by the S. S. the 19th of August 1944, the guardian of the peace André Perrin), under which a graffitist added, *PAIX à son âme"* (Peace to his soul). The city decorates these plaques with flowers on holidays, such as VE Day on May 8, Bastille Day on July 14, the Liberation of Paris on August 25, and Armistice Day on November 11.

These markers are placed by an official organization: the state. They are not temporary, and even though they mark tragedy, they often do not take an overtly political stance on it. Unlike public spontaneous shrines, official monuments rarely challenge the government or critique its role in a tragedy.[4] For instance, these plaques avoid implying that there was *not* enough French resistance to the Nazis, an argument both the oral and print traditions sometime posit. Official shrines themselves are rarely performative in terms of political critique and are primarily public and communal rather than personal and private. However, because of the limited nature of their communicative commemoration, official markers sometimes unintentionally invite the unofficial back again—in the form of words and objects—because these unofficial *assemblages* can tell *more* of the story of loss (see Santino 1992a: 158 on *assemblage*). So in America, for example, people leave C rations, toilet paper, dog tags, and "Grandma for Peace" signs at the Vietnam Veterans Memorial (see Hass 1998: 27–29). They carry flowers and teddy bears to the empty chairs that memorialize the Oklahoma bombing victims; and, in Paris, someone scrawls the word *"Paix"* on one of these streetside plaques.

Death and Love on the Highway

In other parts of the world, such as Ireland or the American Southwest, the sides of the road mourn—unofficially. Spontaneous shrines are erected that represent the loss of loved ones who died on a particular stretch of road. Depending on the area, these markers are sometimes removed by officials in charge of the roadways because they see them as distracting and adding to the danger already present in the treacherous parts of a road. According to Slyvia Grider, "Roadside shrines and crosses which people erect to mark the sites of fatal car wrecks are spontaneous shrines on a smaller, more personal level" (2001: 1). Holly Everett says that the tradition in the American Southwest dates back to the era of Spanish exploration and settlement (2000: 91). Unlike the Diana shrine in Paris, roadside shrines usually mark the loss of a private citizen in a private tragedy—in this, the roadside shrines are similar to graveside shrines. Indeed, I saw a roadside shrine in Ireland made permanent through the placement of a very headstone-like marker with a picture of a man riding a motorcycle; engraved on the stone was: "Harry O'Reilly, 1964–1997 / A willing smile / A helping hand / For those he loved / don't understand / the reason why / you are gone / but in my heart / you go on and on."

Roadside shrines differ from graveside shrines in their very public marking and consecration of sites where tragedy occurred. In contrast to graveside shrines, roadside shrine indicate the cause of death. Some of these shrines simultaneously remind of tragedy *and* cleanse the site: that is, they work to take the horror out of the site where a loved one died. They turn a place where earlier there was only tragedy and pain into a space of love and memory. Unlike the roadside shrine, the graveside shrine usually does not have to cleanse or remake public places into commemorative ones. In the cemetery, most of the space is already dedicated to memorial.

Roadside shrines mark the sites of "bad deaths" (see Kozak and Lopez 1991: 8). They recall auto accidents: sudden, violent deaths that extinguish life too soon.[5] Graveside shines do not indicate the *sites* of bad deaths, and they can commemorate both bad deaths and deaths that are viewed as natural or even "good deaths," such as those due to old age for example. Roadside shrines are performative; they hope to intervene in traffic deaths, to remind people to be more cautious when driving. They can serve as places of reflection and grieving for those who witnessed fatal crashes (see Everett 2000: 94, 101). Graveside shrines do not share similar functions. However, Everett points out that in the Austin, Texas, area there is a relationship between the roadside and graveside shrines; roadside shrines may be a focus of *assemblage* especially when cemeteries have restrictive decoration policies (2000: 98–99). She notes that, often, "After a few years, when activity at the roadside appears to decrease or stop altogether, the greater part of memorialization activity may have moved to the cemetery or home" (2000: 102).

Generally then, roadside shrines usually commemorate the violent or "bad" death of a private citizen. They are similar to graveside markers, but they differ in terms of their very public marking of a private death. Unlike graveside shrines, by their very nature, roadside shrines communicate the cause of the person's death and they can demonstrate the wish to intervene, to remind drivers to proceed with care. While the shrine to Diana in Paris could be classed a roadside shrine, it is not at the exact site of the accident, it does not emphasize the physical manner of her death, and it does not offer a caution about traffic safety. Instead, like other public spontaneous shrines, it mourns her loss and emphasizes the political meaning of her death through its conspiracy theories. Like public spontaneous shrines, roadside shrines can also work to consecrate or purify a mundane place or the site of horror. However, roadside shrines tend to focus on personal and private connections to a greater extent than do many public spontaneous shrines—although not to the same degree as do graveside shrines for private citizens.

Greeting Cards for the Afterlife

In the United States, Max's family and friends mourn him; he died in October 1999 at the age of 29. I photographed his grave in Salt Lake City, Utah, at the end of January 2000, just shortly after his birthday. It was rich with personalized offerings of love including flowers, numerous bottles of Bud Light and Keystone Light beer, Squatter's ale (a local microbrew), Jose Cuervo tequila, yard art such as wooden flowers and a little yard-art-mole statue placed so it was burrowing up out of his grave, two volleyballs—one pink and one white, and a Native American rock art figure (Kokopelli) on skis. Several greeting cards had been left at the grave. One showed a picture of a happy dog (figure 2.3); it said, "I hope you get everything you want for your Birthday. . . . And I hope you weren't counting on me for any of it. This card and a pack of dental floss pretty much torpedoed my savings. Happy Birthday." Written inside this card was: "Holy Shit!!! 30 . . . . Anything that has that many years behind it needs a cane. Just kiddin Bro, you're the youngest thirty year old I know. I hope that your B-Day is better than it ever was in the past. You are an inspiration to me, and I'm going to

Figure 2.3   Greeting card left at graveside shrine, Salt Lake City, Utah.
Photo by: Jeannie Banks Thomas.

try and follow in your footsteps the best I can. It will be tough, but it will be a good tough. I just want to wish you a Happy Birthday and simply say hello. I love you so much Max!!! Stay Gold!!!"

Max's mother also left him a birthday card, and in it she said, "Dear Max, Thirty years ago today I held you in my arms for the first time. You were so tiny but you still filled my heart and soul so full of emotion it felt like I was overflowing with love. Every day after that the bond grew more intense. I love you my baby, my boy, my wonderful man child. The tremendous, precious love and pride will continue to grow and reach out to you until the time when I can hold you again. If I only could touch you. Love, Mom."

Part of yet another card read, "Happy Birthday Baby! I keeping thinking of the beautiful beaches in Jamaica we were supposed to be on celebrating your 30th. Now I would simply be happy seeing your wonderful face anywhere." There was also a postcard on the grave addressed to "Max,

Heaven and Earth" it said, "I hope the snow is good so you can go skiing. I love you now and always. Grandma."

Notes such as these are left at the last earthly address of the person mourned; as the address on the postcard left by Max's grandmother indicates, the gravesite becomes a conduit between heaven and earth. Other types of spontaneous shrines can also function in the a parallel fashion (see Santino 2001: 80; Zeitlin 2002: 5). However, a shrine constructed at a graveside often allows for easier and more private communing with the deceased than do some of the other types of shrines, such as the roadside shrine or public spontaneous shrines, which are located in busier, more trafficked areas.

The poignant offerings left at Max's grave tell much about Max as a person; they also reveal some of the aspects of this type of shrine. Graveside shrines for private citizens share traits with other spontaneous shrines. The graveside shrines are emotional and personal, as are other public spontaneous shrines. Such is the case with some of the New York shrines that emerged in response to the September 11, 2001, terrorist attacks. Steve Zeitlin recorded some of the notes that were left at these shrines: "To Lee . . . We came here today to tell you how much we love & miss you. We are trying to remember all of the good times. We're just saying hello because there will never be goodbyes." Strangers leave notes to the victims as well: "I miss you./We never met" (Zeitlin this volume).

In contrast, just family and friends usually leave the offerings at graveside shrines. The casual visitor may be moved by the site but is much less likely to contribute to it, especially if it is dedicated to a *private* citizen, because they know little about the person's life and death. Anyone can contribute to public spontaneous shrines, and even strangers know something about the victims' deaths, if not their lives. Roadside shrines work in a similar public fashion. Also, Zeitlin notes that the poems left at the September 11 spontaneous shrines in New York bore indications of a greater awareness of a large and varied audience: "Particularly in the weeks after the disaster, most of the poems were anonymous. Now, months later, new poems still appear, but these are stamped with copyright notices and posted web sites" (2002: 6). In general, public spontaneous shrines are more collective and address a wider audience than graveside shrines. Typically, contributions to these shrines are made by people who are unknown to each other.

The graveside shrine constructed for a private citizen—as opposed to those dedicated to public figures such as Jim Morrison—are frequently the most personal and intimate of all the types of communicative commemoration that I've discussed. For instance, people left *flowers in the colors that they liked* at the spontaneous shrines to Diana in London (Francis, Neophytou, and Kellaher 1999: 118). The offerings left by family and friends on Max's grave clearly *included things he liked*. Other graveside shrines evince this pattern as well; I asked a woman who helps maintain a graveside shrine in the Smithfield, Utah, cemetery about the significance of the offerings. She told me her family tries to leave things the family matriarch Felisitas, who died at age 81, would like and they select items in colors she favored. Over the years and months, several generations regularly appear at her grave to contribute to the shrine or just to visit. On one occasion, I saw a boy and girl ride their bicycles around the cemetery, laughing; ultimately they stopped at Felisitas's grave, where they sat meditatively on the grass in front of the grave. After a while, the boy gently pressed the flat of his hand against the front of the marker and held it tenderly there, as if he were touching the cheek of his grandmother.

Because graveside shrines are more revealing and intimate, they are distinct from simpler and more generic grave decoration, such as flowers left on Memorial Day—although such discernment cannot always be made on solely a visual basis.[6] It is frequently clear from the objects left at the grave that the deceased is being directly addressed through the specific tokens left at the site. Not only is it officially consecrated but the ground in the cemetery is also holy because it holds the last earthly traces of loved ones. The graveside shrines function to mark this sacred space; they work as do the altars and *ofrendas* associated with Day of the Dead. Kay Turner and Pat Jasper define an *ofrenda* as "a domestic altar made especially for the Day of the Dead to hold offerings for deceased loved ones . . . . Traditionally, an altar is a threshold; it marks a sacred site between heaven and earth that pro-vides access of each to the other. An *ofrenda* partakes of the altar's general def-inition as an active threshold between earth and heaven, but the *ofrenda* is specifically created as a site of encounter between the living and the dead. All the things on an *ofrenda* have a quality of action that makes them able com-municators between humans and the spirits of the deceased" (Turner and Jasper 1994: 134, 140–141). While all graveside offerings do not emerge out of this custom and culture, nor do they share all the features of Day of the Dead altars, they do share salient characteristics. Specifically, I see the grave-side shrines functioning as *idiosyncratic altars*—they are tailored to the dead, and they mark a sacred site where the living and the dead have access to each other. They are more likely to be extensions of preexisting, domestic, indi-vidual, and intimate relations with the deceased, particularly if the deceased is a private citizen. They have a specific and usually relatively small group of creators (or even just a single creator) and a limited audience—as opposed to public spontaneous shrines and roadside shrines. Public spontaneous shrines (and often roadside shrines) can be described as communal altars; they are usually built by a larger or broader community than are the idiosyncratic altars created at the graves of private citizens.

Cenotaph Offerings

In the same cemetery where Max's friends and family left their offerings of love and pain is a bronze statue of an angel with aspirations of the official. This sculpture does not actually mark a grave, rather it is a cenotaph. Richard Paul Evans, who wrote a slim book called *The Christmas Box*, commissioned the statue. Evans's book deals with a woman whose child died and it includes a reference to the statue of an angel in a cemetery (Dimmitt 2000: 68–69). After being queried about the location of the statue and finding out that the book's distributors were frequently asked the same question, Evans decided to build the statue in the Salt Lake City Cemetery, where it stands today. Engraved on the base is, "Our Little Angel," and, "The Christmas Box Angel. With hope in its wings, the Angel Monument was dedicated December 6, 1994 as a place of love and healing for all those who have lost children. I invite all to leave a white flower at is base. RPE." This is an official monument that deliberately invites folk behaviors, such as the construction of a spontaneous shrine—although, in harmony with its official nature, the statue suggests the proper objects to leave: white flowers.

However, true to their folk roots, members of the public do not limit themselves to just white flowers. They use the site to create a public spontaneous shrine through their leavings of stuffed animals, baby bracelets, toys, notes, and flowers. When I visited the angel, there was a piece of paper taped to the statue; it had a photograph of baby in a Santa Claus suit on it, and it said, "Red & Sliver Ribbons . . . Shaken Baby Syndrome / In Memory of Elijah Carson Fisher. Red represents broken hearts and lost promises. Silver represents the angel's wings as they soar toward heaven. The angel represents the purity & complete innocence of SBS children. Tho no longer with us on this earth. We lost a grandbaby Dec. 24th, '98 to Shaken Baby Syndrome. He is forever our 'Christmas Angel.' Email me for his memory site."

Even though this marker is in a graveyard, it is not a graveside shrine. Instead, it is a *communal* monument created and viewed by a diverse audience; it is a public spontaneous shrine. Like other public spontaneous shrines created near or in response to official shrines (such as those at the Vietnam Veterans Memorial), it marks untimely deaths and calls direct attention to the manner in which some of the lives were lost. The Cenotaph spontaneous shrine also provides a place for public comment on social issues, such as shaken baby syndrome, and through their offerings, people hope to have some impact on this problem. Even though when I visited it, Max's grave was every bit as visually noticeable in the Salt Lake Cemetery as was the angel shrine, and even though it was obvious to the casual observer that the shrine at Max's grave communicated grief at the loss of a child, others visiting the cemetery who mourned such deaths (like baby Elijah's) did not leave offerings at Max's grave. They went to the angel instead. Their actions show that they recognize, at some level, that these kinds of shrines are distinct; each has its own set folk rules, and therefore each calls for slightly different behaviors.

Official shrines are formally designated and designed. Everyday people, acting without an official mandate, create graveside, roadside, and public spontaneous shrines. Official shrines are wholly intended for the public—unlike graveside shrines, which often lean toward the private—or public spontaneous shrines, which can have elements of both the private as well as the public. However, official shrines, such as the Christmas Angel Cenotaph or the Vietnam Veterans Memorial, invite the construction of public spontaneous shrines.

Sharing the Holidays with Dead Pets

Some miles north of the angel and Max's grave is a small cemetery that is also notable for some its of graveside shrines. While it looks like any other cemetery in the area, the names on the markers tell a different story. They belong to Fluffy, Frisky Watson, Kodiak, Sodapop, Scooter Jones, Scrounger Owen ("Our Baby Kitty Girl"), Tootsie Hirai, Gizmo, Proud Pretzel, Sandy ("she came for a weekend but stayed 13 years"), Toke, Conan, Studley, Zeus, Tribble Hodgson, Chakeeta, Daisy Graves ("she lies buried in the heart of her master"), Poppie's Fat Boy Reggie, Patches Stede, "Our Loving Cat Snoopy," Yeti Whetton, and Pee Nelson. This is Tiffany's Memorial Pet Cemetery in Ogden, Utah, and Tiffany was a poodle. When I visited this pet cemetery in the winter of 2000, I found the grave of Bernie Dunn, a small dog, whose marker said, "We Love You Son." His graveside *assemblage* included a long poem with a picture of him on it. Part of it read, "I used to sigh and wonder—what's this thing called love?/Then along came Bernie, question asked and answered/our life, our hope, our happiness—more than one should dare dream of. . . . one day our little Bernie crawled into my arms and slowly passed away./Not feeling that as long as it would beat, within my heart only emptiness could reside,/I never again asked what is love, but now I questioned why?"

A note in the form of a poem was also left on the grave a dog named Ocean, who lived a year: "Ocean Botion so full of life / Until one day he had a strife / A short small battle he couldn't fight / His heart so big he saw the light./ . . . you'd think he was a Rotweiler, caught you dead in the dark / No one would argue he was one heavy lad / He'd claw you in the face every morn—oh so bad / He hussled up so fast the trails when he could / . . . All the other dogs were jealous—they wanted to be him / One cold snow day he couldn't take it no more / His heart stopped pumping dead at the core/ . . . His life was fragile—he drank it up!/See you in Doggy Heaven, Ocean/I love you, 'Mommy.' "

A rabbit, "Archie aka 'Dinky-Dog'," had a grave decorated by an elaborate Christmas *assemblage* (figure 2.4). This graveside shrine included a wreath on a stand with numerous cloth ornaments (some apparently handmade), at least two Christmas stockings, and a Santa doll. One stocking said, "Happy Holidays from Kibbles 'n Bits." Archie's marker read, "You brought a lot of / happiness to all of us! Love, Cara, Randy, Amy, Teresa, Joey, and your friends at Archway Youth Services." There was a cat's tombstone that read, "Owner of Peggy Dunn/My Angel Girl/ Boogs 1984–1991." This marker was surrounded by a little green fence decorated with an *assemblage* of various holidays: a marker with "2000," on it, a small inflated Valentine's Day heart balloon that said "I love you," a tiny Christmas tree, and the whole *assemblage* was draped in a metallic, brightly colored star garland.

These graveside shrines indicate that the custom is democratic; it extends from the private citizen to the famous and even to the furry. It is important to include these examples—humorous and trivial as some might find them—because if I were to dismiss them because they belong to animals, I would be overlooking the range of very real grief at loss that people are expressing through their shrines. The notes on the animal's graves are similar to missives I found at Jim Morrison's or Max's grave, including poetic form. They parallel notes left at public spontaneous shrines, too—once again evincing that *all* of these types of shrines are part of a shared language of communicative commemoration. In addition, the graves of Boogs and Archie also introduce a slightly different twist on the graveside shrine: the *holiday* graveside shrine. The holidays can influence the *assemblage* at other types of spontaneous shrines. Holidays are particularly relevant to shrine construction because of their temporal nature; holiday imagery indicates the passing of time—specifically, time and festive occasions that are no longer shared with the deceased. So, in the commemorative language of shrines, holiday decorations speak concretely to the time and shared experience that is lost when a love one dies.

In some cases, seasonal graveside *assemblage* can also communicate the deceased one's favorite holidays.[7] Seasonal *assemblage* at the graveside shrine of a private citizen is likely to signify bereavement felt at a holiday that would have been shared with the deceased when he, she, or it was alive. One can reasonably assume that Archie was missed at Christmas and that Boogs'

Figure 2.4   Graveside shrine for a deceased pet, Ogden, Utah.

Photo by: Jeannie Banks Thomas.

owner thought about her during the Christmas, New Year's, and Valentine's holidays. Perhaps the creation of Boog's holiday graveside shrine helped her owner "share" the holidays to some extent with her beloved cat. Graveside shrines like Max's also bespeak the celebration *with the deceased* of personal holidays such as birthdays. In this way, such holiday shrines are metaphysically performative; they hope to have a spiritual effect.

Many different types of love are made material through the construction of graveside shrines: mother for child, child for parent, owner for pet, and lover for lover. Shrines use the sensory language of candles, flowers, notes of love, and meaningful objects to communicate the physical, and even sensual loss, experienced at the death of a loved one. For example, the Montparnasse cemetery in Paris houses several modern sculptures including an original of Brancusi's "The Kiss." I photographed a grave that had a reproduction of this sculpture on it, plus flowers, candles, pages from a book written in Spanish, and photos of a loving couple. The grave stood out; in Paris, grave *assemblages* often are not as ornate as those in the United States. The lushness and richness of this graveside shrine conveyed the palpable and physical sensuality and love of this couple—and its loss to the world of the living. Whether a pet, a family member, or a lover, graveside shrines pointedly and poignantly communicate, in material ways, the nature of loss.

Consumerism and Spontaneous Shrines

Spontaneous shrines and the behaviors associated with them, which I have described herein, can be seen as expressive of consumer culture and the breakdown of the borders between elite and popular culture (see Jameson 1991: 1–3). They reflect the influence of multinational capitalism; we can now afford more objects, and mass-produced objects are increasingly important in our expressions of self (see Santino 1996: 151–159; Thomas 2003). Ironically, at these spiritual sites, capitalism and mourning collapse into each other. Erika Doss presents blatant examples of this in her study of the shrines created by Elvis fans[8] (1999: 69–113). Another illustration is the shrine to Diana that was erected in Harrods in London, a department store owned by the father of her companion, Dodi Fahyd, who was also killed in the car crash (see Bowman 1999: 225). The shrine is not in or near a church; instead such a traditional sacred place is replaced by a shopping space. It could be argued that the mourner–tourist who appears at Diana's Paris shrine signifies the shallowness of contemporary culture. Grief is replaced by tourism, which is a central ritual in consumer culture.

The contemporary " 'degraded' landscape of schlock and kitsch" (Jameson 1991: 2) is manifest in the endless, repetitive jumble of cigarettes, plastic objects, and Metro tickets at Morrison's grave.

Some visitors trek to Morrison's grave not because they like his music but because the grave, like Disneyland, is *a place to visit.* The construction of Jim's *fame* is more real to some of the young faces in the photos left on his grave than either his life or music. The expense evident in the carvings and *assemblages* on the pet gravemarkers seem reflective of culture that has capital to burn—even on something so trvial as to be named "Boogs" or "Pee." Finally, the concept of buying a Hallmark card for the dead seems absurd—but *only* when spoken of out of context. In the cemetery, with the words of Max's mother on it, it is anything but absurd.

A consideration of the context of all of the aforementioned shrines, with their varying folk dynamics, is an important and needed complication of the sometimes facile picture of contemporary consumer culture.[9] The media attention given to shrines related to famous people or events has aided the spread of these shines, but perhaps so too has a greater comfort with multiculturalism and expressions that earlier might have been seen as the purview of only one group or religion, such as Mexican American Catholics. Today's mourner may also be a tourist, as were some of the pilgrims of history, but there is also more real emotion evidenced and expressed than not—even by the tourists—at the various kinds of shrines I've examined.

Consider also one of the most visible spontaneous shrines in recent history: the one that people created to commemorate the loss of life in the terrorist attacks on the World Trade Towers. The Towers themselves are now indelibly symbolic of staggering tragedy, their absence and our continued recall of them is a sign of our times. Prior to the destruction of the Towers, Frederic Jameson's classic work argued that the Westin Bonaventure Hotel in Los Angeles was the architectural symbol of postmodern times. The hotel presents more surface than depth, and people lose their way in the building (1991: 44). In contrast, our continued reference to the absent Twin Towers and our painful, phantom reconstructions of them signifies not the architectural postmodern but the architectural abject. This pain is deep, and there is too much emotion, too much horror for one site to contain. According to the terrorists, this violence was their critique of American culture, its foreign policy, and its global capitalism, and part of their goal was to wound the U.S. economy. However, the victims experienced it as abject murder—the same as the victims of history's terrors always have. In the face of such horrific disintegration, a response that reassembles things—even consumer commodities—to form a new creation is not mere pastiche. It is an *assemblage* of the realities of felt experience; it is the pain and suffering of the human subjects of history manifest symbolically and concretely. It is active and political: it is about the realness of grief and love—all of which are often apparent and made concrete again in the detail and shared work in the creation of spontaneous shrines.

These are the shrines of our times, but, ultimately, they are also the shrines of all times, too.[10] The scale may have changed: the difference is that consumerism—our greater access to material goods—is more apparent in our shrines. However, the shrines of our postmodern world still communicate the same human searchings, feelings, and meanings as have shrines for centuries. All of these different kinds of contemporary shrines frequently and clearly communicate an old and necessary human longing. It is spoken of in the notes addressed to Jim, Diana, and Max. It is a yearning for a state of being whose centuries-old evasiveness and ongoing importance is manifest through flowers, notes, laborious poetry, personal objects left behind, and anonymous graffiti. In a word, it is scrawled by the graffitists on the official shrines that mark how war wrought death on the streets of Paris; simply, profoundly, and out of a vexing necessity, they write and wish for "*Paix.*"

Notes

Grateful thanks to Nancy Banks for the numerous "French lessons" and her translation of the French texts quoted in this article.

1. Mr. Mojo Risin' is a code name that Morrison supposedly developed with his manager; if he disappeared and wanted to contact his manager, he was supposed to use this alias to let the manager know he was still alive. I have retained the original punctuation in the notes.
2. Estimates indicate that a least a million people left flowers at Kensington Palace (Francis, Neophytou, and Kellaher 1999: 119). There were some who felt this mourning to be pressured and excessive, and they describe these shrines as a kind of "floral fascism" (Walter 1999: 31).
3. The custom is not to display the flag unless the reigning monarch is in residence (Santino 2001: 103).
4. Erika Doss discusses an example of an attitude projected by an official shrine: Frederick Hart's *Three Fightingmen*, the figural addition to the Vietnam Veterans Memorial, which she says, "uncritically affirms the neoconservative position that the Vietnam War was an honorable episode in American history" (1995: 30).
5. David Kozak and Camillus Lopez speculate that the Tohono O'odham reservation of southern Arizona "may comprise the single most densely commemorated area" in the Southwest (1991: 10). Due to auto accidents, part of the countryside has become a landscape of death, so the O'odham have built

"shrine-chapels," as a means of counteracting the troubling trend of highway deaths. The chapel-shrines are another folk response that attempts to ameliorate bad death (1991: 13, 18).

6. Sometimes it is difficult to discern from items left at a gravesite whether the person was merely following social convention and decorating the grave with flowers that are without any special meaning to the deceased.

7. Seasonal *assemblages* left at the spontaneous shrines of famous people by members of the general public (not family and friends) may simply be expressive of the cultural tradition of the use of holiday motifs as decoration. See Gundaker (1994) and Posey (1998) for discussion of holiday imagery in graveside shrines.

8. I would characterize the Elvis shrines in private homes that Doss describes as domestic shrines dedicated to a famous person; there are also domestic shrines dedicated to private citizens. Both of these types of shrines are similar to graveside shrines.

9. This is not a critique of Jameson; his views are nuanced and not facile, though he has little to say about the folk aspects of postmodernity.

10. They often employ old forms as well (see Chandler 1999: 151–154).

Bibliography

Bowman, Marion. 1999. "A Provincial City Shows Respect: Shopping and Mourning in Bath." In *The Mourning for Diana*, ed. Tony Walker, 215–225. New York: Berg.

Chandler, Jennifer, 1999. "Pilgrims and Shrines." In *The Mourning for Diana*, ed. Tony Walker, 135–155. New York: Berg.

Dimmitt, Barbara Sande. 2000. "The Angel for Lost Children." *Reader's Digest* January: 66–72.

Doss, Erika. 1995. *Spirit Poles and Flying Pigs: Public Art and Cultural Democracy in American Communities*. Washington: Smithsonian Institution Press.

———. 1999. *Elvis Culture: Fans, Faith, and Image*. Lawrence, Kansas: University Press of Kansas.

Everett, Holly. 2000. "Roadside Crosses and Memorial Complexes in Texas." *Folklore* 111: 91–118.

Francis, Doris, Georgina Neophyton, and Leonie Kellaher. 1999. "Kensington Gardens: from Royal Park to Temporary Center." In *The Mourning for Diana*, ed. Tony Walter, 109–134. New York: Berg.

Grider, Slyvia. 2001. "Preliminary Observations Regarding the Spontaneous Shrines Following the Terrorist Attacks of September 11, 2001." *New Directions in Folklore* 5. <http://www.temple.edu/isllc/newfolk/shrines.html>.

———. "Roadside Shrines." *Encyclopedia of Religion and American Cultures*. Santa Barbara: ABC-CLIO (forthcoming).

Gundaker, Grey. 1994. "Halloween Imagery in Two Southern Settings." In *Halloween and Other Festivals of Death and Life*, ed. Jack Santino, 247–266. Knoxville, Tennessee: The University Press of Tennessee.

Haney, C. Allen and Dell Davis. 1999. "America Responds to Diana's Death: Spontaneous Memorials." In *The Mourning for Diana*, ed. Tony Walker, 227–239. New York: Berg.

Hass, Kristin Ann. 1998. *Carried to the Wall: American Memory and the Vietnam Veterans Memorial*. Berkeley: University of California Press.

Jameson, Fredric. 1991. *Postmodernism or, The Cultural Logic of Late Capitalism*. Durham, North Carolina: Duke University Press.

Kozak, David and Camillus Lopez. 1991. "The Tohono O'odham Shrine Complex: Memorializing the Locations of Violent Death." *New York Folklore* 17: 1–20.

Monger, George. 1997. "Modern Wayside Shrines." *Folklore* 108: 113–114.

Posey, Sandra Mizumoto. 1998. "Grave and Image: Holiday Grave Decorations in a Southern California Memorial Park." *Folklore Forum* 29: 51–63.

Rowbotton, Ann. 1999. "A Bridge of Flowers." In *The Mourning for Diana*, ed. Tony Walker, 157–172. New York: Berg.

Santino, Jack. 1992a. "The Folk *Assemblage* of Autumn: Tradition and Creativity in Halloween Folk Art." In *Folk Art and Art Worlds*, ed. John Michael Vlach and Simon J. Bronner, 151–169. Logan, Utah: Utah State University Press.

———. 1992b. " 'Not an Unimportant Failture': Rituals of Death and Politics in Northern Ireland." In *Displayed in Mortal Light*, ed. Michael McCaughan. Antrim: Antrim Arts Council.

———. 1996. *New Old-Fashioned Ways: Holidays and Popular Culture*. Knoxville, Tennessee: The University of Tennessee Press.

———. 2001. *Signs of War and Peace: Social Conflict and the Use of Public Symbols in Northern Ireland*. New York: Palgrave.

Thomas, Jeannie Banks. 2003. *Naked Barbies, Warrior Joes, and Other Forms of Visible Gender*. Urbana, Illinois: University of Illinois Press.

Turner, Kay and Pat Jasper. 1994. "Day of the Dead: The Tex-Mex Tradition." In *Halloween and Other Festivals of Death and Life*, ed. Jack Santino, pp. 133–151. Knoxville, Tennessee: The University of Tennessee Press.

Walker, Tony. 1999. "The Questions People Asked." In *The Mourning for Diana*, ed. Tony Walker, 19–47. New York: Berg.

Young, James E. 1993. *The Texture of Memory: Holocaust Memorials and Meaning*. New Haven, Connecticut: Yale University Press.

Zeitlin, Steve. This volume.

Chapter 3

Mourning in Protest: Spontaneous Memorials and the Sacralization of Public Space

Harriet F. Senie

When Malice Green, an unemployed African American former steel worker, was beaten to death by two white Detroit police officers early in November of 1992, a spontaneous memorial was created on the spot. It consisted of "written messages, flowers, candles, shells, bibles and other objects associated with veneration in African and Christian traditions."[1] The site was framed by crosses with messages addressing Green's perceived martyrdom. A mural was painted on a nearby wall some five days after his death,[2] and soon afterward a mirror was placed so that visitors could see themselves and Green at once (or as one). As the memorial became a destination for motorists as well as local residents, a space was demarcated by two orange traffic cones, providing a place to view the now sacralized site of Green's death.

When international celebrity Princess Diana was killed suddenly in a traffic accident in September 1997, the spontaneous memorial phenomenon was spectacular, generating websites, worldwide news, a televised funeral, a dedicated song, and acres of flowers. Until recently, at the Place de' l'Alma above the tunnel in Paris where the princess was killed, people continued to leave objects and messages around a replica of the torch held by the Statue of Liberty, a gift to the French people from the *International Herald Tribune* on its centenary in 1987, intended "as a symbol of French–American friendship."[3] Here the usual floral and candle tributes were joined by messages in French, English, Spanish, Arabic, Russian, and other languages. Barricades kept people from descending into the vehicular tunnel; here, as in Detroit, road markers delimited another contemporary pilgrimage site.

The chain-link fence that marked off the site of the bombing of the Alfred P. Murrah Federal Building in Oklahoma City on April 19, 1995, held handwritten prayers, poems, children's drawings, teddy bears, and flowers. It separated the ground of death from the land of the living, much as cemetery entrances "announce a special realm dedicated to the departed."[4] The local fire chief put rubble from the building in buckets around the site so that those who grieved could take tangible evidence—relics—of the destruction. Governor Frank Keating gave each mourner a state flag and a diary; families of the nineteen children killed in the bombing were also given statuettes of praying angels.[5] A memorial chapel was built nearby; objects were left there as well.[6] Two years later at the grass covered spot where the building once stood, mourners observed 168 seconds of silence, one for each victim. The names were then read aloud at ten-second intervals and the ground covered with flowers. The governor encouraged people to leave mementos: "That fence has become our shrine and it is fitting that on this second anniversary we adorn it with tributes and memories."[7]

When twelve students and one teacher were shot at Columbine High School in Littleton, Colorado on April 20, 1999 by two classmates who then took their own lives, the actual scene of death was roped off as a crime scene. Almost at once people created a "shrine the size of a football field" across the street in Robert F. Clement Park. The day after the shooting, people hung messages for the victims from paper chains between trees. Thirteen crosses were planted in the grass, one slightly larger for the teacher who had been shot. And just as headstones in country cemeteries often note the profession of the deceased, a memorial for one student centered on her car, an indicator of the defining role of cars in contemporary suburban culture.[8] The omnipresent flowers were constantly replenished.[9]

Open the newspaper any morning or catch the late-night news on television, and you are likely to find an image of another spontaneous memorial—photographs of those deceased, clusters of flowers, candles, notes and cards, an array of gifts for the dead, and, if children are being mourned, a cluster of stuffed animals. Whether commemorating a single victim of a drive-by shooting or Princess Di, the many deaths in the Oklahoma City bombing or the Columbine High School "massacre," the response is identical—a rush to mourning manifest in traditional cemetery rituals. Sacred spaces are demarcated, objects are left, and people gather to grieve.

It is hard to know when this now widespread practice began. Certainly it gained national attention with the response to the Vietnam Veterans Memorial on the Mall in Washington. Even before the monument was dedicated on Memorial Day in 1982, people began leaving mementos alongside its black granite walls. A Navy officer dropped his dead brother's Purple Heart into the foundation trench even as the concrete was being poured.[10] Since then visitors have left over 30,000 objects, not including flowers and flags.

The ritual of leaving tributes occurs also at the five half-size replicas of the memorial known as the "traveling walls" that circulate around the country, functioning as its icon although they are smaller, flimsier, and never quite touch the ground.[11] The space around the memorial (and its facsimiles) is treated as sacred, dedicated to remembrances of the Vietnam War. Visitors file by in silence. In January 1991, a demonstration held against the Gulf War terminated at the D.C. monument; a Vietnam vet asked that protest banners be left outside the parameters of the memorial. All complied.

The objects left at the Vietnam Veterans Memorial[12] and at its offshoots, at spontaneous memorials and burial grounds in cemeteries, reveal an array of personal relationships with the dead as well as a variety of ethnic burial practices and civic messages. Specific objects may be relics of the dead or gifts for them; some reflect aspects of shared experience; others offer social commentary.[13] At the Vietnam Memorial these last include objects, letters, journals, photo albums, and works of art that address issues of the war as well as the participation of gays and women in the military.

Like the ground on which they rest, these ritual objects are seen as somehow sacred—as artifacts that should not be destroyed. The objects left at the Vietnam Veterans Memorial are collected regularly by National Parks Service rangers and stored in nearby Lanham, Maryland, at the Museum and Archaeological Regional Storage Facility (known by its acronym MARS). The tributes gathered at the traveling walls are stored in local historical societies. In Littleton, wilted flowers were used in compost, and fresh flowers were made into bags of potpourri for victims' families; the potpourri was intended to be sold to raise money for a permanent memorial. Other objects, including "homemade art work, handwritten poems wrapped in plastic, teddy bears, team shirts, votive candles and wind chimes," remarkably similar to those left at the Vietnam Memorial, were catalogued by volunteers organized by the Colorado Historical Society.[14] Without a community conditioned to consider its history worth preserving or a local institution to store it, most spontaneous memorials (like Malice Green's) are left to decay.

Although the bodies are buried elsewhere, almost every detail of spontaneous memorial practice revives the role cemeteries historically played in public life. The dead were once buried in the center of town, where they served as a daily reminder of the fate awaiting us all. As J. B. Jackson observed, "Located in the center of the village, concealed by no planting, plainly visible to all, [the graveyard] was a group monument, a constant reminder to emulate the virtues of the dead and to follow the precepts of the faith."[15] This unsettling experience was briefly recalled in June 1999, when bones were discovered for the third time during the renovation of City Hall Park in New York.[16] Reconstruction proceeded slowly around the skeletons in our midst, as they were temporarily covered with green plastic sheets to "preserve the dignity of the dead" and protect the sensibilities of the living. Regardless of our religious beliefs and changing burial customs, we do not tread lightly on the remains of the dead.

Since colonial times, for health, cultural, and economic reasons, local and national burial sites have gradually moved from plots in backyards, churchyards, and town commons to cemeteries further removed from the living, as well as from the prime real estate that can be used for other purposes.[17] In the early decades of the nineteenth century, a park-like setting outside the town became the model for the modern cemetery, as exemplified most famously in the United States by Mount Auburn in Cambridge, Massachusetts, with its emphasis on the landscape, symmetrical family plots, and wide, graceful paths for easy circulation. With this cemetery New Englanders hoped, among other things, to create a cultural institution that would help instill middle-class values in a growing working-class populace that regularly visited the cemetery along with mourners to enjoy the gardens.[18]

But by the end of the nineteenth century, the cemetery was no longer a public venue. It had become a private "place where wealth and family piety could assert themselves."[19] During the twentieth century, perhaps in reaction to earlier perceived excesses of grieving, or maybe in response to the unprecedented devastation of the two world wars, burial practices changed. By mid-century, death and mourning had almost become taboo, too uncomfortable for public expression, and many cemeteries were neglected.[20] Although there are still a few examples such as Arlington National Cemetery in the United States and Pere Lachaise in Paris that are visited regularly, today it is hardly possible to imagine the cemetery as a significant cultural institution.

Mourning in a cemetery has become a private, family affair. In marked contrast, spontaneous memorials invite the participation of a community; if the number of dead is significant or the victim is famous enough, such memorials attract pilgrims from afar, as was the case with Oklahoma City and Princess Di. But the subjects of most spontaneous memorials are individuals who become known only briefly in death.

Spontaneous memorials are populist phenomena, ways for people to mark their own history. They create a public place for individuals and communities united in grief and often anger. And they create, for a while, sacred ground, ground that has been, like a battlefield, the scene of violent death.[21] Victims of sudden death and their mourners have no time to prepare, no opportunity to say goodbye. While subjects or objects of commemoration or celebration in our multicultural society are often contested, death and mourning are beyond debate. They are universally understood.

As did older cemeteries in town centers, spontaneous memorials serve communal as well as personal needs. As Janice Mann has suggested, the drive-by memorial to Malice Green provided a place for peaceful public gathering and consolation for the community.[22] This may be because spontaneous memorials are inherently also expressions of protest, calling attention to the underlying conditions that led to the random death(s) being commemorated. The memorial to Malice Green was also a protest against police brutality; the Oklahoma shrine was a wailing wall at the destruction of random terrorism; the creation of the symbolic cemetery in Colorado was accompanied by cries for gun control and the study of violence in youth culture. The astonishing outpouring for "the people's princess" was widely understood as a demonstration of the desire for a less remote, more accessible monarch. And more directly, the spot where Margaret L. Mitchell, an African American woman in Los Angeles, was killed by Hispanic police officers was surrounded by written comments about the problems of mentally ill homeless people.[23] Unlike early cemeteries constructed for the civic purpose of moderating the behavior of the working classes, spontaneous memorials are often messages to those in control from the populace they govern.

Because we don't think too much about cemeteries today, their ritual practices have slipped relatively unnoticed into our midst. But it may be precisely because cemeteries and the function they once served have receded from civic consciousness that the practice of spontaneous memorials has flourished. Grieving in public expresses the need to have private loss socially acknowledged and shared.[24] The bereaved and their community, as well as the deceased, demand recognition. Those who mourn the victims of society briefly lay claim to public space and attention.

Although, perhaps even because, public experience in our culture has been rendered private by television and the internet, many of us feel an overwhelming need to make real what is increasingly mediated—to recapture the here and now. To stand on the ground where something happened is to feel the reality of the event—to feel meaningfully linked to others and to history. This connection, through feet that stand on hallowed ground or hands that touch a sacred wall, is experienced viscerally. The Hebrew practice of *Gal'ed*, by which a place of commemoration is marked with stones, derives from the ancient word meaning "a stone or a heap of stones that witnessed an event, [that] have been marked off and have become sacred."[25] One writer has referred to Israel as "hot rocks which have seen more holy murder, rape and plunder than any other place on earth."[26] Another, standing atop Gestapo ruins in Berlin observed, "You sense that the stones of this rubble somehow hold the moans and screams of decades ago."[27]

There is pervasive evidence that we believe the ground we walk on holds the content of its history—offers us direct access to what has occurred there. Mourners at spontaneous memorials often act as if the bodies were buried there. But not only are spontaneous memorials built on this premise. The Imperial War Museum in London is situated on the site of the former Bedlam, and so much is this a part of its institutional identity that the director defines the museum as "an unusual place in many ways—a museum devoted to modern war housed [on the grounds of] an ancient lunatic asylum . . ."[28]

The museum in Caen built after World War II is called a "memorial for peace" and features a garden built directly over the site of the headquarters of the German commander during the Nazi occupation of Normandy. The museum catalogue describes the collection of portrait busts assembled there as an "An Alterative History of the 20th Century: the Nobel Peace Prizewinners."[29] Arguably, by burying and obscuring its past the museum itself is trying to accomplish just that. On a smaller scale, when events are experienced as too painful, a place may be destroyed. The town council and local community in Stirling, Scotland, decided to tear down a school gym where sixteen children and their teacher were shot by a man who also took his own life.[30] At both the French museum and Scottish school, the decisions were based on the unstated supposition that the site itself contained the content of its past, not only when the memory was fresh, but indeed forever.

Spontaneous memorials are not, however, for eternity, although evidence suggests that they are especially vivid for those who believe in the hereafter. Many typical memorial objects are linked to the customs of Catholic Latino communities.[31] However, the practice is not restricted to any religion or ethnicity, as the memorials to Diana, Malice Green, and the victims in Oklahoma and Colorado clearly attest. Spontaneous memorials are the sign of an engaged populace responding to personal need for public mourning and civic protest. Fulfilling the functions once provided by cemeteries, such memorials seem to have appeared just when Maya Lin's design—a symbolic cemetery on the National Mall—was chosen to commemorate the war that challenged "the very mythos of America [sic], its blessed and exceptional character"[32] with a symbolic cemetery on the Washington Mall. The Vietnam Veterans Memorial called attention to a rift in perceptions of national identity much as spontaneous memorials mark a localized rent in civic cohesion. In prompting an unprecedented and unexpected public response, both the war and its memorial generated a national upheaval of protest. And the wall, as intended, like many spontaneous memorials, has worked to heal, bringing people together in grief over the consequences of a war that had once divided them in politics.

A Difference in Kind: Spontaneous Memorials after 9/11

Sometimes a difference in degree is a difference in kind. And sometimes apparent similarities mask critical distinctions. That the greatest destruction of 9/11 hit New York at the actual center of international trade, finance, and communication, and the symbolic center of U.S. capitalism guaranteed that everything connected with it would be newsworthy and resonate around the world. Perceived at once to be an event of profound historical significance and symbolic magnitude, it was writ large in all media.

But on September 11, 2001, with U.S. airspace closed for an indefinite future, the nature of the event was barely grasped, the magnitude of public response huge, the death toll uncertain, and the missing presumed to be just that. All this, for a time, changed spontaneous memorial practice.

When people gathered initially and in the days that followed at Union Square, the closest open public space to Ground Zero, the number and identity of the casualties was unknown. This was reflected in the nature of the objects left. There were few things associated with individuals since it was not yet known who had been killed and who might still turn up alive. The only thing gone for certain were the twin towers and there were a number of anthropomorphic depictions and effigies of those, immediate icons for what was lost.[33]

Similarly, there were no gifts for specific individuals or objects of shared experience.[34] But evidence of commentary was everywhere, transforming this symbolic cemetery in-the-making into "a forum to publicize grievances and to right wrong," an echo of the role cemeteries once played in nineteenth-century United States.[35] There were personal expressions in poetry and prose written on the ground or in the huge rolls of paper provided for that purpose. American flags, which soon became ubiquitous throughout the city,[36] appeared draped in front of the statue of George

Washington and in his hand. Henry Kirke Brown's sculpture, the second equestrian monument to be cast in the United States and the city's first outdoor bronze sculpture, dedicated on July 4, 1856, functioned as the symbolic locus of the state and national power.[37] Covered with comments of love and peace, the statue conveyed a decidedly mixed message.[38]

The crowds that gathered day and night at Union Square appeared intent to create a communal space, a place providing comfort in numbers in the most uncertain and frightening of times. As one young man remarked, "You get a little hope in togetherness."[39] In a few days the nature of the gathering at Union Square changed, becoming more of a festival reminiscent of 1960s happenings.[40] Early on, the Department of Parks in consultation with the Art Commission decided to remove the graffiti from George Washington and restore Union Square to its pre-9/11 state. This process of desacralization, what Kenneth E. Foote calls the rectification of a site, implies "no lasting positive or negative meaning" will be associated with it.[41] And while there are no remaining visible signs, the transformation of Union Square in the wake of 9/11 and the weeks that followed are an indelible part of personal memory and undoubtedly will figure in subsequent written histories of the event and of the site.

By early November, when lower Manhattan was partially reopened, the main site of the spontaneous memorial shifted to St. Paul's Chapel of Trinity Episcopal parish, a block from the trade center site on Broadway. (Immediately after the 9/11 attacks and for some eight months the church became a refuge for relief workers at ground zero.[42]) When the public began congregating at the site, the church hung huge canvas drop cloths from the surrounding fence so visitors could sign their names and leave messages, creating what was called "the world's largest guest book." A year later some neighborhood residents began requesting the removal of the mounds of material that could now "be mistaken for a camp for derelicts."[43]

While Union Square and St. Paul's were the primary loci of spontaneous memorials, their widespread proliferation especially at firehouses, marked local sites of loss. For a while it seemed possible to feel that New York itself had been turned into a temporary shrine, but that experience was determined by where in the city you happened to be. There were significant shrines in Grand Central and Port Authority terminals. And just as after the sudden death of Princess Di people gathered at those sites she had frequented in life, so New York's spontaneous memorials clustered at places once inhabited by those who perished on 9/11.

Photographs are a common feature of spontaneous memorials, assuming or standing for the aura of the deceased.[44] Beyond their fragile materiality and symbolic resonance, these images conflate private and public space in a dramatic and significant way. After 9/11 photographs were taken briefly from the intimate frame of the family album or mantle display, copied and paired with personal information on paper posters that provided the vital statistics of those initially presumed missing. The sheer magnitude and proliferation of these images affixed to neighborhood fences, storefronts, subway stations, and lampposts transformed the anonymous character of many New York public spaces. People gathered and paid attention as they rarely do in this city of millions, suddenly participants in some kind of communal wake, often silent, sometimes asking strangers, "Did you know . . . ? How is . . . ?" As the presumed missing were acknowledged dead, the photos became memorials to strangers that had already somehow become more than that.[45]

Photography after 9/11 also assumed another role, enlarging public participation, recording the actual event, details of the destruction, and aspects of the recovery. The impulse to document was immediate for many, prompted by the realization that this was a historic moment. Instead of running for cover many grabbed their cameras and rushed to rooftop vantage points. Photography provided a way to participate and perhaps also acted as a safety valve, a quasi-professional shield, a protection of sorts from the actual horror of reality.

Many of the works of these amateur photographers/historians, as well as their professional counterparts, were quickly displayed in an impromptu exhibition, "Here Is New York: A Democracy of Photographs."[46] Images were scanned, printed on archival paper, pinned to the walls and hung from strings at eye level at the 116 Prince Street Gallery in Soho. There were no frames and no names. Anyone could buy a print for $25 and many did. In the first two months more than half a million dollars in net proceeds were donated to The Children's Aid Society for its World Trade Center relief efforts.[47] The exhibition evoked the chaos of memory, the visual, sensory, emotional overload of jumbled images, fragments that even when put together couldn't quite capture the whole. Subsequently, like the AIDS quilt, a portion of the exhibition traveled in segments to the Museum of Modern Art and the International Center of Photography in New York as well as venues in Chicago, Washington, and elsewhere in the United States, and several cities in Germany, London, Paris, and Tokyo.[48] At each venue where I viewed it, public response was stilled, contemplative, and profoundly emotional.

In November 2001, the New York gallery Exit Art issued a website-based open call for personal responses to 9/11 expressed on an 8 1/2 × 11 inch piece of paper. From January 26 through March 30, 2002, over 2,500 responses were displayed on free-standing supports and in loose-leaf binders at the Soho venue.[49] "Reactions" included poetry, musical scores, texts, letters, drawings, paintings, collages, and photographs, an echo and extension of the objects already gathered at spontaneous memorials in more public spaces.

Around the same time (January 17–February, 2002), an exclusive invitational exhibition at Max Protetch Gallery in Chelsea featured 61 submissions that reimagined the World Trade Center Towers in ways that never strayed far from the original.[50] Even though "The New World Trade Center: Design Proposals" was barely more than a rehash of the old,[51] the public came in droves (it was crowded even on weekday mornings) and stared in rapt attention at visual evocations of a world that suddenly no longer existed.

The need for temporary memorials beyond the spontaneous was clear. Early on the proposal for "Phantom Towers" featured on the cover of the *New York Times Magazine* on September 23, 2001 seemed to strike a resonant note for many.[52] Realized through the efforts of Creative Time and the Municipal Art Society, it was at first called "Towers of Light" and eventually renamed "Tribute in Light" to shift the focus away from the towers that had come to symbolize the 9/11 loss. But the beams of light that illuminated the night sky for a month in 2002, no matter what they were called, only confirmed the iconic power the towers had come to assume.

The last steel column from the rubble left at the World Trade Center site, covered with graffiti, became like the survivor tree at Oklahoma City, a relic of great symbolic value. On May 30, 2002, in a ceremony marking the official end of the recovery effort at ground zero, the 58-ton beam from the south tower was towed from the scene wrapped in black muslin and an American flag.[53] A symbolic body if there ever was one, carried out to the sound of taps played by buglers from New York's Fire and Police Departments and "America the Beautiful" played on bagpipes was now inextricably linked to national identity.

A View from the Bridge

On 9/11 and for some time thereafter much of downtown Brooklyn was covered with dust and office paper from the World Trade Center. The view of Manhattan from the Brooklyn Heights Promenade, the definitive view in so many films and photographs, now too provided a vantage point but little emotional distance from lower Manhattan. People immediately attached posters and messages to the fence at various focal points where clusters of candles were lit and relit until they gradually melted into puddles of wax. A huge, hushed crowd gathered to observe the inaugural lighting of the

Tribute in Light and again to celebrate its last night.[54] Today the only remains of the spontaneous memorial is a single framed photograph of the twin towers, hanging from the fence at the end of the Pierrepont Street entrance, marking the spot where their absence is most visible. Everything else was cleared away by Parks department employees on May 30, 2002, the day that marked the official end of the retrieval of remains from the World Trade Center site.

Coda

Although the remains of the World Trade Center were buried in effigy in the form of the last I-beam, a longing for the towers remains. It was evident in the runner-up proposal for the rebuilding of the site, THINK's emblem of open twin towers, clearly evoking the missing skyline markers. These fantastical obelisks for the future, empty of all but scale and ambition, were perfect symbols for a culture of denial.[55]

The spontaneous memorials, created out of a fleeting experience of community, focused on personal and national loss, are a thing of the past—both time and site specific. They cannot be moved, displayed, or organized.[56] The whole is indeed greater than the sum of its parts. They are a grass-roots public response to a private need, personal messages meant to be shared although not necessarily heard by the powers that be. Although stringently policed, especially in New York, the worldwide protests on February 15, 2003 against President Bush's then pending war on Iraq[57] captured something of the atmosphere of spontaneous memorials after 9/11—a merging of individuals who reflected the spectrum of the world's populations, civic engagement on an international scale prompted by a profound fear of the future, and a need to stand together. One home made sign in particular continues to resonate for me: "OUR GRIEF IS NOT A CRY FOR WAR."

Although the difference in scale of spontaneous memorials post–9/11 signaled a difference in kind, all spontaneous memorials are democracy in action and as such they suggest a range of critical questions for those commissioning and building permanent official markers for history. How can memorial designers tap into the profound personal response and civic commentary evidenced by the practice of spontaneous memorials? What kinds of content do our built memorials now impugn to the ground on which they are built? Which history are we burying or incorporating in their foundations? Can we create permanent memorials that actively engage a society so clearly in need of them?

Notes

1. See Janice Mann, " 'Malice Green Did Like Jesus': A Detroit Miracle Story," in Dawn Perlmutter and Debra Koppman, eds., *Reclaiming the Spiritual in Art: Contemporary Cross-cultural Perspectives* (Albany: SUNY Press, 1999).
2. For a discussion of memorial walls see Martha Cooper and Joseph Sciorra, *R.I.P.: Memorial Wall Art* (New York: Henry Holt, 1994). Memorial walls are related to the practice of spontaneous memorials. Both are prompted by the local community and provide a focus for mourning and remembering. However, since the memorial walls are commissioned works executed by a single artist (albeit with community input), they are, by definition, more formalized. And since they require a wall surface, they cannot always mark the precise place of death.
3. See Craig R. Whitney, "Paris Adds a Garden to Diana's Thriving Memorials," *New York Times*, August 30, 1998. A particularly provocative article about the role of contemporary relics in the sanctification process is Joan Juliet Buck, "Diana's Relics." *The New Yorker*, September 22, 1997, 104–105.
4. Kenneth T. Jackson and Camilo Jose Vergara. *Silent Cities: The Evolution of the American Cemetery* (New York: Princeton Architectural Press, 1989), 72.
5. Jane H. Lii, "For Families Of the Dead, A Pilgrimage To the Scene," *New York Times*, May 7, 1995, 36.
6. John Kifner, "Despite Oklahoma Charges, The Case Is Far From Closed," *New York Times*, August 13, 1995, 1, 24.
7. Sam Howe Verhovek, "A Look Back and Ahead At Oklahoma City Site," *New York Times*, April 20, 1997, 20.
8. Jackson and Vergara, *Silent Cities*, 13, observed that old grave markers in country graveyards that were often decorated with images indicating the deceased's occupation "such as axes, saws, sickles, plows, and hammers" had recently been "updated to images of vehicles or farm equipment."
9. Many articles in newspapers and magazines documented the memorial activities at Columbine High. See especially Gustav Niebuhr and Jodi Wilgoren, "From the Shock of Violent Deaths, New and More Public Rites of Mourning," *New York Times*, April 28, 1999, A24; James Brooke, "A Neighborhood Park Draws Littleton Pilgrims," *New York Times*, May 6, 1999, A26.
10. See Thomas B. Allen, *Offerings at the Wall: Artifacts from the Vietnam Veterans Memorial Collection* (Atlanta: Turner Publishing, 1995), 10.
11. Various individuals and organizations circulate the half-size versions of the Vietnam Veterans Memorial, including the Vietnam Veterans Memorial Fund, which commissioned Maya Lin's sculpture. At each site there are local ceremonies; all are marked by the practice of leaving mini-shrines to individuals near their names. I discuss the practice and implications of the traveling walls in "From the Center: The Vietnam Veterans Memorial as Centripetal and Centrifugal Force" in Edward von Voolen and Gabi Dolf-Bonekamper, eds., *Denkmale und kulturelles Gedächtnis nach dem Ende der Ost-West-Konfrontation* (Berlin: Akademie der Kunste and Jovis Verlag, 2000), 251–264.

12. For a detailed analysis of the objects left at the Vietnam Veterans Memorial see Kristin Ann Hass, *Carried to the Wall: American Memory and The Vietnam Veterans Memorial* (Berkeley: University of California, 1998).

13. I discuss this idea in more detail in "Objects Left, Individuals Remembered: 'Making Memory Real' at the Vietnam Veterans Memorial," in Wessel Reinink and Jeroen Stumpel, eds., *Memory and Oblivion: Acts of the XXIXth International Congress of the History of Art, Amsterdam 1996* (Dordrecht, The Netherlands: Kluwer Academic Publishers, 1999), 1085–1090.

14. Photo caption, *New York Times*, May 5, 1999, A18, and James Brooke, "A Neighborhood Park Draws Littleton Pilgrims," *New York Times*, May 6, 1999, A26; James Brooke, "Teacher of Colorado Gunmen Alerted Parents," *New York Times*, May 11, 1999, A14.

15. J. B. Jackson, "The Vanishing Epitaph: From Monument to Place," *Landscape*, Winter 1967–1968, 23.

16. Dan Barry, "Ghosts from a Long-Ago Poorhouse in City Hall Park," *New York Times*, June 11, 1999, B3.

17. See Jessica Mitford, *The American Way of Death* (New York: Simon and Schuster, 1963) for a critique of the materialistic aspects of the funeral industry.

18. Stanley French, "The Cemetery as Cultural Institution: The Establishment of Mount Auburn and the 'Rural Cemetery' Movement," *American Quarterly*, v.26 (March 1974), reprinted in David E. Stannard, ed., *Death in America* (Philadelphia: University of Pennsylvania Press, 1975).

19. Jackson, "The Vanishing Epitaph," 24.

20. For a description of this development, see Philippe Aries, "The Reversal of Death: Changes in Attitudes toward Death in Western Societies," trans. Valerie M. Stannard, in Stannard, ed., *Death in America* (Philadelphia: University of Penn Press, 1975), 134–158.

21. For a discussion of battlefields as sacred space see Edward Tabor Linenthal, *Sacred Ground: Americans and Their Battlefields* (Urbana and Chicago: University of Illinois Press, 1991). Linenthal focuses on Lexington and Concord, the Alamo, Gettysburg, Little Bighorn, and Pearl Harbor.

22. See Mann. Evidently local law enforcement agencies were concerned that the death of Malice Green might spark riots in Detroit similar to those in Los Angeles after the failure to convict the officers who had apparently beaten Rodney King.

23. See Todd S. Purdum, "A Police Shooting Death, a Study in Contrasts," *New York Times*, June 5, 1999, A9.

24. My thanks to Elke Solomon for this observation.

25. Mira Engler, "A Living Memorial: Commemorating Yitzhak Rabin at the Tel Aviv Square," *Places*, v. 2, 2 (Winter 1999) note 2, 11. My thanks to Wendy Feuer for this reference.

26. "Via Dolorosa: Walking on Sacred Soil and Doing Battle Over It," *New York Times*, April 10, 1999, B11.

27. Lesley Hazleton, "Berlin, A Fast Car, Nightmares," in Elinor Nauen, ed., *Ladies Start Your Engines* (Boston: Faber and Faber, 1996), 147.

28. Alan Borg, "Introduction," *The 'New' Imperial War Museum* (London: Imperial War Museum, 1994 edition), 1.

29. Claude Quetel, *A Memorial for Peace* (Paris: Editions du Regard, 1993), 193ff. All subsequent quotes pertaining to the peace garden are taken from this source.
30. "Scots Raze School Gym Where Children Died," *New York Times*, April 11, 1996, A16.
31. Cooper and Sciorra, *Memorial Wall Art*, 10, suggest that Latino artists predominate in the practice of memorial walls and that crosses marking the spot of suddenly dead Catholics reflect the belief that those who have not received the Last Rites remain in "purgatory's purifying flames" until the soul is released to heaven through prayer.
32. Rowland A. Sherrill, "American Sacred Space and the Contest of History," in David Chidester and Edward Linenthal, eds., *American Sacred Space* (Bloomington: Indiana University Press, 1995), 326.
33. John Kifner and Susan Saulny, "Posting Handbills as Votive Offerings," *New York Times*, September 14, 2001, A9 describe a postcard featuring an image of the twin towers covered by a handwritten message: "They are missing. I am looking for these two great brothers of New York."
34. Gifts for the dead usually appear around major holidays and birthdays, continuing a ritual practice of life. Objects of shared experience are more general, often pertaining to sports, spirits or smokes, and sometimes more intimate activities.
35. Jackson, "The Vanishing Epitaph," 120.
36. Flying the flag seemed another spontaneous response. Images appeared in the *New York Times*, September 14, 2001, A1, A14–15, with the following captions: "Flying the Colors: Americans responded to the attacks by displaying the flag;" "A Symbol Offers Comfort On New York's Streets;" "Americans at home and overseas confronted this week's terror attacks with one simple gesture, flying the flag. The displays seem as much acts of defiance as of patriotism." Flags sold out in many stores and were difficult to obtain in some areas. Over time the flags eventually morphed into more frivolous fashion statements and patterns on sheets, among other things.
37. For a general discussion of the sculpture see Margot Gayle and Michele Cohen, *Manhattan's Outdoor Sculpture* (New York: Prentice Hall Press, 1988), 91–92. Its gesture derives from Michelangelo's Marcus Aurelius monument at the Capitoline Hill in Rome although the implicit comparison to a Roman emperor would have been anathema to Washington and unknown to most contemporary viewers.
38. See, for example, "Peace Signs Amid Calls to War," *New York Times*, November 20, 2001, A20.
39. Quoted in Michael Kimmelman, "Offering Beauty, and Then Proof That Life Goes On," *New York Times*, December 30, 2001, AR35.
40. See, for example, Michael Kimmelman, "In a Square, A Sense of Unity," *New York Times*, September 19, 2001, E1.
41. Kenneth E. Foote, *Shadowed Ground: America's Landscapes of Violence and Tragedy* (Austin: University of Texas Press, 1997) designates four categories for the treatment of such sites: sanctification, designation, rectification, and obliteration.

42. For a description of the early activities inside the church see David W. Dunlap, "Polished Marble and Sacramental Scuffs," *New York Times*, August 25, 2002, Sect 11, 1, 6; Daniel J. Wakin, "Chapel and Refuge Struggles to Define Role," *New York Times*, November 28, 2002, B1, 7. The church produced three videos for sale on its role in the relief process.

43. See Michael Wilson, "How to Say 'Enough' Gracefully," *New York Times*, October 11, 2002, B1.

44. See Elizabeth Edwards, "Photographs as Objects of Memory," in Marius Kwint, Christopher Breward, Jeremy Aynsley, eds., *Material Memories: Design and Evocation* (Oxford and New York: Berg, 1999), 226, for a provocative discussion of the role of photographs as relics as well as the significance of their material forms.

45. For a discussion of this transformation process see Geoffrey Batchen, "Requiem," *Afterimage*, January/February 2002, 5.

46. The exhibition was organized by Alice Rose George, Gilles Peress, Michael Shulan, and Charles Traub.

47. Handout published by the International Center of Photography in conjunction with a series of exhibitions titled "Aftermath: Photography in the Wake of September 11," np. The exhibitions were on display January 11–March 17, 2002.

48. For a review of the exhibition at the Museum of Modern Art see Sarah Boxer, "Prayerfully and Powerfully, New York City Before and After," *New York Times*, March 6, 2002, E1. For reception in Germany, see Otto Pohl, "September 11 Photo Exhibition Touches a Nerve in Berlin," *New York Times*, July 7, 2002, 8. In addition to Berlin, the exhibition was seen in Dresden, Dusseldorf, and Stuttgart. Other venues continue to be added.

49. Exit Art is directed by Papo Colo and Jeanette Ingberman who conceived of the project.

50. The exhibition was curated by Max Protech, Aaron Betsky, the staffs of *Architectural Record* and *Architecture* magazines, and other architecture professionals.

51. For a more detailed review of the exhibition at the Max Protetch Gallery, see Harriet F. Senie, "National Icon: The Transfiguration of the World Trade Center Towers," *Sculpture*, October 2002, 81–82.

52. Initially the concept of Paul Myoda and Julian LaVerdiere, the "Towers of Light" eventually also included the work of John Bennett, Gustavo Bonevardi, Richard Nash Gould, and Paul Marantz. See "Filling the Void: A Memorial by Paul Myoda and Julian La Verdiere," *New York Times Magazine*, September 23, 2001, 80. The two artists had been working on a project about the buildings from their temporary studio on the ninety-first floor of the north tower. The eventual month-long existence of the 88-searchlight sculpture extinguished on April 15, 2002 attracted worldwide attention. Response appeared unanimously positive. See, for example, Andrew Jacobs, "In Morning Sky, Seamless Exit for Twin Beams," *New York Times*, April 15, 2002, A12, photo A1.

53. This ceremony was widely recorded on radio and television and in the press. See, for example, Charlie LeDuff, "Last Steel Column From the Ground Zero

Rubble Is Cut Down," *New York Times*, May 29, 2002, B3, photo A1; Dan Barry, "Where Twin Towers Stood, A Silent Goodbye," *New York Times*, May 31, 2002, A1, B6.

54. My thanks to Iris Klein for her observations of this site made during a seminar titled "Capturing Memory: Strategies of Contemporary Art" that I taught at the Graduate Center, CUNY during the spring 2002 semester. Even though only a single shaft was visible from Brooklyn, at first glance suggesting airport tower transmissions rather than the towers that were, its symbolic resonance was evident.

55. It remains to be seen whether the winning proposal, Daniel Libeskind's cluster of angled buildings and broadcast observation tower (intended to be the world's tallest structure), will satisfy the sense of loss so many still seem to feel for the World Trade Center towers. Preliminary critical reviews have been positive. See, for example, Paul Goldberger, "Eyes on the Prize," *The New Yorker*, March 10, 2003, 78–82; or Marvin Trachtenberg, "A New Vision for Ground Zero Beyond Mainstream Modernism," *New York Times*, February 23, 2003, AR 54. At the time of this writing it is not possible to know how much of the design will actually be built as proposed and what significant changes or modifications may be required.

56. Exhibitions such as "Missing: Streetscape of a City in Mourning" at the New York Historical Society (March 12–June 9, 2002) which contained a selection of the objects left at Union Square and other sites had none of the energy or immediacy of the spontaneous memorials. For a review, see Glenn Collins, "Vessels of a City's Grief," *New York Times*, March 9, 2002, B1. On collecting of 9/11 artifacts in general see, James B. Gardner, "Collecting a National Tragedy," *Museum News*, March/April 2002, 42–45; 66–67. At the time of the first anniversary of 9/11, New York City officials circulated plans to capture new shrines in temporary structures intended to protect them from the weather. The public failed to respond.

57. The various protest activities of February 15, 2003 were documented in numerous articles that appeared in the following two days in the *New York Times*.

Chapter 4

"We'll Watch Out for Liza and The Kids": Spontaneous Memorials and Personal Response at the Pentagon, 2001

Margaret R. Yocom

September 22, 2001. Lying on the lawn with many other memorial tokens, a mustard-yellow t-shirt with a small "NAVY DIVING & SALVAGE TRAINING CENTER" insignia and a handwritten message printed in black magic marker

FOR MY FRIEND,
CAPT. BOB DOLAN, UNITED STATES NAVY.
THEY, WHO DID THIS WILL
HEAR OUR BATTLECRY OF *FREEDOM*
HOO YAH DEEP SEA!!
YOUR PAL
CAPT. H.T. HELMKAMP, *USN*
"KAMPER"
WE'LL WATCH OUT FOR LIZA & THE KIDS.[1]
(see figure 4.1)

* * *

58

Figure 4.1 At the memorial, Capt. H.T. Helmkamp promises his fallen friend, "We'll watch out for Liza & the kids."

Source: Photo: c Margaret R. Yocom.

September 22, 2001. Hanging on the black metal fence of the Arlington National Cemetery across the street from the t-shirt, a six-foot red sign with white letters plastered with cutouts of red, white, and blue hands:

PEACE

St. Bartholomew's School

(see figure 4.2)

* * *

There is no place that is not haunted by many different spirits hidden there in silence, spirits one can "invoke" or not. Haunted places are the only ones people can live in.

—Michel de Certeau

* * *

The first time I ventured down to the memorial I heard was growing near the Pentagon crash site, I didn't go alone. In fact, the times I did go, I always went with friends or family—my husband, John, or my cousins. My friend and fellow folklorist Mary Hufford and her daughter Katherine went with me the first time to see what we, as folklorists and as Virginians who live near the Pentagon, could see there.

Figure 4.2 St. Bartholomew's School poster features the hands of their students. Damaged wall of the Pentagon appears in background.

Source: Photo: c Margaret R. Yocom.

It is never easy for me to visit the spontaneous memorials that dot our northern Virginia landscape. And it's especially awkward to travel with a camera in tow. Sometimes when I read and then photograph the displays, no matter how reverently I move through the site, I feel like a voyeur. Like someone unworthy of entrance, or someone too much a stranger to the dead.[2] I never know who the other people around me might be. Friends of the deceased? Family, maybe? For some years now, though, I've been teaching about these memorials in my folklore classes, curiously drawn to them as are many of my George Mason University students. And though I've made my pilgrimages[3] to several in the area, I am never prepared for what I see.

It's not that I am unused to visiting memorials; I've visited many. After all Washington DC, the place where I live is a city of memorials. People the world over visit the figurative statuary erected in honor of George Washington, Thomas Jefferson, Benito Juarez, African American Civil War veterans, Mary McLeod Bethune, Albert Einstein, Eleanor Roosevelt, the Korean War dead, the Iwo Jima flag raising, the World War II dead, John F. Kennedy, the Vietnam War dead, the astronauts lost on the space shuttles Challenger and Columbia, and many more.[4] On grassy knolls, in marbled buildings, and under spreading trees, the statues sit and stand, often appearing larger than the people they commemorate did in life. Thanks to their stone or metal exteriors, they stand stoically like stalwarts through rain, sun, and snow.

The spontaneous memorials of the region are something quite different, and they easily outnumber official monuments. Flowers, crosses, teddy bears, poems, messages, and more decorated the corner where 17-year-old Tandy Leigh Fitzgerald was killed by a drunk driver on October 22, 1995, on Annandale Road in Falls Church, just minutes from her home. Friends decorated the locker of 17-year-old Oxon Hill High School honor student Charles Marsh with flowers, bows, cards, and more after he died from a stray bullet. He had been waiting in line for the school bus to take him home when a stray bullet shot by a masked youth trying to steal a jacket from another student hit him on December 14, 1995. After their friend Devin Fowlkes was killed by a stray bullet in Washington DC as he walked out of a school pep rally and dance on the afternoon of October 30, 2003, fellow students wrote messages to him all over his bedroom walls (Blum 2003: B1,5).

One of the largest and most complex of these memorials began to take shape shortly after the September 11, 2001, 9:45 a.m. plunge of American Airlines Flight 77 into the west face of the Pentagon, just a river away from Washington DC, two miles from the White House, and three from the Capitol. Fifty-nine passengers and crew, and 125 people in the Pentagon, ranging in age from 3 to 71, lost their lives that day. By that evening, a site lying just west of the gash in the Pentagon had become a place to leave offerings.

Some people, especially writers for the popular press, have called such sites "makeshift memorials,"[5] but there is nothing makeshift about them. These places where people visit, linger, and sit for hours in silent contemplation have a rhythm, a precision, an aesthetic arrangement, and a set of behaviors all their own. These encounters, these acts of witness, these experiences in places carved from the roadside compel many of us. Why do we go to such sites as the Pentagon memorial, and what experiences do we have once we're there? What do the tokens we leave signify? And what lasting influences do the memorials have on us?

The Pentagon Spontaneous Memorial

To drive to the Pentagon memorial, I had to go closer and closer to the twisting eight-lane highways that could, given one false turn, send me spinning across Washington DC into the Potomac River instead. The spot lay just west of the Pentagon, at the juncture of Columbia Pike, Southgate Road, and Joyce Street, but where the boundaries of Arlington National Cemetery, the Navy Annex, and the Pentagon do not quite meet (Hufford 2001: 5).

Arriving on September 22, just 11 days after the attack itself, I was amazed to see how large the memorial had already become.[6] Two main components formed the memorial. One was a wall of messages superimposed on the iron and masonry fence that forms the southeastern boundary of Arlington Cemetery. The second was a spreading array of flowers, wreaths, candles, and posters across Southgate Road from the Cemetery, on the lawn below the Navy Annex building. Displays clustered around trees and hung from branches. They covered the large wooden message board that stood on the right. They spread up the slightly sloping lawn and stretched over to the left, toward the open lawn where nothing had yet been laid.

By November, a third component appeared even closer to the torn side of the Pentagon. Recalling the tokens left on fences at so many other sites of tragedy such as the Murrah Building in Oklahoma on April 19, 1995, people had found several ways to leave messages on the heavy metal fence that cordoned off the bulldozers, excavators, and other equipment being used for reconstruction from the lawn that rolled back toward the Navy Annex.

Just yards away from busy Route 395 that borders the Pentagon, people pinned messages, posters, flags, and flowers on the fence and fastened others to the ground with rocks.

This entire site was, as Mary Hufford wrote later, a "plot of grass and trees at the conjunction of highly administered worlds, facing the site of physical impact, [where] signs of impacts that are spiritual, emotional, and psychological pile[d] up" (2001: 5).

On that September day, Mary, Katharine, and I were three of about eighty people quietly walking through the site. Many lingered as they walked gingerly around the many tributes. Silence was broken only by passing cars, occasional soft whisperings, and the click of cameras. Visitors[7] stood nearby the fence by Arlington National Cemetery in the golden afternoon light, taking photos of the distant blackened wall of the Pentagon with its gaping hole.

Some visitors had brought messages. Some came with no plans, but ended up leaving a note or a signature. Some had brought tokens, not knowing whether they would leave them behind or not. A tow-headed 10-year-old dressed in a black and neon-green Mt. Vernon soccer team t-shirt clutched his black and neon yellow soft-cloth fireman figure whose foot and a half length seemed glued to the boy's body. He had gotten it earlier, his mother told me, and it had quickly become a favorite.[8] He came thinking he wanted to leave it at the site, she explained, in memory of the firefighters in New York who lost their lives, but now, faced with setting the figure down and walking away, the boy had begun to think he couldn't part with the fireman after all (see figure 4.3). When I returned eight days later, his fireman was standing watch over a new plaque that displayed the names of the Pentagon dead.

Some visitors came with humor: a mother and her older son posed for my camera, as they smiled under their tall, floppy Dr. Seuss-like hats that were decorated with the bold stars and stripes of the American flag. The younger son sported camouflage wear; the older son and the girlfriend of the mother displayed Old Navy t-shirts with American flag and "United States of America 2001" beneath it.

Instead of walking the site, some people chose a spot for themselves and rooted themselves there, keeping vigil. One couple wore complementary flag shirts: red and white stripes covered his; hers was blue with stars. When they sat side-by-side, leaning against a pole at the edge of the lawn just a few feet away from Columbia Pike staring at the blackened hole in the Pentagon, they formed one flag. They were there when I arrived, and an hour and a half later, they were still there.

Similarly, a couple sat by a small shrine they had made. Crying softly, they lighted and relighted two long, white, tapered candles that kept

Figure 4.3 At the Pentagon memorial, a boy gives tribute to firefighters at the World Trade Center.

Source: Photo: c Margaret R. Yocom.

blowing out in the breeze. A manhole cover in the grass formed a base for their mementos, candles, and potted pansies. Like visitors to the Vietnam Memorial who sometimes leave cigarettes and beer underneath names, this couple left a six-pack of Coca-Cola in a gray and red box as well as a yellow jumbo bag of M&Ms that were untouched a week later. A white paper heart whispered, "I miss you. Ann and Michael."

A young girl sat quietly on a plastic folding chair by a tree covered with toy airplanes. Two young women sitting by the large white message board twisted red, white, and blue ribbons into yarn for visitors. Several people stood reading the many written messages on the board. As the golden afternoon sunlight deepened, more people came to walk through these artful offerings at the spontaneous memorial.

Art is universal human behavior, Ellen Dissanayake tells us, just as speech and the skillful manufacture of tools are. Art can best be described as "making special," she claims, and, as such, it transforms our everyday reality:

> In whatever we are accustomed to call art, a *specialness* is tacitly or overtly acknowledged. Reality, or what is considered to be reality, is elaborated, reformed, given not only particularity (emphasis on uniqueness, or "specialness") but import (value, or "specialness")—what may be called such things as magic or beauty or spiritual power or significance." . . . In both functional and nonfunctional art an alternative reality is recognized and entered; the making special acknowledges, reveals, and embodies this reality. (1988: 92, 95)

People engage in such artistic behavior, Michael Owen Jones contends, for many reasons: to experience sensory pleasure; to pose and perhaps resolve an intellectual puzzle; to preserve a way of life; to feel a connectedness to past eras, family, or community; to develop, express, clarify, or reconstruct their identity; to gain therapeutic benefits; and more (1995: 254–271). And such art, as Robert E. Walls suggests, also affords people the opportunity to communicate ideas that they may not be able or willing to speak in words (1990: 107).

We learn about people's responses to the events of September 11 at the Pentagon by investigating their artistic behavior that produced the memorial. What did people emphasize as they wrote messages on signboards, and who were they addressing? What images did people turn to over and over again as they left tokens on fences, lawns, and tree branches? And, what do these messages and images tell us about why people came to the Pentagon memorial with the art works they did?

The Public's Message Boards:
Addressing the Living and the Dead

Each time I visited the site, people stood reading the many word-filled posters and reading and writing on the large wooden message board that dominated the hillside component of the memorial. Shaped like the gable end of a house and painted white, its back was propped up by three firmly rooted pieces of lumber. Identical 5 × 7 inch paper USA flags dotted the face of the message board, and people had written their messages, most unsigned, all along the white stripes: "The tree of liberty must often be watered with the blood of patriots. Thomas Jefferson. The sad reality" and "God Bless America. Soon to be Vets of the Terrorist War God Bless You All." Others had pinned cards, messages typed at home, newspaper articles, a scarf, and even a baseball hat to the board. Someone had fastened a fulsome white bow festooned with $\frac{3}{4}$ inch tall green plastic soldiers pointing rifles at invisible targets, and trailing red, white, and blue streamers. As the crowded message board filled, other visitors placed posterboards of articles with photos by its side: the Twin Towers in flame, FDNY firemen raising a flag, and the Pentagon—one of the very few images of the building at the site.

Addressing Each Other, the Military, Grieving Families, and Friends

By September 30, people had covered every inch of the back of the message board and its wooden support beams with black ink. Urgently, often as if there were no time to lose, visitors addressed each other, citizens in the military, and friends and family of the dead. Some, like Jeanine Nesselt, offered comfort: "May God bless us all!!! Please be with us through difficult times. Trust God. I love you all. . . . 9–28–01." The Provost family of Knoxville, Tennessee, left a note saying "Comfort and Courage to the families who are grieving" (Dart 2001: 2).

Others called both members of the military and civilians to action. One person sought to spur on those Americans in or about to be in the military: "Beat 'em B.A. Boys! Be Careful. God and America and V.B."[9] And Charles H. Evans urged others with his handwritten poem "Remember September 2001," which he had handwritten on a red posterboard and laid it on the green lawn:

THE GALL OF THE PERPETRATORS
SURELY MUST GALL US ALL

IN SOLIDARITY WE RISE
SO TERRORISM MAY FALL

PEOPLE
HEAR THE CALL
AND
MAY GOD BLESS US ALL
          Charles H. Evans

Dedicated to ALL who may read these words AND ESPECIALLY THOSE
DIRECTLY AFFECTED BY THE TRAGEDY OF (9–11–01)

Many writers never clarified who the "we" of their messages were. They
preferred the powerful ambiguity that hinted that more than one person
authored the words of the sign as they called out to passersby to join in
the effort: "WE WILL NEVER FORGET SEPTEMBER 11, 2001" some-
one had printed on an $8\frac{1}{2}$ by 11 inch red, white, and blue plaque, edged in
silver pop-beads.

Addressing Fellow Americans

For other message writers, though, clarifying the "we" for other visitors was
one of the most critical priorities; in fact, many post–1965 immigrants to
the United States understood that their lives depended on getting the
understanding of those who walked the Pentagon site.
    On the grassy bank, someone had laid a handprinted sheet of $8\frac{1}{2} \times 11$
white paper:

    The Palestinian
    Community sends
    condolences to the victims and their
    families. God Bless
    Everyone

        From the Sudanese Voice for Freedom: "As refugees who have found
    home in this country we stand in solidarity with this great nation to
    denounce and fight terrorism" (Hufford 2001: 6).

The Washington DC area, home to 5,000,000 people of whom 832,000
(16.9 percent)[10] were born outside the United States, is one of the most
international areas of the United States. But even in this culturally diverse

milieu, new immigrants, especially those whose skin color set them immediately apart from European Americans, certainly felt their difference and their vulnerability. And, in a series of attacks, new Americans had that difference horribly pointed out to them. While listening to President Bush memorialize victim of the September 11 attacks during a service at Washington National Cathedral, for example, Michael Johnson asked deliveryman Mustafa Nazary if he were Afghani. When Nazary, a 10-year citizen of the United States said he was, Johnson threatened him, followed him to a shopping center parking lot, and punched him repeatedly (Jenkins 2002: 1,2). On the first of November 2001 in Manassas, Virginia, two men from Waynesboro berated their cab driver, a Pakistani American, because he was of Middle Eastern descent, refused to pay him, threw him to the ground, and kicked him repeatedly in the head (White 2001: 1). A Dumfries woman and her son led a mob attack against two Afghan American teenagers, people attacked local mosques, broke windshields, and smashed mailboxes. An airline security screener at Baltimore-Washington International Airport forced a Muslim teenager to remove her headscarf while allowing a fully covered nun to pass through. Some Arab Americans went to court to change their names to help avoid harassment. A series of Nazi rallies with swastika-clad marchers have been held in Washington, DC. Bigoted violence and vandalism increased fourfold in Fairfax County, Virginia, since September 11; in nearby Montgomery County, Maryland, hated incidents jumped 76 percent.[11]

The Pentagon memorial, discussed as it was in regional newspapers, gave new Americans one way to publicly mourn their fellow Americans and announce their allegiance to America, even an America that had become increasingly nativistic. Most of the signboards from ethnic and international communities appeared early in the life of the spontaneous memorial.

Displays from Thai, Lao, and Cambodian Americans stressed that they, too, mourned for the loss of their fellow Americans: "WE MOURN ALL THE LIVES THAT HAVE BEEN LOST IN THE TERRIBLE TRAGEDY AND MOURN FOR AMERICA. THAI ALLIANCE," announced the heavy, 11 × 17 inch sign with thick, black printed letters, leaning against metal legs of a tall stand. A wreath of light yellow mums, bright yellow and purple orchids topped the sign. Nearby on the grassy knoll, a plain white canvas board with heavy, black, printed letters stated, "THE CAMBODIAN COMMUNITY UNITED AGAINST TERRORISM PRAYS TO THE VICTIMS." In late November, a white canvas board sign with its bright, bold red letters stood on the green lawn. Held high by a wooden stand and decorated with an American flag, it declared,

LAO AMERICANS FOR AMERICA
LAO COMMUNITY AND

OTHER COMMUNITIES
PRAY FOR 9–11–01 VICTIMS

Several Latino groups and individuals brought displays to the spontaneous memorial. Each one clearly linked their new country and their home-
lands in friendship by using overt claims of brotherhood and by writing in
both Spanish and English. One sign read, "God Bless America: El Pueblo
Latino American Esta Con Los Hermanos de U.S.A."[12] (Hufford 2001: 6).
A second one, written with black ink on cardboard by Luisa, Silvia, Raul,
Roberto, and Rosa Linda, announced

> Viva Freedom, Peace, and Love
> Sep. 18-2001
> Guatemala Love USA
> Nuestro Dolor Con Las
> Personas Que Han Perdido
> Sus Familiares
> Dios Salve America[13]
> We Love USA Too

Another sign spoke of the ultimate sacrifice for one's new country. On
the grassy bank with many other displays around it, lay the *Washington Post*
obituary of Sgt. First Class José Orlando Calderon, 44, of Annandale, who
was born in Puerto Rico and served in first Persian Gulf War. An American
flag, flowers, and handwritten note on an $8\frac{1}{2}$ × 11 sheet of white paper
signed by the Familia Calderon and the Puerto Rican Community of
Metropolitan Washington accompanied the obituary: "Our prayers are with
you. Puerto Rico will always be with you. Neustras [*sic*] oracuones [*sic*]
siempre eştaran con ustedes. Boricue [*sic*] los queremos."[14]

Broadcasting to the World

In addition to addressing those visitors close at hand, sign-writers also
broadcast their messages further afield. Many messages seemed to speak to
the world at large: "GOD SPEED AMERICA" "God Bless America. Stay
Strong. Stephanie White"; "LAND OF THE FREE GOD BLESS. KURT
HELFRICH '01"; "AMERICA IS STILL FREE. WE WILL *NEVER*
ACCEPT TERRORISM."

Speaking to God

Like new Americans, many other visitors to the memorial invoke God.
"Have mercy on me O God for in you I will take refuge under your wings

until this disaster has passed," someone penned on the message board. Church fellowships came in vans to the site to bless the air with their words as they prayed for the living, the relatives of victims, and the firefighters and police working in the debris of the Pentagon (Cho and Stockwell 2001: 2). Buddhist monks wrapped in rust-colored robes led about 250 followers in prayers for the dead (Cho and Stockwell 2001: 2). Prayer flags made of brightly colored fabric squares of red, green, blue, and yellow with images of Buddha and text written in Sanskrit fluttered from three parallel cords strung along the Arlington National Cemetery's black metal fence. And a visitor had brought the Mourner's Kaddish in Hebrew and a poem in English; six rocks arranged on the corners held down the $8\frac{1}{2} \times 11$ sheet of white paper the poem was printed on.

> So say the words that must be said
>> Prayer for the beloved dead
> And as our precious tears are shed
>> We shall remember
> Death and loss are what we pay
> For finding love along our way
> A gift forever, sweet bouquet
>> A rose in December.

Talking With the Dead

Some visitors came as they would to an altar or a shrine: to be with the dead. And here, at the memorial site, people could come as close as possible to the spot where loved ones had drawn their last breath. "Renee," a friend wrote to Renee May, a flight attendant on American Airlines Flight 77, "I've thought of you and your engagement and upcoming wedding" (Dart 2001: 2). "TO THOSE WHO DIED," someone wrote in black ink on the message board, "MAY GOD BLESS ALL OF YOU AND YOUR FAMILIES." On a large paper flag with many handwritten messages, Joe & Sue Brearley wrote, "Your sacrifice will not be forgotten"; "Your sacrifice is not in vain," added CPO Cash & family. And in words painstakingly printed by someone still practicing her letters: "To Dad from Faith. I love you Daddy. I miss you Daddy" (Dart 2001: 1).

The creators of these signs that sprawled throughout the site believed in the power of their words to travel, for their signs created a place that spoke way beyond the Navy Annex. The memorial enabled them to speak to other visitors, to the grieving families, and to visiting soldiers, but it also gave them access to the world, to God, and to the dead themselves. People did not stand by their signs and seek out face-to-face encounters with other visitors; rather, they trusted that the written messages they left on the lawn, the message board, and the fences would speak well enough on their own.

Clusters of Meaning: The Airplane Tree

One striking display at the Pentagon site did not depend on words for its power but rather on the accumulation of objects that people perceived as similar to one another. Among the branches of one of the trees, visitors hung airplane after airplane. "My father put this together," a young girl told me as she pointed to what I came to think of as the airplane tree. On September 22, she sat protectively on a bright yellow plastic chair wearing a red t-shirt decorated with "F-14 TOMCAT" and a picture of the fighter plane. She planned to stay awhile: a willow basket filled with snacks and a water bottle rested in the grass by her side.

Someone, perhaps the girl's father, had written "#1 USA / GOD BLESS AMERICA" across the wings of a model jet plane, its gray body festooned with flags decals and miniature flags and fastened it to the tree. A small bright-white jet hung by its side. Wired to the tree trunk just below was a camouflage-colored jet; and above, two more jets—one bright blue and gold, a second light and dark gray—lay motionless in the tree's lowest branches. Though tied fast to the tree, all the jets pointed nose-up, ready to blast into the sky. Those same branches also supported two signs. In a photo, military pilots by their plane stand in a row with a young boy; the caption read, "MINI ASTRONAUT & FUTURE PILOT, Isilay Davaz." The other sign proclaimed, "YOUR [sic] STILL BEAUTIFUL AMERICA." Around the base of the tree, someone had sunk metal stakes in the ground and surrounded the airplane tree with a cord to prevent other visitors from coming too close.

Within the cord's perimeter, someone placed a child's poster that screamed, "NO MOORE." On it, the Twin Towers of the World Trade Center stands erect, marked with multiple American flags, as a plane heads straight toward them, hotly pursued by two USA helicopters. Across the top of the sign "#1 USA / GOD BLESS AMERICA" flanks a large American flag. Cut flowers, plastic flowers, lighted candles, and a dizzying array of small flags cover the ground. And President Bush, the American flag behind him in an official photo, smiles out from among these tokens at the tree's base.

Eight days later, another white jet and a model of the space shuttle Atlantis, nose-up, had been fastened in the airplane tree's lower branches. By late November, the flags at the airplane tree multiplied; they fluttered around the base, twined up the trunk, and hung from the lowest branches.

Four three-foot tall spikes also bore American flags at their tops and were wound around with red, white, and blue ribbons. Two more smaller planes had been tied on the lower branches. And around the large white shuttle, someone had wrapped a navy blue ribbon of cloth with "TURKISH AIR FORCE" stamped on it in bold white letters.

At the airplane tree, visitor after visitor followed the pattern established by one family. People added additional planes, flags, and flowers, but they kept intensifying their messages through the repeated image of the United States fighter plane. No one placed models of commercial planes, such as those involved in the attacks, on the tree. It was fighter planes, similar to those absent from the skies over New York and Washington in the fateful hours of September 11, that became the focal point of the display, as visitors clustered messages about American military power, achievements in flight, patriotism, international cooperation, and protection. Visitors to the site took pleasure in creating this constantly changing display, especially one that was driven by community purpose, wordlessly agreed on.

Multiple Fragments: The Body in Pieces

At the Pentagon memorial, visitors created displays with multiple images of similar fragments more than any other kind of display. Using representations of heads, hearts, hands, thumbs and feet, people turned to these resonant forms to evoke both human presence and human loss. The "redundant repetition" of these multiple-image displays, as Ellen Dissanayake reminds us, also signals a ritualistic and artistic intent to make something special (1988: 85).

Linked Together: Faces, Signatures, and Chains

Presenting the reality, if not the enormity of the tragedy, several of the displays lined up face after face of the dead. "In Memory of our Friends and Family / Flight 77," a bulletin from a memorial service read, and printed on the bulletin were the photos of the faces of all on board the American Airlines carrier.[15] On one laminated piece of white paper, a visitor had printed photographs of the faces of all the crewmembers on Flight 77 and Flight 11, the flight that crashed into the World Trade Center's North Tower. Also on the lawn stood a framed plaque with a government seal, a photograph of the Pentagon in flames, and the typewritten names of all those who died in the Pentagon attack, with a photo of the building in flames, smoke billowing from the top. Like the Vietnam War Memorial, the plaque's protective surface was so shiny that visitors who kneeled before it to read the names saw their faces reflected on its surface. People left flowers and flags all around the base of the plaque.

A far greater number of the multiple-image displays featured representations of the people who were sending their condolences: their faces, their signatures, and more. On a laminated, foam-core poster standing erect on metal supports, the faces of Native Americans from Marysville, Washington, superimposed in rows on a large American flag stared out at visitors, a candle to the right of their faces as if all of them were holding a vigil for the dead.[16] "TULALIP BINGO-CASINO EMPLOYEES WILL NEVER FORGET SEPTEMBER 11 2001," the poster read. Affixed to the poster, a letter announced that their Nation had sent $100,000 "to the families in need from the terrorist tragedy—to symbolize and illustrate our support as an independent Native Nation to the Nation of the United States" (see figure 4.4).

Another group of people brought a chain made of hundreds of laminated paper links, each with a message and a signature. As I arrived on September 30, 10 people from a Hair Cuttery salon in Baltimore, Maryland, were debating whether to string their chain along the Arlington Cemetery fence, given the warning of a visitor's BE ADVISED sign that

Figure 4.4 With a foam-core poster of their faces, Native Americans from Marysville, Washington, tell visitors to the memorial that "TULALIP BINGO-CASINO EMPLOYEES WILL NEVER FORGET SEPTEMBER 11 2001."

Source: Photo: c Margaret R. Yocom.

told of and protested the removal of the displays along the fence. "After all our work and the promises we made to others," they told me, "we don't want to just throw the chain away." Their customers had decorated the links. When the hairdressers saw the metal chain on the perimeter of the grassy lawn, they walked across the street and strung their paper chain along it, securing their red, white, and blue paper links to the metal ones with plastic twisty strips. "Most of our customers wrote 'God Bless America' or 'United We Stand,'" one of the women told me. Every so often, a single star dangled from one of the links.

Hearts, Hands, Feet, and Thumbs

Another predominant multiple-image display at the Pentagon site were the large rectangular signs covered with images of body parts—especially hearts, hands, feet, and thumbs—as many as they could possibly fit on the paper. Some creators signed their names; others let their hands and feet speak for them.

Images of hands predominated. "The future's in our children's HAND'S [*sic*]," announced a bed-sized white cloth sign that ballooned out from the black fence spokes along Arlington National Cemetery's edge, catching the breeze on September 22. Decorated with the American flag, red handprints formed the flag's stripes, and yellow stars and blue handprints in a blue square created the flag's upper left field. The friends of an 11-year-old from Leckie Elementary School in southeast Washington DC had pressed their hands on this cloth, and one of them had handprinted "In Remembrance of Bernard Curtis Brown" below the last red stripe. Winner of the National Geographic Society's award for scholastic achievement, Bernard, along with two other DC students, was on his way to California aboard Flight 77 (Hufford 2001: 7). Some of Bernard's classmates and their parents also signed the flag: "Our hearts are with you. Love, Cheryl and Matt" and "The language of children is the language of peace."

The Woodbridge Run Community Playgroup hung a large white canvas sign along the Cemetery fence, too, with "To America's Heroes" handprinted on top in read and blue and "From America's Children" on the bottom. Red and blue handprints, with names trailing along side, filled the spaces in between: "Tyler Henley-3," "Hannah Tesmond-2," "Shamiek Aetis." Along the very bottom in small script, someone had written, "In loving memory of those lost and injured in the attack at the Pentagon on September 11, 2001."

"GOD BLESS THE FAMILIES / AND FRIENDS WHO LOST LOVED ONES / BY TERRORIST ATTACKS" read a yellow poster on the lawn. Students had traced the outlines of their hands and had written messages on the palms and fingers, one word per finger. "GOD / Bless / ALL / Of / You," one student's fingers read; across the palm appeared "MELLOW Valley 6th Grade ABBEY JONES."

Some featured feet or a combination of hands and feet. On the lawn, fastened down by candles, the children of Winwood's Jr. Kindergarten, Fairfax, Virginia, laid a large white paper sign in the shape of a foot on which they had pasted red or blue stencils of the patterned bottoms of their shoes. Below the heel they wrote their names: "Graham," "Austin C.," "Zoe W." "PEACE . . . one step at a time," their sign read. Combining handprints and footprints, the children of Learn As You Grow from North Syracuse, New York, made a flag with about a square yard of white paper. They had obviously slathered their hands and feet with paint before walking on the paper to form the red stripes. In the flag's blue field, they had lain their white-painted hands. The shaky letters of one beginning writer provided the only words: "UNITED WE Stand."

Other visitors turned to thumbprints or hearts.[17] In late November, a flag made by students and staff of Yelm Middle School, Yelm, Washington, lay on the lawn. Made from heavy paper, the flag's blue field had fifty white-paint thumbprints on it. Dark blue thumbprints filled in around them. Students had painted the board with white and red stripes, and in the red stripes, students had pressed their black-painted thumbs, side by side. "Our thumbprints / in rememberance [sic]," someone had written in the white stripes. An unsigned flag on the lawn in late November was made completely of hearts. Blue and white hearts interlocked to form the starred portion of the blue field. Similarly, rows of white interlocking hearts and rows of red interlocking hearts alternated to form the stripes.

These images of hearts, hands, and feet appear regularly in art of all kinds.[18] Linda Nochlin in her study *The Body in Pieces: The Fragment as a Metaphor of Modernity* affirms that the trope of the body fragment has long had a "central" role in European and American iconography from the late 1700s through the twentieth century. Nochlin cautions, though, that this popular icon has "ever-shifting, polyvalent" meanings (1994: 54, 56). Visitors to the Pentagon used the fragment in their own way: to evoke compelling dialogues between presence and absence, the infinite and the finite.

Why People Came

In some ways, all the displays at the Pentagon were alike. All addressed some imagined reader or readers. All were fragmentary. Even the writing was brief, as if the writer had more to say but held back to leave space so others could comment, too. All seemed multiple since one written comment rested by another, one item was piled beside others similar to it. What can we learn from these messages, multiples, and fragments about why people came to the Pentagon memorial and left the artful tokens they did?

What Did Not Bring People to the Memorial? Protest and the Image of the Pentagon Building

The displays at the spontaneous memorial indicated the reasons that did not bring visitors to the Pentagon: they did not come to protest the approaching storm cloud of war, and they did not come to declare the Pentagon a much-loved building and mourn the harm done to it.

In my visits to the site, I saw no messages that overtly criticized the United States' international policies or its plans for war in Afghanistan. The message board would have been a perfect place; someone could have blended their message in among the others, in print as small or large as they felt comfortable using. Instead, messages called on visitors to agree with one another and, presumably, the George W. Bush administration policy. "United We Stand," wrote Susanna Zarbough, "God Bless America." And John Green told visitors, "As long as the ties that bind us together are stronger than those who would tear us apart, all will be well." Schoolchildren wrote the great majority of messages for peace; their words were soft-edged, gentle on the eyes of visitors. Very few messages appeared that called on visitors to be aware of other political issues. One white poster with black print announced in late November, "freedom from gun trauma 1-800-RINGING THE BELL CAMPAIGN www.bellcampaign.org."

Voices did appear after September 11 that criticized United States policies and called on Americans to consider why Middle Eastern terrorists might have flown planes into the World Trade Center and the Pentagon, symbols of American economic and military might. Immediately, though, other voices rose not just to argue with protestors, but to silence them. The American Council of Trustees and Alumni, for example, distributed a November 13, 2001, report that listed 117 American university professors who they deemed were insufficiently patriotic because of comments they made or the peace rallies they organized (Eakin 2001: 1). And the *Wall Street Journal* singled out for attack the Middle Eastern Studies Association of North America (Jones 2001:1).[19]

At the Pentagon memorial, though, no one aired these issues overtly. Or, if they did, others removed the signs before I saw them. Clearly, Pentagon memorial visitors, unlike some visitors to New York City memorials,[20] thought that messages critical of United States policy were not appropriate at this memorial, that personal mourning took precedence over and must be protected from what they saw as the potential discomfort and divisiveness of debate. Visitors may also have feared that others might accost them if they posted a political message that challenged the status quo.[21]

The absence of alternative political messages at September 11 memorials, however, did not go unnoticed. In "Before I start this poem," poet Emmanuel Ortiz (2002) critiques the many "moments of silence" being observed at services held for victims of the September 11 attacks as the poem's narrator reminds fellow Americans of places where United States policy has lead to thousands of deaths as well:

> Before I start this poem,
> I'd like to ask you to join me in
> a moment of silence
> in honour of those who died
> in the World Trade Centre
> and the Pentagon
> last September 11th.
>
> I would also like to ask you
> a moment of silence
> for all of those who have been
> harassed, imprisoned, disappeared,
> tortured, raped, or killed
> in retaliation for those strikes,
> for the victims in both
> Afghanistan and the U.S.
>
> And if I could just add one more thing . . .
> A full day of silence
> for the tens of thousands of Palestinians
> who have died at the hands of
> U.S.-backed Israeli forces
> over decades of occupation.
>
> . . . .
> You want a moment of silence
> You mourn now as if the world will never be
> the same
> And the rest of us hope to hell it won't be.
> Not like it always has been
>
> . . . .

In the memorials that sprang up after September 11 in New York City, postcards, newspaper photos, and hastily made models of the World Trade

Center towers were everywhere, as people mourned the loss of a beloved city building. Even the buildings' nickname, the "Twin Towers," draped humanity around the otherwise inanimate skyscrapers. At the memorial within sight of the Pentagon, however, not a single postcard lay among the thousands of commemorative objects. Many items spoke of the Towers; and when people did mention the Pentagon, they linked the building to the Towers. "Honor the innocent who passed away in the terrorist attack on the pentagon and twin towers," one visitor wrote in black magic marker on cherry construction paper. On the plaque with the names of the Pentagon dead, a visitor leaned a plastic envelope that held a single rose, a photo of the Twin Towers, and a poem he or she had written to the Towers themselves:

. . .
You were once a symbol that put us above
the rest
Now you are one of the symbols that will
bring us all together.
The world will unite in a common cause
Peace

Visitors were clearly affected by the sight of the charred Pentagon. They took countless photographs, and they walked the twenty minutes that it took to get as close to the building as they could. At first, we might think that images of the Pentagon weren't needed since the building itself lay in view, but the lack of Pentagon imagery and the preponderance of representations of the Towers at the memorial signals something more.

The allure of spectacular images, especially those of the Twin Towers, influenced visitors to the Pentagon memorial as well as people the world over. Considering the "Kodak Moments / Flashbulb Memories" of September 11, Barbara Kirshenblatt-Gimblett suggests that the "sheer spectacle of the World Trade Tower collapse (and magnitude of the casualties) overshadows the attack on the Pentagon and the plane that crashed into a field in Pennsylvania. Many witnesses to the collapse of the Towers reported a sense of unreality. They felt like they were watching a movie they had seen before" (2002: 7). After pointing out the many pre- and post-9/11 computer games that enabled players to zoom between the Towers or shoot down would-be terrorists, Kirshenblatt-Gimblett suggests that, over New York City, the "sky was the ultimate big screen" (2002: 9).

In comparison to the Towers, the Pentagon is not a spectacular building, even though it has three times the floor space of the Empire State Building (The Pentagon 2001). Low to the ground and folded in on itself, the intrigue of its architectural pattern becomes more clear, ironically, from the air. Unlike the Washington Monument, it does not loom large either on the landscape or in the architectural imaginary of the people in the nation's capital. Its five floors do not give it the compelling, paradoxical image that feminist critic HelénⅡ Cixous paints of the Towers. "I loved the T.T. tenderly," she writes:

> As did millions of human beings. As Windows on the World one could believe for a few instants one was equal to the gods. Image of triumph, soaring, jubilation, beauty, detachment. And: trembling. I only went there with a person I love. Fearing for life. . . . And yet what caused the seduction of the T.T., the fascination they exerted in the entire world? Sexual ambiguity. The representation at once obvious and hidden of the mystery of the *Phallus*. The towers *embodied* phallic power in all its ever disquieting complexity: there is nothing as fragile as the erection, properly or *figuratively*. The T.T. were the figure par excellence of triumphant, therefore threatened, power. To tower over: as soon as one towers one attracts castration. . . . The T.T. attracted looks, desires, love, *therefore*, they aroused the death drive. (2002: 431)[22]

For many Americans, new immigrants, and visitors to the United States before and after 9/11, the Towers stood for American exceptionalism and capitalism, for better lives in a new world, for genius and enterprise and more.[23] "I wanted to see it because that was the building that I loved," said Ayatollahi Tabaar, who visited the Towers as soon as he moved to New York from Iran four years ago. "When I saw them burning, for me it was like two people were dying. I feel like I've lost a relative" (Bahrampour 2001: 1). The Towers were a place for dreams and a place that symbolized the realization of dreams: "I went to the top floor," Leticia Velasquez who grew up in Honduras and moved to New York 12 years earlier remembered, "and for me it was like dreaming. Every time someone came here, I always brought them here" (Bahrampour 2001: 1). In the end, they had become a symbol, a myth of America itself.[24]

The Pentagon arouses different feelings and associations. Many Americans referred to the Pentagon as a symbol of freedom, strength, and the protection of American ideals.[25] For many, though, the Pentagon has been a focal point for protest, symbolizing war (Pershing 1996). Above all, it is a building that few people know. Although tours of the Pentagon are available, the building is identified more with limited access and layers of security and secrets that mirror the layers of its infolding architecture. The building neither seeks nor offers a high profile. "A building," suggests phenomenologist Edward Casey, "condenses a culture in one place. . . . Within the ambience of a building, a landscape becomes articulate and begins to speak in emblematic ways" (1993: 32). The limited number of images of the Pentagon proceeded from many peoples' lack of familiarity with the building, their ambivalence toward the activities within its walls, and the deflection of their eyes to the more spectacular Towers.

Why People Came: Being Present, Individually and Collectively

If people did not come to protest or to mourn the Pentagon building, the mementos they left suggest that one of the reasons they came was to be present at the site, both as individuals and as members of a group of mourners. Being present, though, is not a simple act. It was so important to many people to be present, for example, that if they couldn't come in person, they sent a tracing of their hand or foot instead. Being present involves many acts of attention available to memorial visitors, among them doing, seeing, caring, and forming both individual and shared memories.

Some visitors felt they *had* to do something in the days after September 11, and the memorial became their focal point. Like visitors to the New York City memorials,[26] people whose help had been turned away elsewhere found their way to the Navy Annex site. Sitting on a blanket by the large wall, Jenny Riley, from Mt. Airy, Maryland, and Justine Smith from Centreville, Virginia, came to make red, white, and blue yarn ribbons and distribute them to passersby who would place a money donation in their box marked for the Red Cross. Wanting to do something to help, Jenny had approached both the Red Cross and the Salvation Army, but they both said no. So she and Justine came to the memorial. They made 250 pins as they sat at the site on the weekend of the fifteenth. By the afternoon of the twenty-second, they had made 400, and they intended to stay several more hours.

Many came to burn images in their minds, to try to comprehend what felt so incomprehensible. Through sight, sound, touch, feel, and smell, those "five rivers"[27] of the senses, visitors could begin to reach toward experiencing the reality of September 11. The materiality of the memorial, its sensual substantiality, beckoned.

On the curb where the memorial's lawn met Columbia Pike, a man viewed the breach in the Pentagon wall through binoculars that he then passed to a friend. "It takes your breath away, doesn't it?" he asked (Hufford 2001: 7). Seeing is not believing, of course, but it is the beginning of believing. One of the ways we come to understand dramatic events, philosopher Avishai Margalit suggests in *Ethics of Memory* is to insert ourselves into the event. "The significance of the event for us," Margalit writes, "depends on our being personally connected with what happened, and hence we share not only the memory of what happened but also our participation in it, as it were. . . . [W]e find it important to report (even falsely) the channels by which we become related to a shared event when that event is of immense importance to us" (2002: 52–53). Walking throughout the memorial and carrying away stories of their experiences at the site allowed visitors to participate more intimately in the events of September 11.

People also came to the Pentagon memorial to bear witness to the tragedy, to show their care and respect for the dead, and to signal their intent to remember. One woman visitor reading the messages on the large white board told a journalist, "I can't talk about it, but I don't want to forget about it either. And I'm afraid we will" (Dart 2001: 2). Caring, philosopher Margalit notes, is intimately linked with mourning and memory since even the word to "care" used to mean to "mourn" (2002: 31). In order to care for someone, to give someone the attention that is implied by caring, we need to be able to remember him or her. Caring, Margalit stresses, "is a way of living in time" (2002: 33, 35). Spontaneous memorials provide people with a way to deepen the caring, to impress images into the mind that will find their way, eventually, to memory.

The desire to be in the company of others who had also turned their hearts and minds toward the events of September 11 also drew people to the Pentagon site. People sensed that their lives had been changed forever, and this perspective and their need to be witness to it united them, even if their politics divided them. People may have initially come for an individual experience, but even as they tried to find a parking space and saw all the others walking toward the memorial and the Pentagon with its black gash, they would have begun to sense their communion and, perhaps, hunger for more.

Individual memories can become shared memories, and philosopher Margalit describes the process. "A *common* memory," he suggests, ". . . aggregates the memories of all those people who remember a certain episode which each of them experienced individually." A "*shared* memory," though, ". . . integrates and calibrates the different perspectives of those who remember the episode . . . each experiencing only a fragment of what happened from their unique angle on events—into one version" (2002: 51–52). Perhaps it was the desire for such a "shared memory," that lead visitors to the Pentagon to eschew overt messages of protest and accept only those messages that would provide a feeling of unity in a time of need.

Claiming Space, Hallowing Ground

With the site clearly bearing such meaning to people, it is no wonder that people believe firmly in their right to claim the space and hallow it as a memorial to the dead. People snarled traffic coming in numbers that they did, parking their cars in lots and on the sides of streets when the lots overflowed. They walked across curvy access roads that were never meant for pedestrian access. Their walking, along with their laying down of mementos, is as Michel deCerteau suggests, a "process of *appropriation* of the topographical system . . . a space of enunciation." Walking "makes [possibilities] exist as well as emerge" because, as it "alternately follows a path and has followers, [it also] creates a mobile organicity in the environment . . . [it] is an effort to ensure communication. . . . Walking affirms, suspects, tries out, transgresses, respects, etc., the trajectories it 'speaks' " ([1984] 1988: 97–99).

When visitors realized that authorities were threatening those claimed rights by removing memorial tokens, they interpreted the removal as a violation of both them and the dead. "BE ADVISED," the thick white foam-core board shouted as it leaned against the stone-wall part of the Arlington Cemetery fence on September 22:

JOHN METZLER, SUPERINTENDENT OF
ARLINGTON CEMETERY HAS
TWICE THIS PAST WEEK ORDERED THE
REMOVAL AND *TRASHING* OF ALL THE
MEMORIALS PREVIOUSLY PLACED ON THIS
FENCE AND WALL!

APPARENTLY, THE FEELINGS OF THOSE WHO
WISHED TO EXPRESS THEIR GRIEF OR THEIR
SYMPATHY FOR THOSE WHO LOST THEIR LIVES AND
THEIR LOVED ONES MEANT LITTLE TO HIM!

On top of this sign was another with many signatures and messages; at its feet lay a small bouquet of fresh flowers.

The creators of this BE ADVISED display clearly believed that their signs should be honored, not molested, especially since they addressed grieving Americans and the dead.[28] They had brought signs that evoked the powerful healing of hands and their warm touches, yet here was handiwork of another order. To visitors, their signs and the spaces they claimed had been made sacred.[29] Similarly, my George Mason University students reacted viscerally when I told them about a photographer who had taken home one of the most meaningful signs she had seen in New York City because she did not want it to be destroyed or taken by another. "No matter what the reason," my students said to me later, "taking that sign away was like desecrating a grave."

Even before this threat by the Superintendent, visitors understood how fragile their claim to this space was. They sought to preserve its boundaries and constantly attend to its sacredness by acts of special ritual maintenance.[30] Eyyup Davaz, for example, who lives nearby, went to the memorial each day at 3 a.m. to straighten all the American flags that had fallen or been knocked over (Dart 2001: 3). Members of the group Free Republic kept vigil over the memorial to protect the mementos that people had left there (McCaslin 2002).

The flowers, t-shirts, and signs on the grass symbolized the remains of the dead, lying as they did within sight of the incinerated ruin of the Pentagon, which held the ashes of the victims' actual bodies. And as visitors walked amidst the mementos, they could see themselves there, rooted to the site by these self-referential images: faces frozen onto paper stared out their visitors' faces, hands on signs recalled visitors' own touches as they placed handmade tokens on the ground, images of feet mirrored their feet. For the visitors, then, these tokens rested in their proper place. The messages, especially those on the ground, hallowed a cemetery-like space that visitors strongly believed should have been left to itself.

Conjuring Absence: Fragments and their Dialogues of Absence and Presence, the Finite and the Infinite

Like walking a sacred maze or a circle, visitors who walked the grounds of the Pentagon memorial came to meditate on death. One visitor, for example, haunted by thoughts of the passengers on the doomed planes, left a letter to them, asking, "What did it feel like to look death straight in the eye?" (Dart 2001: 1). The voices that visitors encountered at the site, made material by the repeated images of body fragments, led visitors to experience within themselves, to dramatize internally, the paradoxical feelings that death and catastrophe conjure up.[31] These symbolic images of multiple faces, hearts, hands, thumbs, and feet contained several internal dialogues—especially between those of presence and absence, and the finite and the infinite—not as opposites, but as complements that "mean," as folklorist Henry Glassie suggests, "in association" (1982: 178). These compelling fragments with their oscillating messages electrified people as they walk the grounds of the memorial, offering to them an experience they craved in the weeks after September 11. Here were no simple palliatives. What people found, rather, were the richly allusive, ragged edges of meaning's fragments.[32]

Fragments—and the terrain of loss that results from them—have been seen by many as the wellspring of art, the bloody ground from which art gives birth to itself. Art "is born of a wound that does not heal," surrealist writer Georges Bataille notes in his article on "Sacrificial Mutilation and the Severed Ear of Vincent Van Gogh" (qtd. in Nochlin 1994: 49). Sociologist George Simmel reminds us of another way fragments are essential to art. Art's work, he suggests, is linking fragments to a totality: "The essential meaning of art lies in its being able to form an autonomous totality, a self-sufficient microcosm out of a fortuitous fragment of reality that is tied with a thousand threads to this reality" (qtd. in Frisby 1986: 39). Art critic Lucy Lippard also focuses on the fragment's role in creating a new kind of whole: "Fragmentation need not connote explosion, disintegration. It is also a component of networks, stratification, the interweaving of many dissimilar threads, and de-emphasis on imposed meaning in favor of multiple interpretations" (qtd. in Turner 1999: 99–100). With fragments, Linda Nochlin reminds us, the "issue of 'relationship' " gets posed, sometimes in "new and paradoxical way[s]" (1994: 43).

The fragmented mementos at the memorial pressed visitors to experience presence and absence in conversation with one another. By sending replicas and tracings of the hands, thumbs, and feet, people surely meant to leave the most earnest token of their physical presence and their personal concern that they could. "Our thumbprints in remembrance," the children and adults from Yelm, Washington, had written. Memento creators verified their seriousness of purpose not by signing in blood but by offering replicas of parts of the human body—finger-, hand-, and footprints—that are often used for identification. And, through the images, they make present and visible the vulnerable body parts that humans usually keep hidden from another's gaze: upturned palms, exposed hearts, the exact print of the soles of feet, and the soft bottom cushion of thumbs. The posters with multiple fragments on them—red footprints forming a red stripe of a flag, for example—also testify to people's desire to be physically present at the site, to show up as a "body," a substantial aggregate of people who want to substantiate, to make visible, their intent. Such repetition in art, one image after another similar image, also witnesses to their ritual intent (Dissanayake 1988: 87).

Though these fragmented tokens conjure up people's purposeful presence, the images also convey absence. To look closely at the handprints and footprints on cloth at the memorial was to see images that looked like they could fade away at any moment. The paint was not evenly distributed over the hands, for example, so the edges of the hand appeared and retreated; white spaces slivered the palms and gaps severed the fingers into two to three parts. Fingers floated just above the palm, unconnected, as if drifting away. Thin drops of paint trailed down the cloth, as if the image were dissolving in front of visitors' faces. The prints evoked muddy handprints left

on a wall where they will soon be wiped off or the, chalky sidewalk prints
that will wash away with the rain.

In addition, the images of hands and feet were replicas; as such, they
remind visitors of the actual, flesh-warm hands that are not present. Among
their many meanings, they represent the promise of bodily touch but not
the embrace; the echo of footsteps, but not the arrival. And since fragments
serve in figurative language as synecdoches, as parts that symbolize wholes,
the hands and feet evoke the full body of the person even as they signal the
person's absence from the Pentagon site. Similarly, the images of body fragments on the grassy lawn may well have reminded visitors of the very real
body fragments that lay less than a mile away in the charred rubble of the
west face of the Pentagon. Through such juxtapositions,[33] these images
referenced the whole bodies lost forever in the September 11 attack and
reminded visitors, unintentionally, that the body was the site of suffering
for so many.[34]

Along with the dialogue between absence and presence, that between the
finite and the infinite coursed through the trope of the fragment at the
memorial, especially because the fragments appeared as multiples: a hand
alongside another hand; a foot, after a foot, after a foot. "The fragment,"
philosopher and poet Edmond Jabîls muses, "is our only access to the
infinite. . . . Only in fragments can we read the immeasurable totality" (qtd.
in Waldrop 2002: 18). Even seemingly whole objects such as the fighter jets
on the airplane tree, for example, take on the nature of fragments when
arrayed next to others of their kind, forming a collection. Remove one from
the series, and that plane would then appear incomplete, fragmentary.
To play with individual items displayed as multiples, as Susan Stewart warns
in her study on the collection, "is play with the fire of infinity" ([1984]
1993: 159).

At the Pentagon memorial, infinity and finality lay all around. Jets kept
multiplying on the airplane tree. And if 10 people laid bouquets of flowers
by the plaque that announced the names of the dead, then tens and tens
more appeared. The posterboards were filled with many, many hands placed
close by one another; counting them would have made visitors dizzy as they
tried to distinguish one from another in the tightly packed arrangements.
Although only a finite number of hands could fit onto one poster, the multiple hands seemed to shout that their numbers could go on forever, that the
finite boundary of the posterboard was really just an artificial one. Placing
one item alongside a similar item quickly became a representation of the
enormity of what had happened, of the thousands dead and the millions
who grieved. If images representing all who died in the attacks and all those
who grieved had been placed in one spot, the immensity would have been
terrifying. Boundaries like those offered by the posterboard serve a purpose,

Stewart suggests: "In the collection the threat of infinity is always met with the articulation of boundary" ([1984] 1993: 159).

Boundaries, through these expressions of the finite, also invited images of infinity at the Pentagon memorial. Certainly the site presented visitors with few boundaries, and the mementos stretched eastward across the grassy slope and sprang up along the fence just across the freeway from the Pentagon building. The boundaries that did exist, however, quickly became sites of resistance and of intensified display. The black metal fence that marked the start of the federally protected Arlington National Cemetery, for example, was draped with message after message. And it was by this boundary line that visitors displayed the "BE ADVISED" sign protesting the removal of mementos and where others heaped tokens all around that placard in support of its sentiments. When another fence blocked visitors' access to the ground closest to the Pentagon building itself, visitors piled signs of hands and bouquets of flowers there, as well. These fragments and all the others at the Pentagon memorial, with their ability to conjure the finite and the infinite, absence and presence, provided the most hauntingly evocative images at the Pentagon site for those who had come to meditate on life and life's end.

Disruption, Transformation, and the Promise of Renewal

Feeling the rupture that the events of September 11 had brought to their lives, people also came to the memorial's informal ritual space with its evocative mementos for an experience that would help them find a way into a much-changed world. Such times of personal disruption and, especially, of the move toward reintegration are the most intense, philosopher John Dewey suggests. "Life itself consists of phases in which [a person] falls out of step with the march of surrounding things and then recovers unison with it—either through effort or by some happy chance," he explains. "And, in a growing life, the recovery is never mere return to a prior state, for it is enriched by the state of disparity and resistance through which it has successfully passed. . . . The moment of passage from disturbance into harmony is that of intensest life" ([1934] 1980: 14, 17).

The mementos at the memorial help with such a journey, since objects, Dewey suggests, help people in their quest for reintegration. "Desire for restoration of the union," he writes, "converts mere emotion into interest in objects as conditions of realization of harmony. With the realization, material of reflection is incorporated into objects as their meaning" ([1934] 1980: 15). Objects especially help people move from disturbance through harmony because they themselves, Dewey suggests, are often born of such a passage: "Since the artist cares in a peculiar way for the phase of experience in which union is achieved, he does not shun moments of resistance and tension. He rather cultivates them, not for their own sake but because of their potentialities, bringing to living consciousness an experience that is unified and total" ([1934] 1980: 15).

At the memorial site, people could leave their artistic tokens, look over others filled with symbolic meanings, walk through the others on the ground and the fences, watch over the offerings to keep them safe, and speak with the dead and the living. This ritual space, they sensed, offered a place of encounter where anything could happen. Here, they could experience these moments of "intensest life" and they could reach toward harmony and renewal—for here, transformation was possible.

The site, after all, made the process of transformation material. The lawn amidst all the government buildings was no longer a lawn and the chains and the fences were no longer merely boundary lines of properties. The physical space, itself, became an example of the possibility of transformation. To walk in it was to walk a landscape of transformation—but not to their pre-9/11 selves, but to something new, a ritual passage, the chance to move from everyday to changed site and take the experiences in that liminal place back home and use them to reintegrate our lives.

The memorial also charted the passage of time and guided people through their days by the ritual moorings of the symbolic objects. Here they could reach toward transformation and yet be anchored in time. In late September when the pumpkin sellers, as always, brought their autumn wares to the shopping center parking lots throughout Northern Virginia, memorial visitors placed an uncarved pumpkin on the lawn and surrounded it with small American flags, bouquets of flowers, and a "God Bless America" sign. Reminding visitors of Halloween and of all the approaching holidays in the Christian, Judaic, and Muslim calendars, they wrote on the pumpkin in bold, black letters: "For the children who won't carve pumpkins this year."

Walking through the artistic ritual environment at the memorial also lead people toward transformation by offering them new ways to see past, present, and future. Strangers' faces on a posterboard become fellow-mourners; finger-painted images of children's hands metamorphose into icons of witness. "Our lens is refocused" by making special work of both ritual and art, says Ellen Dissanayake. She explains that

> A new figure or ground is established in regard to the former topology and we will probably respond emotionally with stronger feelings than we would to

"nonspecial" reality. Reality is converted form its usual unremarkable state—in which we take it or its components for granted—to a significant or specially experienced reality in which the components, by their emphasis or combination or juxtaposition, acquire a meta-reality. (1988: 95)

It was to refocus the everyday, to move through disruption toward harmony, and to receive the blessings of ritual that people also came to the memorial. Their visits offered them an encounter with death as well as the promise of renewal. And it is such an encounter and such a renewal that poet Christopher Howell places before us in "Blessing's Precision" as he tells of a group of people who emerge from tree line in an unnamed land and chance upon a dying lion with a man-angel by his wounded, bloody side. Like those who visited the spontaneous memorial, the people of the poem must consider how to respond to the horror—and the wonder—they see before them. Once separate but now brought unexpectedly into communion with one another, the people experience, through ritual, a transformation of their own

Finally we decided to make a ritual
for passing by a wounded lion and an angel
when you come upon them
by accident
and one of them is watching his heart's blood
run bitterly away, in spite of the sweetness
it had always brought before.
And so we held our faces up against the sky
and said our benedictions
and gave up each a bead
from our own red estuaries. And a caress
we might have saved
we placed in the man's palm
till his hands overflowed with little stones
smooth as a lion's ear.

Then we left the both of them there, dying
I suppose, and many of us have been speechless
since then, curiously
simplified in a kind of sunlight asleep
in a kind of shade. Since then
we have begun to build this rose,
this village of our days
where every breathing thing must be received
and tended, because mercy, now, locks our arms

out wide, and nothing, not even happiness,
is ever turned away. (1996: 28–29)[35]

*   *   *

By the time the six finalists for the official Pentagon Memorial were chosen
and the exhibit of their designs and 78 others had opened at the National
Building Museum in Washington DC on October 30, 2002, the spontaneous memorial was much diminished.[36] Its effects, however, were still
being felt. The memorials at all three September 11 attack sites inspired
several of the top designs for the official Pentagon Memorial.[37]

On February 26, 2003, "Light Benches" by Julie Beckman and Keith
Kaseman, two graduates of Columbia University architecture graduate
school, learned that their entry, "Light Benches" would memorialize the
184 lives lost in the Pentagon crash. The site is a two-acre preserve just to
the west of the Pentagon, immediately in the path followed by American
Airlines Flight 77. One hundred and eighty-four cantilevered benches of
anodized aluminum will rise out of the ground and jut out over individual
pools of water that trace the path of the jet. Each bench will have an
engraved nameplate and, perhaps, something more about the person whose
life was lost. Expected to be finished in the fall of 2004, it will cost about 5–7
million dollars, to be raised by private donations. Countless people the
world over sent tokens to workers in the Pentagon that were very similar to
the ones left at the spontaneous memorial (Kunkle 2002a: 1); June Forte of
the Pentagon's Office of Public Affairs of the Secretary of Defense curated a
quilt exhibit (Martinez 2002), and Pentagon workers gave other quilts and
mementos to families of those who died (Papadopoulos 2004). And two
years after the attacks, the sketch of the winning design for the New York
City's official memorial shows spontaneous memorial tokens lining the wall
of one of the spaces (Forgey 2004: A1).

Those of us who visited the spontaneous memorial at the Pentagon have
our photographs and our memories; the wooden message board, the signs
from new Americans, the flag made of little footprints, and the rows of faces
still appear before us. Certainly our reasons for visiting that roadside site
were many, but, for whatever reason, we could not just pass by. Like the
travelers in "Blessing's Precision," we, too, decided on a ritual practice: a
visit to the memorial and the possibility of transformation that such a visit
offers. Anything may happen at these roadside shrines: grieving may begin,
healing may come, or we may publicly promise to care for a dead comrade's
family. Although the intense personal mourning and reflection at the
spontaneous memorial for the Pentagon muffled voices of protest, the deep

yearning for change in a world torn asunder may lead to one other transformative possibility: more of us may decide to walk the path of peace.

Notes

1. Quoted messages and descriptions of the Pentagon spontaneous memorial site and other memorial sites come from my fieldwork journals and photographs in my personal collection, unless otherwise indicated. Many thanks to my colleague Debra Shutika for reading an earlier version of this paper and for her translations of the memorial messages in Spanish. My thanks also to my graduate research assistant, J. Michael Martinez, for help with web-based research, and to my colleague Amelia Rutledge and my folklore student Ieva Cucinelli who sent me 9/11 articles that contributed to my research.
2. For a discussion of photography, 9/11, and New York City, see Kirshenblatt-Gimblett who claims that "[p]hotography materialized the morally ambiguous activity of watching" (2002: 5).
3. For comparisons of visits to spontaneous memorials with pilgrimages, see Grider (2001: 3) and Duke (2002).
4. To locate 148 of the monuments and memorials in the Washington DC region, visit <http://www.kittytours.org/thatman2>. For information on the February 2004 and the May 2004 memorials to the Columbia astronauts and to the World War II dead, respectively, see White (2004), and Reel (2004).
5. See, for example, articles by Bob Dart (2001) of the Cox New Service and David Cho and Jamie Stockwell (2001) of *The Washington Post*. A search of Lexis-Nexis shows the dominance of the term "makeshift memorial." See Grider (2001: 3–4) who also decries the use of the term.
6. Two other spontaneous memorials closely linked to Pentagon families would later appear at different sites. One was created by families of the Pentagon dead as they were ushered to the spot where their relatives died by Pentagon officials on September 17. Families left flowers, wreaths, balloons, notes, and large posterboard signs inside the Pentagon compound; see White and Davis (2001) and Papadopoulos (2004). Another spontaneous memorial for the Pentagon dead was also created at the Family Assistance Center in the Sheraton Crystal City Hotel, organized for families of the victims by Meg Falk, director of the Office of Family Policy for the Office of the Assistant Secretary of Defense at the Pentagon. The memorial grew to encompass six tables of mementos such as photographs and locks of hair; see Kunkle (2002b) and Papadopoulos (2004). People throughout the metropolitan area, though, erected additional spontaneous memorials to the 9/11 dead; see Gowan (2001), Gowan and Thomas-Lester (2001), and Toto (2001).
7. "Visitor" is hardly an adequate word for the people who came to the Pentagon memorial. Although I use the term for clarity throughout this essay, visitors were also artists, cocreators, and ritual practitioners. See also Hufford (2001: 7).

8. Although Fisher-Price had been promoting police officers and firefighters since 1998, by mid-November 2001, 100,000 of the "Billy Blazes" FDNY action figures, just one of the "Rescue Heroes" figures by Fisher-Price, started to arrive in Toys R Us stores instead of the 20,000 originally planned (Hamilton 2001: E1).

9. The memorial offered a site where the workings of a wartime gender system could be seen. Even before President George W. Bush announced the start of the "War on Terror" to a joint session of Congress on September 20, 2001, and before the first strikes on al-Qaeda military installations in Afghanistan on October 7, visitors to the memorial understood that such violent attacks on United States soil would lead to battle. One visitor left a copy of an editorial cartoon from the San Diego *Union*: "GETTING READY," it read, as an angry bald eagle sits on a stool, hacksaw in claw, sharpening one of his talons. "War must be understood as a *gendering* activity," Margaret Higonnet and her coauthors insist, "one that ritually marks the gender of all members of a society, whether or not they are combatants" (1987: 4). At the Pentagon memorial, young women made ribbons to wear, reminiscent of the yellow ribbons of the first Gulf War. Children spoke for peace. Soldiers were described as "B.A. (bad-assed) boys" though women now serve in the military. And, one of the white paper posters placed adjacent to the message board featured an upright Uncle Sam dressed in red, white, and blue, holding in his arms a Statue of Liberty, her eyes closed, her torch still in her hand and glowing, but lowered, her body clothed in a long, light green, body-clinging dress that revealed every contour of her female body.

10. For statistics on immigration to the Washington DC Metropolitan area, see the Federation of American Immigration Reform (2004).

11. See White (2001), Shaver (2002), Associated Press (2002), and Novick (2002). For information about nativism in the form of yellow ribbons during the first Gulf War, see Pershing and Yocom (1996).

12. "The Latino Community Supports Our U.S. Brothers."

13. "Our Sympathies to Those Who Have Lost Their Families / May God Help America Overcome [this tragedy]."

14. "Neustras [*sic*] oracuones [*sic*] siempre eştaran con ustedes. Boricue [*sic*] los queremos" is a Spanish translation, with several errors, of the English sentence that precedes it.

15. The use of multiple images here is reminiscent of the NAMES Project's AIDS Memorial Quilt panels where multiple names appear, sometimes upward of one hundred, to show devastation in numbers: people who once acted on Broadway, people who lived in one small town in Texas, for example.

16. Even though the face is a body fragment, it, along with the brain and the heart, is strongly iconic of the entire person and of his or her identity. See Tangherlini (1998: 63).

17. Hearts, hands, and faces also predominate on New York City's many memorial walls, painted in tribute to people who have died, usually violently. See *Cooper and Sciorra* ([1994] 2001). Many memorials were also painted after 9/11 to honor the dead and the living. See Cotter (2002) and Kirshenblatt-Gimblett (2002: 2).

18. Elementary school children's art today is filled with images of hearts, hands, and sometimes feet. The state of Virginia offers its citizens, for example, a license plate with images of children's hands like the ones at the Pentagon memorial. On the plate are the words "KIDS FIRST." The evocative symbol of the empty shoe, like the foot, has been used in many public displays as a synecdoche for a person. See the display of victims' shoes at the Holocaust Museum in Washington DC, gravestones with images of loggers' boots (Meyer [1989] 1992: 67), or the recent spontaneous memorial for U.S. soldiers killed in Iraq (Brinkley 2003). The shoe as container for the living especially evokes both absence and presence.

19. As the *Washington Post* recently reported, the monitoring and distrust of Middle Eastern Studies continues. See Dobbs (2003).

20. See Schneider for a report on several antiwar messages at the Union Square memorial in September, including one person whose sign read, "The war is over, if you want" (2001: 1).

21. Concern about censure and personal safety routinely affects public displays. University of Massachusetts professor Jennie Traschen, for example, received death threats and more after September 11, 2001 when people learned that she had recommended on September 10, a day *before* the attacks, that her town of Amherst not display great numbers of flags on its downtown streets, since the flag was, in her opinion, " 'a symbol of terrorism and death and fear and destruction and oppression" (Abel 2001). Likewise, the furious reactions to the comment about President Bush made by the country music group the Dixie Chicks was, likewise, broadcast widely by the media (St. John 2003). During the first Gulf War, many people who questioned the war and left their doors and yards undecorated felt pressure from neighbors to display yellow ribbons (Pershing and Yocom 1996). See also the discussion earlier in this article about the displays brought to the memorial by DC area international communities.

22. Barbara Kirshenblatt-Gimblett notes additional linkages between towering buildings and ominous imaginings of destruction. She describes the " 'intimation of mortality' " that E.B. White writes of in his 1948 essay as he considers how a "flight of planes . . . could burn the towers" as well as a report Adolf Hitler's fantasy of burning New York and seeing its " 'skyscrapers being turned into gigantic burning torches, collapsing upon one another' " (2002: 11).

23. See Gillespie (1999: 4,138), Kumar (2001: 5), and Smith (2003: 2).

24. See Gillespie (1999: 4,138), Bahrampour (2001: 2), and Smith (2003: 2).

25. See Novick (2001: 1) and the *Milwaukee Journal Sentinel* (2001: 1).

26. "Every attempt I made to donate something was foiled, which made me feel horrible," Corinne Kerr of New York City admitted. "I tried to give blood. I tried to volunteer. . . ." So Kerr went to the Union Square memorial with a candle: "At least you can help in spirit and give your energy" (Wartofsky 2001).

27. From the poem "The Plum Trees" by Mary Oliver ([1978]1983: 84).

28. Kirshenblatt-Gimblett writes about New Yorkers' reactions as city officials removed the spontaneous memorials at Union Square on September 19: "People posted photographs of the memorials that were once there, with messages protesting their removal" (2002: 12).

29. In 1993, Steve Zeitlin wrote that the ground of memorials had been hallowed by the death of the people there. At the site by the Navy Annex, people had to make hallow the ground within sight of the dead, but it was not the ground on which people died.

30. My ideas here about the perceived fragility of ritual space and the need for continuous maintenance at spontaneous memorials are adapted from Arjun Appadurai's discussion of the production of locality ([1996] 2003: 179).

31. Amy Shuman has suggested that folklorists could conceive of their discipline as one that focuses on "catastrophe," on "the conditions in which cultures clash, and though not demolished, are forever changed" (2003: 5).

32. My use of "dialogues" here refers to Mikhail Bakhtin's concept of the dialogic, which I have written about previously in regards to the study of material culture. See Yocom (2000).

33. See Kirshenblatt-Gimblett for examples of such "random juxtapositions—and their unintended ironies" in the displays in New York City. She reports on a missing person notice, for example, affixed to an advertisement for Continental Airlines that offered " 'dependable service, time after time' " (2002: 6).

34. By September 18, 2001, the remains of 97 people had been pulled from the wreckage, and 11 of the 124 Pentagon employees unaccounted for had been identified. One burn patient had been released from Washington Hospital Center; nine more remained there, six listed in critical condition (Morello and Vogel 2001).

35. My thanks to Professor Christopher Howell of the Master of Fine Arts Program at Eastern Washington University, Spokane, for permission to use his luminous poem.

36. The memorial has had a long life. When a storm threatened the displays on September 28, 2001, Pentagon workers gathered up many of the items for safekeeping. Many of the memorial items are under the care of the Army Center of Military History (Papadopoulos 2004). During the week of February 18, 2002, a fire of unknown origin swept through the memorial destroying almost all of its displays (McCaslin 2002: 2). Occasionally, in 2004, mementos have appeared at the site on the Navy Annex lawn.

37. The committee received 1,126 entries in the Memorial competition. The 11 judges and one alternate, including artists, architects and landscape architects, two former secretaries of defense, and relatives of the victims, selected 45 top entries and then the finalists. One of the entries in the exhibit openly credited spontaneous memorials as their major influence. On their 30 × 40 inch competition poster, Brandon Padron of Miami, Florida, with team member Jason Frantzen, showed visitors walking into a chamber formed by two dark towering walls, leaving their candles and flowers at the walls and taping photos and notes on the walls. Padron and Frantzen explained,

> The events of September 11 have had a profound impact on the world, both through the horrendous carnage of the event itself and the subsequent revaluation of the world in its aftermath. On a secondary level, they have

also made transparent the rituals of the grieving process, illustrating our desire to come to terms with this tragedy through collective acts of mourning.

The temporary memorials which sprang up in New York, Washington, and many other locations in the country can be understood as perhaps the most democratic and genuine representation of this need. Deprived of even the remains of the victims, many families erected small shrines to their loved ones, often times composed of personal artifacts from the victim's daily life. Similarly, the outpouring of flowers, messages, and candles on these sites from concerned strangers all over the world makes apparent the symbolic need for active participation in order for the healing process to begin. These memorials became intensely personal environments, opening up what is usually a very private act to the public so that all may begin to understand. In the process it brought a certain sense of corporeal reality to a tragedy which seemed so unreal through its endless replay in the media. The overwhelming personal intensity of these artifacts conveyed the universal sense of loss felt throughout the world more effectively than any memorial with a specific form in a singular meaning.

With this understanding, the Pentagon memorial was conceived as a pair of abstract open-air meditation chambers in which this grass-roots grieving process can continue. Like the Vietnam memorial on the Washington Mall, these spaces will act as a container or cabinet for the myriad of smaller, personal monuments which visitors erect, its meaning will emerge out of the multitude of expressions of sorrow and evolve over time.

All of the six finalists' designs featured close interaction with visitors, just like the spontaneous memorial did. For example, the entry by Jean Koeppel and Tom Kowalski of Brooklyn featured an arrangement of 184 inner-lit glass slabs, one for each of the victims, which would be cooled to allow visitors to leave temporary messages in the condensation. A "continuous 'tabula rasa,' " the team called it. "We have witnessed human nature in its finest hour," they continued,

> as we joined together, united in expressing our love and respect for one another. It is this wonderful act of human expression that led us to our concept for the Pentagon Memorial. . . . We believe that the memorial should be a place where people not only come to visit, but come to find comfort through interaction with one another and with the monument itself. It is the people who will ultimately fuel this memorial. (Forgey 2002)

Similarly, finalist Jacky Bowring of Centerbury, New Zealand, with team members Peter England, Richard Weller, and Vladimir Sitta, designed 184 metal-clad units in orderly rows, like gravestones. Metaphorically, each of these "life recorders" is a transformation of the airplane's "black box," as well as a grave marker. Each will contain a mirror, a little pool of water, and a family memento or two (Forgey 2002).

Works Cited

Abel, David. 2001. America Prepares Domestic Impact; Campuses See a Downside to Unity Civil Rights Stifled, Some Professors Say. *The Boston Globe*. October 6, 2001. <http://web.lexis-nexis.com> (January 14, 2004).

Associated Press. 2002. Some Arabs in U.S. Change Names. *Chattanooga Times Free Press*. March 21, 2002. <http://web.lexis-nexis.com/universe> (October 28, 2003).

Appadurai, Arjun. [1996] 2003. *Modernity at Large: Cultural Dimensions of Globalization*. Minneapolis: University of Minneapolis Press.

Bahrampour, Tara. 2001. The Farther Away, They Larger They Loomed. *The New York Times*. September 23, 2001. <http://www.nytimes.com> (September 26, 2001).

Bakhtin, Mikhail. 1981. *The Dialogic Imagination: Four Essays*. Trans. Caryl Emerson and Michael Holquist. Austin: University of Texas Press.

Blum, Justin. 2003. Teen's Room Turned Into a Tribute: Friends Cover Walls With Words of Love and Grief, Memories of Student. *The Washington Post*. November 1, 2003: B1, 5.

Brinkley, Joel. 2003. At a Base in Iraq, American Troops Honor 15 Who Lost Their Lives. *The New York Times*. November 7, 2003: A1, 8.

Casey, Edward. 1993. *Getting Back Into Place: Toward a Renewed Understanding of the Place-World*. Bloomington: Indiana University Press.

Cho, David and Jamie Stockwell. 2001. *The Washington Post*. September 16, 2001. <http://web.lexis-nexis.com> (January 15, 2004).

Cixous, HéllIne. 2002. The Towers: *Les tours*. *Signs: Journal of Women in Culture and Society* 28(1): 431–433.

Cooper, Martha and Joseph Sciorra. [1994] 2001. *R.I.P. Memorial Wall Art*. New York: Thames & Hudson.

Cotter, Holland. 2002. Amid the Ashes, Creativity; Responses to 9/11, From Shock and Grief to Visions of the Future. *The New York Times*. 2002: B33, 35.

Dart, Bob. 2001. Makeshift Memorial Grows Overlooking Pentagon Site. Cox News Service. October 2, 2001. <http://web.lexis-nexis.com> (January 15, 2004).

De Certeau, Michel. [1984] 1988. *The Practice of Everyday Life*. Berkeley: University of California Press.

Dewey, John. [1934] 1980. *Art As Experience*. New York: Perigee (Penguin Putnam).

Dissanayake, Ellen. 1988. *What Is Art For?* Seattle: University of Washington Press.

Dobbs, Michael. 2003. Middle East Studies Under Scrutiny in U.S.; Watchdog Groups Allege Left-Wing Bias. *The Washington Post*. January 13, 2003: A1, 8.

Duke, Lynne. 2002. The Pilgrimage to Ground Zero: Officials and Tourists Walk A Fine Line on Solemn Ground. *The Washington Post*. February 27, 2002: C1,10.

Dwyer, Timothy. 2003. How To Remember / Building the Pentagon Memorial: Tribute Design Rose From Emotional Depths. *Washington Post*. May 25, 2003: A1, 14–15.

Eakin, Emily. 2001. An Organization on the lookout for Patriotic Incorrectness. *The New York Times*. November 24, 2001. <http://www.nytimes.com> (November 27, 2001).

Federation for American Immigration Reform. 2004. Metro Area Factsheet: Washington, D.C. PM. <http://www.fairus.org/Research/Research.cfm?ID= 751&c=9> (February 2, 2004).

Forgey, Benjamin. 2002. Pentagon Memorial: Six Finalists in Search of Closure. *The Washington Post*. October 30, 2002: C1, 10.

————. 2004. Making A Design More Winning: Revisions Add Strength To the Final Choice for Trade Center Memorial. *The Washington Post*. January 15, 2004: A1, C1, 4.

Frisby, David. 1986. *Fragments of Modernity: Theories of Modernity in the Work of Simmel, Kracauer and Benjamin*. Cambridge, MA: MIT Press.

Gillespie, Angus Kress. 1999. *Twin Towers: The Life of New York City's World Trade Center*. New Brunswick, NJ: Rutgers University Press.

Glassie, Henry. 1982. *Passing the Time In Ballymenone: Culture and History of an Ulster Community*. Philadelphia: Pennsylvania.

Gowan, Annie. 2001. Letters of Comfort to Family's Friends; Victims Sent Postcards Before Flight. *The Washington Post*. September 24, 2001. <http://web.lexis-nexis.com> (January 15, 2004).

Gowan, Annie and Avis Thomas-Lester. 2001. Family Was Starting Exciting Adventure; Send-Off Proved to Be Last Farewell. *The Washington Post*. September 20, 2001. <http://web.lexis-nexis.com> (January 15, 2004).

Grider, Sylvia. 2001. Spontaneous Shrines: A Modern Response to Tragedy and Disaster. *New Directions in Folklore*. October 5, 2001. <http://www.temple. edu/isllc.newfolk/shrines.html> (January 29, 2004).

Hamilton, Martha McNeil. 2001. A Timely Toy to the Rescue; One Action Figure Stands Tall in Newly Complicated Kids' Market. *The Washington Post*. October 3, 2001. E1, 11.

Higgonet, Margaret et al., eds. 1997. *Behind the Lines: Gender and the Two World Wars*. New Haven: Yale University Press.

Howell, Christopher. 1996. *Memory and Heaven*. Cheney: Eastern Washington University Press.

Hufford, Mary. 2001. A Spontaneous Memorial Near the Pentagon. *Folklife Center News* 23(4):5–7.

Jenkins, Chris L. 2002. *The Washington Post*. March 8, 2002. <http://web. lexis-nexis.com> (October 28, 2003).

Jones, Michael Owen. 1995. "Why Make (Folk) Art?" *Western Folklore* 54(4): 253–276.

Jones, Shannon. 2001. New Attacks on Academic Free Speech in US. *World Socialist Web Site*. November 22, 2001. <http://www.wsws.org.articles/2001/ nov2001/univ-n22_prn.shtml> (October 31, 2003).

Kirshenblatt-Gimblett, Barbara. 2002. Kodak Moments, Flashbulb Memories: Reflections on 9/11. <http://www.nyu.edu/classes/bkg/web> (January 27, 2004).

Kumar, Sameer. 2001. Letter to the Editor. *Immigrant's Weekly*. September 17, 2001. <http://web.lexis-nexis.com> (February 3, 2004).

Kunkle, Frederick. 2002a. Mementos Strengthen A Stricken Headquarters; Pentagon Workers Comforted by Tokens of Support. *The Washington Post*. February 6, 2002: B1, 5.

Kunkle, Frederick. 2002b. Key Pentagon Official Hailed For 9/11 Role; Amid Disorder, Manager Set Up Assistance Center. *The Washington Post*. June 13, 2002: A35 <http://web.lexis-nexis.com> (January 15, 2004).

Margalit, Avishai. 2002. *The Ethics of Memory*. Cambridge: Harvard University Press.

Martinez, Barbara E. 2002. Stitches for Broken Hearts: "Pentagon Quilts" Go on Exhibit. *The Washington Post*. September 5, 2002: C1, 4.

McCaslin, John. 2002. Inside the Beltway. *The Washington Times*. February 26, 2002. <http://web.lexis-nexis.com> (January 15, 2004).

Meyer, Richard E. [1989] 1992. Images of Logging on Contemporary Pacific Northwest Gravemarkers. In *Cemetaries & Gravemarkers: Voices of American Culture*, ed. Richard E. Meyer. Logan: Utah State University Press.

Milwaukee Journal Sentinel. 2001. Condemnation; Attack on America; Condemnation, condolences are major themes for lawmakers. September 13, 2001. <http://web.lexis-nexis.com> (February 3, 2004).

Morello, Carol and Steve Vogel. 2001. Slowly, Signs of a Return to Normalcy; Scattered Evacuations, Pentagon Search Are Lingering Reminders. *The Washington Post*. September 18, 2001. <http://www.washingtonpost.com> (September 18, 2001).

Nochlin, Linda. 1994. *The Body in Pieces: The Fragment as a Metaphor of Modernity*. New York: Thames and Hudson.

Novick, Abe. 2001. The Spirit of the Twin Towers Still Stands. *Capitalism Magazine*. September 22, 2001. <http://web.lexis-nexis.com> (February 3, 2004).

Novick, Michael. 2002. Leading the Edge of the Wedge: Anti-Immigrant Racism & Repression. *Ethnic News: Turning the Tide* 15(3): 13 <http://web.lexis-nexis.com> (October 28, 2003).

Oliver, Mary. [1978] 1983. *American Primitive*. Boston: Little, Brown and Company.

Ortiz, Emmanuel. 2002. Before I start this poem. Idaho Indymedia Center <http://idaho.indymedia.org/news/2003/04/1800.php> (October, 2003).

Papadopoulos, Randy. 2004. Conversations and E-mail with the author, 3–xx February. Author of forthcoming "Pentagon 9/11: An Analysis of the Response." Washington DC: Government Printing Office.

The Pentagon: Headquarters of the United States Department of Defense. 2001. About the Pentagon. January 16, 2001. <http://www.defenselink.mil/pubs/pentagon/about.html> (February 3, 2004).

Pentagon Memorial Competition—Stage One Entry Display. 2002. <http://www.nbm.org/Exhibits/current/Pentagon_Memorial_Competition.html> (November 9, 2002).

Pershing, Linda. 1996. *The Ribbon Around the Pentagon: Peace By Piecemakers*. Knoxville: University of Tennessee Press.

Pershing, Linda and Margaret R. Yocom. 1996. The Yellow Ribboning of the USA: Contested Meanings in the Construction of a Political Symbol. *Western Folklore* 55(1): 41–85.

A Photographic Tour of the Statues, Monuments, and Memorials of Washington DC. <http://www.kittytours.org/thatman2> (January 13, 2003).

Reel, Monte. 2004. Marching Toward a Shining Salute: Construction Entering Final Stages for WWII Memorial's Debut. *The Washington Post*. February 3, 2004: B1, 8.

Schneider, Craig. 2001. "Give Peace a Chance!" Is War Cry in N.Y. Park. Cox New Service. September 21, 2001. <http://www.lexis-nexis.com> (January 15, 2004).

Shaver, Katherine. 2002. Hair Uncovered, Apology Sought; BWI Screening Prompts Complaint From Muslim Teenager in Va. *The Washington Post*. January 9, 2002. <http://web.lexis-nexis.com> (October 31, 2003).

Shuman, Amy. 2003. Cultural Exports: Straining for Aura in an Age of Mechanical Reproduction. Paper read at the annual meeting of the American Folklore Society, 8–12 October, at Albuquerque, New Mexico.

Smith, Jessica. 2003. Lecture Informs on Twin Towers: A Professor Discusses the World Trade Center as a Symbol Of America. *The Shorthorn Online*. September 12, 2003. <http://web.lexis-nexis.com> (February 3, 2004).

Stewart, Susan. [1984] 1993. *On Longing: Narratives of the Miniature, the Gigantic, the Souvenir, and the Collection*. Durham, NC: Duke University Press.

St. John, Warren. 2003. The Backlash Grows Against Celebrity Activists. March 23, 2003. <http://web.lexis-nexis.com> (January 26, 2004).

Tangherlini, Timothy R. 1998. *Talking Trauma: Paramedics and Their Stories*. Jackson: University Press of Mississippi.

Toto, Christian. 2001. Bethesda Vents Grief on Unity Wall. *The Washington Times*. September 16, 2001. <http://web.lexis-nexis.com> (January 15, 2004).

Turner, Kay. 1999. *Beautiful Necessity: The Art and Meaning of Women's Altars*. New York: Thames & Hudson.

Waldrop, Rosmarie. 2002. *Lavish Absence: Recalling and Rereading Edmond Jab1ìs*. Middletown, CT: Wesleyan University Press.

Walls, Robert E. 1990. Folklife and Material Culture. In *The Emergence of Folklore in Everyday Life: A Fieldguide and Sourcebook*, ed. George H. Schoemaker, 107–119. Bloomington, IN: Trickster Press.

Wartofsky, Alona. 2001. In Manhattan, Makeshift Memorials Honor the Lost, Comfort the Living. *The Washington Post*. September 15, 2001. <http://web.lexis-nexis.com> (January 15, 2004).

White, Josh. 2001. Beating of Pakistani Cab Driver Called a Hate Crime; Two Passengers Charged With Assault. *The Washington Post*. November 4, 2001. <http://web.lexis-nexis.com> (October 28, 2003).

———. 2004. "Our Heroic Columbia Astronauts": Seven on Shuttle Remembered at Arlington Cemetary Ceremony. *The Washington Post*. February 3, 2004: B1, 8.

White, Josh and Patricia Davis. 2001. FBI Takes Over at Pentagon Site; Search for Evidence Continues; Bush Declares Vicinity a Disaster Area. *The Washington Post*. September 22, 2001: B4. <http://web.lexis-nexis.com> (January 15, 2004).

Yocom, Margaret R. 2000. Exuberance in Control: The Dialogue of Ideas in the Tales and Fan Towers of Woodsman William Richard of Phillips, Maine. In *Northeast Folklore: Essays in Honor of Edward D. Ives*, ed. Pauleena MacDougall and David Taylor, 265–295. Orono: University of Maine Press.

Chapter 5

Oh Did You See the Ashes Come Thickly Falling Down? Poems Posted in the Wake of September 11

Steve Zeitlin

"There are some things about which nothing can be said and before which we dare not keep silent."

—T.S. Eliot

"26 letters is all we've got to make sense of the space between the canyons in our hearts."

—Jerry Quickly, "Crisis"

"In a crisis, poets lose words . . . You can find them here." With these words, poet Bob Holman, who watched the Towers collapse from his apartment just blocks away from the Trade Towers, provided an opening salvo for City Lore's online call for poets of all denominations to contribute a line to a collaborative poem.

> Topfloor. Hold eyes. Hold hands. Take wing.
> Better to fly than do nothing.
> Out the window, PS 234, "Teacher, the birds are on fire."
> Fire turns into sky,
> Better to fly than do nothing, better to fly.
> Soaring eagles spy glowing ember -
> The pyres of the Phoenix and the Turtle burn wholly.

Wailing whispers. Lost angels
Wrapped in dust drift down,
An avalanche of ash disappears the world,
With every breath, a shower of shoes.
The day's sandwich is uneaten.
Fear rips out my tongue.
The dead race for the sky . . .

Follow us as we run up streets.
How fast can you run, tough rubber boots?
The fireman's feet blister,
Dogs listen, breathing pain.[1]

In the days and weeks that followed, streets lay eerily quiet and deserted.
The avalanche of ashes from the Towers, a black and paralyzing snowfall.
Hours and days fell out of kilter.

Back in the City Lore offices, a week later, as the numbing eased, the idea
for a collaborative poem came to us—two word towers of 110 lines, one
for each story of the World Trade Towers. 220 poets, one line each. Tower
One (from which the above lines are taken) would be created on the web,
inviting contributions from anyone; Tower two by invitation. Poet and
close associate Bob Holman would edit the entries to Tower One, and invite
established poets to contribute for Tower Two. The two word towers
describe the events with the vividness of the videographers who captured
the Towers' collapse, and an emotional depth that is poetry's purview.
The invited poets of Tower Two:

A tremendous roar came over our shoulders, ratcheting our heads slightly to
the right, a huge what looked like a 747 at eye level & moving, then steel
into steel, glass into glass.
Women in the Middle East knew nothing about it. They were washing clothes.
Planes crashing on the windowsill.
"Did the pilots get hurt?" asked the lover of pilots, a young boy still in love
with heroes, when the second plane hit.
She held her breath—but, more, wished to hold his. Him. A hymn. A him of
words.
I, no victor, saw birds in flames. What were their names?
Victor's daughter dances the deck of the red tugboat, marks of embers on her
arms, soles of his shoes molten.
We have become the heat-slick melt of infrastructure,
into the residue of those screams and shouts unheard in the multilayered
collapse revealed again and again via satellite as above and below the crea-
tures deny the supremacy of architecture,

a lock of flame-red hair or a spoke from her wheelchair
Dusty seagulls, powdered roaches, gray-flecked squirrels, ashy mice.
White birds with brown bellies high against the blue sky in Brooklyn, escape
of the charred memos.
We are breathing the dead, taking them into our lungs as living we had taken
them into our arms.
"We are all just walking each other home."[2]

The self-conscious, incisive words of the poets traveled the internet, each line seeking its own original take on the tragedy, describing, analyzing, and codifying personal and collective feelings. The streets were awash with simpler emotions. The first memorials written in the dust and debris—on a car hood, a single word, "Pray."[3] On the window of the McDonalds a block away, "we are not afraid." In the first hours and days, family members and friends, in their grief, coming as close as they could to Ground Zero, the place where loved ones died, where souls may have lingered. Written by a child in the dust of a shop window close to the scene, "Daddy, I came here to find you." Another, "God Be With You Dana—Love, Mom," seen by Dan Barry, a reporter for the *Times* (Barry 2001).

The city did not wait for the poets. As streams of water poured over the smoke at Ground Zero, the city hosed down with words. Distraught and bereaved New Yorkers scrawled missives in the ash. In the early afternoon of the first day, Jordan Schuster, a student from NYU laid out a sheet of butcher-block paper in Union Square, the first of many to inspire his fellow New Yorkers to set down their thoughts. "My friends and I," he told us, "went to get the paper, pens, and tape, and met at Union Square at 3:00 on September 11. We taped down the first two pieces of butcher paper and started writing. People walked up and we'd offer a pen and say 'Do you have something that you want to share?' 'Do you feel like getting anything out?' And some people would say 'Yeah.' And they'd take the pen and write. And some people would say, 'I just kinda want to watch.' And that was fine, too. And some people would say, 'I don't really know what to say.' And we'd say, 'Well, write that down, cause that's definitely a valid opinion, too.' And it just started growing. It grew really quickly. Like, within half an hour there were probably 50 people there. Within an hour there were about 250 people. Within two hours about 500. . . ."[4] In Union Square words gave birth to words, and proliferated into a barrage of written feeling that vented rage and offered solace.

From the first day's writing, September 11: "Strength through diversity in the most diverse place the world has ever known. Tim, born Sept. 11, 1971."[5]

In chalk in Union Square, September 13: "Hate breeds hate/Love breeds love."[6]

Posted on an index card in a Times Square storefront, September 14: "Bastards!"[7]

Posted on Canal Street, September 17: "I felt as if the Twin Towers were injured, and they fought hard to stay up as long as they could, they couldn't hold out any more, but we can! USA"[8] (see figure 5.1).

By the time the staff of City Lore were able to get back into our downtown East Village office a few days later, we already had email messages asking us to document the spontaneous memorials and collect stories. Our photographer, Martha Cooper, had been documenting the streets since the day after the tragedy. The decision was made before we had time to think about it. We decided to document the memorials and the posted poems in order to plan for an exhibit that would chronicle and share this unfolding tribute to the City's indomitable spirit. As participants in grief, New Yorkers as well as folklorists, photographers, and historians, we saw our work as a tribute to this great city where, despite all its potential for anonymity and alienation, people seemed to be able to create places where humanity could re-stake its claim.[9]

Brightly colored, candlelit improvised shrines and memorials cropped up in every corner of the City. In a cathartic burst, emotions etched themselves onto the cityscape—on chain link fences surrounding Ground Zero, index cards in a store window on Times Square, ribbons on Canal Street,

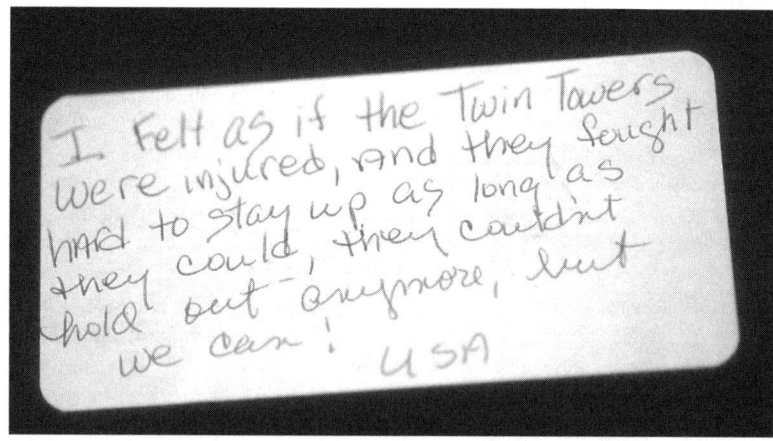

Figure 5.1   The Twin Towers personified.
Photo Credit: Martha Cooper/City Lore.

Figure 5.2   Posting Poems on Canal Street.
Photo Credit: Martha Cooper/City Lore.

chalk on the sidewalk, and on tiles as part of a memorial project at 7th Avenue and Greenwich; inscriptions from Gandhi to Jerry Garcia. Even scraps of paper that blew into the air after the explosions were interpreted as poems. On Marilyn Jacobson's patio in Brooklyn, a balance sheet from an unidentified company showed a profit of several million dollars—an ironic poem of sorts (see figure 5.2).

Posters of the "missing" were taped to walls throughout the City, posted on telephone booths, plastered on firehouses, and wall to wall at Ray's Pizza in Greenwich Village. Hopes dimmed, but the posters proliferated. Kinko's offered free copy services and soon mailboxes, bus shelters, telephone booths, and subway station walls became bulletin boards. Snapshots and wedding photos pleaded with passersby, along with detailed descriptions of clothing and jewelry worn by the missing persons on September 11. Date of birth, height, weight, tattoos, and other distinguishing personal details were also provided.[10] Sometimes a heartbreakingly cryptic line, pleading for a special dispensation: "had no hate in his heart for anyone," "expecting first child this week," or "please help me find my daddy." As one person put it, "If I just put up enough of these flyers, maybe there will be a miracle" (Waldman 2001).

But in only a few days, *New York Times* reporter Amy Waldman would write, "Manufactured in hope, the flyers have now transmuted into memorial . . ." (Waldman 2001).

On the streets, ordinary people started the memorials, sustained them, and made them meaningful. Thousands took part. They neither asked permission from city officials nor waited for religious or civil authorities to tell them how to respond. New Yorkers showed an amazing instinct and ability to use public spaces all over the city to gather and express themselves, and, in many cases, to give others an opportunity to do the same. After Oklahoma City was attached, shrines grew up in great numbers on the chain link fence that surrounded the Alfred P. Murrah Federal Building.[11] After September 11 in New York, the plethora of shrines and memorials were notable in their dispersion across all five boroughs and beyond, unlike Oklahoma City, or the Vietnam Memorial, where the improvised shrines were centralized. New York City sprouted a vast memorial garden. Sacred spaces cropped up on street corners, housing projects, and beside handball courts. So often characterized as Godless, unfriendly, and cold, New Yorkers created places where the language spoken was so often poetry (see figure 5.3).

Figure 5.3   "Goin' Home"—Union Square.
Photo Credit: Martha Cooper/City Lore.

On September 15, four days after 9/11, a ten-year-old boy stood outside the Firehouse of Squad 1 in Park Slope, Brooklyn passing out a poem. Naomi Person, who passed the poem on to us, never found out if the boy wrote the poem, for no name appeared on the page:

In the graveyard,
The gravestones are silent,
The people are even more silent
This tragedy will leave all of us
With unhealable wounds
That only an angel can heal.
That, my friend, is the angel of hope,
An angel of light,
An angel named phoenix
That angel will find you;
Together, we will rise up
Out of the dust
Out of the ashes
And out of the dark.

Particularly in the weeks after the disaster, most of the posted poems were anonymous. In the months that followed, new poems still appeared, but these were stamped with copyright notices and posted web sites.

All space is contested space. As John Urry writes, "the spatial dynamics of conflict can be explained by the fact that no two objects can occupy the same point in space" (Urry 1985: 30). A Jewish grandmother expressed a similar sentiment—one tuchas cannot sit in two places at the same time. Inspired by Michel Foucault who insisted, "space is fundamental in any exercise of power" (Foucault 1984: 252), David Chidester and Edward T. Linenthal write, "Sacred space is often, if not inevitably, entangled in politics. . . . Sacred places are always highly charged sites for contested negotiations" (1995: 15, 16). No need to tell any New Yorker who has ever tried to rent an apartment, to commandeer a parking spot, or paint a mural on the side of a building about contested space. But after September 11 all over the City (with the notable exception of Union and Washington Square), an unspoken partnership sprung up between landlords, the city, policemen, and the grieving public. Behind every shrine, a swath of property owners and city authorities expressed their tolerance, choosing not to contest the space, and not to impose their vested authorities.

After September 11, by the neighborhood handball court on 207th and Seaman Avenue, friends of Brian Monaghan waited for four days and nights for Brian to come home. Eventually, Ray Martinez and Mick Fitzgerald lit a candle on the street, neighbors began to contribute objects and poems, and the street corner became a place for people to gather. Eventually a discarded bookcase was found to hold the objects. Overflowing with messages and memorial objects, a shrine evolved over four months, encompassing a good portion of a city block. Police and sanitation departments issued no summonses but allowed the shrine keepers the space to grieve. With the notable exception of Union Square and Washington Square where in the name of restoring normalcy, the city sent sanitation workers to clear the park several times in the first few weeks that followed 9/11, city agencies and landlords allowed New Yorkers to express their sorrow. They allowed the city to become a memorial garden on their property. The magnitude of these public expressions of grief seemed to approach the enormity of the loss.

In the weeks that followed, arrangements were made for the families to visit Ground Zero. The existing Policeman's Memorial in Battery Park turned into an improvised shrine. Families left teddy bears, thousands of them—along with photos and messages to loved ones. We too made our pilgrimage down to Ground Zero, to the ghost town of Lower Manhattan, where the smoke had not yet cleared. Standing in front of the Battery Park shrine lined with so many teddy bears—selected perhaps for the way they bring comfort to children, and perhaps for Smokey the Bear, who survived fires—we shook our heads in wonder. What kind of a shrine is this that pays homage to the teddy bear?

But on that wet and cold October 20, what seemed silly and sweet took on significance as we started to read the inscriptions. This shrine at Ground Zero and the shrines in all five boroughs had become portals where the living and dead touch one another. "To Lee," one inscription read, "We came here today to tell you how much we love you & miss you. We are trying to remember all of the good times. We're just staying hello because there will never be goodbyes." At the memorial in Inwood for Brian Patrick Monaghan, put together by his friends, many of whom played handball at the adjoining court on 207th and Seaman, a girl casually addresses Brian from across the grave. "What's up Babe. It's me, ROSIE—I'm here in the corner looking at all your pictures and candles."

Many of these missives from the living to the dead were written as poems—this one from the Battery Park shrine, spoken from a wife to her husband:

Where did you go?
You gave me a beautiful little angel,
But didn't stay to see her grow.

On one of the missing person flyers put up on the memorial at Grand Central Station, this one for Clyde Frazier, Jr., a visitor added this post-it, a sentiment felt by all of us haunted by the beautiful faces of fellow New Yorkers on these missing posters that were put up with such desperate hopes in the days after September 11 and gradually transmogrified into memorials for the dead.

> Every morning I see you smiling. I miss you. We never met.

But the shrines were also places where the dead speak to the living—often in verses posted as anonymous; this one was found at many of the different NYC memorials including Grand Central's memorial wall and Union Square:

> Do not stand at my grave and weep
> I am not there, I do not sleep.
>
> I am a thousand winds that blow
> I am the diamond glint on snow.
>
> I am the sunlight on ripened grain
> I am the gentle autumn rain.
>
> When you wake in the morning hush
> I am the swift, uplifting rush
> of quiet birds in circling flight.
> I am the soft starlight at night
>
> Do not stand at my grave and cry.
> I am not there. I did not die[12]

Or again, the dead speaking to the living:

> If you could see where I have gone
> and the beauty of this place
> And how it feels to know you're home
> to see the Savior's face
>
> To wake in peace and know no fear
> That joy beyond compare
> While still on earth you miss me yet
> You wouldn't want me there.

We read one of the most striking missives at the Memorial set up in Grand Central. Alicia Vasquez, whose name appears at the end, seems to be writing to a loved one. This is a section from it,

> don't look for me anymore
> it's late and you're tired

your feet ache standing atop the ruins of our twins
day after day searching for a trace of me
your eyes burning red
your hands cut bleeding sifting through rock
and your back crooked from endless hours of labor

It's my turn
I'm worried about you
watching as you sift through the ruins of what was
day after day in the soot and rain

I ached in knowing you suffer my death
rest in knowing that my blood lies in the cracks and crevices
of these great lands I loved so much . . .

don't look for me anymore
hold my children as I would
hold my sisters and brothers for me
since I can't bring them up with the same
love you gave me
and I'll rest assured
you're watching my children

don't look for me anymore
go home and rest

Mircea Eliade suggests that sacred space is set apart from ordinary, homogenous space. As center or axis mundi, it allows for passage between different levels of reality.[13] The improvised shrines became places where the living and dead are conjoined. In the poetic language of the shrines, the living and dead talk to one another. At the same time, images and miniatures of the Towers suggest an axis mundi, symbolically penetrating the universe, allowing a passageway between worlds. I am reminded of Haitian culture, in which followers of *Vodou* believe that our world and the world of the dead and the spirits are joined at the crossroads, where a great tree penetrates the earth to create a passageway from our world to the land of *Les Invisibles*, the spirits. At every ceremony, this world tree is symbolized by a *port manteau*, a pole in the center of the prayer space, enabling the spirits to pass back and forth between worlds. Temporary exhibits like the two "towers of light," attest to this World Trade Towers' role as a kind of *port manteau*.

The shrines of 9/11 provided portals through which the living and dead communicate. Likewise, shrines served as portals to talk directly to the dead—and to the terrorists, whose remains also lay in the Ground Zero rubble. This one is from the memorial wall at Grand Central:

Well you hit the World Trade Center, but you missed America
You hit the Pentagon,

Again you missed America
You used helpless American bodies to take out other American bodies,
but like a poor marksman, you still missed America

Why? Because of somethings you guys will never understand
America isn't about a building or two, not about financial centers not about
military centers

America isn't about a place, American isn't about a bunch of bodies
America is about an IDEA.

An idea that you can go someplace where you can earn as much as you can
figure out how to, live for the most part like you envisioned living, and
pursue Happiness
(no guarantees that you'll reach it, but you can sure try . . .)![14]

And some of the poems are about a communion with the living and the
dead, as this one posted anonymously in a number of the memorials:

As the soot and dirt and ash rained down,
We became one color.
As we carried each other down the stairs of the burning building
We became one class.
As we lit candles of waiting and hope
We became one generation.
As the firefighters and police officers fought
their way into the inferno
We became one gender.
as we fell to our knees in prayer for strength
We became one faith.

As we whispered or shouted words of encouragement,
We spoke one language.
As we gave our blood in lines a mile long,
We became one body.
As we mourned together the great loss
We became one family.
As we cried tears of grief and loss
We became one soul
As we retell with pride of the sacrifice of heroes
We became one people.

Although the City cleaned up Union Square repeatedly, and tried to dis-
perse the vigil that was always part peace rally and political protest, they did
save the objects they gathered, creating a large pile of memorabilia stored in
the women's locker room of Hamilton Fish swimming pool on the Lower
East Side. We had a chance to go through the materials for our exhibit at the

New York Historical Society. We were touched by these anonymous verses on a weather worn sheet of paper, cleaned up by the Parks Department, probably from Union Square.

To the Towers Themselves

They were never the favorites,
Not the Carmen Miranda Chrysler
Nor Rockefeller's magic boxes
Nor The Empire, which I think would have killed us all if she fell.

They were the two young dumb guys,
Beer drinking
Downtown MBAs
Swaggering across the skyline,

Now that they are gone,
They are like young men
Lost at war,
Not having had their life yet,
Not having grown wise and softened with air and time.

They are lost like
Cannon fodder
Like farm boys throughout time
Stunned into death,
Not knowing what hit them
And beloved
By the weeping mothers left behind.

Standing, the Towers symbolized New York, its capitalism, affluence—but destroyed they were continually transformed through art into a kind of axis mundi—a symbolic world tree around which the earth turned, as they were recreated in miniature sculptures and art in thousands of shrines in all five boroughs. At those sites, the living could still speak with the dead, and address them directly, often through poetry.

In our culture, we think of art as taking elements from what passes for real life, rearranging them, and offering them as a comment—metaphorical or lyrical—about our lives. After September 11, poems were written with the urgency of art but put back into the flow of life to take their place anonymously with ritual objects that were part of the mourning process. On the memorials, words were forged into poetry not for art's sake, but to pierce the very barrier that separates the living from the dead. In this worldly city, along our secular sidewalks, stoops, and parks, in all five boroughs, New Yorkers spoke to one another in a language of symbols and ritual acts, refusing to give death the last word.

In December, 2001, we received an email from Hillary North, describing a self-styled, personal memorial that she had completed for her coworkers at the AON corporation who perished.

How My Life Has Changed
Hillary North

I can no longer flirt with Lou.
I can no longer dance with Mayra.
I can no longer eat brownies with Suzanne Y.
I can no longer meet the deadline with Mark.
I can no longer talk to George about his daughter.
I can no longer drink coffee with Rich.
I can no longer make a good impression on Chris.
I can no longer smile at Paul.
I can no longer hold the door open for Tony.
I can no longer confide in Lisa.
I can no longer complain about Gary.
I can no longer work on a project with Donna R.
I can no longer get to know Yolanda.
I can no longer call the client with Nick.
I can no longer contribute to the book drive organized by Karen.
I can no longer hang out with Millie.
I can no longer give career advice to Suzanne P.
I can no longer laugh with Donna G.
I can no longer watch Mary Ellen cut through the bull shit.
I can no longer drink beer with Paul.
I can no longer have a meeting with Dave W.
I can no longer leave a message with Andrea.
I can no longer gossip with Anna.
I can no longer run into Dave P. at the vending machine.
I can no longer call Steve about my computer.
I can no longer compliment Lorenzo.
I can no longer hear Herman's voice.
I can no longer trade voice mails with Norman.
I can no longer ride the elevator with Barbara.
I can no longer be happy about Jennifer's pregnancy.
I can no longer walk with Adam.
I can no longer say hello to Steven every morning.
I can no longer see the incredible view from the 103rd Floor of the
   South Tower.
I can no longer take my life for granted.

On the day of the disaster, a copy of Shelley's "Ozymandias" crisscrossed the ether of the internet to an expanding aggregate of strangers and friends, suggesting that if the World Trade Center were ever to be rebuilt, it should bear a plaque with the inscription "*My name is Ozymandias, king of kings:/Look on my works, ye Mighty, and despair!*" (Smith 2001). The poems left at the shrines seemed reminiscent not of the Sphinx, but of the poems carved into the tombs of Egyptian Pharaohs and dignitaries, poems that are named according to where they were found: the Pyramid Texts and the Coffin Texts. The poems "rescued" by the Parks Department as they swept Union and Washington Square repeatedly in the month following 9/11, stored in the women's locker room at the Hamilton Fish swimming pool took on the look of archaeological artifacts.

A few weeks after September 11, a gallery in SOHO opened their *Here is New York* exhibition. Like many New Yorkers, Elaine Norman, a friend of ours visited repeatedly. She told us of one image that moved her to tears each time. The photo of a chain link fence near Ground Zero with a note pinned to it (see figure 5.4). The note, addressed to one of the tragedy's victims, read:

> Dear Steven I never met you . . . I don't know where you are Steven. I don't know if I'll ever meet you . Based on what little I know about you, it's hard to imagine how you could have gotten out alive. People who are heroes every day, in all those small and unnoticed ways in which true heroism resides tend to act in character in times of cataclysm and disaster.
>
> If there's some way I can communicate that to you, that's all I need, all I wanted to tell you. I'm not terribly religious. Religion, for me, has always meant fly fishing. But I'd like to believe that if I write this and place it on this wall, with a flower, a candle and a model car, that someone will tell someone and that eventually it'll get back to you. You are my role model, Steven Sr . . . And in that way, I'll get to see you every day.
>
> Love
> Jeff

After September 11, the bereaved spoke to one another in a language that cut across gradations of belief. Whether their religion was Catholicism or fly fishing, whether they considered flowers and candles, as many Catholics believe, a way to speed arrival of a persons soul in heaven, particularly if they have not received Last Rites, or whether they placed the objects in a spirit of commemoration or simply to mark a spot, mourners communicated with one another in a shared language of symbols. Borrowing from sixties flower children, roadside shrines, urban memorial walls, and the customs of many religions, New Yorkers created a unique response to their own unique tragedy. As Ilana Harlow writes, "At shrines, red, white and blue candles flickered alongside Christian votive candles, Jewish memorial 'Yahrzeit' candles and offertory candles petitioning a range of intercessors

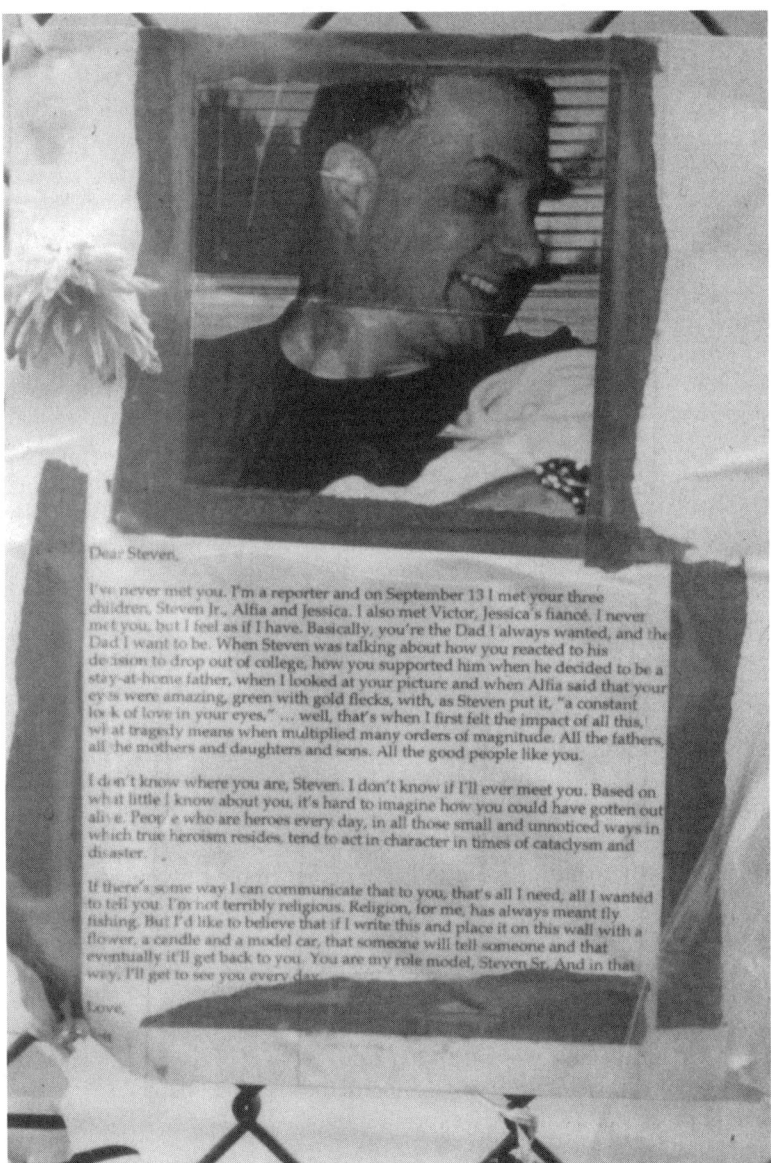

Figure 5.4 "Dear Steven, I Never Met You."
Photo Credit: Martha Cooper/City Lore.

from St. Anthony to the Virgin of Guadalupe to the 'Siete Potencias de Africa' of the Afro-Cuban religion of Santeria. The candles dripped into and onto each other, as our differences seemed to melt away" (2001).

Beyond borrowing modes of mourning, mourners drew upon essential human responses and religious impulses that suggested forms of expression regardless of involvement in traditional religion. Drawing on the work of Gerardus van der Leeuw on the phenomenology of religion Chidester and Linenthal suggest that ideas about sacred place are formed around a "recursive series of metaphoric equivalences (1995: 7)." The sacred site is to the city as the heart is to the human body. In the poetry that followed September 11, the Towers were to the City as the heart to the body. New Yorkers had not confronted anything like this tragedy—many had to learn, and learn quickly, how to express their grief—even if they did not know anyone who was killed. They drew both on religious customs, their own and others, and on a series of metaphoric equivalences to make the loss equivalent to losses in their own personal and family lives.

The 9/11 poems employed the metaphor of family and anthropomorphized the Towers. One poster read "Missing, two beautiful twins, Age 27." In "To the Towers Themselves," they were depicted as two swaggering MBAs. Poetry was utilized rhetorically to suggest that in grief, "we are one." (*"As we retell with pride of the sacrifice of heroes / We became one people."*) Images and words were used as symbols and metaphorical equivalences to mitigate New Yorker's two greatest losses—those who died, creating a symbolic portals between the living and the dead—and the Towers themselves, employing anthropomorphizing metaphors of family and kinship. The poems found along the streetscape used language rhetorically to mend ruptures between the living and the dead by addressing the dead directly, and speaking as the dead to the living; and to personalize the loss of the physical towers by humanizing them so that everyone in the city could be said to have suffered a personal loss—the loss of those physical structures that were not appreciated half so much in their lifetimes.

The literary poets whose work appeared in newspapers across the United States, and also published lines in our collaboration poem (published on www.peoplespoetry.org), sought to move outside these well-worn ideas. Instead of lines spoken directly to the dead, the lines of the poets invited to contribute to Tower Two were far more self-conscious. Many describe the painful process of trying to give form to feeling.

> I hold these syllables like hands on a clock feeling the sound of time
>   through its fingers.
> With one sullen syllable, I peel back a segment of sky,
> Afraid of syllables used to attach wings to breaths,

The words irreversible, unmistakable, come to me. Invincible leaves.
Words on page, mete out this woe; words on page undo sorrow.[15]

Many of the poets sought striking and original metaphors:

Eliot Weinberger: "The emptiness at the center has made the city sacred" ("Crisis," Tower Two, line 40, www.peoplespoetry.org).

Galway Kinnell: "That is our own black milk crossing the sky" (line 41, published solely on www.peoplespoetry.org).

The poet and undertaker Thomas Lynch: "A maze of grace? How great the art? We shall overcome?" (line 70, published solely on www.peoplespoetry.org).

Danny Shot: "Future Day of Remembrance: They tried to destroy us. They didn't. Let's eat" (Line 88 published solely on www.peoplespoetry.org).

The poets searched for metaphors—both accessible and obscure. This is the last line of the Tower Two poem by poet Adrienne Rich, " 'Love should be put into action,' screamed the dirty hermit of another poem" (line 110, www.peoplespoetry.com).

The poetry of the streets had a different kind of work to do. It addressed the ruptures in time-tested ways that sought to make the horrific bearable. The dead are still with us. The Towers can be recreated in our hearts. We are all one family in the wake of tragedy. Kill the bastards who did it. The folk poetry of 9/11 engaged the City in a rhetoric that affirmed and reaffirmed these simple points. As in much folk poetry, giving these sentiments a personal reality through repetition seemed more important than expressing original ideas in an original way.

Yet, both the literary poets and those who inscribed their feelings on the streetscape relayed the sentiment on a sign seen posted at the U.C. Berkeley Extension Art Annex in San Francisco in the days after 9/11: "the only cure for life is art."

Notes

The essay grows out of City Lore's research and documentation in the days, weeks, and months that followed September 11, as well as the exhibition Missing: Streetscape of a City in Mourning that ran from the New York Historical Society. For research, interpretation, and poetic turn of phrase, I am deeply indebted to my two cocurators and partners in the project, Marci Reaven and Martha Cooper, to field researcher Elena Martínez and to cocurator of the Peoples Poetry Gathering, poet and poetry activist, Bob Holman.

The title quote was found by Steve Zeitlin on September 25, on a handwritten scrap of paper pinned up near the entrance to the subway at Union Square.

1. "Crisis," Tower One, lines 8–23. The poets in the order of their lines: anonymous, Jan McLaughlin, Bob Holman, Rob, Jan McLaughlin, Penni Moore, Susan Katz, anonymous, Roberta Singer, Rennie/Georgia A. Popoff, Kristin M. Petersen, Heather Bourbeau, Klonskyj, Stargazer Lilly, Gary Mex Glazner. The full text of "Crisis," both the Tower One and Tower Two poems are posted on the web site <www.peoplespoetry.org>
2. "Crisis," Tower Two, lines 10–21. The poets in the order of the lines: Maureen Owen, Naomi Shihab Nye, Joe Dobkin, Jill Bialosky, Kimiko Hahn, David Lehman, Kathleen Masterson, Ed Friedman, Bob Hershon, Ntozake Shange, Hettie Jones, and Alex Jacobs. The full text of "Crisis," both the Tower One and Tower Two poems are posted on the web site <www.peoplespoetry.org>
3. From a photograph taken by C. Mills (CK).
4. Personal interview with Jordan Schuster, November 2001.
5. The September 11 quote was taken down from a sheet of butcher-block paper set down by Jordan Schuster on the day of the tragedy. Others are taken from photos of posted messages by Martha Cooper.
6. From a photograph by Martha Cooper, September 13, 2001.
7. From a photograph by Martha Cooper, September 14, 2001.
8. From a photograph by Martha Cooper, September 17, 2001.
9. I would like to thank exhibit co-curator and my colleague at City Lore, Marci Reaven, for this insight.
10. Drawn from City Lore photographer Martha Cooper's observations and images.
11. See Edward T. Linenthal, *The Unfinished Bombing: Oklahoma City in American Memory* (Oxford: Oxford University Press, 2003).
12. This poem, ubiquitous after 9/11 are the lyrics from a song by Mary Frye, composed in 1932.
13. See Mircea Eliade's *The Sacred and the Profane: The Nature of Religion* (New York: Harvest Books, 1968); and *The Myth of the Eternal Return* (Princeton: Princeton University Press, 1971).
14. Taken down by Steve Zeitlin at Grand Central Station's memorial wall in New York, September 15, 2001.
15. "Crisis," Tower Two, lines 92–96. The poets in order of their lines: Quraysh Ali Lansana, Patricia Smith, Saba Kidane, Mary Ann Caws, and Maggie Balistreri. The full text of "Crisis," both the Tower One and Tower Two poems are posted on the web site, www.peoplespoetry.org

References Cited

Barry, Dan. 2001. *The New York Times*, September 25, 2001.
Chidester, David. and Edward T. Linenthal. 1995. *American Sacred Space*. Bloomington: Indiana University Press.
Foucault, Michel. 1984. Space, Knowledge, and Power. In Paul Rabinow (ed.), *The Foucault Reader*. New York: Pantheon.

Harlow, Ilana. and Steve Zeitin. 2001. How Much of the City's Grief Should We Preserve, *Newsday*, Sunday, October 14, 2001.

Leeuw, Gerardus van der. 1986. *Religion in Essence and Manifestation*. Trans. J.E. Turner, foreword by Ninian Smart. Princeton: Princeton University Press. Orig. German ed. 1933.

Smith, Dinitia. 2001. *NY Times*, "In Shelley or Auden, In the Sonnet or Free Verse, the Eerily Intimate Power of Poetry to Console." October 1, 2001. Sec. E. p.1, col. 3.

Urry, John. 1985. Social Relations, Space and Time. In *Social Relations and Spatial Structures*, ed. Derek Gregory and John Urry, New York: St. Martin's Press. Quoted in David Chidester and Edward T. Linenthal (eds.), *American Sacred Space*. Bloomington: Indiana University Press, 1995, 2001. 18.

Waldman, Amy. 2001. *The New York Times*, September 29, 2001.

Chapter 6

Louisiana Roadside Memorials: Negotiating an Emerging Tradition

Maida Owens

Roadside memorials have attracted attention from both researchers and the general public in recent years. These memorials evoke strong feelings since they remind us of our own mortality. While this tradition has a long history in many parts of the world, it has proliferated in recent years, spreading into non-Catholic and even non-Christian communities. In the last twenty years, these roadside memorials[1] commemorating sites of violent death have spread into the American South, including Louisiana. But, not all traffic fatalities result in a memorial that is then maintained over time. I investigate factors determining whether a memorial is built or not and whether it remains or not, particularly focusing on the negotiation process.

Providing an alternate location for graveside traditions and as a part of a complex of memorial practices, roadside memorials are most likely to be erected following the accidental death of a relative, especially a teen or a young adult, if the death site is close to the family home. Further, the memorial is likely to remain if the site does not involve private property, the family constructs the memorial in such a way that it does not create a safety hazard, and they regularly maintain it. Most roadside memorials[2] in Louisiana have remarkably consistent physical traits. They are usually white wooden or metal Latin crosses with arms of unequal length, and those in Louisiana do not include any larger constructions such as those found in Mexico, Greece, and other areas with a much longer tradition. Technically, all of these memorials are placed illegally if they are in the highway right of way.

This memorialization transforms the death site into a positive place by transferring grave traditions and incorporating new ones. The proliferation has coincided with several other phenomena in American culture. In recent years spirituality and supernatural beliefs have become more acceptable and now more likely to be perceived as positive. For example, some narratives that previously featured ghosts now have angels. There has also been a depersonalization of some graveyards with adornments restricted or prohibited in many cases to ease maintenance of the space. This may not provide as effective a means for the family to grieve a death and as a result they may turn their attention to the death site.[3] At the same time, there is increased public awareness of drunk driving affecting driving safety. These phenomena may reinforce and assist in the proliferation of roadside memorials. Media coverage has supported the spread of this tradition. All of these have resulted in the cross, a common christian symbol, becoming a more generalized symbol for death in this tradition of erecting a memorial at the place of death.

Since roadside memorials marking traffic fatalities are relatively new in Louisiana—even in Catholic south Louisiana—we have an opportunity to examine a tradition while it is emerging, in particular the process whereby a new tradition is negotiated. Roadside memorials began appearing in south Louisiana in the mid 1980s and proliferated in the 1990s. But they were not unheard of in south Louisiana prior to the 1980s. I remember a small French metal cross in Baton Rouge in the 1960s, but this was unusual. In contrast, they were not seen at all in north Louisiana until the mid-1980s.

While I found no studies linking the tradition historically to the American South, the region seems to have been at least predisposed to embrace this spreading tradition. And, while the tradition was not significant enough to be noted in 1989 in the *Encyclopedia of Southern Culture,* Charles Reagan Wilson does state there that, "Southerners in general have been more outgoing in their grief than Northerners. . . . While the American way of death downplayed such emotional grief, sentimental Southerners typically nurtured it" (Wilson 1989:479). Comments by a grief specialist in Alabama illustrate both the predisposition of the South and the assumption—not confined to the South—that the tradition is limited geographically: "Like pulling to the side of the road during a funeral procession, erecting a cross or memorial at the site where a loved one has died is largely a Southern phenomenon" (Archibald 1996).

Examining the circumstances surrounding the erection and maintenance of the Louisiana memorials reveals new information. In these new locales, no established protocol exists for the family to follow, requiring negotiation to determine how they will proceed. For each memorial, families and friends must negotiate among themselves, with bureaucrats, and, at times, other community members for a memorial to remain in place. There are two phases of negotiation. The first is among family and friends and is part of the private grieving process. For each death, they must negotiate to determine whether they will place a memorial at the death site and what it will consist of. The second phase is between the private world of the grieving and the public: The deceased's family and friends must negotiate with the landowner or the agency responsible for the highway right of way. At this point, they are, in effect, negotiating their private grief with public issues.

Over a four-year period between November 1994 and October 1998, I gathered information about 149 memorial sites in Louisiana, 139 of which included crosses. During this time, I personally experienced a family member's death in a traffic accident. The data below concentrates on the 93 sites with crosses for which I have photographs. I traveled most of the major highways and interstates and many back roads—some areas more intensively than others[4]—but all quadrants of the state were covered. In addition to photographing the crosses and the surrounding area, I maintained written records describing the placement and adornment of the crosses. I noted death circumstances obtained from the memorial or secondary sources. I also maintained a map indicating all roads traveled during the research period. A literature search revealed existing documentation of memorials elsewhere. The Internet listserv, Folklore-L, and personal communication provided anecdotes on geographical distribution, and finally, a newspaper search revealed patterns in the media.

During this time, I investigated 93 memorial sites, which involved parking, getting out of the car, experiencing each space, noting details, and photographing the site. Through this repetitive process and having a personal experience with unexpected death, I came to realize that several factors determine whether a memorial will be erected and then maintained. First, I concluded that a cross is likely to be placed and maintained only if the death occurred in the general vicinity of the family's home and especially if the grieving family or friends pass the site periodically. This became clear when my own brother-in-law died at the age of 45 in 1995 in an auto accident in front of a house in a neighboring town, about 15 miles away from his wife and mother. Our family did not even consider placing a memorial, and I did not bring up the subject. Our decision, or really lack of a decision, was consistent with what I noticed investigating the roadside crosses. All the stories collected about crosses that continue to be maintained reveal that the family lives in relatively close proximity. Maintaining a cross provides a means for the grieving family to cope with their loss, especially if they have to pass the death site on a regular basis.

Figure 6.1   Memorial to Jerry and Todd maintained by the family members.
Photo Credit: Maida Owens.

Referring to the cross her family erected following the death of her father (Jerry) and 12-year-old brother (Todd), (see figure 6.1) Christy Hollingsworth of Alexandria, Louisiana, stated in a newspaper article, "By my driving by it four or fives times a day, it's a way of saying, 'I love you, and I miss you.' " The article continues that,

> Seven years after that tragic accident, a small memorial to both of them continues to stand at the intersection. . . . Susan Hollingsworth Wilson, who lost her husband and her son in the accident, said the first wooden cross was placed at the intersection about two months after the accident. The agriculture department at Tioga Junior High School where Todd attended school donated the cross. After that cross wore down with weather and age, a metal cross was given by a family friend and placed there. The memorial eases the grieving process which continues still today. . . . The entire family takes part in the upkeep of the memorial site. Wilson, who drives by the site every day, said she places fresh flowers two or three times a year. . . . H.C. Hollingsworth, the father and grandfather of Jerry and Todd, respectively said he continues to cut the grass and make sure the area is kept clean. (Conrad 1997: 12C)

This scenario is typical of other Louisiana sites for which I know the circumstances of the death.

The second determining factor is the age of the deceased. Families are most likely to place a memorial for a teenager or a young adult. Of the 28 crosses for which I know the deceased's age, 24 were between the ages of 15 and 25—deaths considered before their time. Putting up a cross may be a way of coping with the extreme grief of the death of one's child or classmate. Perhaps the parent is more likely than other relations or friends to maintain a cross or memorial,[5] but classmates have participated in constructing, erecting, or decorating several crosses.[6]

With the third factor, the negotiation moves from among the family and friends to the public sphere. The third factor is the site of the death which determines whether a memorial once placed will remain. A memorial is only likely to remain if it is placed in a space perceived to be what I refer to as "neutral"—spaces not involving inhabited private property. This is supported by narratives about the crosses in addition to the fact that of the 139 sites, only 17 appear directly in front of homes, churches, or businesses. All others appear in neutral spaces: public highway medians, urban intersections, in front of vacant land, planted fields, pastures, forested land, parks, and riverbanks. In Louisiana, memorials can be found in rural, suburban, and urban settings. Nonetheless, the deciding factor is still whether the space is neutral. Numerically, they, most often, appear along roads in rural settings, but 17 of the 139 cross sites identified are in urban and suburban locales, and 18 are in small towns. The relatively smaller amount of road frontage considered neutral in highly populated areas decreases the likelihood of urban memorials, and the proliferation of roads in urban areas make their appearance more difficult to identify.[7]

A Baton Rouge resident told me about an accident near her suburban home in which a 20-year-old man driving at a high rate of speed was killed when he lost control of his car. The next night, his friends came at 1 a.m., the same time that the accident occurred, where they:

> erected a cross, attached notes to it, and sat where he had died through the night. They kept a vigil [and burned candles]. The man who owned the property let them do so for two nights. Then the subsequent nights he asked them to leave, removed the candles, [and] left the cross with notes. They kept returning for a week. It was moving, but disturbing to those of us who lived on the street. (Roberts 1997)

The homeowner said that while he sympathized with the boys, he felt that leaving the cross might affect his property value. Also he did not want the reminder that this death had occurred in front of his property (Roberts 1996).[8]

While property values are certainly an issue, I suspect that discomfort with death could be an even more significant one. Traffic fatalities are the great equalizer. It can happen to anyone anytime for no reason. Getting in a car is the most dangerous thing that most people do. Having a memorial on your property that you are not otherwise connected to serves as a daily reminder that: "There but for the grace of God, go I."

Many memorials have a short life span such as this. They often consist of only floral arrangements and mementos. Some crosses reported to me were removed before I was able to get there to photograph them. For example, one was reported in St. Martinville that was supposed to be attached to a business in front of the church square. By the time I got there two months later, it had been removed. While I do not know the reason that it was removed, its removal is consistent with the pattern, since this was not a neutral space.[9]

Other crosses have a longer life span that seems to play itself out. I observed the entire life span of several crosses maintained for several years. In 1989, I noted a cross erected following a highly publicized death on Perkins Road in Baton Rouge, another road I regularly drove. Diane Upp Simino (Upp 1992) was killed when two teenage boys threw a concrete cinder block at her windshield, killing her instantly. The family erected a simple, white wooden cross along the road in front of a vacant field. The cross remained for approximately three to five years. In the first few years, the grass was kept cut, but then it became overgrown and evidently not maintained. The cross remained until the property was sold and a commercial building constructed.

The fourth factor is whether the memorial's construction techniques and placement meet highway safety standards so that the memorial does not cause another death. If construction does not meet the approval of those in charge of the highway right of way, or, occasionally, does not meet the approval of community members, the authorities will remove the memorial. The crosses found in Louisiana vary according to materials, condition, adornment, and number of crosses at each site, but with few exceptions, generally do not create a safety hazard. Construction methods and materials range from simple, wood slats nailed together to more finely crafted wood and metal structures.[10] The most common form is a relatively simple wooden cross approximately 24 to 36 inches tall, but many variations exist. The wooden crosses can be made from driftwood, wood slats, two-by-fours, and treated lumber. They employ varied construction methods, including nailed, screwed, and fitted joints with chamfered edges. The metal crosses include welded rebar, angle iron, iron pipe, or more finely constructed pieces including three small French-style crosses.[11] Some of the more substantial iron crosses use breakaway construction so that the bolts connecting the cross to a base will break first, minimizing damage to a vehicle.

Forty-nine crosses are medium size, approximately 24 to 36 inches tall, but 33 are small, about 12 to 18 inches tall, and 11 are large ranging up to eight feet in height. Most are driven directly into the ground, but four have metal rods or concrete bases to ensure longevity. Four are attached to trees, fence posts, or telephone poles. The large crosses that do potentially pose road hazards are either placed several feet from the road, are on back roads, or are situated in such a way that hitting the cross is secondary to other hazards. The best example of this is a cross of welded pipe with a concrete base located beside a bridge in a river basin. If one doesn't hit this cross, one will end up in the river.

One cross was constructed from the tree that the boy hit. A relative said that his cousin and the boy's girlfriend,

> both high school seniors, were traveling from Bayou Gauche to Paradis; they were attempting to pass a car when an oncoming car appeared. So, he took to the shoulder of the road, striking a tree and killing both occupants. The impact split the tree in half. Within two days of [the] accident [and] (before the funeral took place), his friends used the splintered tree to form a rough cross at the accident's site. . . . The group of friends planned to replace this impromptu memorial with a more formally constructed one later on, [but I don't] know if the replacement marker ever went up, or if the original marker survives. (Swann 1997)

A fifth factor is whether the family and friends maintain the memorial. At least 71 sites are in especially good condition and evidently maintained, while only seven are in poor condition with overgrown grass, rusted metal, and faded adornments. The relatively fewer number in poor condition is most likely due to road maintenance crews removing any that do not appear to be maintained.

One sign that the site is maintained is the changes made in the decorations. Many crosses are more elaborate with decorations changed on the death anniversary and holidays. I photographed ten crosses twice, indicating that the site is maintained and decorations periodically changed.

Twelve have holiday decorations for Christmas, birthday, Valentines, Mardi Gras, Thanksgiving, or Fourth of July. One cross photographed February 11, 1996 along with its Christmas decorations included toys still in their packaging and a shot glass with a cigarette lighter in it. Another outside of Lafayette has Christmas tree lights and a battery pack, although I never observed it lit. One photographed outside Jennings on the Cajun prairie included a Cajun Mardi Gras mask[12] (see figure 6.2).

Other adornments are typical of many grave traditions[13]: flowers which may be plastic, silk, fresh, or wooden; vases; ribbons; bows; wreaths; Catholic

Figure 6.2   A cross outside Jennings on the Cajun prairie with a Cajun Mardi Gras mask.

Photo Credit: Maida Owens.

items such as rosaries, scapulas, crucifixes, and images of Jesus; statues of angels; photographs of the deceased; and other presumably personal mementos. These include Mardi Gras beads, necklaces, vanity license plate, model car, shot glass, cigarette lighter, and rebel flag. Floral sprays on tripod stands are frequently placed beside the cross or occasionally on a nearby tree.

Decorations not typical of graves include red and blue reflectors, reflective letters, and white reflective paint. Three crosses have auto parts arranged at the base: windshield wiper, dealership nameplate, and parts of the front grill.[14] Another two are enclosed by a small fence or sandbox. While two Louisiana sites did have food (satsumas and another had fast food containers), more research is needed to determine the meaning of the food offerings.

Only seven sites have more than one cross ranging from two to five crosses per site. At these sites, some crosses are identical while others differ in style and size. One site had a cross with one vertical and three horizontal bars to mark three deaths. Ten of the 20 crosses indicated the death date, which reveals that the crosses range in age from one to nine years, with eight aged three or four years old. Of the 18 memorials I documented in the 1990s in the greater Baton Rouge area, only four remained by 2004. Three involved more substantial construction that would not deteriorate with time and the fourth erected in 1999 did not appear to be maintained.

Forty-two crosses have writing of some sort, either handwritten using a marker, carved into the wood, stamped into iron, or a brass or bronze plaque. The writing most often indicates the deceased's name, but may also include the deceased's birth and death date or messages from family and friends. One iron cross painted white is covered with handwritten names, presumably of classmates. One wreath had a note card with a letter to the deceased enclosed.[15]

One of the more elaborate crosses that has been carefully maintained for several years is placed in the median of I-49 near Opelousas (see figure 6.3). The large white cross is carefully constructed of angle iron with holes placed so that silk flowers can be wired in place to cover the entire cross except for the crucifix in the center. At the base are carefully arranged parts of the car's grill from the accident. A 40-foot section of median is regularly mowed. The construction of the base is significant in that it will break away if hit, which dramatically decreases its hazard to drivers.

Another elaborate cross, also carefully maintained, is located on Drucilla Drive in Baton Rouge in front of a city park. Parents erected this cross following the death of their four teenagers killed while in the back of a pickup truck drag racing (Kay 1999), and they continue to maintain it in 2002. This medium-sized wooden cross is also white, but of wood construction and has a bronze plaque stating the names and birth dates of the

Figure 6.3   An elaborate cross in the median of I-49 near Opelousas.
Photo Credit: Maida Owens.

four teenagers and "Killed at this Location by a Negligent Drinking Driver May 22, 1988." Plastic flowers placed at the base are surrounded by white metal rods driven into the ground marking the space.

When I first started asking folklorists and the general public in Louisiana about the roadside crosses, they generally stated that they thought this tradition originated in Mexico as a Latino Roman Catholic tradition that was spreading to Louisiana. Existing documentation by folklorists, cultural geographers, and anthropologists (Barrera 1991; Griffith 1992; Henzel 1991; Rajković 1988; West 1988; and Zimmerman 1997)[16] confirm that death site memorials have a longstanding history that is not limited to either Catholics or Latinos and has spread into predominately non-Catholic areas. Until recently, many folklorists and the general public were not aware of the extent of the tradition and assumed that the tradition was limited geographically or even unique to a region (Barrera 1991: 279; Henzel 1991: 95; Rajković 1988: 172).

As I documented roadside memorials in Louisiana, other researchers and friends became aware of my research. They started reporting to me about memorials in other states and mailing me newspaper articles, photographs, and even existing research. When Folklore-L, a listserv with a worldwide subscription base, discussed the subject, I realized that this medium offered an unprecedented opportunity to get a relatively quick sense of the extent of the phenomenon. So I queried the list and received, over a period of two years, almost 100 responses from 29 American states, five Canadian provinces,[17] four Latin American countries,[18] and seven other countries[19] confirming that this is an extensive phenomenon. It is often a Latino Catholic tradition,[20] but has historically existed in non-Latino Catholic areas as well. For example, roadside memorials are described as "standard in South Dakota, especially on Indian reservations" although today they do not occur "with the same frequency" (Kemnitzer 1995). Likewise, crosses were "very common on the Blackfeet Indian Reservation in northwest Montana in the 1960s, much more so than in the British/African American areas adjoining" (Stanley 1995). Death site memorials are part of a larger cult of the dead among the Tohono O'odham in southern Arizona (Kozak and Lopez 1991).

Roadside memorials also appear in predominately Eastern or Greek Orthodox areas such as Yugoslavia where crosses are only one means of marking roadside fatality sites. Rajković notes that,

> it is difficult to judge to what extent the cross is chosen to mark roadside memorial signs to traffic victims as a Christian symbol, and to what extent it is simply a symbol of death, perhaps without any conscious, underlying religious feeling. Those cases where the cross is crudely fashioned, unsightly and hardly visible under the wreath lead one to consider that the cross's sole purpose is to hold up the wreath. (Rajković 1988: 168)

Other sources confirm that the tradition has now spread into predominately Protestant areas such as east Texas (Carson 1997). And finally, roadside memorials, without crosses, are constructed by non-Christians including a Jewish woman in Tucson, Arizona (Griffith 1992: 187) and neo-pagans in Mendocino, California (Tannen 1995).[21] In Japan, accidental deaths are marked, but without crosses (Ohta 2004).

The Louisiana data corroborates this pattern. Of the 139 sites, 74 appear in predominately French/Cajun/Creole (Catholic) areas, 48 in British/African American (Protestant) areas, and 17 in urban areas with diverse populations. The narratives I collected about the Louisiana crosses indicate that Cajun, Italian, British American, African American, and Latino families have constructed them.[22] In addition, crosses appear in areas of the state with very low Catholic populations. Even though 62 crosses appear in predominately Catholic areas, only five have artifacts that are specifically Catholic such as crucifix, scapula, or rosary. Some crosses known to be maintained by Catholic families did not have specifically Catholic items when documented.

Local and national media, through television and newspapers, have influenced the spread of this tradition with both high profile, out-of-state cases and local sites considered newsworthy.[23] Between January 2, 1994, and March 15, 2004, the *Baton Rouge Advocate*, ran 27 articles about roadside memorials, 19 with photographs. Seven appeared on prominent pages: 1A, 2A, or 1B. Twelve were Associated Press stories, while eleven were news articles or photographs written locally about local crosses, one was a local feature article, three were a syndicated columnist addressing the phenomenon, and one was an arrest report concerning the removal of a cross related to a high profile murder case.

One article and photograph reported the Baton Rouge community's response to the murder of a 20-year-old prostitute found in the undeveloped fringe of a shopping mall. During the month it took to identify the woman, there was an outpouring of concern. After the victim was finally identified, the newspaper reported that "four . . . friends gathered Sunday around the spot where Arnold's nude body was found last month to leave flowers and a cross and to hold hands and pray." A photograph of the friends and the cross appeared on the front page of the *Baton Rouge Advocate* (Baughman 1995). Friends and strangers continued to maintain the cross for a few months until mall management removed it.

Associated Press articles about out-of-state crosses that appeared in the *Baton Rouge Advocate* concerned an accident in Hermleigh, Texas, that killed ten people ("Deadly Day" 1995: 5B); a bus accident in Fox River Grove, Illinois (Webb 1995: 2A); and the incident at Waco, Texas (Landsberg 1995: 9A; Davidians' 1996: 19A). Other stories featured spontaneous memorials that did not highlight crosses, but did feature elaborate displays of flowers and gifts left by mourners: the Susan Smith murder case in Union, South Carolina (Holland 1995: 1A), TWA Flight 800 accident in

Montoursville, Pennsylvania ("Flowers and a . . . "1996: 15A), the death of Princess Diana, and the Oklahoma City bombing.

The phenomenon of roadside memorials even attracted the attention of columnist Judith Martin, known as "Miss Manners." On Sunday, September 1, 1996, with the headline, "New Customs help the Bereaved, but nosy questions still out of place," she endorsed "the new 'etiquette of catastrophe' where the site of the disaster . . . becomes a sort of chapel for the bereaved and sympathizing public, who offer prayers, condolences and memorial tributes. . . . In just a few years, these trappings of grief have become as standard as black plumes and arm bands once were." She considers "the changes to be in the best tradition of evolving etiquette by modernizing customs while retaining their spirit. Ribbons serve as well as crepe to symbolize that one is in mourning and the site of death may serve as well as the tombstone to make one feel near to the dead person." She goes on to say that she "is gratified that any attention is still paid to ceremony and symbolism in death" (Martin 1996). In 1997, she states that shrines "is now an established mourning tradition" (Martin 1997). By 2003, she needs to address how to remove memorials tactfully once they are not maintained (Martin 2003).

During the week of March 17, 1997, the national television news covered the fact that Bill Cosby put up a cross in memory of his son, Ennis. The Associated Press picked up this story and while the *Baton Rouge Advocate* did not run it, the *Ruston Leader* did. Cosby "had a small cross-shaped sign bearing the message, 'Thank you, friend' placed at the site of his son's slaying. . . . The message was derived from the manner in which Ennis Cosby would greet people" ("Bill Cosby" 1997: 2A). Only a few weeks previously, a television program dealing with America's most deadly highways focused on crosses on a highway in Connecticut.

The memorials have attracted widespread interest. After a few years, my research started to attract the attention of other types of researchers and artists. A playwright in New York requested a copy of my research as background for a play she was writing, and a performance theory graduate student at Louisiana State University asked for leads on crosses because she was focusing on performative aspects of shrines for her dissertation (Kennerly 2002). The crosses have captured the imagination of at least one Louisiana visual artist, Chris Hero, who had an exhibit, "Roadside Shrines: Sacred Spaces on Tragic Foundations" in New Orleans in 2000.

The research came full circle when I was interviewed by a journalist for a local newspaper feature story for the *Baton Rouge Advocate* Religion section about roadside crosses in Baton Rouge. This enabled me to hear about the impact such an article can have on the family (Kay 1999). In addition to quoting me and other professionals, the journalist tracked down people familiar with several memorials in town. The full-page article included four color photographs. In the weeks following the article, I learned about some of the fallout from it. An acquaintance related that one of the photographs featured the memorial cross for a friend of hers, a young man who had died in an auto accident only three months prior. The young man's mother had not been aware that her son's roommate had placed the cross at the death site until she learned of it in the newspaper. She became extremely upset and insisted that the cross come down immediately, which it did. This case illustrates how ownership and protocol of the tradition is still being negotiated (Powenski 1999). It is still being determined who is the appropriate person to place a memorial and whether someone else would need to ask permission to do so.

Since 2000, the *Baton Rouge Advocate* and other local media have shown less interest in this issue. Whereas 22 articles appeared between 1994 and 1999 including all but two of the Associated Press wire stories, only five appeared from 2000 to 2004. The emergence of the memorials during the 1990s was newsworthy, but not thereafter. Even though the news coverage faded, the memorials continue to be placed by families and friends.

I can personally testify that roadside memorials often mark hazardous road conditions, a fact I discovered while trying to photograph them. Road safety is often the focus of newspaper articles because the crosses provide a visual means of addressing the issues either for specific roads or safety in general.[24] As a result, several Baton Rouge newspaper articles illustrate the media's use of roadside crosses to address road safety concerns. For example, one particularly winding, narrow portion of LA 42 in Ascension Parish was the focus of both a Baton Rouge WBRZ–TV newscast and a newspaper article. Using the crosses as evidence to support their cause, local residents complained that the road should be straightened because several deaths had occurred. Five crosses occur on this stretch. One cross was photographed next to a "Drive Carefully Substandard Roadway" sign in the newspaper with the caption,

> A double warning beside LA 42 near Oak Grove in Ascension Parish informs motorists to be careful when driving. The road sign warns of substandard road conditions. The small white cross bearing a little bouquet of flowers, is a more stark reminder to travel with caution. Such roadside crosses are sprinkled across south Louisiana roads to mark where a traffic fatality occurred. ("Still Reminders" 1994: 3B)

Another incident followed a car–train wreck that killed two women and three children and prompted a debate about unguarded railroad crossing safety. The Baton Rouge newspaper ran a story entitled "Officials discuss

Pontchatoula train safety" with a large photograph of the five crosses beside a speeding train ("Officials discuss . . ." 1995: 3B). In Houma, a family of five was killed, and five crosses appeared in conjunction with the relative's campaign to get a caution light installed at the intersection, which was accomplished after a few years (Service 1995).

Another front-page article in the *Baton Rouge Advocate* (Frink 1999), also used a photo of two crosses to illustrate the immediate need for roadwork.

> Out on US 190, just west of the Erwinville truck scales and under a blinking caution light, two crosses rise from the ribbon of guardrail that separates the traffic streaming east and west. The crosses memorialize some of the people who've died in accidents at the South Winterville Road intersection. Finding out exactly who those crosses stand for would be dangerous and difficult. Dangerous because the median is only about two feet wide and offers no room to avoid speeding traffic. Difficult because in the last three years at least four people died at that spot.

The article continues with details about efforts to "widen and improve that deadly stretch of highway" and lawsuits concerning some of the deaths. These two crosses are particularly unusual because they remained in place during road construction through Summer 2002, but were removed once construction was completed.

Internet listserv members reported similar cases focusing on particularly noteworthy sites. For example, several mentioned sites with either many crosses at one site or many on a particular highway: the Carrollton bus crash in Kentucky, Route 101 between Portsmouth and Manchester, New Hampshire, or US 27 from Oxford to Cincinnati, Ohio, known as "killer highway," "Highway to Heaven," or "Highway of Death."

Such newspaper articles also reveal that while crosses are technically illegal on medians and rights of way, Louisiana local and state road maintenance crews frequently allow them to remain since the crosses assist in reminding drivers to drive carefully, illustrating that there is a difference between official policy and bureaucratic attitudes. Louisiana state and local governmental attitudes are publicly stated in another newspaper article appearing in the *New Orleans Times-Picayune* focusing on five St. Bernard Parish wreaths. With the headline, "Roads Sprout Wreaths, Highway deaths are remembered," the article noted that,

> such memorials are a growing phenomenon throughout the New Orleans area according to Bob Roth, district maintenance engineer for the state Department of Transportation and Development. "They seem to be more common than five years ago. . . . Technically, some of the roadside wreaths violate state rights of way, especially ones on the neutral ground [median] of

state highways. . . ." But . . . Roth and St. Bernard officials say they are reluctant to remove the wreaths, especially if they aren't a safety hazard and there aren't any complaints about them, because they are part of the grieving process of relatives and friends of the victims. "You hate to fool with them," Roth said. "It's helping people deal with their grief." Some are hazardous and must be removed, he said.

The article continues with statements from Bob Turner, director of the parish Department of Public Works, which

> "has been trying to handle it compassionately. We try to let them go as long as they aren't an eyesore or become a safety hazard." Maj. Richard Baumy of the St. Bernard Sheriff's Office said such memorials can remind passers-by to drive carefully. "It could deter some traffic violations," he said. "it's a reminder of what can happen." Baumy doesn't know of any safety hazards caused by wreaths along St. Bernard highways." (Cannizaro 1996: B1)

Similar sentiments from a district engineer appeared in the *Lafayette Sunday Advertiser* (Stanford 2001).

The Louisiana bureaucracy's compassionate approach was also noted in a *Wall Street Journal* article, which quotes the Louisiana State Police Captain Ronnie Jones as saying, "we're not going to go around kicking over memorials on the highway" (McCarthy 1997).

Wondering how officials in the State Department of Transportation and Development that have jurisdiction over maintaining clear highway medians and rights of way viewed the situation, I contacted John Collins with the Maintenance Division. He stated that in Louisiana, the State does not have the authority to issue permits for memorials on state highways and that technically, the memorials are illegal. He also took a purely practical approach and said that with nine state employees to handle all highway permits for the entire state, the staff does not consider memorials a significant enough problem to warrant their attention. Collins stated, "The memorials don't end up making a difference. They fade out over time anyway. We don't want to interfere with people grieving" (Collins 1997).

A highly publicized case involving an abducted toddler's murder (purportedly by his sitter) further illustrates the degree to which the tradition can be supported by a community, including the police. The *Baton Rouge Advocate* reported that the toddler's mother,

> was arrested early Saturday in connection with the removal of crosses erected in memory of the child . . . [The mother] . . . was booked into Livingston Parish Jail on one count each of theft and simple criminal damage to property. . . . She posted a $1,000 property bond. . . . [The mother] and

two men were seen removing the roadside crosses, which were recently erected by . . . the child's natural father. . . . "A car behind them saw them do it" and called officers from a cellular phone. (Matthew Populis 1995: 3B)

Note that, ironically, the police arrested someone for removing something that was illegally placed!

Newspaper articles and the Folklore-L Listserv discussion reveal that governmental policy varies from state to state. The Alabama Department of Transportation takes a stance similar to Louisiana, where spokesman Barry Fowler stated,

the memorials appear all over Alabama. . . . If they are too close to the road or pose a hazard to drivers, they must be removed. . . . Otherwise the department looks the other way. "We don't encourage it, but we try to be very conscious of what it means. Sometimes you just have to do things out of kindness toward your fellow man." (Archibald 1996: 1A, 2A)

This policy probably contributes to the fact that Alabama is another state where the crosses are reported to be abundant.

This attitude contrasts with those in other states where the memorials are viewed as problematic. This approach was the primary focus of the *Wall Street Journal* article mentioned above. Bureaucrats in some other states take a different approach. In an article appearing next to the story about the Hollingsworth cross in Alexandria, Louisiana, mentioned above, the governmental policy in Florida was featured in the Baton Rouge newspaper. After describing a dramatic nine-foot concrete cross on Interstate 75 north of Naples, Florida, the article in which Carol Matthews emphasizes that she wants her son remembered continues that,

As poignant and understandable as Matthews' sentiments are, that memorial and others like it have created a predicament for Florida officials who have decided to clamp down on the proliferation of roadside memorials on state highways. "We understand the intentions of people who put these up," said Dick Kane, spokesman for the Florida Department of Transportation. "But these shrines are starting to take on a life of their own. It's a safety issue." But DOT's plan to replace homemade memorials with a standardized marker has raised another controversy. Just days after state workers last month began to replace roadside shrines with a simple, two-foot white plastic marker, civil rights groups complained that it looked too much like a cross. "In fact it was a cross," said Arthur Teitelbaum, Southern area director of the Anti-Defamation League, "and it raised a constitutional concern of church–state separation." Eventually, DOT Secretary Ben Watts ordered highway workers to pull up the first dozen or so roadside markers and proposed a new design, a circular memorial featuring the words "Drive Safely" and a space for the

name of the deceased. . . . But a few family-sponsored memorials have become
elaborate traffic hazards. "We had one concrete cross that took three men to
remove, and our maintenance men aren't wimps. It would be a tragic irony if
someone died after hitting a nine-foot concrete cross." (Clary 1997: 12C)

In all honesty, the Louisiana bureaucrats would also have to remove such a
memorial, which could also end up being controversial.

Even though Louisiana has evaded large-scale controversy concerning
this issue, it has been an issue in at least one community (DOTD 2003). In
2003, state workers removed memorials to aid mowing. An Associated Press
story reported the conflict because families of the deceased complained.
This was the site of two accidents killing six people in three months.

Other states have taken on the responsibility to provide crosses at
accident sites, but later discontinued the practice for undetermined reasons.
James Griffith (1992: 103) confirms that the state of Arizona erected crosses
for a time during the 1950s, but discontinued the practice. Similar, although
more tentative reports about seeing plain crosses of uniform size and design
supposedly erected by state highway departments as a safety reminder in the
1960s are from New Mexico, Nevada, and Washington State.

In 1996, the controversy expanded to include separation between
church and state and class differences in a situation near Houston, Texas, in
Harris County involving confrontation between two communities. White
metal crosses commemorating accidental deaths were erected by county
officials upon request until a controversy arose. Precinct Commissioner
Steve Radack approved a cross following a death of a Sommerall man in
front of Copperfield village caused by a DWI Copperfield resident.

Some Copperfield residents had complained to AMI [the management
concern that oversees Copperfield and seven neighborhood villages] that the
cross was a depressing reminder of [the] death and that it might hurt their
property values. "Copperfield has no problem with these kinds of markers,
but not in residential areas," AMI administrator Kate Loefler said. Radack
was promptly bombarded with telephone calls and letters. "Did you give in
to the BIG MONEY of Copperfield and disgrace your constituents by
removing the cross marker?" a Pasadena man wrote to Radack.

Following a legal opinion that the county had the right to put up the
marker,

county workers reinstalled the cross. But about 10 hours later, they took it
back down. The county's attorney's office . . . had found a different element
to the issue. . . . "It is my understanding that residents of Copperfield contacted your office to have the sign removed because they thought it was

devaluing their community," a woman from the Sommerall subdivision wrote. "It just so happens that it was one of their residents who was charged with that DWI."

The article continued by editorializing, "Should a governmental entity be in the business of putting up any kind of religious symbols for any reason? The matter is now in the lap of the attorney general" (Makeig 1996: 25A, 29A).

Some crosses involve successful negotiation within a community. Suzanne Finkelstein-Winn of Dartmouth, Nova Scotia, reported a cross that became entangled with legal proceedings, providing a good example of a situation where the community negotiates until the cross is placed in a space perceived to be neutral before it can be maintained for an extended period of time.

> In July 1995, two sisters, Danielle and Renee Orichevsky, were sitting by the bus shelter with their boyfriends when a car went out of control and hit them. They died at the scene. Two crosses were erected almost immediately and for a whole year, they remained in the very spot where the girls died. Last summer around the time the trial was held, it was decided that the two crosses would be moved about 50 feet further away from the street to a crest of a hill. The property where the bus shelter was located was on the very edge of a church lawn. It was decided (with the parent's agreement) that a small park with benches and the two crosses would be designed with flowers and shrubs as a small contemplative park. (Finkelstein-Winn 1997)

Many areas report a tenacity of the tradition, despite governmental policy or public opinion. There also is a long history of attempts to suppress the tradition. Griffith cites a 1783 letter from Father Kieran McCarty in which he urges people to stop erecting crosses where Apaches have killed settlers because they only further encourage the Apaches (1992: 101). More recently, an observer in Germany reported that, "[One] stone cross was set in place in the spot where two farmers had killed each other. Later, someone tried to move the cross to another location, but it kept reappearing near the road, so today that is where it is" (McMahan 1995). More recently and more systematically than in Florida, roadside memorials continue to flourish in Yugoslavia, despite governmental mandates and aggressive publicity campaigns (Rajković 1988: 167).

By 2000, media coverage and public controversy forced some states to address the issue and create public policies and procedures to regulate roadside shrines. By 2000, Wisconsin, Virginia, Wyoming, Colorado, West Virginia, and Placer County (California) formally addressed the issue by instituting formal procedures to allow shrines for two to five years and have applications online. In 2004, Nevada was studying the issue with public meetings.

After 2000, diverse responses to the shrines were evident. While Maryland atheists argue for separation of church and state (Brown 2003), others consider them tacky (Tinotopia 2003). Some, including Christians, tell their family and friends that they don't want a memorial if they die in an accident (Snyder 2003). Reports of vandalism have increased (Powers 2003). Websites offer ready-made crosses to purchase (Roadsidemarkers. com 2002), virtual memorials (Roadside Memorials 2004), and virtual exhibits (Sampson 2004). Other websites ridicule the tradition (Let's 2004), suggest vandalism, or creating your own as a prank (Personalize 2004, Rotteneggs 2004), or argue that roadside crosses are an effective form of stealth ministry to promote Christianity (Baker 2003). Tinotopia (2003) argues about the underlying issue thus:

> the reality is that getting into a car is the most dangerous thing most people will ever do. More "premature" deaths in the United States (and, probably, in most industrialized countries) are caused by car accidents than by anything else. Roadside memorials can communicate this hazard to drivers better than any Slippery When Wet or speed limit sign ever does: they say, "Someone died here doing just what you're doing now."

Porkjerky.com (Let's 2004) argues the same point, though with a mocking tone. Why is this so prevalent and persistent from Japan to the United State? This coincides with escalating traffic fatalities and drunk driving. In Texas, Mothers Against Drunk Driving (MADD) provides crosses. Why do the memorials make people uncomfortable and cause controversy? Is it because the real issue is that we don't want to admit that the most dangerous thing that most of us do is get in a car? But do we value our freedom and mobility too much to address it? For example, why has no one focused on the fact that Princess Diana wasn't wearing a seatbelt? She was in the back seat and much less likely to die in an auto accident.[25]

In summary, the evidence overwhelmingly shows that roadside memorials provide an alternate location for graveside traditions and are most likely to be erected following the accidental death of a relative, especially a teen or a young adult, if the death site is close to the family home. Further, the memorial is likely to remain if the site does not involve private property, the family constructs the memorial so as not to create a safety hazard, and they regularly maintain it. At the same time, there is increased public awareness of drunk driving affecting driving safety. These phenomena reinforce and assist in the proliferation of roadside memorials into new communities without an established tradition. Each family must negotiate their own protocol in their efforts to give the death site a sense of place, to make sense of something that doesn't make sense—an untimely, violent death.

Notes

I am indebted to Rosan Jordan, Susan Roach, Barry Ancelet, Carl Lindahl, Carolyn Ware, Nalini Raghavan, and Jocelyn Donlon for their comments, especially for John Laudun's recommendation to focus on negotiation. I would like to thank those who provided information about memorials and newspaper articles; the Folklore-L listserv for providing feedback about distribution and leads on articles; Fabio Mugmaini for providing a copy of Zorica Rajković's article; and Costantinos Grivas for identifying Carsten Holbraad's book.

1. This study of roadside memorials does not include the following sites with crosses: (1) three, 20-foot blue and gold crosses strategically placed at vistas in many eastern states erected by The Rev. Bernard Coffindaffer, (2) the French Canadian crosses marking the establishment of a church or community documented by Paul Carpentier (1976), (3) crosses in Mexico and southwestern United States that mark traditional resting places on funeral routes called *descansos*, which do not indicate a death site (West 1988: 236; Barrera 1991: 279; and Anaya 1995), (4) some Greek memorials, which may also be erected by survivors of auto accidents (Holbraad 1998), or (5) spontaneous memorials resulting from violent deaths of public figures (Haney 2001).

2. In Louisiana, the sites generally mark traffic fatalities, but three mark murder sites, and one a death resulting from an airplane crash.

3. Everett (2000a) credits restrictive cemetery rules regarding decorations with "greater activity at a roadside cross" in Austin, Texas.

4. The areas covered include (1) the Cajun/Creole prairie north of I-10 (predominately Cajun/Creole Catholic), (2) northeast Louisiana between Monroe and Ferriday (predominately British/African American Protestant), (3) the greater Baton Rouge area (a diverse urban area), (4) parts of the Florida Parishes (predominately British/African American Protestant), and (5) LA 1 south of Baton Rouge (predominately Cajun/Creole Catholic).

5. In Austin, Texas, Everett (2000b: 149) found that the "parents, and especially the mothers of the deceased . . . often assume the more mundane tasks of clearing trash from the site, repainting or replacing a cross and clearing weathered floral displays."

6. In Kentucky, Zimmerman (1995: 39) also found that immediate family members made most memorials, but friends made some.

7. A similar perception that they tend to be located in rural settings was noted outside Louisiana. Most reports do concern rural locations, but urban sites are noted. Urban areas reporting crosses include "a multicultural part" of Atlanta, Georgia; Madison, Wisconsin; Columbus, Ohio; Huntsville, Alabama; Taos, New Mexico; San Francisco, California; Buffalo, New York; and New Orleans, Louisiana. Only one was reported in Columbus, Ohio, and "the first was seen" in Huntsville, Alabama in 1993 (Chavers 1995). In New York City, Joseph Sciorra documented memorial walls in Harlem and Manhattan (1991). Everett's (2000a) study of memorials in Austin, Texas, revealed a "distinctly urban" phenomenon.

8. Everett (2000b: 32) and Zimmerman (1995: 101) also report cases where the family unsuccessfully negotiated with private property owners. Everett tells of a medical center offering "to replace the cross with a horizontal granite marker. While the marker is more permanent than the wooden cross it replaced, its message to passers-by is less clear." Zimmerman reports of a "cross [that] was destroyed by the owner of the land. . . . The owner apparently did not feel that it was appropriate to have a death memorial in his front yard. . . . The current memorial was placed on the property owned by a nearby country store."

9. Folklore-L listserv members also reported that many memorials were only temporary. A resident in England reported that he had, "seen flowers placed by an accident site, but the memorials . . . lasted as long as the flowers" (Alexander 1997). Monger (1997) reports a longer history in England. In 1995, an Australian reported that wreaths had recently appeared in the past few months, but not crosses (O'Dea 1995).

10. In northern Mexico, some memorials are comparatively large stone monuments resembling grave markers. None like this were found in Louisiana. Also, wrought iron crosses with intricate designs are more abundant there (Henzel 1991: 100–101).

11. Memorials in Yugoslavia with significant influence of communism display a wider range of shapes and sizes, with memorial slabs or plaques being the most common (Rajković 1988: 169). Other symbols also appear in Yugoslavia including the five-pointed star painted red to symbolize Communism and a steering wheel or tire symbolizing death by traffic accident (Rajković 1988: 174–175).

12. Ritual visitation for renewal of decorations is also reported in Mexico, southwestern United States, and Yugoslavia.

13. Refer to Nakagwa (1987) for information on grave decorations throughout Louisiana.

14. Placement of automobile wreckage near the memorial is also reported in Yugoslavia (Rajković 1988), Austin, Texas (Everett 2000b: 85, 131) and Arizona (Griffith 1992: 104). In Yugoslavia, the steering wheel and tires are often incorporated into the design of more elaborate sites (Rajković 1988).

15. The amount of identifying information on a memorial varies within the south. In Kentucky, Zimmerman (1995: 116) reports memorials often have less information compared to Louisiana. Only one memorial had a full name on it, and it was "the one most hidden from public view. Other memorials are coded using nicknames or other language that has meaning only to those who can translate it into a meaningful form." Thus, they are private, not communal, memorials. The memorials in Austin, Texas, described by Everett (2000b) more closely resemble those in Louisiana and are more likely to have identifying information about the deceased, such as names and dates of birth and death.

16. Articles about the phenomenon in Brazil have also reportedly been written in Portuguese.

17. Listserv members reported memorial crosses in 29 states in the 1990s, but described crosses as abundant in only nine: Alabama, Arkansas, Louisiana, Tennessee, Kentucky, Texas, New Mexico, Arizona, and southern/central California. Other states with crosses reported, but not described as abundant

include Virginia, Mississippi, Georgia, Nevada, Utah, Idaho, Washington, Wyoming, Montana, South Dakota, Nebraska, Wisconsin, Indiana, Ohio, New York, New Hampshire, Connecticut, Massachusetts, and Hawaii. In Canada, most of the French areas report memorial crosses (Nova Scotia, Ottawa, Ontario, Quebec, St. John Valley).

18. In northeast Brazil, crosses are common and called *Santa Cruz de beira de estrada*. At least a few were spotted in Panama, Costa Rica, and the Yucatan state of Mexico. Other states of Mexico report a proliferation of crosses, including the northern states and Sinaola on the Pacific coast. A long history of the tradition and ex-voto use of crosses is reported in both Brazil and Mexico.

19. In Australia, wreaths have recently appeared in the past few years, but not crosses. In Europe, crosses were common in southwestern Germany and Ireland, but rare in eastern Germany. Conflicting reports come from England. Some report that they are rare, but Monger (1997) reports a longer history that includes crosses. The only non-Western area reporting crosses was a Christian area of Sumatra (Alexander 1997). Yugoslavian memorials are documented in Rajković (1988). Roadside crosses have also been reported as abundant in Greece (Zachariou 2002) and documented by Holbraad (1998) but many Greek roadside shrines commemorate the survival of an accident along with fulfilling of a dream, or inauspicious places. Shrines are reported from Turkey, but less abundant.

20. From Buffalo, New York, "spontaneous altars [have been] set up in areas where drive-by shootings have happened, especially in the Hispanic part of town (Piatkowski 1995). From California,

> A group of Hispanic men recently discovered and excavated the cockpit impact site of Joe Walker's F-104. They brought cockpit artifacts and human remains to the [US Air Force Flight Text Center] history office [at Edwards Air Force Base, California] along with large pieces of XB-70 collected elsewhere. They erected a memorial cross to Walker at the site. ("Pete" 1995)

21. Tannen (1995) reports,

> Here in Mendocino, [California], where the roads are curvy and the fog is thick, people frequently die in automobile accidents. Not all of them are Christians, however, so flower wreaths, photos of the person who died, bottles of beer (when it was an alcohol-related accident . . .) are often left. The first semester I taught here, one of my students died in a car crash while cutting class. We heard the ambulance siren, but didn't know who it was until later. Her women friends did a ceremony at the spot, invoking the four directions and the Goddess—your basic neo-pagan ritual—and left flowers and one of those plastic wallet cards of La Diosa Del Mar on the tree she had crashed into.

22. Everett (2000a) found that,

> Austin area memorials may be read as a manifestation not only of grief and affection for a loved one suddenly departed, but also as highly representative

of the region's cultural syncretism, ...Contemporary memorials in Austin are erected by people of varying religious affiliations. Indeed, most of my principal informants were Protestants of various denominations who did not identify roadside memorialisation as a practice "belonging" to any specific group.

23. Rajković reports that media coverage about memorials in Yugoslavia also contributed to the spread of this custom since the 1960s (1988: 177).

24. Kozak and Lopez (1991: 7) report that the proliferation of death memorials commemorating violent deaths among the Todono O'odham correlates to the high annual death rate from traffic fatalities which is "four times the rate for Anglos in Arizona and double the overall Arizona Indian rate." It also correlates to high alcohol and drug abuse and economic hardship. Monger (1997) and Smith (1999) also credit memorials in England and New South Wales, Australia, respectively, as warning travelers of dangerous road conditions. Smith further reports that while officials at first discouraged the memorials, they came to tolerate them "when they became seen as possible curbs on speed. Current . . . policy is to show respect for the bereaved, but if the memorial is dangerous or an obstruction, then it will be removed. In practice memorials are only removed when they have fallen into neglect."

25. See Kennerly (2002: 245) for more details about the media's involvement with spontaneous shrines, online developments concerning shrines, and opposition to roadside shrines.

References Cited

Alexander, Guy. 1997. Email. January 31.

Anaya, Rudolfo, Juan Estevan Arellano, and Denise Chávez. 1995. *Descansos: An Interrupted Journey*. Photographs by Juan Estevan Arellano. Albuquerque: El Norte Publications/University of New Mexico Center for Regional Studies.

Archibald, John. 1996. Roadside memorials: Families mark spots where loved ones died in accidents.*Birmingham News*, Monday, December 2: 1A, 2A.

Baker, Don. 2003. Roadside memorials promote Christianity. From <www.christianitymem.org/roadside-memorials.shtml> Printed March 24, 2004.

Barrera, Alberto. 1991. "Mexican-American Roadside Crosses in Starr County." In *Hecho en Tejas: Texas–Mexican Folk Arts and Crafts*, ed. Joe S. Graham, 278–292. Denton: University of North Texas Press.

Baughman, Christopher. 1995. Four friends mourn victim, recall dreams. *Baton Rouge Advocate*, Monday, September 25: 1A.

Bill Cosby. 1997. *Ruston Leader*, Monday, March 19: 2A.

Brown, Steve. 2003. Maryland Atheists Want State to Remove Roadside Memorials. From website March 24, 2004, posted on October 27, 2003, FreeRepublic.com from CNSNews.com.

Cannizaro, Steve. 1996. Roads sprout wreaths: Highway deaths are remembered (St. Bernard). *Times Picayune*, January 18: B1.

Carpentier, Paul. 1976. La Survivance des croix de chemin: mythe ou realitie. *Culture & Tradition* 1: 43–53.

Carson, Gary. 1997. Email. March 3.

Chavers, P. J. 1995. Email. October 9.

Clary, Mike. 1997. Officials concerned about safety issues (Florida). *Baton Rouge Advocate*, Thursday, February 6: 12C.

Collins, John. 1997. Personal Communication. April 1.

Conrad, Jeff. 1997. Crosses symbolize tragic loss (Alexandria, La.). *Baton Rouge Advocate*, Thursday, February 6: 12C.

Davidians' anniversary (Waco, Texas). 1996. *Baton Rouge Advocate*, Thursday, February 29: 19A.

Deadly day (Hermleigh, Texas). 1995. *Baton Rouge Advocate*, Monday, July 3: 5B.

DOTD: Memorials distract drivers. 2003. *Baton Rouge Advocate*, May 14: 10A.

Everett, Holly. 2000a. Roadside Crosses and Memorial Complexes in Texas. *Folklore* 111: 91–118.

———. 2000b. Crossroads: Roadside Cross Assemblages in Contemporary Memorial Culture. M. A. thesis. Memorial University.

Finkelstein-Winn, Suzanne. 1997. Email. January 29.

Flowers and a newspaper clipping . . . (TWA Flight 800). 1996. *Baton Rouge Advocate*, July 21: 15A.

Frink, Chris. 1999. U.S. 190 revamp planned. *Baton Rouge Advocate*, July 11: 1A.

Griffith, James. 1992. *Beliefs and Holy Places: A Spiritual Geography of the Pimeria Alta*. Tucson: University of Arizona Press.

Haney, C. Allen, Christina Leimer, and Jiliann Lowery. 2001. Spontaneous Memorials: Violent Death and Emerging Mourning Ritual. *Tombstone Traveler's Guide*. <http://home.flash.net/~leimer/spont2.html> (cited March 21, 2002). *Omega: The Journal of Death and Dying*, 35(2): Fall 1997.

Henzel, Cynthia. 1991. *Cruces* in the Roadside Landscape of Northeastern Mexico. *Journal of Cultural Geography* 11(2): 93–106.

Holbraad, Carsten. 1998. *Ellinika Ikonostasia (Small Greek Shrines)* Athens, Greece: Trohalia.

Holland, Jesse J. 1995. Jury weighs verdict today (Susan Smith trial). *Baton Rouge Advocate*, July 24, 1995: 1A.

Kay, Julie. 1999. Seeking a sense of peace: Families, friends place markers to honor victims. *Baton Rouge Advocate*, Saturday, February 27, C1–2.

Kemnitzer, Luis. 1995. Email. May 31.

Kennerly, Rebecca M. 2002. Getting Messy: In the Field and at the Crossroads with Roadside Shrines. *Text and Performance Quarterly* 22(4): 229–260.

Kozak, David and Camillus Lopez. 1991. The Tohono O'odham Complex: Memorializing the Location of Violent Deaths. *New York Folklore* 17: 1–20.

Landsberg, Mitchell. 1995. Davidian siege site attracts tourists, pilgrims, revolutionaries (Waco, Texas). *Baton Rouge Advocate*, April 30, 9A.

Let's Mock the Dead: They Would Have Wanted It That Way. 2004. <www.porkjerky.com/rip.htm> Printed March 24.

Makeig, John. 1996. State's next to take up Copperfield cross controversy. *Houston Chronicle*, Thursday, October 10, 25A, 29A.

Martin, Judith (Miss Manners). 1996. New customs help the bereaved, but nosy questions still out of place. *Baton Rouge Advocate*, Sunday, September 1, 3H.

———. 1997. Sidewalk shrines express human need for communal form of behavior. *Baton Rouge Advocate*, October 19, 3H.

———. 2003. Getting street memorial dismantled calls for tact. *Baton Rouge Advocate*, August 6, 2C.

Matthew Populis' mother arrested (Livingston, La.). *Baton Rouge Advocate*, Sunday, September 10, 3B.

McCarthy, Michael J. 1997. Roadside Memorials Bring Some States A New Kind of Grief: Markers for Accident Victims Create Traffic Hazards, But Families Stand Tough. *Wall Street Journal*, Monday, March 10.

McMahan, Faye. 1995. Email. May 30.

Monger, George. 1997. Modern Wayside Shrines. *Folklore* 108: 113–114.

Nakagawa, Tadashi. 1987. The Cemetery as a Cultural Manifestation: Louisiana Necrogeography. Ph.D. dissertation, Louisiana State University, Baton Rouge.

O'Dea, Julian. 1995. Email. October 7.

Officials discuss Pontchatoula train safety. 1995. *Baton Rouge Advocate*, December 23: 3B.

Ohta, Kazuko. 2004. Personal Communication. January 3.

Personalize. 2004. Personalize Your Own Roadside Memorial: You Would've Wanted It That Way. <www.porkjerky.com/crosmaker.htm> Printed on March 24.

Pete. 1995. Email. December 18.

Piatkowski, Nancy. 1995. Email. May 30.

Powenski, Kathleen. 1999. Personal Communication. March 1.

Powers, Lenita. 2003. Vandals target roadside memorials. *Reno Gazette-Journal*, October 6. From a printout March 24.

Rajković, Zorica. 1988. Roadside Memorial Signs for Traffic Accident Victims. *Narodna Umjetnost: Annual Institute of Folklore Research*, Special Issue 2: 167–180.

Roadsidemarkers.com. 2002. RoadsideMarkers.com: A Tribute to the many lives lost on our nations highways. <www.roadsidemarkers.com/detail.html> Printed on August 8.

Roadside Memorials. 2004. <www.funeralguy.com/roadside.html> Printed on March 24.

Roberts, Robin. 1996. Personal Communication. November 10.

———. 1997. E-mail. March 31.

Rotteneggs. 2004. Roadside Memorial Prank. <www.rotteneggs.com/se/2684392.html> Posted 12/07/03. Printed on March 24.

Sampson, Bill. 2004. Roadside Memorials: A Photographic Documentary. <www.roadsidememoria.org/> Printed on March 24.

Sciorra, Joseph. 1991. "In Memoriam: New York City's Memorial Walls." In *Folklife Annual 90*, ed. James Hardin. Washington, DC: Library of Congress, American Folklife Center.

Service, Donna. 1995. Personal Communication.

Smith, Robert James. 1999. Roadside Memorials—Some Australian Examples. *Folklore* 110: 103–105.

Snyder, Tommie Lou. 2003. Personal Communication. December 25.

Stanford, Judy. 2001. Roadside Remembrances: Crosses are reminders of those who die on the highway. *Lafayette Sunday Advertizer*, December 2: 1D.

Stanley, David. 1995. Email. June 14.

Still reminders. (Oak Grove, LA). 1994. *Baton Rouge Advocate*, January 9: 3B.

Swann, Fenwick A. III. 1997. Email. March 27.

Tannen, Holly. 1995. Email. June 3.

Tinotopia: Roadside Memorials, June 3, 2003. <www.tinotopia.com/log/archive/000329.html> From a printout on March 24, 2004.

Upp, Dr. James R. 1992. Getting On With Life. *Guidepost*. March.

Webb, James. 1995. Signal being checked when train hit bus (Fox River Grove, Illinois). *Baton Rouge Advocate*, Friday, October 27: 2A.

West, John O. 1988. *Mexican-American Folklore: Legends, Songs, Festival, Proverbs, Crafts, Tales of Saints, of Revolutionaries, and More*. Little Rock: August House.

Wilson, Charles Reagan. 1989. "Funerals." In *Encyclopedia of Southern Culture*, ed. Charles Reagan Wilson and William Ferris, 479. Chapel Hill, NC: University of North Carolina.

Zachariou, Stelios. 2002. Personal Communication.

Zimmerman, Thomas. 1995. Roadside Memorials in Five South Central Kentucky Counties. M.A. thesis. Western Kentucky University.

———. 1997. Sites of Public Death: Roadside Memorials in South Central Kentucky. Paper presented at the 1997 American Folklore Society, Austin, Texas.

Chapter 7

"Like a Trace": The Spontaneous Shrine as a Cultural Expression of Grief

Hege Westgaard

In Norway, as in many other places in the world, we have become used to seeing flowers and lit candles on places where people have lost their lives in accidents or where other tragic deaths have occurred. Sometimes small notes, letters, or even objects which can be related to what has happened, are placed among the candles. Especially when children die, we can observe toys, teddy bears, and other plush animals among the flowers and candles. The spontaneous shrines are simple but moving demonstrations that express compassion and participation in connection with tragic deaths. The acts are strongly symbolic and the candles and flowers clearly convey that this is a place where someone has been killed in an accident.[1]

Spontaneous shrines that have gained much attention in Scandinavia are those dedicated to the Swedish Prime Minister Olof Palme (Källstad 1987 and Scharfe 1989) and to the Norwegian King Olav (Aagedal 1994b and Bringager 1992). These shrines were special because they were characterized by the position these two persons held in the consciousness of the entire population. My work has focused on spontaneous shrines made in the memory of "ordinary" people. The shrines become the centre of attention both to the public as well as in the media, not so much because of the people they concern, but because they commemorate dramatic situations, such as murder or fatal traffic accidents involving young people.

In this article, I wish to discuss what spontaneous shrines can tell us about how people of today regard and encounter death and sorrow in general, as well as how they deal with sudden and unexpected death. What does creating a spontaneous shrine mean to the participant, and which references of meaning are attached to it? Which concepts related to grief and death are reflected in the shrine? Is it possible, through the phenomenon of spontaneous shrines, to see a change in our way of expressing grief today?

A Ritual Perspective

Regarding the spontaneous shrines as rituals has been the pivotal point in my understanding of the phenomenon. To call acts "ritual" is to exoticise them, put them in a new light, and make it possible for them to be analyzed (Klein 1995: 12, see also Ehn and Löfgren [1982] 1994). The concept of ritual is many-faceted and can signify everything from empty repetitive acts to deeply transforming experiences.

By employing the term "ritual" to label the act of constructing a spontaneous shrine, it is possible to grasp the assessing and interpretive aspect of the act (see Klein 1995. See also Skjelbred 1994 for a discussion of rites of passage). Using the ritual concept, we may place the acts, the attitudes, and the ideas of the participants into settings that enable us to interpret what they say and what they do in the light of their desire to express something that goes beyond the mere situation itself.

Within the area of religious studies, ethnology, and folkloristics, acts that were religious in content or pertained to religion were for a long period of time labeled as rituals. In view of this light, rituals are acts that are not only formalized, repetitive, or in accordance with a particular pattern, but moreover phenomena that have sacred or magic overtones. In the 1970s, many anthropologists tried to broaden the ritual concept. Sally Falk Moore and Barbara Myerhoff introduced the concept "secular ritual" and thus ventured to steer the religious and magical connotations away from the ritual as a concept. They were motivated by the wish to grasp the ritual behavior that was not attached to belief systems, thereby making it an object of research on the same level as ritual acts that were connected with religion (1977; see also Klein 1995). (For a Nordic discussion see Frykman 1979; Honko 1976; Selberg 1989, 1991, 1993, 1995; and Skjelbred 1972, 1989, 1994.)

In my work, the central issue is the communicative aspect of the ritual. In connection with the spontaneous shrines it may be rewarding to regard rituals as acts that communicate something and that signify something more than the acts as such. A ritual may be regarded as a symbolic, expressive aspect of behavior that communicates something about social relations, often in a relatively dramatic or formal manner (Wuthnow 1987: 99 and 109, 184–185).

A Constructivist Perspective on Death

The interpretation of spontaneous shrines is ultimately grounded in a constructivist perspective on death. This means that death is regarded as a socially, culturally, and historically constructed phenomenon. From this point of view, both death and the reactions to and attitudes toward it are thought to be changing and variable in the context of time and culture.

The French historian Philippe Ariès has studied the history of death in the Western world from the middle ages to the present day (1977). In his analysis he has made use of a varied source material. He has utilized literature, folk tradition, art, testaments, and tombstones in his study of the changing attitudes toward death. Ariès' fundamental hypothesis is that the attitudes toward death have changed in parallel with the changes in attitudes toward individuality. These changes imply the transition from previous times when the individual was only significant as a part of the community, to the times when the individual and individuality as such are meaningful in themselves, independent of the community. Ariès is of the opinion that through increasing individualization, the attitudes toward and the experience of death have changed from the acceptance of death as a part of one's destiny (the tamed, approachable death) up until the present day to the tabooing and suppression of death (the wild and forbidden death). Death in the premodern world was ritualized, prepared, and undramatic— it was a familiar death. Today, however, death is a concealed and hidden death which one meets unprepared and alone (Ariès 1977; see also Alver 1994a: 68ff and 1996: 18–19; Eriksen 1984; and Frandsen 1985: 13ff). Ariès' work on death represents a criticism of modernity that has conveyed a view on death as something frightening and dangerous (Ariès 1977; see also Frandsen 1985).

Ariès has been criticized for his analysis. The critics have, among other things, claimed that his source material has provided a too fragmentary basis upon which to draw the conclusions that he has drawn (see for example Hodne 1980). The historian Norbert Elias, has passed the most fundamental criticism on Ariès. He is of the opinion that Ariès is prejudiced in his theories on how people in previous times encountered death; furthermore, that his nostalgic attitude determines his choice of source material (1985). Ariès may well be criticized for his selection of sources and the way he employs them, but the Danish scholar of cultural studies Finn Frandsen regards Elias' criticism as harsh and not entirely just. In Frandsen's opinion Elias ignores Ariès' fundamental hypothesis about the parallel changes of people's attitudes toward death and the human's self-awareness or perception of individuality. He also means that Elias underestimates the critical aspects of Ariès' work (Frandsen 1985: 23–24).

Ariès' analyses on death have inspired a considerable number of researchers. In Norway, the folklorists Bjarne Hodne (1980) and Bente G. Alver (1994a, 1994b, and 1996) have discussed his work. Hodne is critical toward him because of his nostalgic approach and his source material, but nonetheless finds that Ariès' views provide a good starting point for comparing present day attitudes toward death with those of previous times. Alver regards Ariès' hypothesis as a valuable contribution to the research on death. The moot point is what exactly this changed attitude toward death involves (1996).

The criticism of Ariès is in my opinion just; his hypothesis is nevertheless inspiring in relation to death research. Even though the main objections to Ariès' work have been grounded in methodical and source critical criteria, the debatable point is: what is the nature of the change that has taken place in people's attitude toward death from the middle ages up until today? The Swedish ethnologist Lynn Åkesson is, together with Bente G. Alver, critical to the unbalanced view on death as something tabooed and suppressed (1997). Åkesson argues that a changing attitude toward death not only means disintegration but also innovation. She claims there is a new closeness to death in present day society, a death which rather than being a public affair, is a personal and intimate matter (see also Alver 1994a and b, 1996 and Ladenheim 1993). The spontaneous shrines offer a good starting point for this discussion.

Like a Trace

My research on spontaneous shrines is primarily based on a field study. Additional sources are a questionnaire and material collected from the mass media. The field study was conducted in connection with an accident that happened in a small village in Norway. I interviewed a group of people who had contributed to the making of a spontaneous shrine in memory of a friend, and thus I came into contact with some of the people mourning the loss of a young boy I have called Torstein. Among the people I talked to were Ane and Lisa. They were close friends of Torstein's and knew him well.

Torstein was killed when he collided with the school bus while riding his moped on his way to school. On the bus were school children, classmates, and friends of his. The accident happened right in front of the local primary school. Torstein was immediately taken to hospital but died of his injuries a few hours later. At school, they arranged informal gatherings where the pupils could talk to each other and the teachers. The parson and Red Cross personnel were also present. On the same evening, village youth began visiting the scene of the accident, lighting candles and torches and leaving flowers there. The idea came to many of them simultaneously and there was no clear initiative from any one. The youths had seen such events taking place through the media and found them beautiful and peaceful. At the scene of the accident all of Torstein's classmates came together with many other local youngsters. Looking toward the place where Torstein was killed, they stood in a semicircle around the lit torches and candles and embraced each other before leaving the place. The youth kept on adorning the scene of the accident with flowers and candles the following evenings. Some of them stopped after the funeral while others went there for weeks after.

The spontaneous shrine was not the only ritual related to Torstein's death in which the youth participated. The day after the fatal accident, the school organized a memorial gathering, which ended with pupils, teachers, and the local parson walking together to the scene of the accident. Torstein's funeral was also beautiful and grand and friends and classmates actively participated. They read their own texts in the funeral service and each of them placed a rose on Torstein's coffin. The spontaneous shrine with its fresh flowers and burning candles, however, was more than anything the youth's own ceremony. There they were in charge, they decided the content and chose the ritual elements that would provide the atmosphere they wanted.

I asked Ane and Lisa why they wanted to visit the place of Torstein's accident and adorn it with flowers and candles after his death. They answered that the candles and the flowers were meant to signify that something had happened there, and to make evident that someone cared for Torstein and those who mourned him.

> Because you want it to show. We went to the place of the accident every evening—you wouldn't show it if you'd been there and just stood there. But when you place flowers and candles there—it becomes sort of like a trace.

The candles and flowers were there to show Torstein, Torstein's parents, and people who passed the shrine that they loved the person who had died and that they love each other. The spontaneous shrine stays behind like a trace after they have left the place and evidences the love of Torstein and the compassion for those who mourn him.

Lisa and Ane contributed to the spontaneous shrine and to the other markings related to the boy's death to show that they cared. Torstein's parents and everybody else should see that they were Torstein's friends, that they were fond of him, and that they would never forget him.

Ane and Lisa went to the place of the accident every night up until the funeral. Ane says that she appreciated going there to leave flowers, light a candle, and just stand there contemplating what had happened. With fresh roses and lit candles, they wanted to create something beautiful in spite of the painful events that had taken place there. Together with the flowers and the candles they also left a card on which they had glued a picture of the hand of an adult holding the hand of a child, and on which they had also written the lyrics of a song they had sung a lot together and which they liked. The song had a content they found appropriate for both sadness and joy.

To Ane and Lisa the aspect of communication is the central point of the ritual. The ritual allows them to express themselves, to express what they feel toward Torstein, his parents, and toward the accident itself. The ritual thus becomes an arena for reflection and an opportunity to express ideas and values (see Bauman and Briggs 1990 and Klein 1995: 20–21).

The British anthropologist Allison James argues that like the talk of adults, the talk of children and youth is an activity in itself through which social knowledge is reproduced and created (1995). My young informants also evidence that speaking as such can be an act of self-reflection when they talk about Torstein and the events surrounding and following his death.

Torstein's accident and the spontaneous shrine attracted the attention of the media, and Ane and Lisa have kept the newspapers that wrote about the accident. When we leaf through the papers together, they emphasize that the photographer from the local newspaper, which covered the funeral and the spontaneous shrine, behaved in a way that they much appreciated. He stayed at a distance but nonetheless took photos that depicted what had happened. The photos captured something that was meaningful to look at and hold on to. The girls say that it is nice to have these newspapers to leaf through and thus have a few tangible evidences of that which had happened. In these newspapers they can read about Torstein and about themselves and what they did for him. The text and the photos are concrete evidence of the events they participated in and contributed to.

Death in itself provides a context for thorough self-reflection where cultural values are clearly expressed. When Ane and Lisa tell us about Torstein's death and what happened thereafter, they also tell us about themselves. The narrative about Torstein also relates to their self-awareness. His death has made an impact on their self-image and their feeling of identity. They regard themselves as persons who were made stronger from grieving, who learnt to appreciate other people, and who care about others. Much of what they did in connection with Torstein's death was to communicate to other people that they show consideration and that they care. To Ane and Lisa, talking about Torstein's death is to negotiate a self-awareness related to an event that made a great impression on them, changed them, and did something to them as human beings. It is important to talk about Torstein's death. It represents an active, conscious self-reflection, and a negotiation of identity. With Torstein's accident as a setting, they discuss what a good friend is, the nature of close friendship, and how one may deal with the loss of a friend. Through dealing with grief the youth develop ideals about friendship, intimacy, and relations.

Torstein's death is an evil and incomprehensible death. Ane and Lisa both experienced the loss of a grandfather and a great-grandfather when they were little, but find these experiences irrelevant when faced with the loss of a friend their own age. They can accept that old people die, whereas they are unable to accept the death of young people. It is only natural that old people die, they say, but it is not natural that young people die. The death of young people is an unfair death. This reflects the notion that a good and valuable life equals a long life. That young people die cannot be right, because they are then bereaved of the chance to experience and achieve all the things that old people have when they die. The death of old people may have some kind of existential meaning, while a young death lacks this dimension and therefore becomes an evil and incomprehensible death.

Torstein's accident is mysterious. Ane and Lisa do not know what happened when Torstein crashed with the school bus, and they have reconciled themselves to the fact that they never will. They are not seeking to cast blame for what happened; neither Torstein nor the driver of the bus could be blamed for the accident. To Ane and Lisa, young death is unfair and incomprehensible in itself, and therefore Torstein becomes a victim. It is not unusual that people who are killed in such accidents are described as victims (Köstlin 1992). Torstein is a victim of circumstances. It is not the work of destiny or God, but mere coincidence. The coincidences may also strike back on oneself. Faced with accidental death one is also confronted with one's fear of one's own death.

Ane and Lisa visited the scene of the accident every night up until the funeral. Since Torstein had no grave yet, the spontaneous shrine provided a place where they felt close to him, where they could still feel his presence. It was the last place where Torstein had still been alive. As soon as he is buried, his friends will follow his body and visit the grave. Ane's and Lisa's stories about Torstein's presence reflect notions about the body's ability to sense, feel, and hear after death, and that some of the personality and the soul remains with the dead body (Åkesson 1997: 94–95). The dead body is not only evidence of the person's existence but also of the relationship one once had with this person. The notion of the dead body as a vessel for a person's identity goes beyond the deathbed and the funeral. As time goes by it is the mortal remains that symbolize the person one once was close to (Åkesson 1997: 146–147). When Torstein gets his grave, this will be the place where his presence is felt the strongest. Where his body is, some of him still remains present.

That Ane and Lisa feels Torstein's presence, that they communicate with him, and that they stress the importance of a place to visit after his death, signals a strong connection between body and soul. The dualism of body and soul is not tangible in life where identity and personality, the soul and the self is clearly connected to the body. This connection remains after death, and it makes it easier to communicate with the soul or the self if one knows where the body rests (Åkesson 1997: 150). Now that Torstein's body rests in his grave, this is the place where Ane and Lisa feel most close to him.

Åkesson points out that several metaphors relating to the body may coexist. The body as a worn-out machine is a common simile. At the same time many people believe in a spiritual existence of some kind. The notion of the body as a vessel or container leaves room for this possibility. Through death, the soul is liberated and it leaves the vessel. The soul of the individual is then reunited with this spiritual "something" together with all the other spirits that exist on the same side of death's borders. At the same time as the spirited body is committed to flames, earth, or water, the spirit itself also exists in another place (1997: 150).

A week went by between Torstein's death and his funeral. The funeral marked the end of the week they had dedicated to the commemoration of his death. The funeral confirms the death. Arnold van Gennep introduced the concept "rites of passage" to describe a three-staged transition from one status to another. The three stages of the transition are separation, transition, and inclusion (van Gennep 1960: 10ff). Death may be regarded as such a status transition. You move from the status of a living being, to the status of a dead being and are included among the dead. In the transition phase or the liminal phase, you have no status. Van Gennep compared this phase with the crossing of borders, going from one territory to another with a no-man's-land in between where one "wavers between two worlds" (van Gennep 1960: 15ff, see also Skjelbred 1994: 32). The anthropologist Victor Turner describes this phase as a period "betwixt and between," an intermediate stage, which is neither this nor that. The liminal phase is a period which is ambivalent, paradoxical, and where there is a confusion of the common categories (Turner 1967 and [1969] 1995: 95).

The three stages of the transition rituals, separation, transition, and inclusion, are, according to van Gennep relevant not only in relation to the dead person but also to the mourners. Van Gennep regarded grief as a period of transition, a liminal phase for the bereaved, in which the mourners and the dead person constituted a special group. The transition phase ended with the separation of the mourners from the deceased, where the mourners reentered the world of the living to be included anew, whereas the deceased crossed the metaphysical borders to be included in the world of the dead (van Gennep 1960: 146–147. See also Åkesson 1997: 122). The burial ritual is soothing in that it commits the dead to the world of the dead and thereby confirms the deceased's status, while at the same time it confirms the bereaved's status as belonging to this life. The living and the dead are separated and through the ritual, harmony and cosmos are restored once again.

To Ane and Lisa, the week they visited the spontaneous shrine constituted a liminal period. In the course of this week, Torstein was nowhere they could physically reach him. His status was unclear and their status in relation to him was also diffuse; at the funeral, however, when they saw his coffin disappear into the ground, his status as dead was confirmed—and they are left behind as his closest friends. The grave becomes a place where cosmos is reinstored, while the scene of the accident was a place where chaos ruled. Through the ceremonies they tried to reestablish a state of cosmos. When the coffin is lowered into the ground, chaos is banished; the ritual gives peace. Sorrow is then left to the individual alone. The community of mourning is over and each and every one is left to handle their own grief.

The Spontaneous Shrine
As Grief Therapy

Surrounding the youths and the spontaneous shrine were also adults who had different roles in connection with the ritualization. The village parson participated in the school gathering at the scene of the accident, and he also conducted Torstein's funeral. In connection with death, the professional role of the parson is to meet the spiritual needs of the bereaved and to help create existential meaning (Åkesson 1997: 106 and 109). Clergymen define these spiritual needs from their own religious platform and that of their church. The parson is a representative of God and a representative of the church and its common values and views. In general, clergymen are regarded as one of many experts on death and grief in our society and are among many professionals who have particular competence when it comes to meeting dying and grieving people. As professionals, they must have a sense of what people want and they must know what is in demand; how grieving people want to meet death and grief (Åkesson 1997: 20, 104–105).

The clergyman is an authority on death and grief in a society where the notion of therapy is prominent. Therapy as a notion embraces ideas of treatment and self-development, and what is regarded as healthy and sick. In a therapeutical setting the clergyman is a specialist on the self with a particular competence on mental intimacy connected with the longing for something larger than ourselves—a search for God.

In the tension between individual and society, the German educationalist and philosopher Thomas Ziehe ([1989] 1993), finds subjectification to be one of many cultural tendencies in present day society. Subjectification is a therapeutic-moral longing, which embraces thoughts of closeness and mental intimacy and attention on the self. Through the concept of subjectification, phenomena such as conversation groups, counseling literature, and various psychosocial courses have become quite common. It is the therapists—the specialists—who offer assistance in the quest for one's inner being.

As a therapist, the clergyman has notions about what sorrow should be and what a positive sorrow should constitute. Grief may create a feeling of community and solidarity among the grieving. Through grief, relations are established among people; these relations are established through the common loss they have suffered, and grief may thus become a positive experience. The clergyman regards it as his task as a therapist to offer mourners the possibility of experience and the opportunity to do something through participating in ceremonies and rituals. The therapist arranges events in which the mourners may do something meaningful, experience something, and express their feelings and frustrations.

There seems to be a widespread attitude that people in a crisis need the help of a therapist because they are unable to know what is best for themselves. One of the things one needs help for, is to express one's emotions. In the Western world, the dominant view on the body is that of a vessel, a container as it were. Emotions that remain unacknowledged and repressed may in time become dangerous. Subconscious feelings are harmful if they surface uncontrollably (Åkesson 1997: 120; Hockey 1993). The therapist, therefore, creates safe settings in which people can let go of their inhibitions and express their emotions freely in company with other people (compare Featherstone's theories about controlled decontrol, p. 22). From a therapeutic point of view the spontaneous shrine as a ritual may be regarded as something that contributes to the "correct" experience of grief. The positive experience of grief gives mourners the opportunity to deal with the loss in community with other people through evocative and beautiful ceremonies related to the death; for this the help of the therapist is necessary.

Rituals are important in the church's encounter with death and the dead individual. The church represents the standardized and the general, and places restrictions on what can be done within the church framework and under its auspices. Torstein's parson understands the spontaneous shrine as a ritual. He greatly emphasizes the importance of rituals in connection with deaths and points to the special need of a particularly clear demonstration when a tragic and unexpected death has occurred.

The clergyman works with death-related rituals in practice and to him the rituals mainly function as acts that may be of help and support to grieving people in that they offer them something tangible to participate in. The spontaneous shrine at the scene of the accident was, in the parson's opinion, an expression of the youth's need to do something for Torstein and to express their gratitude toward him. This is the practical side of the ritual; to do something beautiful and meaningful, which at the same time can offer peacefulness. However, the parson does not believe that the ceremonies at the spontaneous shrine express a need on the part of the youth for rituals and ceremonies outside those offered by the church. Through the parson's participation in the school gathering at the scene of the accident, the church was also present. The parson thus integrates the spontaneous shrine into the church's own ritualization of Torstein's death. At the scene of the accident he is the representative of the church, the representative of God, and the parson is of the opinion that the spontaneous shrine does not signal that there are ritual needs in the mourners that the church cannot meet.

An ecclesiastical funeral consists of rites that the clergyman alone may administer. In the burial ritual, the dead moves from the world of the living to the realm of the dead and is thus committed to God through the symbolic acts of the clergyman. More than any other ritual, the burial ritual gives the officiator a unique opportunity to fill the ritual with his own presence and his personal interpretation (Åkesson 1997: 117). The parson tells me that he became emotionally involved in Torstein's death. Through the burial ritual, the parson tries to paint a living picture of Torstein—a picture his next of kin will recognize. The funeral shall reflect and call attention to the personality of the deceased and direct our thoughts to the living person who once was, and not to the dead body that rests in the coffin. As a rite of passage, the objective of the burial ritual is to separate the deceased from the living and include him or her in the world of the dead. Through the privatization, intimization, and individualization of death, this has become less evident. The deceased is retained in the world of the living because the emphasis is placed on the dead as being a part of life and not death. This makes the burial rituals all the more important since they mark the transition from living to dead and since they clarify the separation between the living and the dead. At the funeral the clergyman, in capacity of ritual administrator, must outline the borders between the living and the dead (Åkesson 1997: 122–123).

The parson represents something greater than himself and must deal with existential questions, contexts, and meanings. His role as a representative of God is to give hope and strive to convey existential meaning. However, he does not want to impart that there is a higher meaning to everything that happens. He admits that he was unable to see the meaning of Torstein's death. But even if Torstein's death is meaningless, meaningful things happened in the days after the accident. An atmosphere of solidarity and community arose. Amidst all the pain something good was created.

The headmaster at Torstein's school was another adult who played a part in the rituals following the young boy's death. The headmaster dissociated himself from the school's ceremony at the scene of the accident, and emphasized that he participated in the event because as headmaster, he is responsible for every activity that takes place within the school context. He did not sympathize with the emotional behavior the ceremony at the accident scene invited. He stressed the ideal of self-restraint and regarded intense emotional outbursts to be potentially dangerous, even unhealthy. The headmaster represented a view that considers rituals as known, established patterns that may channel or subdue emotional outbursts. The pattern and the given premises contribute to the control. According to the headmaster, the introduction of new rituals represents a considerable risk.

In the discussion of the parson's role, we were given an example of the dominant Western view of the body as a vessel or container. From the therapeutical approach of the parson, we might regard the body as a container that may suffer a too high internal pressure if subconscious emotions are left unacknowledged and suppressed. Should these subconscious emotions explode uncontrollably they may be harmful. The headmaster, on the other hand, reveals a different view on the body. In his opinion, it is not the subconscious emotions that may cause harm. The dangerous thing, however, would be to let go of one's control and express these feelings. A connection between notions of control and notions of health is evident in the attitude of both the parson and the headmaster.

The headmaster regards the ceremonies at the scene of the accident as an expression of the differences between generations, where the youth bring new elements to the ritualization of death. He regards the ceremonies at the shrine as a way in which young people deal with grief, while they to him represent something unfamiliar and new. In what he refers to as tradition, he finds the controlled and the regulated, while the new and uncontrolled is represented by the spontaneous shrine and the ceremonies at the accident scene. The headmaster makes his judgements about what is good and less so in relation to tradition and the past. He appreciates the "traditional," the old, and views the new with scepticism.

The last of the adults to be discussed in this article, is Torstein's form master. As a teacher, he holds a subordinate position in relation to the parson and the headmaster. The headmaster is his professional senior while the parson holds a superior position by virtue of his expertise on grief and death. The teacher, however, is the one among the three who is most directly involved in the boy's death: he is close to the pupils and knew Torstein better than the two other adults. His closeness to the pupils thus stands apart, and he includes himself in the grief. He had no particular role in the gathering the school arranged at the scene of the accident. He silently stood there together with the others. The teacher saw the ceremony as something that belonged to both children and adults and he greatly appreciated it. They were all equals there, he felt, and he joined the youth in their grief. He regarded the spontaneous shrine as a positive demonstration of this community. Through the grief and loss of a classmate and friend, the teacher experiences a new and more intimate atmosphere in the class after the accident. Out of pain something good arises, and the teacher finds that in this new fellowship; Torstein's death is existentially meaningful in much the same way as the parson's notions of grief.

Therapy and Experience

The spontaneous shrine was, as mentioned, part of an extensive ritualization related to Torstein's death. The youngsters themselves were responsible for much of the ritualization, while other ceremonies resulted from the interest of committed adults. All the rituals related to Torstein's death, however, represent a striving for closeness, intimacy, individuality, and authenticity. They are the result of an effort on part of the contributors to express what they regard as Torstein's personality. The spontaneous shrine is the evidence of this search and through the shrine and the other ceremonies and rituals the youth create a space wherein these feelings are accommodated. The parson—the ritual administrator—sees to the ceremonies and rituals he is in charge of and helps to arrange these qualities.

The adults' experience of the ceremonies differs from that of the youth's and their intentions behind the ritualizations are also different. The differences in experience and attitude may be illustrated by what Ziehe calls the concept of intimacy and the concept of intensity. To Ziehe, these concepts represent two opposites as concerns one's mental attitude toward, and desire for, experience.

The basic idea behind the concept of intimacy is the commendability of opening up to other people, giving other people insight into one's inner life, showing authentic emotions, sharing emotional interests—and thus the idea reflects a need for mental intimization. For instance there is a wish to make public situations private. The concept of intimacy is an expression of a therapeutical motivation, a desire to reach the others, as it were ([1989] 1993: 74ff).

The concept of intensity does not strive for emotional intimization but for common experiences in given situations. This approach signals the desire not to meet the whole personality of the other individual, but rather his or her immediate personality. One does not desire authenticity at all costs, as Ziehe expresses it, but rather the partial richness of a given situation, not the whole person. The desire for these common experiences is governed by aesthetic motives rather than therapeutical motives (Ziehe [1989] 1993: 76–77).

While the parson has therapeutical intentions behind the experiences he contributes, the youth, perhaps Ane and Lisa in particular, have a different motive. They want to experience something strong, something beautiful, they want to express themselves and their emotions by observing their own participation. The parson regards grief therapy as the main drive behind the ritualization, while Ane and Lisa participate partly to see themselves as participants in a beautiful ritual.

The Power to Define and the Will to Create Time and Space

The spontaneous shrine was a result of the fact that many youngsters had the same idea in the course of the day of Torstein's death. At nightfall they gathered around the flowers and candles they had brought to the scene of the accident.

Nobody had arranged for this ritual to take place, neither was there a defined, common purpose behind it. It was simply beautiful and gave the youth an opportunity to mourn their friend together. The spontaneous shrine they created the night they learned that Torstein was dead, and which they continued to adorn night after night, was the *youth's* own ritual. They themselves defined its form, its content, and its duration.

The day after Torstein's death, the school arranged a memorial ceremony during which the participants went in procession to the scene of the accident, bringing flowers to leave there. This was the official arrangement of the school. The teachers, the school management, and the parson had discussed the form and content of the ceremony. The event was designed and directed by the adults, the school, and first and foremost the parson. They planned this event in the afternoon before they knew that the youth would visit the place by themselves. As a professional, the parson contributed to the clear, therapeutical motivation behind the ritualization: grief will disappear if it is handled right. To the therapist, the duration of grief is limited.

Even if the adults, the school, and the parson defined the ceremony, Ane and Lisa experienced it as their own. Within the given framework, they created a space they defined as their own, and thereby made the ceremony their own as well. To the young people, the period of mourning is extended. They bring grief into the space they have created and guard it from those who do not understand.

The Places of Death

Rituals do something to places. The use of public space as an arena of a ritual produces not only participants but also spectators. Rituals taking place in a public space are undoubtedly rendered visible. Through the ritual one wants the spectators to see oneself, one's group, or one's intentions (Klein 1995: 17). However, there might be different ideas about what should be openly expressed by the one and the same ritual. As previously mentioned, at the school's ceremony the day following Torstein's death, different participants try to define the ritual as theirs. Besides the wish to express their own grief, the adults, the entrepreneurs, want to express interest and compassion and to demonstrate that they are attentive to the grief of the youths and the grief of Torstein's family. The main point for the youth is that the grief for their friend is made visible. They want it to show that they care for him, for his family, and for each other, and they want it to be visible that something dreadful had happened at this particular place.

Through the ritualization the place is redefined and transformed from a neutral scene to the scene of an accident. Through the ceremonies and symbols, the youths change this scene from a place of pain and horror to a beautiful and peaceful spot. Through the ritualization they claim the place and make it their own (see Klein 1995: 23).

Related to Torstein's death, there are several "places of death": the scene of the accident, the grave, his desk at school, and his home. There are also several participants who try to define and give these places content and meaning. In addition to the ritualization, one may also say that the youth create a "space of intensity," which they bring with them to various places. This space may contain the personal, both regarding Torstein and themselves, the emotional, the beautiful, and the self-reflecting. They bring this space of intensity to the school ceremony at the accident place, they bring it into the classroom, to Torstein's desk upon which they have placed candles, flowers, and a photo of him, and they bring it to the grave, which in time becomes the only place that is connected closely with Torstein.

The youngsters do not bring their space of intensity into Torstein's home, however. The home and the boy's room belong to the private sphere and is therefore out of their reach. In addition, they may feel that the home is not directly relevant for them to visit, since the Torstein who is present there is not *their* Torstein but his parents'. The tension between public and private may also be evident at the scene of the accident. One may claim that the school's ceremony taking place there is considered by the adults to be a public ritual in a public place, while the youth experience it as a private ritual in a public place.

The Spontaneous Shrine as a Cultural Expression of Grief

The questionnaire[2] provides a broader framework within which to understand and interpret the material from the field study in relation to Torstein's spontaneous shrine. The questionnaire reveals how the spontaneous shrine is experienced as a cultural expression of grief. The respondents have become familiar with the phenomenon of spontaneous shrines mainly through the media, but some of them have also seen such shrines in their own community. A positive attitude toward spontaneous shrines represents the strongest tendency that can be read from the material. However, some of the answers are negative, there are also ambivalent answers, while some of the respondents have no opinions on the matter whatsoever.

The respondents who were negative toward the spontaneous shrine, were critical because in their opinion the shrine represents an unpleasant reminder of death. Some respondents also react to what they feel is worshipping or idolization of the dead. The ritual of the spontaneous shrine is also experienced by some to be exaggerated and evidences that some mourners seem unable to cope with grief. Some of the respondents also find the shrines objectionable because they are public.

To these respondents, grief is something that is not to be demonstrated in public. It belongs to the private sphere and does not concern others than those directly involved. One respondent is concerned that sad and solemn occasions like these may be used by some as an opportunity to express opinions on different matters. When the rituals are moved out into the public arena, grief alone is not the main issue. Some participants may use the tragic death to demonstrate their position in a public matter. Since the ritual takes place in the public space, by the roadside or in other public places, the respondents fear that the intensity of the event disappears and that the grief and the emotions become less sincere.

Some respondents regard the spontaneous shrine as a commemorative event or as clerical acts and therefore feel that they belong in the context of the church—not outdoors or by the roadside. To them, the spontaneous shrines represent religious ceremonies that take place at the wrong scene. The lighting of candles and other ritualized acts belong within the framework of the church. These respondents react to the context, not the ceremony itself.

However, several of those negative toward the spontaneous shrines have participated in similar rituals, but in another context. In their homes, they have placed lit candles and flowers next to photos of the departed, they have also tossed flowers into the open grave directly after the funeral. The respondents regard this as something entirely different from the spontaneous shrines. The reason for this may lie in the context, that the act takes place in the private arena and that they were closely related to the deceased. Their ritual resembles that of the spontaneous shrine but is adapted to their ideas of grief and death and how to demonstrate them.

How can we understand these attitudes? The Norwegian folklorist Bjarne Hodne has discussed the attitudes to death in Norway in a historical perspective (1980). He emphasizes that people in the past suppressed neither death nor grief, and claims that his source material evidences that grief reactions were both accepted and tabooed. This means that the collective attitudes toward grief were subjected to norms that clearly allowed for sorrow, but within clear limits (1980: 139–140). In some communities it was even demanded that emotions were displayed openly. Crying related to bereavement evidenced love for the deceased and sorrow because he or she was gone. The main tendency is nonetheless that demonstrations of grief should be somewhat subdued. One ought not to lose control and succumb to grief. Religion was also employed to relieve grief; one ought to mourn as Christians (Hodne 1980: 140–141). Grieving too much was to oppose God's will. God presides over every individual destiny and refusing to accept someone's death was seen as a protest toward the predestined.

Behind the tradition, which concerns the regulation and standardization of grief, there are conceptions that claim that strong grief, longing, and excessive crying did not give the deceased peace. It could on the contrary bring them back for a short while (Hodne 1980: 140–141 and Alver 1971). In her article "Conceptions of the Living Human Soul in the Norwegian Tradition" (1971), Bente G. Alver points out that it was believed that one could long for a departed to the extent that the deceased came back from the realm of the dead for a short while, and that the bereaved's longing made life in the grave impossible to endure. This notion of the power of longing is clearly demonstrated in the folk song "Den døde fæstmand," "The dead betrothed" (literally translated):

> For huer en gang du greder for mig,
> din hu giøris mod:
> da staar min kiste for inden fuld
> med lefret blod.

> For huer en gang du qveder,
> din hu er glad:
> da er min graff for inden omhengt
> med rosenblad.
> (DGF 90, 495, st. 17 and 19, rendered in Alver 1971).

> Every time you weep for me
> In times of your adversity:
> my coffin is soon filled
> with clotted blood.

> Every time you sing to me
> and you are joyous:
> then my tomb is adorned
> with rosy leaves.

In these stanzas the dead fiancé speaks on behalf of society. No one is allowed to succumb to grief and longing (Alver 1971). The strong regulation and social control of grief concerned the importance of keeping a tight rein on sorrow and that one should control oneself and one's emotions (Hodne 1980: 140–141). The tradition is dominated by a negative attitude toward exaggeration and a preference for subdued and controlled grief. Thus it becomes evident that reserved grief is not something new.

The Norwegian anthropologist Marianne Gullestad has analyzed the concepts of "peace" and "quiet" as cultural categories in Norway ([1989] 1993). Peace and quiet mean control over one's emotions and actions and concern self-restraint and self-control. Peace and quiet as a notion is about the absence of anxiety, passionate emotions, chaos, disorder, unregulated and uncontrollable actions, and emotions. In addition to encompassing the notion of absent negative emotions, the concept also concerns the presence of positive emotions such as fulfillment and harmony. The words peace and quiet have many meanings and are also used as synonyms. The concept of peace which according to Gullestad is the most important one, seems to concern relations among people. Peace means that you are not disturbed by others. Peace also means quiet, which concerns a state of mind. Quiet represents among other things immovability, reserve, control, and balance (Gullestad [1989] 1993: 125–130).

The notion that peace and quiet constitute a cultural category means that the concepts influence the structuring of thoughts, emotions, and to a certain degree, actions. This in turn means that the cultural category peace and quiet holds standards for what is real, important, and right. Peace and quiet represent among other things a view of humanity in which self-control is of the utmost importance. Central in the Norwegian culture is the notion of sameness, in which sameness to a substantial degree is defined as equality, in the sense of being of the same status (Gullestad [1989] 1993: 116–118 and 129).

As a category, peace and quiet influences our attitudes to events and actions. However, a cultural category is not unambiguous. The context in which an act takes place influences to a significant degree how that act is experienced. Furthermore, what is considered to define peace and quiet in a given situation is subject for disagreement. In connection with the spontaneous shrine related to the death of Princess Diana, journalists and others alike experienced and commented on the silence that seemed to dominate the event in spite of the enormous number of people present at any time.

Gullestad opens up for a possible connection between religious ideas and the peace and quiet of everyday life. She claims that Norwegian pietism represents some kind of secularization of the contemplative silence and secluded life of the convents ([1989] 1993: 138). As mentioned, Hodne argues that religion was used to rationalize subdued grief. However, one may also consider that moderation, self-restraint, and self-control rather than being related to convent life, are typical traits of protestantism and that they furthermore represent a mentality influenced by the dominating religious practice in Norway (see also Weber [1920] 1973). This idea may contribute to explain why these attitudes have remained so stable over long periods of time.

The questionnaire respondents who did not approve of the spontaneous shrine as a ritual may easily base their viewpoint on traditional attitudes toward grief, and also by separating the spontaneous shrine as such from the cultural category of peace and quiet. These respondents found the shrines to be emotionally disturbing, exaggerated, and uncontrolled, and therefore the shrines starkly contrast with the content of the cultural category peace and quiet. The respondents also reacted negatively toward what they regarded as worship of the deceased, and this may relate to the idea of sameness, so common in Norwegian and Scandinavian culture. When one person is being honoured in an unusually grand manner, and the spontaneous shrine is an instance of exactly this, it does signal that the person in question was extraordinary. Therefore this conflicts somewhat with the notion that sameness is the same as equality.

The respondents who are ambivalent in their view on the spontaneous shrine lean more toward the negative attitude than the positive, but all of them accept and understand why people make these shrines, and many of the respondents find them beautiful expressions of compassion and care. They understand and accept that people need to *deal* with the deaths by making spontaneous shrines, and also that the mourners use them as a means for *venting* their emotions.

The ambivalent respondents express that they respect that other people wish to make spontaneous shrines in relation to violent and unexpected death. They evidence their acceptance in "psychologizing" language and "therapeutical" terms. When they nevertheless react negatively it is for the same reasons shared by the negative respondents: the spontaneous shrines are too public, too exaggerated, unreal, disturbing, and upsetting, and these are the reasons why these respondents would refrain from participating themselves.

For the most part, the questionnaires express a positive attitude toward spontaneous shrines as a form of expression. The positive respondents all underline that they think that spontaneous shrines are a beautiful way of expressing grief. Typically, they are also of the opinion that young people are the most active contributors to spontaneous shrines.

The positive respondents regard the spontaneous shrine as a solemn event which expresses caring, community and solidarity, and which can comfort people in mourning. The shrine is furthermore a welcome contrast to the undercommunication or even alienation of death so typical of our time. It is also a good way in which to deal with grief. The symbols provide a concrete language that can be of great help when words are hard to find. The spontaneous shrine may also express a desire to be near the deceased as well as the bereaved. In addition, the shrines offer the participants the opportunity to do something actively when a tragic death has occurred, and through this they may vent their emotions. These respondents regard the spontaneous shrines as a kind of "mental hygiene."

To some of the respondents, the spontaneous shrine is an expression of present day concealment and suppression of death as such. In previous times the thought of death was all the more present in everyday life. You were never unprepared, and when death at last came you did not have much chance in trying to avoid relating to it. People died in their homes and the deceased remained there, in the family as it were, until the funeral. In society of old, the social death was a process that began when the biological death occurred and ended with the burial. Today, many people claim that death is tabooed especially considering that the social death, which in many instances precedes the biological death, is ended as soon as possible after the closing down of the biological functions (see Hodne 1980: 133–134 and Aagedal 1994: 13). Today, we look to the community and solidarity of the past evidenced in our traditions' sources, and we assign to them great importance in relation to the dying and the grieving. One is of the opinion that the care one used to show the dying and the dead through communal solidarity and traditional institutions and organizations, contributed to a healthy and correct attitude toward death (Hodne 1980: 134). Hodne nevertheless means that such opinions represent an idealization of the attitudes toward death prevalent in the past. Autobiographical material,[3] for instance, expresses strongly a different attitude. These statements evidence that the way people related to death and the dead in previous times were not necessarily commendable, quite to the contrary, it could be experienced as brutal, especially by children. Hodne therefore warns against the drawing of conclusions on a wrong basis. Knowledge of people's relationship to death in the past, based on the norms presented through traditional practices "gives us no knowledge about *people's individual reactions* to these norms. There can be no doubt that all the different sides of communal fellowship were of great help to the individual. However, we need to be aware that the customs had nothing to do with spiritual guidance. The close relationship to death was forced upon people as a result of the dual function of the norms. This function was to establish the deceased's status as dead, in addition to protect the living against ghosts" (Hodne 1980: 135). (See also Aagedal 1994: 10–11). (Translation by S.F.)

The responses in the questionnaire material hardly represent a desire to go back in time, but they rather express a reaction to the tabooing of *grief* and the ideal of control, which to some extent is present even today.

In the 1960s and 1970s, there was a trend that opposed rituals; rituals were regarded as bourgeois, hollow acts. People expressed their scepticism by privatizing the rituals and by making their own versions or even by parodying them (Frykman 1991 and Skjelbred 1994). In the 1980s and 1990s, rituals had their renaissance and the need for and the importance of rituals have become subject for public discussion (Skjelbred 1994: 29). The attitudes to the spontaneous shrine evidenced by the respondents may be viewed in the light of previous scepticism toward rituals, and an altered and more positive attitude toward the importance of rituals.

The respondents say that the spontaneous shrines offer a chance to do something and to be near, both at the scene of the accident and through the acts at the shrine. This evidences the power and the importance of the rituals. The rites structure and help people to go on and endure adversities. The patterns of the rituals are of help and offer the chance to participate, also emotionally (Skjelbred 1994: 39–43).

In the liminal phase of the rite of passage while the deceased's status as dead is not yet established, it can be opened up for different rules for behavior than the usual. The spontaneous shrine, in the vicinity of which powerful emotional outbursts take place and where the feeling of community is strong, may contribute to demonstrate the transition between life and death. The site of the spontaneous shrine was the last place the deceased was still alive and thus the link between life and death is particularly strong there. On this place, where the deceased was lastly alive and where he or she met death, a liminal space may be created and this opens up for reactions different from what can usually be observed. An example of this is Lisa and Ane's need to be near Torstein at the spontaneous shrine.

The questionnaire material reveals different reactions to what may happen in this liminal space. The respondents who are negative to the shrines emphasize the trauma of seeing such demonstrations and claim that those present at such a shrine seem unable to handle grief properly. They are of the opinion that what happens at the spontaneous shrine is unhealthy. In this light we can understand the headmaster's scepticism toward the spontaneous shrine and the ceremony the school held there the day after Torstein died.

To those ambivalent toward the spontaneous shrines, the making of a shrine offers an opportunity to channel emotions, to express them freely— it functions as a vent. Personally, they would not consider participating in such a ritual; it is something that other people appreciate and seem to need.

The positive respondents regard what takes place in the liminal space as a good way to process grief. By expressing emotions in the company of others, people are given a chance to vent their emotions. To these people, participating in the events at a spontaneous shrine is mental hygiene and it is healthy. The positive respondents show an appreciation of the therapeutical attributes of the shrine similar to the one expressed by Torstein's parson.

The questionnaire respondents, the headmaster and the parson, represent two main positions regarding the reactions that can be observed at a spontaneous shrine. The respondents negative toward the shrines point to the lack of emotional control, while the positive respondents, on the other hand, appreciate that the ritual gives people the opportunity to be emotional. The ambivalent respondents claim the middle position in that they accept that the spontaneous shrine represents an expression *others* need and appreciate.

Among the "therapeutical-sounding," psychologizing terms the questionnaire respondents use to explain their opinions, we find the notions of control and lack thereof. Controlling one's emotions is to refrain from expressing them openly, certainly not publicly. Letting emotional inhibitions go, allowing one's emotions to be expressed freely, is viewed as bad. From one point of view this is negative and unhealthy, from the other it is commendable and healthy. We can take a look at these attitudes from the perspective of history.

From the middle of the 1800s, the disciplined lifestyle gained momentum in the bourgeoisie. The body and its functions became subject to control, restraint, and discipline. One yearned for the cultivated as opposed to the brutish, and emphasized the spiritual instead of the corporeal (Frykman and Löfgren [1979] 1994: 211ff). According to the British sociologist Mike Featherstone (1992), this "civilization process" led to a stronger control over emotions, a feeling of discomfort related to the corporeal and an increased awareness of the need for personal space. The bourgeoisie, the middle class, dissociated itself from the common, "the others." Embedded in this dissociation was also a fascination with "the others" and "the other." The "other" and undisciplined could be experienced and felt for instance in the forest, at fairs and in the theatre, in the circus and in the slum. In these circumstances one were allowed to let go of one's emotional control. Today, we also find such "sites of ordered disorder," somewhat safer and more controlled, where people are allowed to let go of their self-control and their emotions and may behave in ways otherwise not tolerated. Featherstone's point is that decontrol (being allowed to let go of one's emotions) is an active and conscious act on part of the individual. You decide for yourself whether you want to let go of control or not. This is what Featherstone refers to as a controlled decontrol of one's emotions. Featherstone's sites of ordered disorder may be compared to a liminal space or a liminal state. What is experienced as control and lack thereof may be regarded as two forms of control. On the one hand, control over one's emotions, that is restrictiveness and restraint, and on the other hand controlled decontrol over one's emotions, for example visiting a spontaneous shrine and there express one's emotions in community with other people. As mentioned above, both positions express the existence of a connection between notions of control and notions of mental health.

The Spontaneous Shrine and Conceptions of Grief and Death

The making of a spontaneous shrine reflects different conceptions of death. There is a difference between avoidable and inevitable death. The avoidable, unnecessary death is experienced as unfair and unreasonable. The person subjected to the avoidable death is regarded as a victim. This attitude seems to be the main reason why the death is marked by the construction of a spontaneous shrine. Death has an age, and young death is met differently than the death that befalls an old person. The young death is unnatural and when it nevertheless happens it is met with stronger ritualization and a greater acceptance for the open display of emotions as well as less distance to the deceased's body. Through the notions of death we also see ideas about the unity of body and soul, which are connected to the close relations and the intimate and private.

The spontaneous shrine also reflects different conceptions of grief. Grief as such is regarded both as a creative and a destructive force. To those who want to control their emotions and strive for restraint, grief is destructive if it is acted out. In my material, the headmaster controls grief through tradition. Using grief actively is on the other hand creative. The parson uses grief therapeutically and grief is therefore creative as long as it may be controlled through the ritual. Independent of one's opinion of control one may claim that the uncontrolled grief is a bad grief. Through therapy and tradition one strives for an overall control of one's grief reactions. The youth use grief to negotiate identity and thereby seek an inner control and a control within the circle of friends. The conceptions of grief are furthermore connected to ideas of body and health.

People visit accident scenes because that was where death struck. At this place, the connection with both life and death is the strongest. They go there and they create a ritual to evidence that something terrible has happened there, and that they are by no account indifferent to it. They also visit the scene for their own sake. To the youth the scene of the accident is the scene of accidental death and of the young death. It could just as well have happened to them. Through Torstein's death they were given the opportunity to experience community and also to learn from his death. As opposed to the adults who regard the place solely as the scene of an accident, through their realization, the youth experience it as a place of their own, more private than public, perhaps a place of sacrifice. Through the fellowship and the new knowledge, Torstein's death gave life to something good. Through the ritual people seek intimacy and community. Through the symbols, the flowers, the candles, and the words, the space is aestheticized, it is redefined, and reclaimed. It changes from being a place of horror to becoming a place of afterthought. By visiting the scene of chaos, people experience that through the ritual a condition of cosmos is reestablished.

The spontaneous shrine represents a change in the way grief is expressed, a change toward individual and personal ritualization taking place in public space. One does not want to make the public private, however, but it is nevertheless a trait from the private introduced into the public sphere. The spontaneous shrine exists in the tension between public and private. The tension between the two spheres contributes to the meaning and the power of the ritual. The division between the public and the private is not erased by the ritualizations, but voices from the private sphere are aired in the public space.

The spontaneous shrine evidences that even today there are conceptions of the evil and the good death. The good death is the painless and peaceful death of old people—a natural and calm end to a long life. A good death is a death that is rational according to our sense of reality. A death that ends a painful existence and relieves people from suffering, may also be regarded as a meaningful death. The evil death occurs too early, it tears people full of will and zest for life away from their existence. Death by one's own hand is another instance of evil death. This is a meaningless death, it is unnecessary and unfair, and the deceased is therefore regarded as a victim. The making of spontaneous shrines evidences the need to react to the evil, avoidable death.

As previously mentioned, Ariès regarded death in our time to be suppressed and tabooed. This might well be somewhat moderated; one category of death may be more tabooed than another. Taking one's own life and taking the lives of others are examples of taboos. The medicated death of old, lonely people in institutions represents another example of a death that is not easy to cope with. The *shameful* death is the lonely death, which makes one feel inadequate and powerless. The spontaneous shrine shows that the death that is not looked upon as shameful is not suppressed in practice. In the acts related to the avoidable death which is evidenced by a spontaneous shrine, focus is on the *individual*. This regards the deceased as a person as well as gives the mourners' an opportunity to express themselves through rituals. The spontaneous shrine reflects an attention directed toward the *intimate*, that one strives to be near the dead and near to other people, and it also reflects an attention toward the *authentic* and *intense*, that one desires experiences. In the making of a spontaneous shrine also lies a search for *community*. Considering my material, the same key concepts are in focus; intimacy, authenticity, individuality, community, and intensity. The different respondents, however, have their own individual approach to these concepts. The parson regards these concepts as important from a therapeutical point of view, while the headmaster finds them unsettling compared to his ideal of control. The youth hold the key concepts to be central because they are related to friendship.

I will not without reservations claim that people who contribute to a spontaneous shrine have a close relationship with death. Nonetheless, in my material there is a marked difference as concerns attitudes toward death between people who contribute to such shrines and those who are negative toward them. The reactions to the public, the emotional, and the fact that the rituals focus directly on one person, are connected to views on grief and death. Negative reactions to spontaneous shrines may reflect the belief that grief should remain subdued and private and less emotionally expressive. The perspective of the therapist is also made evident through the ritualization of spontaneous shrines, and the attitudes to both death and grief are in many instances colored by a therapeutical understanding. In the therapeutical universe death is suppressed so long as it remains unconfronted, similarly, grief is suppressed so long as one is unable to express it in words or actions.

The way we relate to death is closely connected to the historical, social, and cultural context in which we live. This context influences our feelings toward death. Through the spontaneous shrine as a way to meet death, ideas about death and grief are reflected, and different attitudes connected to different kinds of death are made evident. Whether death is experienced as good or evil, avoidable or inevitable, may be related to the experiences of grief in connection with the different kinds of death. The attitudes toward death are connected with the feelings of those who are left behind. Those are the people in search of meaning—it is they, and we, who shall live on.

Notes

Translation by Siri Fuglseth.

1. These events were the subject of my postgraduate thesis in folkloristics: " 'som eit spor'. Spontanalteret som moderne sorguttrykk i et kulturanalytisk perspektiv." Literary translation: " 'Like a trace'. The spontaneous shrine as a modern expression of grief in a culture analytical perspective." Institute of cultural studies and cultural history, the University of Bergen 1998.

2. The questionnaire was distributed through Norsk Etnologisk Gransking (NEG [Norwegian Ethnological Research]). NEG has for a considerable number of years established a network of respondents all over Norway, who from time to time receive questionnaires concerning a variety of topics. Many of the respondents are elderly people, who have contributed to NEG's activity over many years.

3. At the Institute of cultural studies at the University of Oslo, there are extensive collections of autobiographical material, which deal with different subjects among them death.

References Cited

Aagedal, Olaf. 1994. "Sorga over ein konge og ein krig." In *Døden på norsk*, ed. Aagedal, Olaf, 179–201. Oslo: Ad Notam Gyldendal.

Åkesson, Lynn. 1997. Mellan levande och döda. Föreställningar om kropp och ritual. Stockholm: Natur och Kultur.

Alver, Bente Gullveig. 1971. Conceptions of the Living Human Soul in the Norwegian Tradition. *Temenos* 7: 7–33.

———. 1994a. "Det genvundne paradis." In *I dødens skygge. Tradisjoner ved livets slutt*, ed. Alver, Bente Gullveig and Ann Helene Bolstad Skjelbred, 61–90. Stabekk: Vett og Viten a/s.

———. 1994b. "Døden i billedet." In *I dødens skygge. Tradisjoner ved livets slutt*, ed. Alver, Bente Gullveig and Ann Helene Bolstad Skjelbred, 91–105. Stabekk: Vett og Viten a/s.

———. 1996. "Det genvundne paradis: Oplevelse, fortolkning og fortælling." In *Myte i møte med det moderne*, ed. Lisbeth Mikaelsson, 13–32. KULTs skriftserie nr. 63.

Ariès, Philippe. 1977. Døden i Vesten. Oslo: Det norske samlaget. Norwegian edition of Essais sur l'histoire de la mort en Occident du Moyen Age à nos jours. 1975.

Bauman Richard og Charles L. Briggs. 1990. Poetics and Performance as Critical Perspectives on Language and Social Life. *Annual Review of Anthropology* 19: 59–88.

Bringager, Frithjof. 1992. I lyset fra Slottsplassen. *Norveg* 35: 89–103.

Ehn, Billy and Orvar, Löfgren. 1994 [1982]: *Kulturanalys. Ett etnologiskt perspektiv*. Malmö: Gleerups förlag.

Elias, Norbert. 1985. *The Loneliness of the Dying*. Oxford: Basil Blackwell.

Eriksen, Trond Berg. 1984. "Den usynlige død. *Kontrast* 2: 51–58.

Featherstone, Mike. 1992. "Postmodernism and the Aestheticiziation of Everyday Life." In *Modernity and Identity*, ed. Lash, Scott and Jonathan Friedman, 265–291. Oxford UK & Cambridge Mass.: Blackwell Publishers.

Frandsen, Finn. 1985. "Dødens nekrolog: Philppe Ariès og dødens historie." In *Dødens tårer*, ed. Schøllhammer, Karl Erik and Erik Kr. Sloth, 10–24. Århus: Modtryk.

Frykman, Jonas. 1979. "Rit som kommunikation." In *Kulturell Kommunikation*, ed. Bringéus, Nils-Arvid and Göran Rosander, 59–66. Lund: Liber.

——— 1991. "Mellan mössbränning och champagneyra." In *Svenska vanor och ovdnor*, ed. Frykman, Jonas and Orvar Löfgren (red.), 136–159. Stockholm: Natur och Kultur.

Gullestad, Marianne. 1993 [1989]. *Kultur og hverdagsliv. På sporet av det moderne Norge*. Oslo: Universitetsforlaget.

Hockey, Jenny. 1993. "The Acceptable Face of Human Grieving? The Clergy's Role in Managing Emotional Expression During Funerals." In *The Sociology of Death: Theory, Culture, Practice*, ed. David Clark, 129–149. Oxford: Blackwell Publishers.

174   HEGE WESTGAARD

Hodne, Bjarne. 1980. Å leve med døden. Folkelige forestillinger om døden og de døde. Oslo: Aschehoug.
Honko, Lauri. 1976. "Riten—en klassifikation." In *Nordisk folktro Studiertillägnade Carl-Herman Tillhagen 17. December 1976,* ed. Klintberg, Bengt af, Reimund Kvideland and Magne Velure, 71–84. Stockholm: Nordiska Museet.
James, Allison. 1995. "Talking of Children and Youth. Language, Socialization and Culture." In *Youth Cultures. A Cross-Cultural Perspective,* ed. Amit-Talai, Vered and Helena Wulff, 43–63. London og New York: Routledge.
Källstad, Thorvald. 1987. Rosealteret på Sveavägen. *Syn og segn* 128–136.
Klein, Barbro (ed.) 1995. *Gatan är vår! Ritualer på offentliga plaster.* Stockholm: Carlssons Bokförlag.
Köstlin, Konrad. 1992. Totengedenken am Strassenrand. Projektstrategie und Forschungsdesign. *Österreichische Zeitschrift für Volkskunde* 95: 305–320.
Ladenheim, Melissa. 1993. Å lese kulturlandskap. En analyse av norske kirkegårder. *Tradisjon* 23: 39–55.
Moore, Sally F. and Barbara G. Myerhoff. 1977. "Introduction: Secular Ritual. Forms and Meaning." In *Secular Ritual,* ed. Moore, Sally F. and Barbara G. Myerhoff, 3–24. Assen/Amsterdam: Van Gorcum.
Scharfe, Martin. 1989. "Totengedenken. Zur Historizität von Brauchtraditionen. Das Beispiel Olof Palme 1986." *Ethnologia Scandinavica* 19: 142–154.
Selberg, Torunn. 1989. Massemedienes ritualisering av vårt hverdagsliv. *Norveg* 32: 141–154.
———. 1991. "Kvinder maa ikke komme i berørelse med fiskegreier; thi det volder ulykke." Mannlig og kvinnelig i folkelig forestillingsverden. *Tradisjon* 21: 101–117.
———. 1993. "Folklore and Mass Media." In *Nordic Frontiers. Recent Issues in the Study of Modern Traditional Culture in the Nordic Countries,* ed. Anttonen, Perti J. and Reimund Kvideland, 201–217. Turku: NIF Publications 27.
———. 1995. "Folklore og massekommunikasjon—folkelig kultur og populærkultur." In *Nostalgi og sensasjones. Fokloristisk prespektiv på mediekulturen,* ed. Selberg Torunn, 9–36. Turku: NIF Publications 29.
Skjelbred, Ann Helene Bolstad. 1972. *Uren og hedning. Barselkvinnen i norsk folketradisjon.* Oslo–Bergen–Tromsø: Universitetsforlaget.
———. 1989. Kirkelig og borgerlig konfirmasjon og ungdomsfest. En diskusjon omkring riter og rite de passage. *Tradisjon* 19: 27–40.
———. 1994. "Å være til stede i sitt eget liv—Ritualenes betydning." In *I dødens skygge,* ed. Bente Gullveig Alver, and Ann Helene Bolstad Skjelbred, 29–42. Stabekk: Vett & Viten.
Turner, Victor. 1967. *The Forest of Symbols. Aspects of Ndembu Ritual.* Ithaca and London: Cornell University Press.
Turner, Victor. 1995 [1969]. *The Ritual Process. Structure and Anti-Structure.* New York: Aldine de Gruyter.
van Gennep, Arnold. 1960. *The Rites of Passage.* London: Routledge & Keagan Paul.

Weber, Max. 1973 [1920]. *Den protestantiske etik og kapitalismens ånd.* Gyldendals
Studiefakler.
Wuthnow, Robert. 1987. *Meaning and moral order: Explorations in cultural analysis.*
Berkeley, CA: University of California Press.
Ziehe, Thomas. 1993 [1989]. *Kulturanalyser. Ungdom, utbildning, modernitet.*
Stockholm: Brutus Östlings Bokförlag Symposion.

Chapter 8

A Memorial Wall in Philadelphia

Jonathan Lohman

The stories follow a familiar pattern, like a recurring nightmare. Each woman begins her tale by showing a photograph. "This is my son. . . ." Next, she reports the final moments of her child's life in striking detail. "Well, he and this boy got into an argument. . . ." Rarely was the murder a result of a robbery, and rarely was it premeditated. Instead it seems to always result from some kind of "argument," usually with someone the victim knew, over something that to these mothers must seem so agonizingly trivial—an insult, a joke, or a misplaced look. The mothers tell the story as if they themselves were eyewitnesses to the event, including what, precisely, was said before the trigger was pulled. They freeze those last seconds as if casing the scene for some trace of reason.

Listening, you envision the scene, with the backdrop of some nameless "urban" street. You imagine the look in the eyes of the killer, himself only a child, and wonder if, at that moment, he fathomed any sense of the staggering weight of what he was about to do, and of the vast breadth of the hurt he was about to cause. The scene is fuzzy, almost unimaginable, and quickly disappears, leaving only the face of the mother standing before you and the rising pain in her voice. Tears well up in her eyes, and descend well-worn paths down her cheeks. You understand then that she has been through something you couldn't even begin to imagine—something akin to, as one mother put it, "having someone thrust his hand down your throat to rip out your heart."

Her words come quicker now, and her voice rises, struggling to be heard behind her tears— "And then he just pulled out a gun and shot my baby." Other women are crying now as well, and you know that they are reliving some other argument, on some other street, only it is their child that looks down the barrel of the gun.

Barbara Smolen, "the artist" as she has come to be known around the neighborhood, is crying too. She sits at the table, her painted lips trembling, slowly shaking her head. She listens further as the stories go on to tell of the days, months, and years of grieving that follow each murder. Each story tells another heartbreaking tale of justice not served, of clocks that seem to have stopped, of little brothers and sisters that can't understand. And when they can no longer continue, they hand Barbara the photograph.

"Well, anyway, here's his picture."

At the end of the meeting, the artist gathers the pile of photographs and places them into a paper bag. One young woman offers her only a faded driver's license, another hands her a Xerox copy of her son's death notice in the Philadelphia Inquirer, so dark you can only see the whites of his eyes and his smile.

"I'll do my best," she tells them.

West of 43rd Street

When University of Pennsylvania students arrive in West Philadelphia for their freshman orientation, they are often advised, by fellow students and school administrators alike, to avoid living, or for that matter, even walking, west of 43rd Street. If one were to venture west, however, beyond the boundaries of University Police jurisdiction, past the Ethiopian-owned shops and restaurants that dot Baltimore Avenue, and walk south across the patchwork of occupied and abandoned row houses of 50th Street, where pay phones cease to work, and where graffiti-tagged gas stations cease to offer restrooms, you will come upon a dramatic landscape of rolling hills, spanning the entire block (see figure 8.1).

This mural will likely jar your attention, not simply because of the vibrant colors emanating from its depicted sunrise, in stark contrast to the aluminum sides of the warehouse behind it, but because of the tragic scene painted on its far right. There you will see a mother and father kneeling before a slain child, as an angel descends to recover his soul. The grief on the mother's face is unmistakable, speaking from depths of despair that few of us can truly understand (see figure 8.2).

In the foreground is a long row of columns, which gradually fade out into the mural's horizon, like images of China's Great Wall. At the top of each column is a portrait, too small to make out from your perch across the street. You come in closer. What first strikes you about the portraits are the years posted under their names, revealing the tragic brevity of their lives: *Joseph Jordan, 1974–1998, Robert A. Randolph, 1965–1992, Jeffrey Rushton, 1987–1998.* There are 15 portraits in all, depicting 14 boys and 1 girl, all

Figure 8.1   The mural on 50th and Wood lawn.
Photo by: Jonathan Lohman.

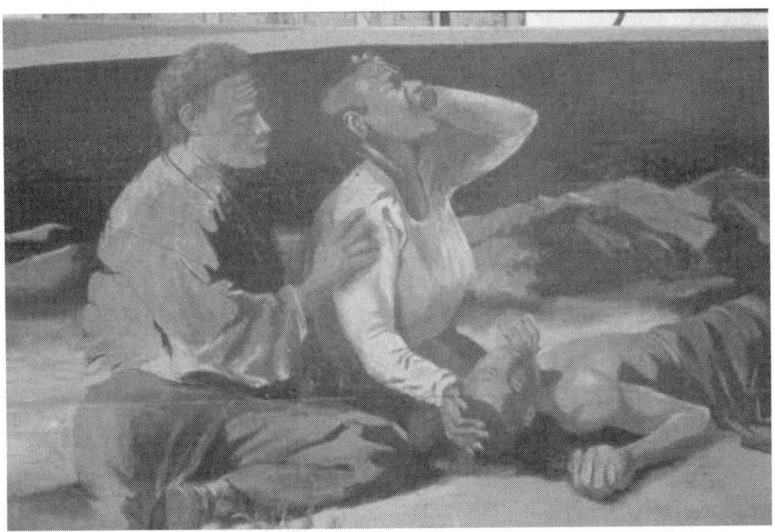

Figure 8.2   Slain child, grieving mother.
Photo by: Jonathan Lohman.

African American, and all dead before the age of 30. These portraits, combined with the arresting scene of the grieving parents, tells a clear, unavoidable story. These young people were murdered.

The memorial mural is one of over 2000 murals painted by Philadelphia's Mural Arts Program (MAP). MAP started in 1982 as "The Philadelphia Anti-Graffiti Network," a public arts program initiated by the then Mayor Wilson Goode to employ convicted graffiti artists to create murals in blighted neighborhoods throughout the city. Since then the program has evolved into one of the premiere public arts organizations in the country, and boasts a roster of some of the country's finest muralists.[1] MAP cooperates with local neighborhoods, involving community members in all phases of the mural-making process.

For the mural on 50th and Woodland, MAP was contacted by Sandy and Garnet Spicer. Sandy and Garnet, who themselves have lost two sons to street violence, operate a grassroots nonprofit organization, Families Are Victims Too (FAVT), out of their home, providing a number of services for grieving parents of murder victims in southwest Philadelphia. Having seen other murals honoring local residents throughout West Philadelphia, the Spicers felt that a mural would be an excellent way to help preserve the memory of their son Donald and the other slain children. They also hoped that the mural would draw attention to the cause of youth violence in southwest Philadelphia, and provide some comfort to the victims' mourning parents and families. "The mural is like the backbone of everything we do," Garnet tells me, "it all comes out of this."

I asked Sandy how she first came up with the idea to apply for a mural.

> Well, I used to stand at my window often and watch the children from Comegys and various schools. They'd take the school children over there, and give the kids a tour of the bus depot. So I just thought that it would be a good idea, to just let them know, that these children—all from this neighborhood—had their lives taken in an untimely fashion. And it's like a deterrent, to tell these kids that that's not the way to go. And maybe, just maybe, if people can get that idea, they might stop and think before they go out and do something horrendous . . .
>
> And, I thought that the wall could also be a way to keep these kids alive, through their portraits, and give their families a chance to live as well. Because they won't be so much in pain because their children weren't forgotten. See, I took my *own* personal feelings, as a mother. And I guess I projected, that other parents will feel the same.

Sandy wrote to Jane Golden, the Director of MAP, about her idea for the mural. Jane was so moved by the letter that she contacted Sandy the following day. Sandy then began working to generate support for the mural.

She posted fliers throughout the neighborhood, leaving them in mailboxes and behind screen doors. She contacted local newspapers, radio and television stations, and politicians.

Yet, for a while it appeared that no one wanted his or her child on the mural, as Sandy describes:

> Well, at first, nobody really responded. And I was a little disheartened. But, I didn't give up. I just kept faxing and faxing and faxing. And finally, people started responding. And it went from there.
>
> I mean, then I started hearing all the stories about the kids. And I really got thrown into it. Because it became a part of me. Those children that passed had become *my* children. So I wanted to do something personally, besides just having the pictures up there. So when I met with the artist, Barbara, I talked to her about my idea. I wanted to get my message out. I told her that it is time that we reach these kids.

Once word got out, the stories started coming in, each telling of young lives tragically cut short, and parents whose lives have forever been blown apart. By the time they were scheduled to hold their first meeting with the artist, Sandy had a list of over 30 names, growing agonizingly larger by the day.

Yet while Sandy was garnering support for the memorial within the neighborhood, she began to receive unexpected skepticism and resistance from others in the city. For in Philadelphia, murals are used as a primary medium to honor the heroes, both living and dead, who claim a connection to the city: great artists such as Paul Robeson (see figure 8.3a) and John Coltrane; important political figures, such as Maxine Waters and Frank Rizzo; and legendary athletes, such as Philadelphia 76er and basketball hall-of-famer Julius "Dr. J" Erving (see figure 8.3b), and the late Philadelphia schoolyard legend Hank Gathers.

Local community activists are honored as well. Murals have been painted to honor block captains, local schoolteachers, and community organizers. Requests come into the MAP office almost daily, suggesting other Philadelphians who "deserve" a mural. Sandy learned, as she was preparing her application for the FAVT mural, that in many people's eyes, her proposed subjects didn't make the grade.

> When I first wanted to see this done, they were telling me, "Oh, no, that shouldn't be done. Why do you want to put those people's face up there? They weren't heroes!" But they were *our* heroes. They were our children. And to us, you know, we loved them. I don't care what anybody thinks. Everybody has dirty laundry, I don't care what walk of life you come from. Not everybody can be the mayor. Everybody can't be some form of dignitary. But you

Figure 8.3 (a) "Paul Robeson" 4502 Chestnut Street. Artist: Peter Pagast; (b) "Dr. J" Ridge Avenue and Green Street. Artist: Kent Twitchell. *Photos by:* Jonathan Lohman.

know, they're still people, and we love them. And I'm not going to let people forget that.

As Sandy quickly learned, when a MAP mural memorializes a neighborhood resident who is otherwise *not* famous, particularly a young person, it is generally assumed that the person was somehow an innocent victim of a tragic circumstance.

This seems to have been the assumption of the FAVT mural's chosen artist, Barbara Smolen, when she began the project. Upon hearing these initial accounts of the lives and deaths of the young people she would soon paint, however, Barbara was confronted with a moral dilemma.

I mean, I went through a whole . . . I mean, I don't know how you would describe it. You see, the way the mural was presented to me, they made me think it was going to be, like, a wall for kids who were caught in cross fire, not for anybody who was involved in criminal activity. And not for people who were shot as a result of the business that they chose to engage in . . . the drug business. So then I was like, can we distinguish between innocent victims who were murdered, like in cases of mistaken identity, from people who were going down a path that was going to lead them to their death? I didn't want to, like, pay tribute to people who made wrong decisions in their lives, and ended up killed as a result.

Barbara was shocked to hear that in some of the cases, the victims were involved in dealing drugs, and many had engaged in violent activities themselves.

Barbara's concern with valorizing the victims addresses larger issues surrounding the vocabulary of mural painting in the city. The Families are Victims Too mural operates within a larger memorializing vocabulary in Philadelphia, carrying with it a host of previously understood meanings. In Philadelphia, as well as other cities such as New York, there exists an assumed dichotomy regarding the subjects of "official" or "professional" city-sponsored, brush-painted memorial murals, and those of the seemingly ubiquitous airbrushed, "graffiti" memorials. For, it is widely understood that the mural is for the heroic, the accomplished, and the innocent. It is certainly not a place for known drug dealers. There are other walls for them.

What It Means To Be
"Up On The Wall"

For the children of Southwest Philly, much like the children living in inner cities across America, the dead at times seem almost omnipresent in the daily lives of the living. The dead are in the music they listen to, the movies they watch, and listed in the unrelenting deluge of notices in the back pages of the *Philadelphia Inquirer*, eulogizing young men and women, boys and girls really, who have fallen victims to street violence. But the dead are even closer than that. The dead are represented by empty desks in their classrooms, and spoken of in stories of fallen brothers, sisters, cousins, and neighbors.

And often, the faces and names of the dead are airbrushed and spray-painted on the walls that comprise the physical backdrop for daily life in the city. Painted by friends, family members, or local artists commissioned by the deceased's loved ones, these spray-can memorials serve as an attempt to ensure the remembrance of the deceased, or perhaps more precisely, to stave off the process of forgetting.

With the prevalence of graffiti memorial walls throughout the city, Philadelphia's young have a highly developed understanding of what it means to be "on the wall." This understanding has manifested itself in everyday vernacular speech, as Sandy explains: "They have this saying, it's like a threat, they say, 'Don't make me put you on the wall!' or 'If you don't watch yourself, you're going up on the wall.' "

Barbara described to me her earliest encounter with local understanding of what it means to be "on the wall":

> I was working on the mural one day, and this guy came by, and he asked me about the mural . . . we talked for a while, and I said, you know, you're such a handsome guy, I'd love to paint your portrait sometime, and he said, "Oh no! God forbid, I'm not ready to be on the wall!"

Joseph Sciorra (1994) studied the spray-can memorials of New York's Lower East Side, a tradition that appears to have predated Philadelphia incarnations. According to Sciorra, these "In Memory" walls began as recently as 1988, and then increased dramatically over the next several years, in close relation to the increased proliferation of handguns and crack cocaine (1988: 8). Like other forms of New York's graffiti, memorial walls began to spread to other American cities, and eventually to Europe and beyond largely due to the increasingly mainstream interest in new urban black music and hip-hop culture in the 1980s (Prigoff 1987: 8).

Sciorra points out that there was a strong Latino presence among the first memorial-wall artists. Sciorra traces the origins of this practice, to other traditions of memorializing in Latino and other predominantly Catholic regions:

> The strong Latino presence reveals a historic precedent for the memorial tradition. The walls are updated versions of the simple roadside crosses often erected at the site of an automobile accident in predominantly Catholic countries. These wood, metal, and cement crosses manifest the belief that the souls of those who die unexpectedly and fail to receive the Last Rites of the Catholic Church are suffering in purgatory's purifying flames. The marker serves then as a lasting reminder for passersby to pray for the person's soul and thus speed its eventual arrival into heaven. (1994: 10)

The strong Latino connection to "In Memory" walls is evident in Philadelphia, where the majority of them can be found in the Puerto Rican section of Fairhill. Recently, however, the "In Memory" walls become increasingly prevalent in black neighborhoods as well. Though Sciorra connects the origins of the Lower East Side's memorial walls to the increased prevalence of violence due to the heightened proliferation of drugs in the inner city, he explicitly points out that not all of the deaths memorialized on New York's walls were drug related. My research into the public perception of these walls in Philadelphia, however, suggests that it is most often *assumed*, particularly among young people, that a victim portrayed in a spray-can memorial was a drug dealer.

To illustrate this point, I will briefly turn to another memorial mural in Philadelphia, located in the North Philadelphia neighborhood often called "the Badlands," because of its reputed legacy of heroin deals and crime. Peaches Ramos, block captain at 9th and Indiana, expressed her frustration over the public misunderstanding of a graffiti-style memorial in her neighborhood, honoring a Latino male, in his early twenties. Viewing me as a representative of MAP, Peaches repeatedly requested that "we" paint over the spray-painted memorial, done by a local artist with money collected from the victim's friends, with a more "professional" MAP mural. Standing in front of the mural with Peaches, she waves a photograph of the deceased young man in the air, barely containing her anger:

> See how that's supposed to be him? Like, what is that? What is that? And that just doesn't look nowhere like him! And, I mean look at him, he's smoking a blunt. And that's so disgusting. And I'm like, "Y'all paid, what, nine hundred dollars for that shit?" Excuse my language, but that is *not* him. That is *not* him. And you know, it's like, "what is *that*?" And to pay so much for this junk? I don't think so.

Peaches' dissatisfaction with the airbrushed memorial proves revealing of the larger relational issues between what could be called "graffiti style" memorial murals, and the MAP murals. First, Peaches criticizes the artist's technical skills, in particular, his inability to capture the likeness of the victim in his portrait. Clearly, Peaches understands the critical role the mural will play in constructing and maintaining collective memory. She knows that over time, the pictured image will, for many, replace personal memory, so it is critical that the artist captures the likeness of the deceased. Also, Peaches contends that the mural's "graffiti style" rendering, as well as its depiction of the victim smoking a "blunt," has caused many local residents to assume that the victim was a drug dealer: "I keep telling everybody, he's not a drug dealer!" Peaches tells me. "Because you know, there's people around here that say, 'If he's sprayed up there, then he's got to be a drug dealer!' "

As Peaches' comments reveal, the assumed connection between memorial walls and drugs has much to do with these walls' aesthetic style. As I discussed earlier, the "graffiti style," triggers a host of cultural assumptions for the viewer, often seen as the visual marker of a youth-dominated street culture. Graffiti, as clearly implied in the broken windows thesis, has often become conflated with other crimes associated with the street culture, in particular drug dealing, as Clare Ignatowski states:

> So, why is graffiti conflated with drug-dealing? Part of the answer is in the way graffiti operates symbolically as an outlaw action and aesthetic form.

The qualities associated with graffiti by mainstream viewers closely resemble those associated with the drug-trade. So, even though there is no necessary, actual connection between the production of graffiti and the selling of drugs, these two activities are conflated on the level of public discourse. (1996: 28)

While the subjects of MAP's memorial murals are usually understood as commemorating those members of society that were heroic, accomplished, and "innocent," those immortalized in airbrush are assumed to be those who made their living on the street, by dealing drugs or through some other criminal means, evoking the larger dichotomous system of classifications of "decent" and "street" families in urban, black Philadelphia, described by sociologist Elijah Anderson (1999: 35).[2]

As Barbara discovered through her repeated interactions with neighborhood residents, the distinctions between "decent" and "street" are often much murkier than Anderson describes. The many stories Barbara heard about the circumstances behind the children's deaths forced her to realize that the "decent" and the "street" exist within a complex web of relationships, operating under the omnipresent weight of joblessness and violence, where her previously held notions of the innocent and, as she put it, "the not so innocent," cease to apply.

I mean, I wanted to just say, "I can't do this." Even Sandy, her two sons were killed, and they were involved in . . . you know, they weren't such choir boys. But you know, I talked to my mom—she's a social worker in the South Bronx—and she said, "It's not your place. You've had all of the advantages." Kids who grow up in this community, you know, it's really hard to judge them. I mean, I think you can say *this* is an innocent victim, and *this* is a victim that's not so innocent. But when you look at the bigger picture you can't really . . . I mean, the whole culture of poverty, and crime, and drugs, and guns. I guess it's hard to put yourself in the place of being a fourteen or fifteen year old kid in this neighborhood. So, I decided I would try not to pass judgment. But yes, sometimes it's still hard. . . .

The Artist

"I told Barbara often," Sandy tells me as we sit on her porch watching Barbara meticulously attend to a portrait on the mural, "that she was commissioned to do this, long before she knew, maybe before she even came into this world. I know in my heart, that she was sent here to do this. Barbara Smolen, she's the one. The one who was chosen to help deliver this message. She's 'the bomb,' as the young people say."

I asked Sandy if the mural matched her original vision:

Oh, completely. In fact, Barbara asked me, "what do you see in this picture?" I said, Barbara, look at the mother there. Look at her. She's in so much anguish. And the father, if no other time he's there for her at that time. To comfort her. And he's looking up, just saying "I wish." "I wish there was an answer to all this senseless crime." And the mother is just . . . she couldn't reach the child. She just couldn't reach him, and let him know that this is not the way.

So, yes, it tells a story. It reflects the children there . . . And it shows the angel coming there to take the soul of the child, and the other angel is leaving, that has already taken a soul. That's what it shows. If people can't understand that, then something's wrong.

In meeting Barbara Smolen for the first time, she strikes you as a rather unlikely candidate to be the one "chosen" to paint the Families Are Victims Too mural. Barbara is shy, soft-spoken, and noticeably uncomfortable as the focus of attention. She could be mistaken for the stereotypical "soccer mom," pulling up to the mural in her white minivan from her home in the Philadelphia suburb of Bala Cynwyd. Inside cans of paint, stacks of canvases, and loose brushes compete for space with child seats and action figures. Like many MAP artists, Barbara was classically trained, having received an art degree from the Philadelphia Academy of the Arts. She painted her first mural for MAP in 1997, "Tribute to Atiya," also a memorial to a victim of violence.

The "Tribute to Atiya" Mural, located in the Latino neighborhood on 17th and North Streets in North Philadelphia, memorializes Atiya Rodrigues, granddaughter of community activist "Dot" Rodrigues, who was brutally murdered by her boyfriend in her home. Ms. Rodrigues contacted MAP Director Jane Golden, a personal friend, to alert her of Atiya's murder, and to request that a mural be done both to honor Atiya and to act as a strong message against domestic violence. Jane designed the mural and participated in the early phases of its creation, then left the project for Barbara to complete, in particular the portraiture of Atiya, as Barbara describes:

The father of the victim gave me a picture of her to work with. And in the picture, she was laughing. She had this great big smile. So, I asked around, and I got two more pictures of her, but she was laughing in those too. I didn't think it would be appropriate, you know, to have her look so exuberant in a mural condemning domestic violence.

Barbara hired a young woman to pose for Atiya's portrait, and directed her to portray a "sorrowful, dreamy, far away look." Barbara painted the woman's portrait in black and white, to express the bleakness of life for one caught up in the vicious cycle of domestic abuse. Barbara's plan was to paint the woman's portrait, then transform it to make it look like Atiya. In mid-process, however, Barbara was confronted by a local resident, who she soon learned was Atiya's godmother:

> She was yelling at me, in Spanish. I had spent some time in Puerto Rico as a child so I could get what she was saying. She was saying, "That looks nothing like Atiya!" And saying that if Atiya was alive, she wouldn't like it. She kept asking, "Why isn't she smiling? Atiya was always smiling!"

Barbara's confrontation with Atiya's godmother was her first of many forays into negotiations with neighborhood residents regarding the content and style of her murals. These type of negotiations often become quite emotionally charged, particularly when such critical issues as public remembrance of the deceased are at stake. As the muralist, Barbara is often commissioned with the difficult task of creating visual images that not only "accurately" depict an aggregate of personal memories, but also that conform to residents' uses for the past in the present. Often, the memorializing objectives of the artist enter into conflict with those of her audience. In this case, Barbara was most concerned with the mural's political message—raising awareness of the tragedy of domestic violence—while members of the community, particularly Atiya's family and friends, were most concerned with the preservation of the vital, joyful woman of their memories. Suzanne Lacy describes a similar situation in her examination of the memorial created for victims of the Oklahoma City bombing:

> Out of whose longing does an artist act? The artist reaches out to restore connection with others through art, and in so doing codifies memory, which is endlessly interpretable. But public memorials by nature are meant to express collective, not individual, memory. Aside from the question of whether collective memory is possible, or perhaps within the context of this question, the role of the artist in the endeavor of constructing history and transforming our experience of the contemporary landscape is contested and politicized. (1996: 8)

While Barbara chose not to make Atiya smile in the mural, she did compromise much of her intended compositional design.

> People in her family remembered her as a beautiful young woman. I realized that while I was trying to send a strong message about domestic violence, that this was a real person here. I was painting her as "the victim" but her loved ones saw her as "Atiya." So, I decided to put her in color. I tried to make her

look as pretty as I could. I gave her lipstick and eyeliner. I even did her nails. So, a couple days later, the godmother returned, and she had this great big smile, and she said—in English by the way—"now that's my baby!" Then, it was like, she totally opened up to me. She told me about how they wanted her to get away from her boyfriend, how Atiya was killed, the way he cut her throat. It was like, once she felt that her goddaughter was remembered properly, then she could talk about it. I think it had kind of a cathartic effect.

In large part due to her experience with the Atiya mural (see figure 8.4) as well as her skills as a portrait artist, Barbara was asked to paint the Families Are Victims Too mural. While the two murals share a central theme, Barbara quickly learned that the similarities largely ended there. Unlike the neighborhood around 17th and North, which is home to a diverse population of residents including Latinos, blacks, Asians, and whites, the neighborhood surrounding 50th and Woodland is exclusively black. Barbara, who is white, found herself the object of much attention and suspicion, being immediately identified as an "outsider." Barbara says she heard some "rumblings" around the neighborhood that a black artist should have been commissioned to paint the portrait. For many, it appears, the boundaries between "insiders" and "outsiders" are racially drawn.

"I think she was a little bit scared at first," Seneca McClendon, whose son Seneca Jr. is memorialized on the wall, told me one day, "I think she only knew about black neighborhoods what she saw on TV. But after a

Figure 8.4   "Tribute to Atiya," 17th and North Street. MAP photo.

while, with me and Garnet and some of the other fellas looking out for her, I think she got more comfortable."

Sandy and Garnet were immediately impressed with Barbara's interest in learning as much as possible about the victims before painting their portraits. Sandy described the long hours of sitting with Barbara, looking through scrapbooks of photographs and newspaper listings that Sandy had compiled over the years. "Barbara, she really puts her whole heart and soul into this mural," Sandy told me, "I mean, this was more than a job to her. She wanted to know all about these kids, how they passed, everything."

Hearing the Stories

The unique conditions of creative production in the public art world of the mural create opportunities for the artist to know her audience, and in consequence, her subjects, in ways unattainable in the art worlds of galleries and museums.[3] From her earliest moments working on the FAVT mural, Barbara was visited by family and friends of the victims, who would often engage her in detailed conversations about their deceased loved ones.

> These people, whose portraits are on the wall, the circumstances of their deaths were so tragic. I mean, each one was like worse than the one before. And you can't . . . you can't paint all of those portraits and not know the stories. That's why I put the scene at the other end, with the mother and the child and the angel. A lot of the parents of these victims live right on this block. One day, when I was painting, this woman came up to me. She was crying. She kept pointing to the mother figure, the one crying over her dead son. She kept saying, "This is me. That woman you painted is me!"

I visited with Barbara one afternoon after she had completed all 15 of the portraits. Walking the length of the mural, her voice quickened, becoming more animated, as she described the tragic details behind each portrait. Seneca, she told me, had just returned home from delivering presents to the poor on Christmas Eve, when he got the call that Seneca Jr. had been killed in an apparent robbery. Another boy, she said, was killed in a drive-by shooting. Another one was killed for his basketball. At several of the portraits, Barbara stopped to tell lengthy stories of her own, describing her own memories of how she learned about a particular child's death while painting the mural.

> One day this police officer came by. And then he started asking me about the mural. We were talking and then he just kind of froze at the sight of one of

the portraits. Then he started telling me all about the boy I had just finished painting, Donald Burroughs.

The cop was working the night Donald was shot. He told me that some guy robbed him, and then shot him, and Donald was laying on the ground bleeding. And this guy said to Donald, "Beg for your life." And Donald Burroughs, who already refused to give him money, refused to beg him for mercy. So the guy shot him two more times, at point blank range. The policeman was saying, that there's a technical term for when a bullet goes from a short distance through someone and right into the ground. And from the ballistics, it was evident that he shot him when he was already lying there bleeding. . . . And the guy who shot Donald knew him, they had grown up together.

We are standing away from the mural now. Barbara is speaking with her hands, creating a visual image of the crime scene for me on the sidewalk. Her breath quickens between words.

So then the policeman starts telling me about his first night on the job. He gets a call over the radio with a report that a man had been shot, in such and such a neighborhood. Well, he finds out later that the man who had been shot was his best friend from childhood. His best friend! Can you imagine? This was the *first* call he got over the radio. So here we are, me and this cop, and we're crying in front of the mural.

As this story demonstrates, the mural becomes an evocative site, not only eliciting memories of the losses depicted on the wall, but of other losses as well.

Barbara shared similar stories for other portraits. During her time painting the FAVT mural, she not only received graphic accounts of the circumstances behind the victims' deaths, but also gained a sense of the families' experiences of trying to cope with the loss. She learned that much of the recovery process is tied in with bringing the perpetrators to justice, an unfortunately all too infrequent occurrence. Both during the painting of the mural and after its completion, Barbara has kept close watch over the various murder investigations and trial proceedings. Most times, Barbara was shocked to learn, the murders remain unsolved. Perhaps worse, the murderer often is found to be a close acquaintance, a friend, and many times, a neighbor. Parents of the perpetrators and the victims often live side by side one another, which set the stage for painful encounters on a regular basis, as Barbara describes:

Imagine living in a community where you have people who are trying to live a more wholesome life, hardworking, have a job, and then living side by side with people who have chosen a different path. And imagine seeing the mother of the person who killed your child, like running into her in the supermarket. And imagine her, the mother of the criminal, making excuses for him, and blaming *you* for putting *her* son on death row!

Through these and other stories, Barbara developed a better sense of the bereavement process, understanding that it is not a linear progression from despair to acceptance, as is often portrayed, but rather a cyclical process, a constant shifting between darkness and light:

> That's another thing I wanted to show in the mural. I had it as night, and then morning, and then night again. So I wanted to represent time passing. And you know, a hope for the future. So I wanted to reflect the pain and the tragedy, but I didn't want to leave it entirely on that note. . . . But I made the sunset not in the middle. Because I wanted to reflect the different emotional states that people go through. That you know, you can have a beautiful morning, but then all of a sudden you're plunged into this darkness. I'm not sure if people will get that. But that's what I'm doing.
>
> And the sunrise, it's meant to be like hope for a tomorrow. I know that sounds like a cliché. But I don't think that the people who have gone through this can really live with their pain, thinking that things are not going to change, and that this is gonna' just keep on going. I think you need to have faith that there's reason to keep on living. You know what I mean? (See figure 8.5.)

Figure 8.5   "Sunrise—hope for a better tomorrow."
Photo by: Jonathan Lohman.

Most often, murals are designed to be viewed from a distance, but Barbara reports that she painted the mural to operate on two levels, viewable both from far away and up close. Barbara painted the landscape to "read" from across the street, while the portraits, painted much smaller, are intended to be viewed from up close. Barbara wanted the mural to literally "draw the audience in," making the viewing of each portrait an intimate experience (see figure 8.5). Barbara also drew upon several classical artistic references for the painting of this narrative scene. She reports that her rendering of the parents kneeling down to hold the head of their slain child was greatly influenced by Michelangelo's Pieta (1499), and the mother's grief-stricken expression, Barbara tells me, was drawn from the anguished contorted expression of the horse in Picasso's 1937 depiction of the Spanish Civil War, "Guernica." Barbara also drew heavily from the narrative style renderings of the French painter Pierre Prud'hon, who often depicted crime scenes with allegorical figures representing virtue and justice. With classical references such as these, drawing more on the works of Michelangelo than from graffiti style, one might assume that the FAVT mural would not be well received by graffiti writers in the neighborhood, yet Barbara reports that this was not the case.

> One day this kid came up to me while I was working on the mural, and told me that it was declared "Top Secret" in the neighborhood. I told him I had no idea what that meant, and he said that it means that nobody better touch that wall. They kind of questioned me at first, but then they saw I was sincere.

The approval among young people in the community of the memorial is further evidenced by the fact that, unlike nearly every other substantial surfaces of the neighborhood's built environment, there is not a single piece of graffiti on the FAVT mural.[4]

But how do the other residents of 50th and Woodland feel about the mural? How is it received by those whose lives have not been personally turned upside down by gun violence? What about those residents who do not have a child on the wall? Visiting with several of the parents one afternoon around the mural, I posed this question to Garnet, who reiterated that he had only received positive reactions among the neighbors. Scanning down the block, he pointed out different families that have left flowers, helped clean up the street in front of the mural, or commented on its beauty: "The couple down the block, they asked me to move my truck at the time, because they wanted to look across and see their loved one," he told me, "they asked me, could I move my truck up, so they could see their boy."

Though Garnet maintained that he and Sandy have heard nothing but positive responses to the mural, I soon found that I needed to look no further than the next door for a dissenting opinion. From the house directly next door to the Spicers, an elderly gentleman walked out to the curb, and began uncovering his Lincoln Town Car, draped in a protective canvas. The sign in the back window read "Ask me about Jesus."

> "What does he think of the mural?" I asked Garnet in a hushed whisper.
> "Him?" He rolled his eyes. "Oh, I don't know . . ."
> "You don't know?"
> "Well, let's just say, you'll have to find that out for your own self," Garnet diverted his eyes from the neighbor, who was wiping down the hood of the Lincoln with a hand cloth.
> "Excuse me, sir," I called to him, "I'm asking folks in the neighborhood about the mural . . ."
> "The mural?" He looked me up and down, then freezes his gaze at my tape recorder. "You don't want to know what I think about it."
> "Actually I do. I'm interested in all types of opinions . . ."
> "Oh, no. You don't want to know what I think about it."
> "You don't like it? You don't want this across the street?"

He shut his trunk, quickly glanced at Garnet and Seneca, and then answered, loud enough for them to hear:

> What do I want to look at dead folks for? Sit up in my house and lookin' at dead people! Why do I want to do that? That's my opinion. Dead people passing 'cross my eyes everyday! In the church everyday I look at dead people. Why I got to look at dead people out my own house?

The neighbor opened up the driver-side door and got in the car. He had already started the engine before Garnet and Seneca could offer a response.

A friend put her hand on Seneca's shoulder, saying, "If that were his son or loved ones over there he'd feel different!"

Garnet stared at the wall, and responded in calm, measured tones, as if he was reading a prepared response to a question to which he had already allotted considerable thought:

> You see sometimes people say things, without thinking before it comes out their mouths. Like, when he says, "Why should I sit here and watch dead folks?" See, these children were not *dead* when . . . these children were among us at the time that these portraits were taken. So it's a portrait of a person that was alive. There's not a dead person on that wall! When they took these pictures, these children were alive! You don't see a dead person over there on that wall.

Garnet is speaking faster now, his argument gaining considerable momentum. Like the many lawyers that he and Sandy have witnessed while accompanying other grieving parents to murder trials, he breaks down the flawed logic of his neighbor's indictment of the mural—

> Sure, they may not be among us any longer, but those children were very much alive. I mean when was the last time you seen a dead person standing up smiling? There's a girl standing there smiling! Jeffrey Rushton, fourth from the left, he's standing there smiling! Now, I never seen a dead person smile before! Now, if the artist went to the morgue, and took a picture of a child laying there on a slab, then you'd have a picture of a dead person. This picture was taken of people that were *alive*.

A Landscape of Loss

Acts of violence not only permanently destroy the social fabric of a neighborhood, but also leave indelible marks on its physical landscape. For the families of the victims, the landscape around them becomes proliferated with sites of tragedy—pervasive reminders of devastating loss, evoking painful and graphic images. At the recent FAVT meeting family members report having to walk past a front porch where their loved one was shot down, or catch the bus across the street from where an argument resulted in their loved one's death. The sister of a young woman, who was murdered and then set on fire, spoke to this:

> And what makes it so bad, (the murderer) lives down the street from my mother's house, so we got to walk past his house every day. Then, we have to catch the El, right across the street from where her body was burned and thrown at. Then, the family of this boy lives down the street. It's like you can't escape it. My sister *knew* the killer. He was her girlfriend's brother. She practically grew up with him.

In sitting with the mothers of young murder victims at the meeting, and hearing them map out their neighborhoods using sites of personal tragedy as their primary landmarks, one can see how these women feel "stalked" and "haunted" by the landscape around them, as Basso (1996) and Stewart (1996) have described.

Understanding this aspect of the daily experience of place for the families of victims sheds light onto Garnet's response to his neighbor who complained about "having to look at dead people" on the FAVT mural. For the neighborhood parents who have lost their children to violence, the landscape is littered with evocative places, triggering devastating images of "what happened" there. They are thus constantly confronted with the faces of "dead people," the faces of their own children. Places trigger memories, sending many of the parents back to the precise moment they received the call, or heard the gunshot, or felt, as many reported, "that cold feeling, when a mother just knows." Time, one of the few things they were told would help them, seems to work against them as well. As soon as a parent "gets past" one significant date, such as her child's birthday, the day he would have graduated, or the day he was killed, she is forced to brace for the next one. Time does not wait for them, the calendar keeps repeating itself, and together with painful visual reminders, creates a landscape of loss, as one mother describes:

> He was shot on a Sunday, at 2:15 in the morning. I was in the bed, and I heard the shot. He fell on *my* porch. When I went outside I called him. And he called back to me and said "Mommy, I'm hit." I'm still feeling it. I re-live Sunday night every night of my life. I *hate* to see Sunday come.

Scholars interested in the notion of landscape have argued that it is a multilayered concept—a complex interweaving of the "physical landscape" of the natural and built environments with the "emotional landscape," the psychological connections to place, attainable only through deeper exploration (Hirsch 1995). The experience of landscape, one's "sense of place," is thus highly individualized, calling upon a depth of personal experiences and memories. To the families of the victims, the experience of the landscape will forever be connected with the tragic losses that these walls have witnessed. The wall on 50th and Woodland was, for them, never "blank" before the painting of the FAVT mural, but rather a space replete with memory and significance.

The memorial, then, could be viewed as a kind of symbolic *reclaiming* of the wall from death. The wall, with portraits that depict the children as their parents most wish to remember them, offers an alternative experience to the persistent images of death which the parents "encounter" daily. It operates, in many ways, not unlike a dream, providing a separate space where parents can once again "visit" their children "face to face." Much as rituals, celebrations, and rites of passage create a "time out of time," the mural, with its dramatic landscape and classical imagery, provides a kind of "place out of place," offering the possibility of a separate, albeit temporary, ontological reality where, as Garnet says, "there's not a dead person on that wall."

Herein lies one of the many paradoxes of the FAVT mural. While to the "outsider" the mural is primarily about *death*, for the victims' families and loved ones the mural is fundamentally about *life*. While the outsider experiences the mural as a memorial to those that *died*, the parents view the mural as a memorial to those that *lived*.

The Dead and the Living

Seneca McClendon stops by the mural on a regular basis. His son, Seneca Jr., is the third portrait from the right. "I come here whenever I can," he tells me. I ask him how visiting the mural helps him in his mourning process:

> I have a son over there. Seneca Jr. It helps me, because I don't have to go to the cemetery to see him. I can come here. Speak to him, talk to him. Face to face. You know? I can come here and speak to him in person! Or call him in person, you know? Speak to his portrait.

Seneca's response highlights one of the more common themes discussed by family members of the victims portrayed in the mural; their preference for visiting their loved one's portrait at the mural over visiting their gravesite. Roxanne Williams, whose son Tyrell is depicted in the memorial, echoed a similar sentiment:

> The mural's just awesome. It made me feel like I don't always have to go to the grave site to visit him. Because, I really don't like to go to there. But we go at least two or three times a year, on his birthday, the anniversary of his death, you know, like holidays. But the wall, I go past it every night, 'cause I go that way to work, and I come past it every morning.

As Roxanne states, she feels compelled to visit Tyrell's grave marker several times a year, most often to mark significant dates in his life. Often during her visits, she will decorate Tyrell's grave marker with various objects—such as balloons, flowers, photographs, and stuffed animals (see figure 8.6). Clearly, however, she prefers to visit Tyrell at the mural, and like many other parents, she decorates his portrait with similar objects as well. Sandy explains that the leaving of objects comprises one of the central year-round activities around the mural:

> It's like they come here as opposed to going to the gravesite. They might just put, you know, like something standard, something small at the grave site if they do go out. But over here, they really do get into it. I mean, they'll be out here all day.

Explorations into African American funerary practices reveal a tradition of not only visiting, but decorating grave markers (see Vlach 1978; Thompson 1983; Haas 1998; and Krepps 1990).[5] In fact, scholarly writings dating back to Melville Herskovits' controversial *Myth of the Negro Past* (1958)

Figure 8.6   Decorated portrait.
Photo by: Jonathan Lohman.

have pointed to African American grave decorations as a poignant example of "African retentions," or as John Vlach (1978: 142) put it, "African antecedents" in the New World.

Investigations into the decoration of grave markers suggest that these alterations, while providing comfort to the loved one's survivors, also reveal deeply felt beliefs regarding the "place" of the dead among the living. Grey Gundaker (1994) describes the practice of physically altering gravesites in the American South, arguing that the alteration of grave markers provides powerful imagery that draws into question notions regarding which types of funerary activities are acceptable and unacceptable:

> Halloween and other grave decorations challenge cemetery rules that attempt to dictate how lively the world of the dead is permitted to be. When families add personal emblems and objects that extend the repertoire of yard decoration to the grave site, they also bring "home" to the deceased family member's space. Seasonal decorations extend this process further, binding the deceased to the annual cycle of living. (1994, 253)

Through this unique form of decoration, the aesthetic is merged with the political in a way that allows for renewed connections with the deceased, while challenging culturally constructed approaches to death. The alteration of grave markers serves not as an element within a Halloween demonstration, but in many ways as the event itself.

> This African American tradition of decorating grave stones and burial mounds, as well as leaving gifts at gravesites, began to decline in the 1920s, largely as a consequence of the movement of many blacks from rural to urban areas. As blacks increasingly moved to urban centers, they were forced to bury their deceased loved ones in professionalized, managed cemeteries. (Hass 1998: 80)

During this period, the process of death was largely moved out of the home and into the hospital setting, and the dead were increasingly laid to rest outside of the urban centers, in suburban cemeteries. Thus, cemeteries increasingly became separate, clearly bounded spaces of the dead, clearly marked from spaces of the living.

Karen Krepps (1990), who explored African American funeral practices in southeastern Michigan, observed that managers of these new cemeteries discouraged visitors from leaving gifts at grave markers in their efforts to maintain a perceived sense of order and uniformity, though often with only limited success. Clashing ideologies regarding the decoration of gravesites became a central point of conflict between newly formed "associations of cemetery managers" and mourning loved ones at the turn of the century, as Kristin Hass states:

> Around the turn of the century, the newly organized associations of funeral directors and cemeterians expressed a good deal of concern about the problem of individuals who wanted elaborate, celebratory monuments erected at the grave sites of loved ones. . . . Cemeteries developed strict regulations and have continued to discourage too much individuation in stone. The cemeterians wanted to streamline their work by requiring clean, uniform grave sites and taking control of the burial out of the hands of the bereaved. (1998: 76)

The declining funerary practice of leaving objects at gravesites, however, appears to correlate with the growing prevalence of left objects at public memorial sites over the last century. One of the most visible and most studied examples of this phenomenon is at the Vietnam Veterans Memorial. Hass (1998: 77–81) draws the often overlooked connection between gift-leaving rituals at the Vietnam Veterans Memorial, and those funerary traditions, "unaffected by Anglo-Protestantism, professionalism, and middle-class aspirations" that have dominated the management of funerary practices since the end of the nineteenth century:

> The impulse to standardize and professionalize the work of burying the dead was not universal. . . . African Americans, Chinese Americans, Mexican Americans, Italian Americans, and Native Americans, among others, have funerary traditions shaped by different cultural needs and forces. These traditions provide an essential part of the vocabulary with which people speak at the Vietnam Veterans Memorial, and they seem, in fact prefigurative of the response to the Wall. Common to all of these traditions and to the offerings at the Wall is the theme of an active, ongoing relationship between the living and the dead. (1998: 77)

Recent attention by scholars has focused on the personal items left at both planned and "spontaneous" memorial sites, such as the recent memorial to Princess Diana and the site of the Oklahoma City Federal Building bombing (see Lacy 1996 and Rosenberg 1999). There are countless, less publicized memorials that become sites for the leaving of object as well. A wall constructed in the wake of the Los Angeles Riots of 1991 quickly became adorned with a myriad variety of personal gifts. Similar walls have been erected in Bedford Stuyvesant, Brooklyn (Hass 1998: 2), New York's Lower East Side (Sciorra 1996), as well as at spontaneously created roadside memorials throughout the United States and abroad (Everett 2000).

Writings offering interpretations of the leaving of gifts at memorials, much like Gundaker's analysis of the decorating of gravesites, tend to

Philadelphia, including accompanying them to murder trial proceedings, helping them to make funeral and burial arrangements, and providing trauma counseling immediately following the murder. Garnet credits the FAVT mural with providing him the opportunity to channel his grief in a positive way, providing comfort to himself through comforting others:

> We have people out here two, three o'clock in the morning. I've come out here to sit with a mother, that might be sitting on a bench crying. I'll come out here, sit down and talk with her, see what I can do. Maybe a cup of coffee, a hug. Sometimes all it takes is a hug just to see that somebody cares.

Most afternoons, Garnet is joined by a group of men—fathers, uncles, and brothers—at the mural. Together they tell stories of their loved ones, and share their theories about "what went wrong," and how they can "take back" their neighborhood.

"We're not asking people to come out and fight no drug lords," Garnet explains. "We're just saying, come out and monitor what your *own* children are doing. If each parent would do that, well, that's the beginnings of a good neighborhood! You see, you can't take a gun out of Johnny's hand, but I bet his dad could."

As Garnet speaks, Seneca silently nods in approval. Though Seneca lives several miles west of 50th, he visits the mural almost daily. I asked him if he was pleased with the way his son's portrait turned out. "Oh yes, very pleased. She did an excellent job. It's so . . ." Seneca paused a moment, searching for the right words, "it's so *life-like*."

The Mother

There is likely no one who has spent more time viewing the FAVT mural than Sandy Spicer. Her's and Garnet's front door is directly across the street from the portrait of their son, Donald. Only Sandy, it seems, can speak in such detail how the mural seems to "glow" when it rains, how the first morning light moves across the faces to the beckoning angel, or how the portraits' stares seem to pierce through the evening darkness:

> I'll come out here late at night, two or three in the morning, and I'll just sit. And I'll look, and I can actually feel the spirits of these kids. I can feel it. I don't feel like they're dead! I can feel them. They wanted to live too, and I'm going to keep them alive.

The desire to "keep them alive" is a repeated motif in conversations with Sandy, and is echoed in conversations with many other parents. On the most basic level, this wish can be interpreted as the desire to keep the *memory* of the victims alive, with their portraits serving as a springboard into a deep ocean of remembered images. Around the mural, the deceased children also are "brought to life" through the sharing of stories, and referenced, much like the living, in daily conversations.

On another level, Sandy's intentions to "keep these kids alive," speaks to her own personal struggles over the fact that she was unable to "save" Donald from his tragic fate. It is not a stretch to suppose that Sandy was talking about herself in narrating the depiction of the grieving mother when she said, "Try as she could, she just couldn't reach the child. She just couldn't reach him, and let him know that this is not the way." Often the parent of a deceased child endures a tremendous amount of guilt, which is compounded when the child is taken by preventable causes, such as a tragic accident, or an act of violence. In these cases, the mother often blames herself, because in her mind she was not able to *protect* the child, thus "failing" to carry out the primary commission of the parent, as Geoffrey Gorer points out in his influential work, *Death, Grief, and Mourning*:

> The most distressing and long-lasting of all griefs, it would seem, is that for the loss of a grown child. In such a case it seems to be literally true, and not a figure of speech, that the parents never get over it. I can only speculate on why this is so. . . . First, it would appear that, at least in a time of peace, it is "against the order of nature" that a child should die before his or her parents; and it seems as though the parents, in some obscure way, interpret this as a punishment for their own shortcomings, a sort of divine retribution. . . . Perhaps a reliance on the orderliness of the universe has been undermined. (1965: 106)

Having been unable to "protect" Donald in life, Sandy now focuses much of her spiritual and emotional energy on trying to somehow keep Donald and the others "alive" in their deaths. Organizing the FAVT mural provides both Sandy and Garnet a certain measure of parental success, while providing a primary motivation to keep moving forward. As Garnet describes:

> Seeing that wall each day gives us the strength to know that we have to go out and continue, and try to fight this endless onslaught of children. You see, when I step out my door and my wife steps out her door and we look over here. . . . It's not only about Donald, anymore. Because *all* these children have become our children. So it gives us inspiration, to just keep on moving forward—to just keep on going.

Keeping Them Alive

"It's real important that people get the message, that families are victims too," Sandy told me during our first visit, "I mean, they're the ones that are left to deal with it. They're the ones whose lives are blown apart." Sandy knows this experience all too well, having endured the loss of three of her own children:

> Well, I have lost two sons myself. In '92 and '93. And I lost a daughter to AIDS in '95. I guess I was always looking at my kids pictures. And at one point I couldn't look at them. And I was trying to think, what could you do to keep these kids alive? Because it's always a thing where these children are slain, and people don't remember, and the families walk around in anguish. And I knew that *I* was feeling a lot of pain, and I wanted to bring awareness. And I thought that maybe, if they had their pictures up there, you know, it's like keeping them living. And they will be alive through the portraits. And, that will give the families a chance to *also* live.

Freud's essay "Mourning and Melancholia" (1917) provides insight into the potential benefits of memorials to the mourning process. According to Freud, while some people are able to endure personal losses, others may crumble under their weight. The latter group Freud termed "melancholic." They are smothered under their grief, which they ultimately generalize so that they are unable to distinguish what has been lost and what endures. In contrast, the non-melancholic mourner does not suffer from overgeneralization, and ultimately is able to experience a measure of closure, and move on from the loss. The melancholic is unable to go through this process, unless there is some mediating element to help isolate the loss, and establish its limits (Winter 1995). The FAVT mural could very well serve as this critical "mediating element" for those closest to the victims.

Drawing from Freud's writings on mourning and monuments, Peter Homans further develops the notion of the monument as a kind of critical "transitional object," for those undergoing the mourning process, allowing them to not only engage in memories of the past, but ultimately free themselves into the present:

> [M]onuments are symbols of separation as well. They not only draw individuals and groups into society and the past; they also free and liberate them from that past, in what seems to be a kind of double action. In doing so they release persons into the present, into what Freud referred to as the "business" and the "hurry" that "modern working conditions demand." In this sense monuments are also a kind of shared transitional object, facilitating a passage

or separation from an imagined lost union with the past, a transition which people are always making together. (1989: 277–278)[7]

Sandy reports many instances when the mural has served as an important transitional ground for parents to begin the mourning process. A telling example was her story about "the woman who lives across the street":

> Let me tell you about the woman who lives across the street. Now this is a woman whose son got killed so long ago. And she told me that she could never cry before. She could never show no emotions, 'cause her feelings were locked up on the inside. But let me tell you, at that dedication, she was crying her eyes out. And she said that's the first time she's felt relieved in a long time. And she came out, and she put that (wreath) up there, and I felt good because I knew, that she's not keeping it all bottled up anymore. She's able to release some of that. To me that's rewarding to see.

The participatory process of creating a memorial mural—from its creative conception, physical construction, to its public dedication, can help bring a measure of closure to the grieving community, helping them to proceed with the mourning process. Both psychoanalytic psychologists such as Homans (1989: 277), and social historians such as Kenneth Foote (1997: 80) suggest that the completion of a memorial can signal, in a sense, that the worst stage of grieving is complete, and the long road of the healing process has begun. I suggested this theory to Sandy, and while she agreed that the mural helps the grieving families move on, she takes exception with the notion of "closure":

> I don't believe in closure. That's the one thing that I'm tired of hearing from people. There is no closure. Because you have people that have died, hundred of years, and they're still remembered by their loved ones. How can you bring closure to love? Love is everlasting. And it's forever. And that's what people have to know.

The mural, then, operates as a kind of paradox, facilitating closure while at the same time stubbornly resisting it.

The Mural as Paradox

Several weeks after the dedication, Barbara walked me through the mural. We stopped at its far left side, near the words "Families Are Victims Too." Behind the letters, Barbara had painted the marble columns so that they appear to gradually fade off into the mural's landscape. "I tried my best," Barbara told me, "to suggest that there are many others. That these victims are not the only ones." Barbara communicated this tragic fact deftly. The mural gives the viewer the sense that the killings, like the columns, delve deeply into the neighborhood's past, and likely will extend out into its future. The unusual dimensions of the wall itself—its unusually short height and expansive length—strongly imply a linear, temporal quality. This expansive quality of the mural is perhaps its greatest source of beauty. Herein also dwells its fundamental paradox, in which, the mural derives much of its heightened emotional force.

The mural is at once beautiful and horrible. When viewing the mural, one can't help but be touched by its beauty, and awed by its expansiveness. At the same time, the viewer is keenly aware that this sense of expansiveness represents a seemingly endless trail of suffering. Unlike, for example, most of our nation's war memorials, the FAVT mural resists closure. Even the Vietnam Veterans Memorial, which reserved room among its list of names for future entries, memorializes a tragedy that has, if not always in the minds of its participants, come to an end. However, as in many urban neighborhoods throughout the country, the scourge of gun violence on the streets of southwest Philadelphia rages on.

Therefore, the FAVT mural operates more similarly to the San Francisco NAMES Quilt, memorializing victims of AIDS. Like the FAVT mural, the NAMES quilt thrusts its viewer into its wrenching paradox, prompting *Village Voice* journalist Jeff Weinstein to ask, "How could you be profoundly affected by this work, by this undeniably beautiful work, and, at that same time, hope it would simply stop, vanish—or wish it had never existed at all?" (1989: 46).

Coda

In my most recent visit to the mural, the street was quiet. It was early evening, so no shouts could be heard from the nearby schoolyard. A light rain had begun to fall, and the block was free of its usual activity. The only action on the corner was the slow idling of a SEPTA bus. Peering up the block, I spotted the boarded up building, which Sandy hopes will one day be the bustling headquarters for FAVT, and the vacant lot where Garnet hopes to build a playground. I wondered what the future might hold for this neighborhood, 20, 30, 50 years from now. Will the current trend of drugs and violence continue, leading more residents to leave the neighborhood? Will yet more buildings become abandoned, decrepit, and torn down? Or will it one day return to the neighborhood that the elders remember—a place where people closely looked out for one another, where kids could be expected to reach adulthood, and where, as Roxanne remembers, "you can leave your doors open?"

What will future generations remember about this neighborhood? And what will they make of this mural? For the mural is intended to reach not only those who pass by it today, but also the audiences of the future, who exist for now only in its architects' dreams and imaginations. The mural is a kind of message sent out to those who will walk these streets long after Sandy, Garnet, Barbara, and their neighbors are gone.

For as we have seen, the painting of a mural is more than an "installation" of art *into* the landscape, but rather a fundamental modification *of* the landscape. And, as material culture scholars have repeatedly asserted, cultures have traditionally modified and altered their physical landscapes not simply to "leave a mark," but to reach across the boundaries of time. Changes to our physical landscape allow us to communicate with those that will come after us, as Kenneth Foote states:

> This concept of memory provides an important bond between culture and landscape, because human modifications of the environment are often related to the way societies wish to sustain and efface memories. More to the point, the very durability of the landscape makes these modifications effective for symbolizing and sustaining collective values over long periods of time. Landscape might be seen in this light as a sort of communicational resource, a system of signs and symbols, capable of extending the temporal and spatial range of communication. (1997: 33)

It has been widely stated that the study of a work of art is ultimately a study of the intentions of its creators. Henry Glassie, in his groundbreaking writings on material culture, has expanded this notion to shed light on the way the study of art provides powerful insights into the values of its "users" as well (Glassie 1999: 143). In the case of a mural, where notions of art, architecture, and landscape converge, and where the audience participates in the work's creation in ways unparalleled in other forms of public art, we are able to grasp a glimpse of what could be called the "collective memory" of a neighborhood (see Lacy 1996). The FAVT mural stands as evidence of a collaborative process in which artist and audience work together to present an image replete with narrative significance, telling a story that they want the rest of us to remember; because it is one they can never forget.

But what will be remembered, and what will be forgotten? Will the stories of these young men continue to be told? Years from now, when the school children who pass the mural no longer say, "I know him!" when

Sandy and Garnet, and the other parents pass on or move away, will anyone know anything about these young men, as I have come to over the last several years?

In attempting to answer the question of the mural's future meaning, we gain great insight by turning to the work of social historian Jay Winter (1995), who explores the social and political significance of memorials erected throughout Europe after the Great War. Winter observed that historical studies into the significance of war memorials focus erroneously on political and aesthetic concerns, rather on their initial intended purpose—to aid in the bereavement process of the fallen soldiers' loved ones. This oversight, he argues, is in part due to the gradual transformations of meanings attributed to the memorials over time—what he calls their "half-life."

> Once the moment of initial bereavement had passed, once the widows had remarried, once the orphans had grown up and moved away, once the mission of veterans to ensure that the scourge of war would not return had faded and collapsed, then the meaning of war memorials was bound to change. They could have no fixed meaning, immutable over time. Like many other public objects, they manifest what physicists, in an entirely different context, call a "half-life," a trajectory of decomposition, a passage from the active to the inert. Their initial charge was related to the needs of a huge population of bereaved people. Their grief was expressed in many ways, but in time, for the majority, the wounds began to close, and life went on. When that happened, after years or decades, then the objects invested with meaning related to loss of life in wartime become something else. Other meanings derived from other needs or events may be attached to them, or no meaning at all. The public experience of fete and civic ritual has also tended to fade away, so that now, seventy-five years after the Armistice, war memorials have become the artifacts of a vanished age, remnants of the unlucky generation that had to endure the carnage of the Great War. (1995: 98)

While he does not state it explicitly, Winter's example reveals the ways in which a memorial transforms over time from a site of *memory* production, to a site of *history* production. Over time, the audience's connection to those memorialized becomes more distant, more abstract. For now, the kids who pass the wall on their way to school see the faces of playmates, of camp counselors—faces of people they knew as living. One day, these victims will only exist to the passing children as faces on the wall—as cautionary reminders of what can happen in "the street," and of the fragility of life in the inner city. Perhaps they will be told some of the stories, with motifs they might find all too familiar—tales of "being in the wrong place at the wrong time," or of "going down the wrong path." The transition from memory to history is by no means a seamless one. At any given time this process is influenced by intermediaries guided, and limited, by their own perceptions and agendas.

So, what will be known of these children, when future audiences view the mural? Will they view these children not unlike the "unlucky genera-tion" lost to the Great War? What will be known about the circumstances of their lives and the tragedies of their deaths? Perhaps, one day, the experience of the FAVT mural will not so much center on what is known or unknown about these children, but on understanding something about those who loved them. In the future, viewers might better understand that with each young life lost in the war-zone that had become much of urban America at the turn of the millennium, an entire community was left grieving in its wake. And perhaps, over time, these memorials will wield their greatest force through their evocative qualities—we will respond to the mural by referencing our own losses, to the memorials housed deep in our memories. In this way, the mural might help others "keep on living," as well.

Or maybe, the mural won't be there at all. The wall, only several years old, has begun to show cracks in alarming numbers, scarring its rolling landscape, and obscuring some of the names. A white substance has foamed up from the cracks, hardening at the surface. The wall is literally leaking.

The average life span of a mural is about 25 years, though they can be maintained to last much longer. The very temporality of murals further engage their audiences—their continued survival, in large part, hinges on their continued relevance. Standing before the mural, I put my finger to its cracks. I felt the hardened airy white rock that has oozed from inside the wall, like lava that had cooled after bubbling up from restless heated ground.

"Kind of like it's crying," Sandy says, startling me.

As was often the case in my visits to the mural, Sandy spotted me from her window across the street. She had brought out some photographs to show me, of the visit to the memorial by the Mayor, the birthday celebra-tion for Shantia, the lone girl on the wall, and a film crew from a local news station. The bustling excitement shown in the color photographs was in stark contrast to the emptiness of the street, as we sat alone on the bench across from the mural. She put the pictures down, and for one of the few times I had visited Sandy, she went a long time without speaking. After a while, she directed my attention to the portrait directly in front of us, one of the few portraits she hadn't narrated to me before, and spoke softly:

That was my son. Donald. My husband says that's the same look he had on his face when he was slain. Donald had gotten his papers for photography. And he was darn good, by the way. And because he had a criminal record, he couldn't get a good job. Now, I'm not saying that to make any excuses. I tried to encourage him to hold on. I said just hold on, your time will come. But, he went out and he robbed a drug dealer. And I think one of the main reasons is, Donald was on drugs at one time . . . And I told him, "If you love me, you'll come off of them." So that's when he came off them and decided to get his life together.

So I guess because he had no respect for the drug dealers, he wanted to rob them as opposed to someone else. . . .

Well, the guy ran him down. And when this guy ran him down, he didn't have nowhere to go. So, he was lying on his back, from what I was told. And he was looking up at the perpetrator. And then the guy just shot him in the head. And the guy didn't do a day.

But I felt sorry for his mother, though. The other boy's mother. I felt sorry for her because, you know, I imagine that as horrendous as it is for a mother's child to be taken, it's also got to be for a mother to be put into a position that her child was someone who took another person's life. Because you'd rather see your child become a lawyer or a doctor, someone who gives something back to society. I felt sorry for her. And I don't hold her responsible.

All she did was bring a child into this world.

Notes

1. Under the tireless direction on Jane Golden, the Mural Arts Program (MAP) has painted over two thousand murals throughout the city of Philadelphia. MAP muralists collaborate with neighborhood residents on the conception and design of each mural. For more information on the Philadelphia Mural Arts Program, see Golden, Jane, Robin Rice, and Monica Yant Kinney, 2004. Philadelphia Murals and the Stories They Tell. Philadelphia: Temple University Press, or visit their website at www.muralarts.org

2. As Anderson describes, many young people assume that the murder of one of their peers must have resulted from a street oriented life, involving drug related activity, in part to "make sense" of the untimely death:

> The younger people take it especially hard. They wonder aloud why this happened, but in fact they know why. They know the boy was a drug dealer. They know that he violated in some way the code of the street and possibly messed up someone's money. "He did somebody wrong," or he "thought he was slick." It was something. Otherwise, the youth's death simply makes no sense. (1999: 139)

3. The term "art worlds" is credited to sociologist Howard Backer, whose systematic analysis of the social networks contributing to the production, identification, and consumption of "art," published in 1982, remains the most ambitious work on the topic to date. In Art Worlds, Becker contends that audiences "are among the most fleeting participants in art worlds," and that their contributions begin

once the artistic creative process is completed. This is clearly not the case with MAP's collaborative creative process or with muralism more generally.

4. Tags, the most pervasive form of graffiti in Philadelphia, are quickly drawn signatures, rendered in markers or spray paint. Most taggers use a pseudonym or nickname as their tag, in part to protect them from law enforcement. Taggers will spray their tags in multiple settings, in an attempt to make their tags as visible and recongnizable as possible. Though these tags might appear randomly applied to the outsider, within the culture there are widely recognized conventions regarding their appropriate placement. Churches and private homes, for example, are generally off limits, while school buildings, recreation centers, and vacant buildings appear to be fair game. Respect is most gained through tagging highly visible sites considered the most "cohallenging," such as highway overpasses. For an in depth exploration into this sub-genre of graffiti see Prigoff, 1987, and for a focus on tagging in West Philadelphia see Drew, 1995.

5. A repeated theme in these studies is the connection between the decoration of grave markers by blacks, particularly in the American South, and African cultural practices, as Robert Farris Thompson states:

> Nowhere is Kongo-Angola influence on the New World more pronounced, more profound, than in black traditional cemeteries throughout the South of the United States. The nature of the objects that decorate the graves there, as well as in places as diverse as Haiti and Guadeloupe in the West Indies, reveals a strong continuity. That continuity might be characterized as a reinstatement of the Kongo notion of the tomb as a charm for the persistence of the spirit. (1983: 132)

6. Kristin Hass's recent work, *Carried to the Wall*, for example, views the leaving of at the Vietnam Memorial largely in political terms.

> I see the gifts Americans bring to the Wall as part of a continuing public negotiation about patriotism and nationalism. These gifts forge a new mode of public commemoration and suggests that ordinary Americans deeply crave a memory, or a thousand memories together, that speaks to ways in which this war disrupted their sense of American culture and their place in it. (1998: 3)

7. Here, Homan seems to use the terms "monument" and "memorial" interchangeably. Some scholars draw distinctions between the two. Danto, for example, believes that there are subtle differences, stating "we build monuments so we will always remember, and we build memorials so we will never forget" (in Haas 1998: 48).

Bibliography

Anderson, Elijah. 1999. *A Code of the Street*. NY: W.W. Norton Press.
Basso, Keith H. 1996. "Wisdom Sits in High Places: Notes on a Western Apache Landscape" in *Senses of Place*, ed. Steven Feld and Keith Basso. Santa Fe: School of American Research Press.

Becker, Howard. 1982. *Art Worlds.* Berkeley: University of California Press.

Drew, Robert S. 1995. "Graffiti as Public and Private Art" in *On the Margins of Art Worlds,* ed. Larry Gross. Boulder: Westview Press.

Everett, Holly. 2000. "Roadside Crosses and Memorial Complexes in Texas." *Folklore,* 111 (1): 91–118.

Foote, Kenneth E. 1997. *Shadowed Ground: America's Landscapes of Violence and Tragedy.* Austin: University of Texas Press.

Freud, Sigmund. 1917. "Mourning and Melancholia." *Standard Edition.* 14: 243–260. London: Horgarth Press, 1957.

Glassie, Henry. 1999. *Material Culture.* Bloomington: Indiana University Press.

Gorer, Geoffrey. 1965. *Death, Grief, and Mourning in Contemporary Britain.* London: Cresset Press.

Gundaker, Grey. 1994. "Halloween Imagery in Two Southern Settings" in *Halloween and Other Festivals of Death and Life,* ed. Jack Santino. Knoxville: University of Tennessee Press.

Hass, Kristin Ann. 1998. *Carried to the Wall: American Memory and the Vietnam Veterans Memorial.* Berkeley: University of California Press.

Herskovits, Melville J. 1958. *The Myth of the Negro Past.* Boston: Beacon Press.

Hirsch, Eric. 1995. "Landscape: Between Place and Space" in *The Anthropology of Landscape: Perspectives on Place and Space,* ed. Eric Hirsch and Michael O' Hanlon. Oxford: Clarendon Press.

Homans, Peter. 1989. *The Ability to Mourn: Disillusionment and the Social Origins of Psychoanalysis.* Chicago: The University of Chicago Press.

———. 2002. "Introduction" in *Symbolic Loss.* Charlottesville: University of Virginia Press.

Ignatowski, Clare A. 1996. "Graffiti Murals: The Appropriation of Geographic and Idelogical Space in a Neighborhood." Paper delivered at the Ethnography in Education Forum, Center for Urban Ethnography, University of Pennsylvania.

Krepps, Karen. 1990. "Black Mortuary Practices in Southeast Michigan." Ph.D. dissertation, Wayne State University.

Lacy, Suzanne. 1993. "Fractured Space" in *Art in the Public Interest,* ed. Arlene Raven. New York: Da Capo Press.

———. 1996. "Love, Cancer, Memory: A Few Stories." *Public Art Review,* 7 (2): 5–13.

Lee, Anthony W. 1999. *Painting on the Left: Diego Rivera, Radical Politics, and San Francisco's Public Murals.* Berkeley: University of California Press.

Lippard, Lucy. 1990. *Mixed Blessing: New Art in a Multicultural America.* New York: Pantheon Books.

———. 1997. *The Lure of the Local: Sences of Place in a Multicentered Society.* New York: The New Press.

———. 1998. "Forward" in *Toward a People's Art: The Contemporary Mural Movement,* ed. Eva Crockcroft, John Weber, and James Cockcroft. Albuquerque: University of New Mexico Press.

Prigoff, James. 1987. Spraycan Art. New York: Thames and Hudson Press.

Rosenberg, Jan. 1999. " 'It's Something To Hold On To': The Murrah Building Memorial Fence." Paper presented at the Annual Meeting of the American Folklore Society, Memphis.

Sciorra, Joseph Umberto. 1996. *Space into Place: Public life, Material Culture, and the Building of Community in New York City*. Philadelphia: University of Pennsylvania Dissertation.

Stewart, Kathleen C. 1996. "An Occupied Place" in *Senses of Place*, ed. Steven Feld and Keith Basso. Santa Fe: School of American Research Press.

Thompson, Robert Farris. 1983. *Flash of the Spirit: African and Afro-American Art and Philosophy*. New York: Random House.

Vlach, John Michael. 1978. *The Afro-American Tradition in Decorative Arts*. Cleveland: Cleveland Museum of Art.

Weinstein, Jeff. 1989. "Names Carried into the Future: An AIDS Quilt Unfolds" in *Art in the Public Interest*, ed. Arlene Raven. Ann Arbor: UMI Research Press.

Winter, Jay 1995. Sites on Memory, Sites of Mourning: The Great War in European Cultural History. Cambridge: Cambridge: Cambridge University Press.

Chapter 9

Twelve Aggie Angels: Content Analysis of the Spontaneous Shrines Following the 1999 Bonfire Collapse at Texas A&M University

Sylvia Grider

Introduction

Spontaneous shrines are not generic; each shrine is unique because each disaster and the individuals who died in it are unique (Santino 1992; 2001). In addition to the ubiquitous flowers and candles, the artifacts of which each shrine is comprised are manifestations of this individuality. For example, the shrine at NASA headquarters following the explosion of the *Columbia* space shuttle featured Israeli flags because one of the astronauts was the first Israeli in space. The preponderance of helium-filled balloons in the NASA shrine metaphorically represented flight, reaching toward the heavens. The shrines in London and elsewhere after the death of Princess Diana were filled with photographs of the princess and depictions of the Queen of Hearts playing card. In recognition of her work with the world's children, the shrines for Diana also contained an extraordinary number of teddy bears and other plush children's toys. Many of the shrines in New York City following the 9/11 attacks on the World Trade Center contained photographs, models, and other artworks depicting the Twin Towers. A large percentage of the artifacts left at the distinctive campus shrines following the fatal collapse of the Texas A&M University spirit bonfire were clearly related to that institution specifically.

Careful content analysis of the artifacts which comprise a spontaneous shrine can reveal previously overlooked information regarding the donors of artifacts and how they use these artifacts to express themselves and their attitudes as they "commune with the dead."

Background and Context

Tradition is the heart of student life at Texas A&M University. Founded by the state of Texas in 1876 as an all-male, land-grant, military institution of higher learning, through the decades the students of Texas A&M University (known as Aggies) have maintained an unusually strong sense of heritage and group identity. The Corps of Cadets, in continuous existence since the school was founded but no longer compulsory, is the primary custodian of "The Spirit of Aggieland" (Adams 2001).

The various traditions that are unique to A&M are known as "good bull" (Hoyle 1990). Some of these traditions have flourished and then faded, according to societal norms and attitudes, although the conservative nature of the university enables some traditions to outlive their original raison d'etre. Of course, as is to be expected over a 125-year span, other traditions no longer exist. One of the most enduring of all campus traditions has been building a bonfire (signifying "the burning desire to beat the hell outta t.u."[1]) to be lit before the annual football game against archrival University of Texas. With few exceptions throughout the decades, this is the last game of the regular season for both teams and is played Thanksgiving weekend (Forsyth 1981; Jacobs 2002).

By the 1970s, building "Bonfire"[2] had become the student focus of the fall semester, involving thousands and thousands of student-hours of labor as well as expensive equipment and supplies donated by businesses throughout the state, which regarded themselves as loyal partners in the Aggie network. Perhaps the most distinctive feature of the bonfire tradition was the student control and leadership, commonly known at A&M as "the other education." A complex student hierarchy emerged in order to provide leadership and continuity in building Bonfire from year to year. However, technical instructions on how to build Bonfire usually were passed down by oral tradition from one generation of "pots" to the next rather than depending on strict or professionally approved written guidelines or plans. ("Pot" refers to the color-coded military helmets the students wore while working on Bonfire, many of which were ceremonially passed down to the following year's student leaders.) As the size of Bonfire exceeded the local wood supply, students cut trees at off-campus sites ("cut") and hauled them back to campus on trucks to build Bonfire ("stack"). In order to complete Bonfire in time for the lighting ceremony, for the last week or so work continued around the clock ("push"). The complex and secretive traditions surrounding Bonfire ultimately led to subtle and cumulative structural changes over the years, not all of which were safe or appropriate (*Final Report* 2000; Petroski 2000).

Despite the potential hazards, in true Texas style students over the years built their bonfires taller and taller until the university attempted to regulate the height to 55 feet and 45 feet diameter at the base, although these regulations were generally disregarded by the student builders. The tallest bonfire reached 109 feet in 1969. The shape of Bonfire changed over time from a chaotic pile of trash into a teepee stabilized by a center pole. By the 1970s, the shape of Bonfire developed further into an iconic, ziggurat-like, stepped cone resembling a wedding cake with six "stacks" and topped by an orange outhouse symbolizing a University of Texas fraternity house. Some say that the outhouse is also a reference to the early years of the tradition when students allegedly stole outhouses from throughout the community and piled them on the fire as well. Most recently, a large flag and an *Austin City Limits* sign with the year of the sophomore class painted on it have been added to the stack (Tang 2000: 10). The burning stack has become the symbol of Aggie spirit (see figure 9.1).

What would have been the 90th annual Aggie Bonfire collapsed in the predawn hours of November 18, 1999, killing twelve student workers (one of whom was a former student) and injuring 27 others (*Final Report* 2000). The A&M Emergency Care Team members who are always on standby at the site immediately began triage of the injured students and put in emergency calls to start the massive rescue operation. Frantic and shocked students were stunned by how unexpectedly and suddenly the stack fell. At 2:45 a.m., only minutes after the collapse, the College Station Fire Station dispatched its first emergency vehicles to the campus. Almost simultaneously other local emergency units began converging on the scene. The massive size of the tangle of approximately 5,000 logs (estimated to weigh 2 million pounds) ensnaring the dead, dying, and injured required a huge rescue and recovery effort ("Report on the Rescue and Recovery . . ." 2000).

Professional engineers were brought in to supervise the precision-moving of the logs with large cranes in order to safely reach students still trapped in the stack without causing the tangled logs to shift. A temporary morgue was set up in a large tent near the collapsed stack to facilitate the identification of dead students. Ambulances and emergency vehicles from throughout the area transported the dead and injured to funeral homes and

Figure 9.1   Aggie Bonfire.
Source: University Relations, Texas A&M University.

hospitals. Injured students who were rescued from the tangle of logs or who had been thrown clear were triaged, and within the first hour of rescue operations 23 of these students had been transported to two local hospitals; five students who remained trapped inside the pile of logs were classified as critical ("Report on the Rescue and Recovery . . ." 2000).

By almost midnight, ten hours after the collapse, the final victim was freed from the stack and removed to the morgue ("Report on the Rescue and Recovery . . ." 2000). Students maintained a vigil throughout the recovery operations and refused to leave the site until the last Aggie had been pulled from the collapsed stack. They maintained their vigil even during the community-wide memorial observance in Reed Arena earlier that evening attended by an estimated 14,000 people. Local TV and radio stations issued requests for blankets and sweaters for these students, many of whom refused to leave long enough to go home and get warm clothing. The Aggie sentiment was that as long as one of their own was trapped in the stack, they were staying too. When the last body was pulled from the stack, a total of eleven students had died in the accident and others barely clung to life in the surgeries and intensive care units of local hospitals.

On November 19, at 2:25 a.m. (nearly 24 hours to the minute after the collapse) the stack had been completely dismantled and the Emergency Operations Center closed ("Report on the Rescue . . .", 2000). At 8:00 p.m. that night, the twelfth victim of the accident, Tim Kerlee, died in a local hospital (Kerlee 2000).

The Spontaneous Shrines Following the Bonfire Collapse

Although it is not possible at this point to determine who brought the first grief offering to the bonfire site, by mid-morning on November 18, 1999, students had begun to bring flowers and other mementos—especially Aggie-related items—to the site in memory of the students who died and were injured. At first these offerings were laid on various logs scattered throughout the perimeter of the area where the EMTs and engineers were working. After all the dead and injured students had been removed from the stack, officials erected an orange plastic security fence around the site and it became the primary armature on which people hung their mementos. For a time people stretched over the security fence in order to lay their offerings on the logs within reach. Others laid their mementos on the ground in front of the fence and some of these assemblages[3] began to spill outward for several feet. In appearance, the A&M bonfire shrine at first echoed the one that developed on the security fence surrounding the Oklahoma City bombing site (Linenthal 2001).

Smaller spontaneous shrines on the Texas A&M campus also developed at the base of the Administration Building flagpole, the base of the statue of Lawrence Sullivan "Sully" Ross west of the Academic Building, and in the Flag Room of the Memorial Student Center (MSC) and elsewhere on campus. Large floral arrangements were lined up and down the halls of the MSC when the Flag Room became overcrowded. The fence at the bonfire site was the largest, most complex, and most frequently visited shrine.

The bonfire shrines attracted visitors from throughout the country during the month that they remained in place on campus. Various groups and individuals in the university community expressed concern over what would happen to the growing accumulation of artifacts. A great many people on their own initiative photographed the shrines, and media reporters not only wrote features about the shrines but also used them as backdrops for interviews and other reports. Clearly the shrines became the emotional core of the public response to the accident, making it essential that the artifacts be collected and preserved. The Bonfire Memorabilia Project was the university's response to this deeply felt need. This project, under the direction of Dr. Sylvia Grider (this author), Principal Investigator and Ms. Patricia Clabaugh, Collections Manager, Department of Anthropology, to date has cataloged and inventoried over 4,000 artifacts from the bonfire shrines, and the project files contain well over 3,000 photographs of the shrine in situ and the collection process, as well as digital photographs of selected artifacts for documentary purposes.

The Bonfire Shrine Artifacts

All of the artifacts from the Bonfire shrines were systematically collected by adapting the methodology for salvage archaeology of gridding the area to create "lots" for reference and then tagging and inventorying every artifact within each grid with a unique number (Grider 2000). The collected artifacts were then categorized, using a special Artifact Type Form, based on the over 4,000 artifacts and over 3,000 photographs which comprise the collection rather than use the AASLH system, which was too broad for our purposes (Chenhall 1989). As analysis proceeds, this categorization system is continually modified and refined. At present, the Artifact Type Form is comprised of seven basic categories (each of which is further subdivided as appropriate): Paper, Cloth, Figurines and Dolls, Religious Tokens, Miscellaneous, Special, and Photographic Media. Each artifact within each category is assigned a unique, coded number. All information about each artifact is entered into a digital database.[4]

Through this artifact type classification system, we established that there were at least three distinct groups of artifact donors: Aggies, children, and Christians.

Aggies

The "Aggie Family" extends far beyond students and former students. Members of the community who did not attend the university nevertheless regard themselves as loyal Aggies, and they attend university sports events and other activities with as much and sometimes more enthusiasm than those directly associated with the university. The university also has wide public support throughout the state, where the university as a whole but especially the Corps of Cadets is a source of pride for most Texans.

This pride and loyalty toward the university is evident in the artifacts left at the bonfire shrines. The presence of so much Aggie memorabilia is a manifestation of what William Bascom calls the "validation of culture," one of the four basic functions of folklore (Bascom 1954). By bringing Aggie memorabilia to the bonfire site and leaving it in the shrine, people were expressing not only their own self-identification as part of the Aggie Family, but also their grief toward the loss of twelve young members of that metaphoric and extended family. Merchandising of Aggie logos is big business, so there are literally hundreds and hundreds of commercially produced items available featuring Aggie logos and the school colors, maroon and white. This merchandise ranges from conventional souvenir items such as coffee mugs and t-shirts to stuffed animals (especially Reville, the school's collie mascot), athletic gear, wrapping paper, baby clothes, and even food and flowers such as specially developed maroon carrots and maroon bluebonnets.

Perhaps the most distinctively Aggie items are "Twelfth Man Towels," which students wave during football games. These white hand towels, on which "Twelfth Man" is printed, refer to an incident during a 1922 Aggie football game when the coach called a student from the stands to suit up because so many players were injured. Although that student did not play in the game, he became known as the "Twelfth Man" and today the entire student body stands in his honor throughout football games, signaling their willingness to go onto the field and play if necessary. Since 12 students were killed in the bonfire accident, these Twelfth Man towels were very common offerings at the shrine. Many students wrote their personal sentiments, poetry, and scripture on the towels before putting them in the shrine. At least 160 of these towels are archived in the collection.

Because 12 students died, there were also a great many assemblages of 12 items, such as 12 maroon carnations or 12 sets of maroon and white ribbon loops. In the days immediately following the accident, local merchants reported that they sold out completely of certain items, including maroon and white ribbons as well as candles. Other Aggie merchandise also experienced a sharp rise in sales at this time. Of course much of this newly purchased merchandise ended up in the shrine.

People also fashioned artworks based on Aggie themes and brought them to the shrine. Especially common were miniature bonfires made of wooden dowels, candles, cardboard cylinders, and cinnamon sticks. The iconic image of the bonfire was included in many drawings and posters, both hand drawn and computer generated.

Other more esoteric bonfire-related items were also common among the memorabilia. For example, over the years students developed the tradition of wearing the same clothes, called "grodes," while working on the bonfire. As the bonfire burned each year, the graduating seniors threw their grodes into the flames. At the shrine, carefully folded and laid at the base of the fence, were several complete sets of grodes, including the students' boots and pots. One assumption is that these sets of grodes belonged to students who would have thrown them into the flames, if the 1999 bonfire had burned instead of tragically collapsing. Hundreds of students placed their pots at the shrine. Students also left many tools that they had used in the construction of the bonfire—axes, axe handles, and wire cutters.

Perhaps the most cherished possession of an Aggie is the class ring, known in Aggieland simply as "The Ring." These class rings are expensive; plain rings cost as much as $600 and the price goes up considerably if the ring is set with diamonds. In addition to the primary shrine surrounding the bonfire site, another impressive shrine developed at the flagpole in front of the Administration Building. Students began leaving their class rings on the elevated base of the flagpole, some adding notes to the effect that since the students who were killed would never get their own class rings, these would serve them instead. There is no record of exactly how many rings were left at the flagpole; estimates are as many as 50. About 30 of these rings were finally picked up by one of the student leaders and delivered to the Former Students Association, which eventually returned the rings to their owners. One other ring was recovered from the main shrine at the bonfire site during the collection process. The owner's name had been filed away so that it could not be identified. This anonymous ring is now part of the Bonfire Memorabilia collection. For an Aggie, there is no greater gesture, no more emphatic validation of culture, than the offering of these class rings to their fallen classmates.

These Aggie items are unique to the bonfire shrine and clearly demonstrate the point that each shrine is carefully constructed to identify the people who died but also those who came to mourn them.

Children

Local children are introduced to the Aggies and to Bonfire when they are quite young and many retain that attachment to the university all their lives. Children regularly attend football games and basketball games wearing miniature Aggie regalia. The yell leaders visit local elementary schools before football games and teach some of the school yells to the children. Many families have sent four generations to study at A&M. So it is not unusual, but rather expected, that much of the memorabilia left at the bonfire shrine was from children.

Many parents brought their children to the bonfire site to help them understand the magnitude of the accident and also to discuss death. Throughout the time that the shrine was in place, one could see parents with their young children solemnly walking along the memorabilia-covered fence, stopping periodically to look at certain items or to kneel and pray. Some parents later reported that their children asked to be taken home so that they could get their favorite toys and bring them back to put in the shrine. We cannot be sure, however, that all of the toys left at the shrine were left by children. Teddy bears are quite common in other spontaneous shrines, such as at Oklahoma City, where 19 children in an on-site day care center died in the blast. Why the teddy bear is the plush toy of choice in spontaneous shrines is an open topic for debate among scholars. However, plush collie toys with maroon vests representing the A&M mascot, Reveille, are certainly unique to the bonfire shrine.

Children at local elementary schools also made colorful posters that were brought to the shrine and hung on the fence. In these posters, children expressed their sorrow at the pain and suffering of the Aggies and also sent get-well wishes to the Aggies who were injured. Drawings of a burning bonfire predominated in these posters. Other shrine collections also contain a large number of children's contributions. The children's drawings in Oklahoma City following the bombing were so beautiful and moving that many were published in two books and are also featured on special postcards on sale at the Oklahoma City National Memorial gift shop (Jones 1997; Ross and Myers 1996). In their foreword to *Dear Oklahoma City, Get Well Soon*, Ross and Myers speak for all children caught up in the aftermath of violence, ". . . throughout this tragedy the voices of America's children were all but lost in the torrent of dramatic stories and images saturating the news. Yet their reactions, expressed in both writing and art, cut straight to the heart of the disaster's impact on all of us." Children also responded to the 9/11 attacks on the World Trade Center by drawing very expressive posters, some of which depicted people falling from the burning towers.

In lieu of books of condolence, such as those for Princess Diana (Jones 1999) large sheets of plyboard were set up at the bonfire site for people to sign. After these boards were dismantled and brought into the lab for processing, we discovered that many children had signed their names along the bottoms of the boards, which were low enough for them to reach. The childish writing is poignant; children wrote not only their names but also tried to express their feelings of sorrow for the dead Aggies. Parents apparently let their children write anything they wanted to. Some of the children's writing at the bottom of the boards are the unintelligible scrawls of the very young who cannot write yet but nevertheless wanted to be part of the activity at the bonfire shrine.

Christians

Contemporary Christian religious artifacts are a generally untapped source of cultural information. For example, the author of *Material Christianity: Religion and Popular Culture in America* wonders "why so little attention is paid . . . to the material manifestation of [contemporary Christian] religion. The artifacts of religious belief and practice exist as a compelling category of evidence, long overdue for informed historical and cultural analysis" (McDannell 1995: 4). Researchers generally have paid closer attention to religious and ritual artifacts from non-Western cultures than to the paraphernalia of modern Christianity as a category of material culture. A preliminary survey of the bonfire memorabilia clearly demonstrates the Christian worldview of many of those who visited the shrine.

The religious artifact assemblage set a reverential tone for the bonfire shrines. The shrine landscape was dominated by two large crosses, a plain one standing twelve feet tall (one foot for each of the students who died) and another more elaborate one only a couple of feet shorter (see figure 9.2). Visitors to the site covered the plain cross with scriptural references and signatures, as high as they could reach. On the crossbar, the students who erected the cross had inscribed John 15:13, "Greater love hath no man than to lay down his life for his friends," implying (rightly or wrongly) that the twelve students who were killed had willingly sacrificed their lives while building Bonfire. The smaller cross was part of an elaborate folk-art tableau: the cross itself was painted maroon and 12 tall votive candles were attached at intervals along both axes of the cross; a "shadow" of white landscaping pebbles stretched in front of the cross. Twelve more tall votive candles were placed within this "shadow" (see figure 9.3). Crowds gathered around this cross at night when all of the votive candles were lit. The people who erected both of these crosses, although they gladly provided contextual information

Figure 9.2   Large plain cross.
Source: University Relations, Texas A&M University.

Figure 9.3   Shadow cross.

Source: University Relations, Texas A&M University.

for our growing files and database, requested that their names not be publicized because they erected the crosses out of deep, personal religious commitment and did not want any credit or publicity for what they had done.

Bibles were another dominant category of Christian artifacts left at the shrines. A total of thirteen Bibles are in the collection, ranging from inexpensive, small "give away" New Testaments to a personal Bible bound in fine morocco leather and filled with marginal notations and personal photographs. Some of these Bibles remained in situ for nearly a month, subjected to the wind and wintry weather (Smith and Grider 2001). People were frequently seen kneeling in prayer and reading from their Bibles at the shrines. Our assumption is that many of the personal Bibles in the memorabilia collection were left at the shrine on a sudden impulse, rather than as a deliberate, thought-out act.

Many Christian artworks, including commercially produced figurines as well as handcrafted items, are included in the bonfire memorabilia collection. Angels are the most common subjects of these artworks. The students who were killed are frequently referred to as the "Twelve Aggie Angels," and many posters and other handcrafted items included sets of 12 angels, each bearing the name of one of the twelve students who died in the accident (see figure 9.4). The collection currently contains 80 angels of various types.

Forty-one rosaries and an assortment of 122 small crucifixes, and saints' medallions form another subset of Christian artifacts left at the bonfire shrines. Our assumption is that people may have left these artifacts at the bonfire site on impulse, which would be consistent with emerging research into the spontaneous shrine phenomenon. For example, at spontaneous shrines following other disasters, coins frequently have been documented among the artifacts; such offerings are apparently simply what people had with them when they stopped by the shrines. Caps and t-shirts or scarves may also be left on impulse.

Written messages constitute the most diagnostic and at the same time the most problematic category of Christian memorabilia left at the bonfire shrines. Paper that has been exposed to early winter weather for a month is extremely fragile. The paper from the bonfire shrines has been dried and put in acid-free boxes and folders, but we have not had time to thoroughly document, transcribe, and analyze the hundreds and hundreds of messages written on paper and poster board. Anecdotal reports from shrine visitors, as well as the experiences of those researchers who have worked with the stabilization and foldering of the paper artifacts, indicate that in addition to scripture and prayers, many of these messages are extremely emotional and many are addressed directly to the students who died. Although there are

Figure 9.4   Set of twelve angels.

Source: University Relations, Texas A&M University.

potential copyright and privacy issues that will have to be considered, the analysis and publication of the written messages should provide one of the most important categories of data for understanding the religious worldview of those who left these messages at the bonfire shrines. Preliminary research indicates that scriptural references, as well as brief messages referring to God and angels, were the most common types of written messages and graffiti.

Material culture specialists have long considered cemeteries—including not only grave markers but also the memorabilia left on graves—as a rich source of cultural information. As Jordan points out, quoting folklorist John Stilgoe, ". . . the traditional Christian graveyard is the work of laymen seeking to objectify the most meaningful elements" of their religious beliefs (Jordan 1982: 7). Spontaneous shrines likewise represent incredibly rich expressions of the deep-held cultural beliefs of the people who visit them and leave offerings. Much of the artifact assemblage from the bonfire shrines, as well as the written messages, clearly reflects the basic Christianity of a great many of the people who visited the shrines and left memorabilia.

Conclusions

Just as archaeologists have for decades excavated and studied ancient grave goods, the contemporary artifacts left at spontaneous shrines can be studied by material culture specialists to get a clearer understanding of emerging modern grieving rituals (Thoms 2000). By the choice of items that they leave at spontaneous shrines, people reveal at least as much about themselves as about those they are mourning for.

Systematic collection of items from spontaneous shrines—as opposed to conventional archaeological sites—is a complex issue because of the lack of clear jurisdiction governing most shrines. Artifacts that are left in spontaneous shrines are technically abandoned, so the donor has no further control over them. Furthermore, once jurisdiction is established and spontaneous shrines are dismantled, families are allowed to take away whatever they want and a selection of the artifacts that remain are then archived or put on display. The Vietnam Veterans Memorial collection, however, took the unique approach of archiving all of the artifacts that were left at The Wall, thus creating a populist collection which was unmediated by aesthetic or other judgments by curators (Allen 1995).

The Bonfire Memorabilia Collection Project followed the precedent set by the Vietnam Veterans Memorial and collected and inventoried nearly all of the artifacts that were left on campus at the various bonfire shrines. (However, some categories, such as melted wax, were only sampled, and wilted flowers were composted.) Because of the systematic methodology utilized during collection and inventory, as well as the completeness of the artifact assemblage, the Bonfire Memorabilia Collection is therefore an important and unique data set for content analysis.

In Memoriam
Miranda Denise Adams
Christopher David Breen
Michael Stephen Ebanks
Jeremy Richard Frampton
Jamie Lynn Hand
Christopher Lee Heard
Timothy Doran Kerlee, Jr.
Lucas John Kimmel
Bryan Allan McClain
Chad Anthony Powell
Jerry Don Self
Nathan Scott West

Notes

1. To show their contempt for the University of Texas, Aggies do not capitalize "t. u."
2. At some point within the past 20 years or so, students began referring to the tradition simply as "Bonfire," always capitalized and with no article.
3. Folklorist Jack Santino (1986) was the first to apply the term, *assemblage*, to the broader material culture landscape rather than restricting the term to the conventional archaeological usage referring to associated artifacts in an archaeological matrix.
4. The data management program for this project is PastPerfect©.

References Cited

Adams, John. 2001. *Keepers of the Spirit: The Corps of Cadets at Texas A&M University, 1876–2001*. College Station: Texas A&M University Press.
Allen, Thomas B. 1995. "A Place for Memories." In *Offerings at the Wall: Artifacts from the Vietnam Veterans Memorial Collection*. Atlanta: Turner Publishing Company.
Bascom, Willliam. 1954. "Four Functions of Folklore." *Journal of American Folklore* 67:266, pp. 333–349.
Chenhall, Robert G. 1989. *The Revised Nomenclature for Museum Cataloging: A Revised and Expanded Version of Robert G. Chenhall's System for Classifying Man-Made Objects*. Nashville, TN: AASLH Press.

Final Report. 2000. Special Commission on the 1999 Aggie Bonfire. College Station: Texas A&M University.

Finley, Greg. 1986. Review of *Material Culture: A Research Guide* by Thomas J. Schlereth. *Winterthur Portfolio* 21: 334.

Forsyth, John A. 1981. *The Aggies and the Horns: 86 Years of Bad Blood and Good Football.* Austin: Texas Monthly Press.

Grider, Sylvia. 2000. "The Archaeology of Grief: Texas A&M's Bonfire Tragedy is a Sad Study in Modern Mourning." *Discovering Archaeology.* 2(3) July/August: 68–74.

Hoyle, John. 1990. *Good Bull: 30 Years of Aggie Escapades.* Bryan: Insite Press.

Jacobs, Homer. 2002. *The Pride of Aggieland: Spirit & Football at a Place Like No Other.* New York: Silver Lining Books.

Jones, Bethan. 1999. "Books of Condolence." In *The Mourning for Diana,* ed. Tony Walter, 203–214. Oxford: Berg.

Jones, Frances. 1997. *A Circle of Love: The Oklahoma City Bombing through the Eyes of Our Children.* Oklahoma City: Feed the Children.

Jordan, Terry. 1982. *Texas Graveyards: A Cultural Legacy.* Austin: University of Texas Press.

Kerlee, Janice Cross. 2001. *The Chance to Say Goodbye.* New York: Writers Club Press.

Linenthal, Edward. 2001. *The Unfinished Bombing: Oklahoma City in American Memory.* New York: Oxford University Press.

McDannell, Colleen. 1995. *Material Christianity: Religion and Popular Culture in America.* New Haven: Yale University Press.

Petroski, Henry. 2000. Vanities of the Bonfire. *American Scientist* 88 November/December: 486–490.

"Report on the Rescue and Recovery Efforts Following the Collapse of Bonfire at Texas A&M University, November 18, 1999." 2000. Prepared by the College Station Fire Department.

Ross, Jim and Paul Myers. 1996. *Dear Oklahoma City, Get Well Soon: America's Children Reach Out to the People of Oklahoma.* New York: Walker Publishing Company.

Santino, Jack. 1986. "The Folk Assemblage of Autumn: Tradition and Creativity in Halloween Folk Arts." In *Folk Art and Art Worlds,* ed. John Michael Vlach and Simon Bronner. Ann Arbor: UMI Research Press.

Santino, Jack. 1992. "Not an Unimportant Failure:" Spontaneous Shrine and Rituals of Death and Politics. In Michael Melaughan. *Displayed in Mortal Light.* Antrim, Northern Ireland: Antrim Arts Council.

Santino, Jack. 2001. Signs of War and Peace: Social Conflict and Public Display of Symbols in Northern Ireland. New York and London: Palgrave MacMillan.

Smith, Wayne and Sylvia Grider. 2001. "The Emergency Conservation of Waterlogged Bibles from the Memorabilia Assemblage Following the Collapse of the Texas A&M University Bonfire." *International Journal of Historical Archaeology* 5(4) December: 309–316.

Stilgoe, John. 1978. "Folklore and Graveyard Design." *Landscape* 22(3) Summer: 22–28.

Tang, Irwin A. 2000. *The Texas Aggie Bonfire: Tradition & Tragedy at Texas A&M*. Austin: Morgan Printing Company.

Thoms, Alston. 2000. "The Emotion Enigma: Today's Grief May Help Explain Ancient Funeral Offerings." *Discovering Archaeology* 2(3) July/August: 72.

Walter, Tony, ed. 1999. *The Mourning for Diana*. Oxford: Berg.

Figure 10.1 Memorial's placement on the bridge overlooking the beach. The shrine was constructed of stuffed animals and bouquets of flowers.
Photo by: Diane E. Goldstein and Diane Tye.

What impressed us most strongly as we stood in front of the small spontaneous shrine was the way it refused to be contained. While it clearly started out on the bridge, it was not confined to it. Flowers and stuffed animals were tucked into the chain links of a fence that ran along the cliff edge from the bridge in both directions, eerily resembling fish caught in a net (figure 10.2). This refusal to be limited (although we did not know it at the time) was an early metaphoric sign of mourning that would refuse containment and resist control at every turn. We came to see the construction of the shrine and its relation to a number of critical actions that took place in Pouch Cove during the days following the drownings as constituting a process of community resistance. Through their challenge of outside interpretations of the accident, these acts of resistance together presented an alternative understanding of the tragedy and by extension of the community and its past. This paper is about a grief, a memory that refused to be contained in a shrine, and it is about the community management of that memory. In many ways, it is about a shrine that provided a first clue, for us, and perhaps for community members, to deaths heavily imbued with cultural resonance and layers of historical meaning, meanings that resisted outside constructions of the cause of the drownings and the characters of the boys whose lives were lost.

Figure 10.2   Flowers and stuffed animals tucked into the chain links.
Photo by: Diane E. Goldstein and Diane Tye.

The Shrine

There was nothing remarkable about the memorial site on the bridge. An initial spontaneous reaction to the disaster, it was likely inspired by media coverage of similar shrines erected in response to the death of Princess Diana, the Oklahoma bombings, the Lockerbie Air crash, and numerous other public tragedies. Many of the bears had been handed out by the Red Cross in hope that they would help the teenagers and children from the community sooth their grief. The stuffed rabbits were most likely items that would have been on hand, considering the proximity of the boys' deaths to Easter. Notes were brief, more of the "Jessie, we love you" order than longer or more specific messages. Candles, holy cards, and the rosary, mimicked the Roman Catholic alter many community members would have in their homes. Beyond all else, the shrine appeared almost stereotypical of the phenomenon.

The incongruity of the generic quality of the shrine and the deeply felt personal loss that community members articulated when interviewed in the media should have been our first clue to its place in an interrelated web of community mourning practices, and its import as a quiet symbolic and political statement. In the context of rural Newfoundland, shrines like the one on the bridge overlooking the beach in Pouch Cove make less sense than their urban and suburban counterparts. The unforgiving climate and relentless wind and snow do not allow such displays to survive for any length of time, nor permit leisurely visitation. Perhaps more significantly, however, the structure of rural community life calls into question the normally assumed functions of spontaneous memorials. Most authors writing on the topic of spontaneous memorialization emphasize the public function of shrines, acknowledging the loss to the larger community, and allowing the inclusion of people, "who are not in the culturally prescribed group of mourners, ie., relatives friends and associates"(Haney, Leimer, and Lowery, 1997: 162). "*Spontaneous memorialization*," argue Haney, Leimer, and Lowery, "extends the boundaries of who is allowed or expected to participate in the mourning process" (Haney, Leimer, and Lowery 1997: 162). Rural communities like Pouch Cove, however, still permit participation of the broader grieving population in other aspects of funeral and memorializing tradition. Community members are family and by extension they participate in the loss. The whole Pouch Cove community and many outsiders actively expressed their grief through preparing sandwiches for search and rescue operations and providing blankets and other supplies to aid in the search, taking care of the families most directly involved through endless cups of tea and visits to their homes, through visiting the funeral home, attending the funerals, decorating the graves, flying flags at half-mast, taking part in school and community sponsored events, and through the online exchange of poems and personal memorials. When it became clear that the small church would not hold the massive number of people who wished to attend the funeral service, the local cable company was asked to film it and the school gymnasium was set up with seats so that the overflow of grievers could watch the broadcast together.

Other characteristics and functions of spontaneous memorials were absorbed into the community's modern adaptations of local traditional death rituals. Haney, Leimer, and Lowery emphasize the inclusive, counter-hegemonic, personal, and eclectic nature of spontaneous memorials[2] and while most of these functions remained significant in the Pouch Cove shrine, they also found expression elsewhere, in adapted tradition. But most significantly, the shrine was an immediate and very public signal that this community regarded the drownings not as an inevitable accident when teenagers play on ice or beside water, but rather as a tragic loss of three young Newfoundland lives claimed unjustly by a cruel sea, the same sea that swallowed up generations of hardworking, heroic Newfoundlanders. And, just as the flowers and teddy bears that made up the spontaneous shrine stretched along the fence and into the community, so did expressions of resistance to the outside management of memory.

Copying

It is unclear whether early reports, which indicated that the boys were engaged in copying at the time of the drownings, came from the fourth boy who accompanied the others but survived or whether the reports were speculative, based on local knowledge of the game as a common springtime activity for Newfoundland youth. The local newspaper reported that copying was the cause of the deaths in their first edition the morning after the boys were lost. Bernie Bennett and Ryan Cleary reported,

> The three boys aged 16 to 18 are presumed drowned. They and another friend were "copying" on the ice pans along the shoreline of the harbor at about 4:30 p.m. when the trouble started. ("Town Mourns Loss," *Telegram*, March 9, 2001: 1)

Certainly, participation in copying is widely reported and warnings to "stay clear of the ice" are common in every spring both as parental admonishments and in the media. While "copying" as a term is used to refer to the game of jumping from ice pan to ice pan, Newfoundland historians have argued that the activity served as training for the work of seal hunting, which would come later in the lives of young male Newfoundlanders. *The Dictionary of Newfoundland English* defines copying (also cobbying, cockeying, conking, cooding, coodying, and coonying) as,

> 1. [a] children's pastime, the action of leaping from one piece of floating ice to another as the participants follow or copy the leader and 2. The action of running over ice-pans, esp during the seal hunt. (Story, Kirwin, and Widdowson 1982: 114)

The dictionary further quotes a note published in 1895 from *The Journal of American Folklore* (viii, 38) written by Rev. George Patterson, which described the activity as "an amusement of boys in the spring, when the ice is breaking up, of jumping from cake to cake, in supposed imitation of the sealers" (Story, Kirwin, and Widdowson 1982: 114). Some authors have argued that copying only occurred when the ice pans were small enough to present a real challenge in jumping quickly from one to the other. If the ice pieces were too big or too stable the game lost its interest. Writer, Farley Mowat (1969) wrote, "If you were jumping from one big pan of ice to another, it was not considered copyin'. It was only copyin' where there was danger" (39).

Few coastal Newfoundlanders would not recognize the term "copying" and many would remember having engaged in the activity themselves.

Nevertheless, media reports that the boys were copying at the time of their deaths were full of condemnation for the activity and their condemnation appeared to extend to the boys themselves. An editorial in the *St. John's Evening Telegram* warned:

> The call of the ice must still be strong . . . Unfortunately, the reality has never changed, and today there is only grief and shock in the wake of such a horrific loss . . . Let us hope that other young people will learn a lesson and not put their lives at risk. Let this tragedy serve as a caution to everyone about the power of the ice and of the ocean, and the respect that we should pay to them, and to our own lives. (Editorial, *Telegram*, March 10, 2001: 10)

Whether or not the media intended to condemn the lost boys through their writings, their comments represented the teens as foolhardy risk takers, an implication that was not missed by members of the community. In a letter to the editor of the *Telegram*, a resident of nearby Holyrood wrote,

> The families of those youths have enough tragedy to deal with, let alone knowing the opinion of many Newfoundlanders, as well as most of the country, is that these kids somehow "should have known better." ("Media Reports Add to Families' Pain," Letters to the Editor, *Telegram*, March 15, 2001: 6)

Resistance

The hasty construction of a spontaneous memorial shortly after the boys were lost began a string of acts of resistance over the days that followed the drownings and culminated with fishermen's defiant recovery of the last two bodies. Some of these subversive actions personalized formal ritual in an expression of the deep personal loss felt by friends and family members. On March 12, following the Roman Catholic funeral service for Jessie Elliott, the pallbearers walked out of the church, carrying the casket, and, surprising everyone, marched past the awaiting hearse, choosing instead to carry their friend on foot up the steep hill to the graveyard.

A few days later, during the funeral for Adam Wall, the teenagers engaged in a more controversial act of defiance. Ignoring Father Puddister's edict that there could be no secular music incorporated in the service, the pallbearers brought their own ghetto blaster to the church and hit the play button as the priest moved to escort the casket down the aisle. All stood and waited for the song, "Wind Beneath My Wings," to be played in its entirety. In the religiously conservative Roman Catholic communities that are typical of Newfoundland, the act of openly defying the priest is nothing short of extraordinary. Several weeks later, Father Puddister, clearly annoyed by these actions, wrote in the church bulletin that secular adaptations of funeral services would not be tolerated in his Parish.

Resisting the depersonalization of funerary tradition (and perhaps death itself) members of the community decorated every aspect of the mortuary process. At the funeral home the coffins were filled with and surrounded by mementoes—on the floor near the casket were displays of the boys hobbies—skateboards, bowling pins, pool sticks, and model cars. The kids pinned items to the coffin liner as they filed past—friendship beads, hemp bracelets, sports medals, poems, and notes. In the coffin were placed small bits of money owed to the deceased, cards, flowers, a baseball cap, and huge quantities of jewelry. According to one of our interviews, Jessie Elliott was covered in 40 or 50 gold chains by the time the coffin was closed. Cards, teddy bears, jewelry, trinkets, and painted rocks decorated the graves (figure 10.3) and a teddy bear was placed in a tree in the yard of a friend of one of the boys. The resistances, small and large, personalized methods of grieving, allowing individuals to reclaim individual involvements with the deceased boys.

Pouch Cove is not unusual in its reactions of resistance to tragedy and death. While other ethnographers of disaster and grief have not specifically focused on the role of resistance in the reclamation and recovery process,

Figure 10.3　Gravesite of Jessie Elliot and Adam Wall.
Photo by: Diane E. Goldstein and Diane Tye.

the data is there, buried but described in the ethnographic context. Richard Burns (1999), in his study of responses to the school shootings in Jonesboro Arkansas, briefly mentions acts of noncompliance with a request by the Governor for area residents to fly flags at half-staff for a two-day mourning period. Burns notes that residents were angered by the Governor's absence at a service of hope and healing organized by the community and thus they refused to comply with his request and created their own methods for expressing grief. Burns writes, "there were many in the community who found comfort in expressive forms not shaped for commercial consumption, but rather reflecting a more personal and community oriented response" (169). People of Jonesboro chose to wear white ribbons instead as a sign of innocence and antiviolence. When they ran out of white ribbon, a widow donated her wedding dress for material, adding an additional layer of meaning to the personalized expressions of grief.

Tad Tuleja (1997) describes the 1991 U.S. Gulf War yellow-ribbon campaign as a sign of national pride for government officials but also notes numerous counter-hegemonic uses of the symbol by those critical of the military action. For at least some of the American population the ribbon became a sign of resistance in the face of tragedy and crisis. In Erica Brady's (1987) description of the "Beau Geste" she describes the burial of a man who had lived a creative and unconventional life but who was given a rigidly conventional funeral. According to Brady, "his brother plotted a harmless rebellion, conspiring to have him buried in a respectable suit but also in his tattered and beloved sneakers—invisible . . . beneath the hood of the casket but a source of comfort, even glee, to the few who were in on the secret" (29).

The small resistances described by these authors, like those found in Pouch Cove, are located in reactions to the external construction and control of discourse, meanings, and subjectivities in tragic events. Resistance in this sense is the contestation of socially established meanings of dominant discourses that define the situation and how it should be managed. These small acts of defiance, nonconformity and noncompliance ("weapons of the weak" in Scott's terms) wrestle away the practices, strategies, representations, and textual devices that are expected in response to crisis and allow participants to manage the continued identities of the tragically affected individuals and the community. The subjectivities that grievers hunger for in times of tragedy are to some extent negated by the conformity of traditional mourning practice. But the re-empowerment process, the process that makes it possible for grievers to go on living, seems to require a certain amount of resistance. While Foucault (1980) argues that where there is power there is resistance, Abu-Lughod (1990) reminds us the reverse is also true and where there is resistance there is power. Resistance reclaims agency and marks the road to recovery.

The Shrine in Retrospect

So what about the bears and bouquets on the beach? Do they fit into this picture of activist mourning? Certainly, those who left the stuffed animals and flowers were commemorating something—a grief, a sympathy, and a personal relationship with the deceased. But the mass-manufactured, supply-oriented, and seemingly nonpersonal nature of the items (the bears provided by the red cross, religious items, and flowers) don't lend themselves to an activist reading. Jack Santino's discussion of shrines erected at sites of violence in Northern Ireland suggests that overt political statements contained within the displays are not common, the shrines themselves are not understood as appropriate places for the expression of angry statements (Santino 2001: 80). But perhaps the very existence of a shrine, there on the beach where the media were reporting that the boys essentially caused their own deaths was in itself an act of resistance. Shrines are not generally constructed for the foolhardy, for those who are responsible for their own demise. While roadside crosses and other displays might be constructed to mark the deaths of drunk drivers or joy riders and therefore stand as a warning to others, these markers tend to evolve sometime after the deaths and not with the same immediacy as spontaneous shrines. Scholars who write about spontaneous shrines often, however, emphasize the wider symbolic nature of the deaths involved. Haney, Leimer, and Lowry (1997) define spontaneous memorialization as "a public response to the unanticipated violent deaths of people who do not fit into the categories of those we expect to die, who may be engaging in routine activities in which there is a reasonable expectation of safety, and with whom the participants in the ritual share some common identification" (161). Similarly Santino (2001) notes that shrines usually commemorate a "sudden, violent or early death" (81). Certainly, there can be no question that the deaths of the boys in Pouch Cove came too early and that the victims were not those we expect to die. But children who die from the flu are also taken too early and fall outside the category of anticipated deaths, yet shrines are not often built for them. Perhaps the very construction of a shrine in this place, following on these deaths was a statement both about the expectation of safety and identification with the victims. As Mary Hayes told us, "to go down on the cliffs and watch the waves come in, there isn't a person in Newfoundland born and bred that has never done that, it's something that you do." Though perhaps not containing any overt political statements in their assemblages, shrines are political and they are narrative. They narrate a tragedy through their very existence, saying in a powerful voice, "this death was not caused by the flu, this death was caused by something of import to us all." Shrines, according to Santino "commemorate the loss of a life, . . . call attention to how the life was lost, and . . . consecrate the place where the unthinkable happened" (77). They make sense of senseless deaths.

And so it was in Pouch Cove. Whether collectively conscious or not, the bears and bouquets on the beach began a re-narration of the tragedy, wrestling the memory of the boys away from the media construction of foolhardy deaths and replacing those images with a very different narrative of heroic bravery. This was a shrine of heroism.

Narrative Constructions of the Heroic

The reconfiguration of the victims as heroic appeared everywhere in the days following the drownings. In this construction, the boys were walking along the beach looking at the ice when a wave came up on shore and swallowed one of the boys. The other boys lost their lives trying to save their friends as successive attempts resulted in the loss of another one of the teenagers. This counter-narrative was supported textually, initiated in one of the early newspaper reports by Royal Newfoundland Constabulary inspector Sean Ryan:

> They were lost but they were heroes . . . They showed you never give up on a friend. It mirrors the boys' honour . . . They're lost but they'll always remain a part of Newfoundland's courage. ("Searching for Closure," *Telegram*, March 10, 2001: 2)

Inspector Ryan's comment that linked the boys' heroism with nationalism—theirs was "Newfoundland courage"—underscores John Roberts's understanding of heroic creation as a process much like culture building and closely tied to group identity. According to Roberts the conception of a "hero" is part of a group's differential identity, that is, a "means by which a group creates and maintains an image of itself to proclaim difference from others by objectifying in its institutions the ideals it claims for itself" (Roberts 1989: 1). Within days heroism was an inseparable part of the discourse of the accident, extending from the victims to the community and to the whole province.

Community members quickly embraced the concept of the drowned teenagers as heroes.

The song friends fought to include in the funeral was a rendition of Bette Midler's "The Wind Beneath My Wings":

Did you ever know that you're my hero?
And everything I'd like to be?
I can fly higher than an eagle,
'Cause you are the wind beneath my wings! (Words and music by Larry Henley and Jeff Silbar 1983, 1988).

In the weeks after the spontaneous memorial on the bridge was dismantled, the locus changed to the gravesites of Jessie Elliott and Adam Wall who are buried in the Roman Catholic churchyard (AJ Sullivan was buried in another community). There carefully arranged stones spelled out "Heroes of the Day" on graves of the two boys buried side by side. The complexities of these constructions is reflected in a belief held by one of the victim's mother that her son's heroism extended past his death. She contends that it was the spirit of her son, who had planned a career in search and rescue, that led the fishermen to the recovery of the other bodies.[3]

Two days following the drownings, and a day after the report quoted above, Inspector Ryan again characterized the victims as heroes. This time, however, he added a survivor to his list: a fourth boy who had tried to rescue his friends by running for help. The item reads:

Micheal Sparkes, the teenager who was with the boys when the tragedy happened is being described as "a hero, a remarkable young man," Ryan said.
"Without him, we'd be merely surmising what happened." ("Search gets tougher," *Telegram*, March 11, 2001: 2).[4]

Not surprisingly others who tried to rescue the boys were also constructed as heroes. Michele Stamp, a Pouch Cove resident who was present during the rescue attempt, described the bravery of those on shore: "all the men . . . put their lives in peril, trying to pull the teenagers from the ocean while standing on ice, waves crashing violently around them." She spoke of the "incredible anguish" on the faces of the men who tried and failed to rescue the boys. "They did everything and they did it without thinking. They were so brave, so courageous." And, she singled out the efforts of one man who ironically restrained the others: "If Tom (Poynter) hadn't of told the men next to him to unwrap the ropes from around their hands they would have been lost, too"("Searching for Closure" *Telegram*, March 10, 2001: 2).

As the search to recover the bodies continued and eventually successfully ended in the fishermen's defiance, the fishermen took on heroic stature.

One of the most widely circulated poems composed in response to the tragedy is by Kim Nolan of nearby Torbay. Titled, "A Pouch Cove Tragedy: God Bless the Fishermen," it reads in part:

> God Bless the men who risked their lives
> they brought some peace and found the boys.
> When all else failed they went out on their own
> and off in their boats the rough shores they did roam.
> These are the Heros of Pouch Cove Indeed
> along with the boys, our hearts they do bleed. . . .

In speaking of the fishermen's recovery of the second boy's body in light of an official decision not to search, Sgt. Bob Garland of the RNC affirmed the heroic nature of the men's actions. His statement recognized the whole communities agency as he thanked the "residents of Pouch Cove":

> "The find today is to the credit of the residents in Pouch Cove itself, to the tenacity in going out to find one of their own and (bringing) him home," Garland said. ("Second body recovered," *Telegram*, March 13, 2001: 2)

Following the discovery of the third body, Garland again spoke to the press, praising the efforts of the "people of Pouch Cove." *The Evening Telegram* reported:

> RNC spokesperson Sgt. Bob Garland was quick to admit there were mistakes made and any blame should be pointed at police, but he was just as quick to credit the people of Pouch Cove.
> "It was their operation (Monday and Tuesday); they did it," said Garland.
> "Thank God the people of Pouch Cove didn't follow the lead. They went with their hearts and their knowledge, and didn't follow scientific evidence.
> We give them full credit for that." ("No more looking," *Telegram*, March 14, 2001: 2)

From Inspector Ryan's identification of the boys with Newfoundland courage in one of the first reports of the tragedy, the victims were closely aligned with provincial character. They became everyman and every Newfoundlander felt the loss according to the heroic construction. "It's a sad day for Pouch Cove," Bob Garland reflected. "It's a sad day for Newfoundland" ("Town mourns loss," *Telegram*, March 9, 2001: 2). The fishermen too assumed the persona of everyman becoming symbolic of the Newfoundland values of bravery, family, and perseverance as this letter to the editor from an expatriate Newfoundlander attests:

> We would like to add we are proud of the determination of the people of
> Pouch Cove in keeping up the search until they found all three bodies.
> It is acts like this that make Newfoundland unique and it only goes to
> show what a close-knit family the province of Newfoundland is.
> Even in the face of such a tragedy, those of us looking from afar and seeing
> a community united can still say we are proud to be Newfoundlanders.
> (Letter to editor by Sheldon and Karen Thorne, former residents of
> Sullivan's Loop, Pouch Cove, Sioux Lookout, Ontario, *Telegram*, March 15,
> 2001: 6)

We explore this heroic discourse not intending to negate or even to diminish the bravery of boys, the fishermen, and the boys' friends and family.[5] Rather, we examine these constructions because as Roberts argues the process of hero making offers insight into important cultural values. Roberts (1989) writes that " . . . folk heroic creation occurs because groups, at critical moments in time, recognize in the actions of certain figures, which may already be known to them, qualities or behaviors that they have reason to believe would enhance culture building (that is, their ability to protect the identity and values of the group in the face of a threat to them)" (5). Always ongoing and remedial, hero creation may be employed by a group to cover cracks in the basic structure of its culture, so that the ideal image of itself can be projected as if it were actual (Roberts 1989: 2). In the case of the Pouch Cove drowning what are those ideal images? What are the cracks they hide?

Immediately identifying the boys as heroes served a practical purpose. Lauding their bravery deflected attention from a debate that surrounded the accident: were the boys washed to sea by a rogue wave as they stood on land bravely trying to save one another or were they jumping from ice pan to ice pan, engaged in the traditional game of copying? Early media reports that described the teenagers as copying were quickly and very strongly challenged by members of Pouch Cove. Some argued that the ice that night was not pan ice but slob ice. It was impossible to jump on. And, they protested further that Pouch Cove is not even a location for copying. Conditions in this harbor usu- ally prohibit it (Robinson 2001; Hayes and Hayes 2001). Nonetheless per- ception, at least outside the community, seemed to be that the boys were copying. By naming the drowned boys as heroes, members of Pouch Cove and of the rescue effort resisted outside interpretations of the boys as reckless and dismissals of their deaths as unfortunate but self-inflicted.

Perhaps one of the reasons that the belief the boys were copying remained current despite resistance of those in Pouch Cove was its symbolic linking of the victims with all Newfoundlanders. For many residents of the province, copying has become a mental tableau of sorts for growing up, especially growing up male, in rural Newfoundland. And, while many children grow up to recall their fun on the "tippy pans" the sea has also been the grave of many Newfoundlanders who ventured out on ice. In reflecting on the poignancy of the Pouch Cove drownings, Mary Hayes commented on the way in which she and other residents of the province could identify with this incident, "But there's so many tragedies of the sea in Newfoundland . . . We all go to the church and pray for the bodies . . . bodies of the sealers whose families were watching them . . . They were on pans of ice. The sea just pretty well carted them. Down goes all the men. Very few communities in Newfoundland are free from tragedy from the ocean" (Hayes and Hayes 2001).

The creation of the fishermen as heroes seemed to gain wider currency as Newfoundlanders living throughout the island and beyond joined residents of Pouch Cove in celebrating the men's bravery. One writer of a letter to the editor of the *St John's Evening Telegram* claimed:

> Newfoundland fishermen from years ago would always recover their own victims of tragedy. Now I guess that it has slipped so far back in the past that we have to do it again. . . .
>
> Stand back, boys, and let the fishermen—the people who know how—do the job and be successful. The brave and determined and devoted fishermen of Newfoundland will show you how.
>
> To the families, I express my sympathy for your loss. To the fishermen, I pat you on the back for a job well done. You are a proud people, you, the fishermen of Newfoundland.
>
> You make me proud to be a Newfoundlander.
> (Letter to the editor, Rodger French, Halifax, *Telegram*, March 15, 2001: 6)

This discourse of heroism emphasized what the fishermen's actions had done for the community. Throughout the media coverage of the drownings, reports stressed the loss suffered by the whole town (e.g., "Town mourns death on ice," "Two communities ripped apart," and "Town mourns loss"). Pouch Cove's mayor, Sarah Patten, declared: "We're too small a community to lose three people like that and everybody not to feel it" ("Searching for Closure" *Telegram*, March 10, 2001: 2). By defying the procedures of the official search, fishermen had found the last two bodies and brought closure for the families. They had reconstituted the community. Their efforts came generalized as those of all seafaring Newfoundlanders who place primacy on kin and community.

Heroic discourses around the Pouch Cove drownings have a distinct Newfoundland character to them. The extension of hero creation from boys to rescue and recovery workers and ultimately to residents of the community and of the province reflects cultural dynamics that have characterized Newfoundland for generations: the primacy of the communal over the individual (e.g., see Pocius 1991). Rural life in Newfoundland is now however, under siege and those very dynamics are threatened. Since the collapse of the cod fishery in 1995 tens of thousands have left the province. No longer able to provide a living from the sea, small communities are dying. The population is aging and those too old to relocate scrape together a living anyway they can—most with the help of some sort of government assistance. It is a bleak picture. In the face of these massive social changes it is lucky there were any boats in Pouch Cove for the fishermen, who should rightly be called retired fishermen, to launch.

Reshaping of the boys and the fishermen as heroes becomes a central act of resistance in its validation for all Newfoundlanders of a way of life that is disappearing. Importantly, this is an emergent process—not simply because each telling is new, but because it reflects on the past in a way that makes sense of the future. The narratives shared here are built on the knowledge that the cod fishery's collapse came despite repeated warnings from fishermen that stocks were in trouble. Scientists disagreed until it was too late. In both the fishery collapse and the search for the boys the fishermen's knowledge was correct and the "authorities" were wrong. And in both cases, nobody listened. Through heroic construction of the boys, the fishermen and by extension the community and the province, Newfoundland of the past is authenticated. Narrating the tragedy confirms the centrality of fishing skills and the importance of following the innate sense of what one knows.

Reclamation

All of the resistances noted here—from nonconformity with traditional funerary practice to the fishermen's defiance of the Constabulary and the redrawing of the tragic narrative—respond through the same mechanism: they assert belief in the superiority of primary knowledges over secondary ways of knowing. Scott Rushforth (1994), in his work on Athapaskan knowledge and authority, distinguishes these by saying:

> Primary knowledge denotes fully justified beliefs that an individual acquires through his or her experiences, including social interactions. Primary epistemic evidence is the foundation of primary knowledge. People employ the former as warrant for the latter. Secondary knowledge is based only indirectly

on primary evidence. Non-epistemic factors such as a speaker's credentials can provide the salient reasons for believing in secondary knowledge. (336)

Primary knowledge is apprehended through direct experience (in this case of the cove, the community, and the boys), while the secondary knowledge, which forms the subject of the resistances, is apprehended through analogy (of search and rescue operations, universal precautions at sea, landscapes and seascapes, and proper grief and mourning). Dominant official outsiders, seen as outside the community or outside the central core of grievers in Father Puddister's case, bear greater secondary knowledge but lesser primary knowledge. The fishermen, on the other hand, resist by asserting their intimate knowledge of the sea and the cove and the family and friends resisted by asserting their intimate knowledge of the drowned boys. Political resistance, writes Carol Gilligan, "is an insistence to know what one knows and a willingness to be outspoken"(1990: 502). That insistence and that willingness gave the bodies of the boys back to their families and the cove back to the community.

The actions of the fishermen became a cause of celebration,[6] even while the community was still reeling from the loss of the three boys. While their success was necessary to the community's ability to have proper Roman Catholic funerals and burials—it was also seen as a triumph of local knowledge over the universalizing forces of official culture. The fishermen accomplished what the Royal Newfoundland Constabulary and the Coast Guard could not; further, they did it in defiance of the orders of those very officials. Mary Hayes, a cousin of AJ Sullivan, told us:

> Those fishermen know . . . all the rocks, all the snags and all the buoys and the sea fairies. They know exactly what can happen. I guess what prompted them most to go out that day was frustration. Maybe they felt that their hands were tied. Maybe they felt that they weren't doing enough. When you walk over and see all of the families going in and crying, the grief was brought to everyone . . . maybe they had a point to prove. You know, the Newfoundland way, with those so-called experts coming in and telling you . . . what to do. We know it best. It makes you kind of determined. (Hayes and Hayes: 2001)

Everyone we interviewed, including those Mary referred to as "the so-called experts" mentioned the role of the fishermen in reclaiming the cove for members of the community, making it possible to wake up every morning and look out at the sea that swallowed up AJ, Jessie, and Adam. Nearly every house in Pouch Cove looks out on the water, and the recovery of the boys partially replaced that vision of tragedy with one of pride. From an analytic point of view, the acts of the boys and the acts of the fishermen suggest an intriguing parallelism. The boys may have lost their lives through the traditional act of copying but the fishermen retrieved them through their traditional knowledge of the sea. In both cases, the intimacy of Newfoundlanders' traditional relationships with the harsh realities of the water is paramount, on one hand resulting in grief—on the other, resulting in joy. The traditions of sea faring cultures—to visit the rocks, to watch the ice, to play by the water, that resulted in the boys deaths—are made from the same knowledge that found the lost boys and reclaimed the Cove. Without that parallel the reclamation might have been still joyful—but less powerful and less loaded with cultural meaning.

The patterns of resistance and reclamation that we trace in Pouch Cove may also provide a critical spin on the role of ritual in recovery. Jack Goody once described ritualized behavior as "repeated, standardized, stylized, stereotyped behavior, that is usually evocative, serious and dramatic" (1961: 142). For some time, folklorists, anthropologists and others have argued that through its predictable sequences of action, ritual encourages stability. We argue here that this statement can only be true if the knowledge, which provides that ritual, can be understood by participants as in some sense primary. Laura Brown, in her book on subversive dialogues, suggests that, "models of personal change must promote resistance"(1994: 24). Perhaps models for coping with disaster must do the same.

The Shrine

So . . . back to our shrine. Set now in a context that recognizes a variety of types of memorializing and remembering as deeply interwoven, our shrine takes on a new life, even as its flowers long ago faded and notes became unreadable. The association of spontaneous memorials with incomprehensible victimization of those who play no role in their tragic deaths, suggests that the initial community response of setting up the shrine on the bridge may have been a preliminary step in reactions of resistance, narrative reconfiguration, and reclamation. While others argued that the death of the boys was through the dangerous and foolhardy activity of copying, the shrine represented perhaps the community's first, but not their only, assertion that the young men were just being young men; their activities were consistent with common vernacular values of tradition, personal safety, life by the sea, and heroism.

At the same time the resistance reading of the shrine points out the dangers inherent in treating spontaneous memorials in isolation. Bold, Knowles, and Leach (2002) distinguish between what they call *hegemonic cultural memory*—"the dominant record of memorializing solidifications of imagined community" (126), and *cultural countermemory*—"the various kinds of oppositional or resistant memory making" inherent in localized shrine activities (126). Based on the work of James Young (1993), Bold et al. argue that dominant hegemonic memorialization culture, present in standardized funerals, monuments and the like, are oriented toward what they call "active forgetting." As James Young notes, "once we assign monumental form to memory, we have to some degree divested ourselves of the obligation to remember" (273); "Instead of searing memory into public consciousness . . . conventional memorials seal memory off from awareness altogether" (272) . . . and reduce the public to passive spectators (274). In Pouch Cove residents reclaimed their community through resources available to them: traditional knowledge as well as material, customary, and narrative practices. To consider the creation of a spontaneous shrine in isolation from the context of these other remembering and forgetting strategies of the community is to risk complicity with the memorializing, monumentalizing forms of dominant culture that claim unique status for the shrine and thereby repress individualism, resistance, and collective involvement. In other words, it risks encouraging the process of active forgetting. The shrine in Pouch Cove reminds us that spontaneous memorialization is not *the* memory and to treat it apart from other expressions of grief and memorialization is to treat it as a strategy of forgetting. In this case the shrine found its primary importance in the first two days after the drownings as an early statement of community refusal to be told either what had happened or how to remember.

The Epilogue

On June 24, 2005 Her Excellency the Right Honourable Adrienne Clarkson, Governor General of Canada, awarded the Medal of Bravery posthumously to Jesse Elliott and Adam Wall. The description of their acts of bravery follows.

On March 8, 2001, 18-year-old Jesse Elliott and 16-year-old Adam Wall lost their lives while trying to rescue a friend who had fallen into the ice-filled bay of Pouch Cove, Newfoundland and Labrador. The cousins and two other teenagers were at the seashore watching the waves from a three-meter-high ice-and-snow-covered rock when a chunk broke off, sending the boy into the seething mass of ice and freezing water. While one teenager ran for help, Jesse jumped in after him and tried to reach his side, but the boy disappeared below the surface before Jesse could save him. Seeing that Jesse was in trouble, Adam then leapt into the Atlantic Ocean. Jesse and Adam, holding on to each other, managed to grab a robe thrown to them from shore when they were struck by a slab of ice and drowned.

Notes

1. Also called a "fish glass." From *the Dictionary of Newfoundland English*, "a tube shaped device with glass in [the] bottom for viewing fish underwater" (Story, Kirwin, and Widdowson 1982: 178).

2. Specifically, they note that spontaneous memorialization is characterized by: not being formally organized thus allowing mourners to make individualized decisions; occurring at a site that is associated with the deceased rather than a prescribed place of mourning; creating a role for those who wish to define themselves but who may not be externally defined as mourners; are composed of eclectic combinations of traditional, religious, secular, and highly personalized objects tailored to the deceased or circumstances of the death; reflect emotions such as anger or vulnerability, which may be felt but typically are not displayed in traditional death rituals; are not constrained by culturally based norms, which prescribe the amount of time allotted for ritual action or appropriate periods of bereavement; and, extend the focus beyond the victim to the social and cultural implications of their death (162).

3. A local poet elevated their status to something near sainthood when she paralleled the boys to Jesus Christ:

   We'll reflect upon the pattern that they followed
   The pattern of Jesus so greatly hallowed
   They reached out to help and to be true to the end
   They could show no greater love than to die for a friend. (Joyce Young, "Tragedy Strikes Again")

4. Ryan elaborates in an article published in a national newspaper:

   "It was an amazing act of courage. For a young man to have such calm in utter chaos and to have the ability to come up with whatever he could to try to save his friends, and that he did that with no consideration for his own life," Insp. Ryan told reporters. "But that heroism was the only ray of light in a dark tragedy." ("Tragedy rips two communities," *Globe & Mail*, March 10, 2001: 1)

5. We examine these constructions of the heroic knowing that we base our reflections on only a sampling of ways these constructions were developed and perhaps are still evolving around the tragedy in Pouch Cove: newspaper reports, local poetry, a student web site, conversations and interviews we've conducted,

and our observation of grave decoration and other funerary ritual. We fully realize that there might well be other expressions that remain closed to us and those we may have missed.

6. Despite the regularity of lives lost at sea in Newfoundland, the Pouch Cove crisis received National media coverage and in an unprecedented decision, all three funerals were broadcast in full on the local cable television network. The tragedy spurred the creation of a disaster fund and inspired numerous shows of support by surrounding schools, grief counselors, clergy people, and community leaders. In part, it is likely that the community's proximity to Newfoundland's capital in St. John's made these particular drownings more accessible to the media than most. But part of what really captured the hearts of the outside community was the incredible acts of the fishermen. Over the days following the drownings, the St. John's newspaper printed letters from locals and people in other parts of Canada expressing praise for their bravery and asserting the importance of local fisher knowledge. Within the community, the fishermen became citizens of special stature—asked to carry the gifts to the alter in one funeral, invited to present a box of notes and mementoes in the school memorial service, and becoming the subject of a number of poems written by community members.

Works Cited

Abu-Lughod, Lila. 1990. The Romance of Resistance: Tracing Transformations of Power Through Bedouin Women. *American Ethnologist* 17: 41–55.

Bold, Christine, Ric Knowles, and Belinda Leach. 2002. Feminist Memorializing and Cultural Countermemory: The Case of Marianne's Park. *Signs: Journal of Women Culture and Society* 28(1): 125–48.

Bong, Laura S. 1994. *Subversive Dialogues: Theory in Feminist Therapy*. New York: Basic Books.

Brady, Erika. 1987. The "Beau Geste": Shaping Private Rituals of Grief. *Folklife Annual*: 24–33.

Burns, Richard A. 1999. "Our Friends Have Given Consolation": Communal Response to the Jonesboro School Shootings. *Southern Folklore* 56(2): 161–179.

Foucault, Michael. 1980. *Power/Knowledge*. Ed. Colin Gordon. New York: Pantheon.

Garland, Bob. Personal interview with Diane E. Goldstein and Diane Tye. June 4, 2001.

Gilligan, Carol. 1990. Joining the Resistance: Psychology, Politics, Girls and Women. *Michigan Quarterly Review* 29: 501–46.

Goody, Jack. 1961. Religion and Ritual: The Definition Problem. *British Journal of Sociology* 12: 142–164.

Haney, C. Allen, Christina Leimer, and Juliann Lowery. 1997. "Spontaneous Memorialization: Violent Death and Emerging Mourning Ritual." *Omega* 35(2): 159–171.

Hayes, Mary and Paula Hayes. Personal interview with Diane E. Goldstein and Diane Tye. April 22, 2001.

Mowat, Farley. 1969. *The Boat Who Wouldn't Float.* Toronto: McClelland and Stewart.

Patterson, Rev. George. 1895 "Notes on the Dialect of the People of Newfoundland." *Journal of American Folklore* 8: viii, 27–40.

Pocius, Gerald L. 1991. *A Place to Belong. Community Order and Everyday Space in Calvert, Newfoundland.* Athens and Montreal: University of Georgia Press and McGill-Queen's University Press.

Roberts, John W. 1989. *From Trickster to Badman: The Black Folk Hero in Slavery and Freedom.* Philadelphia: University of Pennsylvania Press.

Robinson, Jane. Personal interview with Diane E. Goldstein and Diane Tye. June 18, 2001.

Rushforth, Scott. 1994. Political Resistance in a Contemporary Hunter-Gather Society: More About Bearlake Athapasken Knowledge and Authority. *American Ethnologist* 21(2): 335–352.

Santino, Jack. 2001. *Signs of War And Peace: Social Conflict and the Use of Public Symbols in Northern Ireland.* New York: Palgrave.

Scott, James C. 1990. *Domination and the Arts of Resistance: Hidden Transcripts.* New Haven, CN: Yale University Press.

Story, G.M., W.J. Kirwin, and J.D.A. Widdowson. 1982. *Dictionary of Newfoundland English.* Toronto: University of Toronto Press.

Tuleja, Tad. 1997. Closing the Circle: Yellow Ribbons and the Redemption of the Past. *In Usable Pasts: Traditions and Group Expressions in North America,* ed. Tad Tuleja, 311–331. Logan: Utah State University Press.

Young, James E. 1993. *The Texture of Memory: Holocaust Memorials and Meaning.* New Haven, CN: Yale University Press.

Chapter 11

The Missing and Photography:
The Uses and Misuses
of Globalization

Ariel Dorfman

We have grown strangely used to them over the last 25 years, the women with the small photo of a man pinned to their dark dresses, the extended tribe of those whose loved ones, from Chile to Kurdistan, from Argentina to Ethiopia, from Guatemala to Guinea, have been abducted in the night and never heard of again. Mothers and daughters, wives and sisters, demanding to know the true fate of their men, demanding that they be returned to their families alive. They have become a habitual presence, these faraway women on the television screen asking at least for a body to bury, asking that they be allowed to start mourning their dead. A widespread, almost epidemic, image of tragedy and defiance that is just as much a part of our planetary imagination as the brands and logos that pervade us with an opposite sort of message, the Golden Arches of McDonalds, the red glistening cans of Coca-Cola, the Nike symbols of acceleration, the United Colors of Beneton that promise life–everlasting through incessant consumption.

The misfortune of women who search for information about their missing husbands, sons, fathers, brothers, lovers, is as haplessly old as the wars and slaughterhouses with which we humans have disgraced ourselves throughout our history. What is specifically new about the iconic representation of woe, which anyone who owns a television set can now recognize and identify, is not the repression or the pain, but rather the form of spectacle that these demonstrations have taken, how the performance of that pain is only conceivable in the context of present-day globalization. Indeed, those marching women brandishing a black and white photo have become so natural to our eyes, so much a part of the mythical landscape of our time, that we tend to forget that there was a time, not very long ago, when photographs did not constitute an automatic ingredient of that sort of protest.

As far as I can tell the first time photos were displayed as a means of responding to the state terror that uses disappearance as a form of control and punishment was in June 1977 when a group of Chilean women whose relatives had been arrested by General Pinochet's secret police in the years after the 1973 coup, decided to go on a hunger strike to force the military and judicial authorities to acknowledge those detentions. That they chose to do so in the regional offices of the United Nations in Santiago may have initially been due to the relative safety that an international organization provided under a dictatorship but, more crucially, suggests that their targeted audience was potentially the wide world beyond the country's frontiers rather than their own fellow countrymen, most of whom had no way of being informed about even the existence of this rally. I am not sure if the organizers of that protest immediately realized how influential and far-reaching the image they had created was to become in their own struggle and they certainly could not have anticipated the ways in which it would be adopted by people with similar dilemmas all over the globe, from Cyprus to Mexico. What probably mattered most to them was that the exhibition of those photos fiercely expressed the core of their tragedy. The central drama of those women was, after all, that they had no body to oppose to the denial of responsibility by the authorities, no way of countering the refusal of the judges to accept writs of habeas corpus because, to put it bluntly, there was no corpus. No body. Dead or alive. The photo became a substitute for that body that the government officials contended had never been arrested, a way of bringing into visibility someone who was at that very moment being hidden from view, whose corpse, if indeed the detainee had been killed, was being denied the right to denounce the crime committed against it, the only vocabulary left to the dead. When the relatives showed bystanders that replica in celluloid they were making present and material and lifelike what had been phantasmagorically removed from their hands, they were calling attention to a moment that had existed in the past when that loved one had been alive and a finger had clicked on a camera, they were demanding a moment in the future when that loved one could once again stand in front of them, could step out of the photo and into life, could climb out of their memory and into life. It was only in the months and years that followed, as the relatives took their protest into the streets, that they discovered that, beyond telling the essence of their predicament with extreme efficiency and extraordinary poetry, those stark semblances of the missing also answered the needs of the contemporary media, its time constraints, its hunger for visually striking imagery, its audiences with their short attention spans. And when the police attacked the women, jailed them, ripped the photos from their dresses, or kicked the placards upon which the photos had been reproduced, these scenes were then also transmitted over and over to the world. In the violence done to the relatives because they dared to remember and bring their memories into communal spaces, the regime was being forced to publicly reenact the secret, covert outrage done to the original bodies in the dank privacy of jails and basements and concentration camps.

Making that violence globally visible was a particularly apt response to disappearance because that extreme form of repression originated, in fact, in a strategy of the dictatorship that had a global component from the start. The new rulers of Chile were determined to integrate their country into the worldwide market and join what they called the "civilized concert of nations," A membership that entailed two contradictory requirements: On the one hand, the need to terrorize a restless and recalcitrant populace into submission and make it economically and politically pliant for the experiment of what was, quite blatantly, called "shock therapy"; coupled, on the other hand, with the need to present an immaculate face to the international community and therefore distance officials from any acts of barbarism. And disappearances perfectly fit this bill: dissidents and revolutionaries could be conveniently tortured to death without any of their executioners ever being held accountable; terror could reign in the whispers of the mind without the government having to openly admit being the source of those whispers, that terror.

It is this perverse tactic of invisibility that the bodies of the women and the photos pinned to their clothes fracture, that the photos of their resistance and repression further perturb and disrupt, a cycle of visual transgressions that were to amazingly grow into a worldwide movement. It is incredible, after all, that one small gesture by one solitary woman in a violated Chilean home, one woman who looks at the faded image of her absent loved one and comes to understand that its public exposure can keep him alive inside her and in the world, merely that one modest, unpretentious image speaking louder than all the machinery of State, and finally spreading and extending its reach until it is imitated all over the world. The ferocity with which the masters of these many misdeveloped nations have dragged their societies, quite literally kicking and screaming, into modernity is answered by a denunciation of the consequences of that process of forced development, using none other than the central invention of modernity, photography, shrewdly appropriated by the victims. Two possibilities of globalization face to face: the high technology of systematic fear employed by tyrants, their scientific use of torture and censorship and propaganda and, of course, of spying through cameras, confronted with the cunning and defiance of multitudes of humiliated women with their low-tech performances, their snapshots of bodies that refuse to be silenced.

At a time in history where it is all too easy to feel defenseless and passive and irrelevant in the face of a global world profiteering disorder that often seems to even be beyond the control of its most dominant elites, a planetary network that acts according to scarcely comprehensible laws, it is heartening to see how some of the least powerful people on this Earth can score a victory of the imagination against their enemies, can prove that it is possible for the modernity of human rights to defeat the modernity of inhuman authoritarianism. Indeed, I would venture to suggest that the relatives of the disappeared are handing us a model for how other humans can make use of the forces of globalization to make this world a less threatening home for us all.

And yet, a note of caution.

If you go through a little booklet published many years ago by the Association of Relatives of Arrested and Disappeared Persons in Chile, which lists and seeks to portray some of the peasants abducted by the authorities since 1973, you will notice, on the very first page, six names with respective spaces for their photos. Two of these spaces are blank—those meant for Antonio Aninao Morales and Juan Salinas Salinas. Of these two, not even a photograph remains. They are men who lived their twentieth-century lives without once being photographed. Let me repeat this: they were never captured by the process invented by Louis Daguerre more than a 100 years before their birth. It is only the kidnapping of Salinas and Aninao, which paradoxically, calls them at all to our attention among the millions who are too poor or marginalized to have been captured by a camera, who are outside the eyes of modernity. And if you continue to read the booklet, on each page there are several more unphotographed peasants, until the last page where all four of those named are without an image—that deep blankness, the only visual evidence that they ever existed.

These are the true *desaparecidos* of humanity, those who are missing because, in reality, the modern world acts as if, all this while, they had never been there at all, members of orphaned countries that seem to flicker into public consciousness only when they cause trouble, when they upset strategic balances or unhinge the lives of those who watch from the comfort of detached television screens. They were missing before the police came for them. They came late to the distribution of words and techniques and knowledge and, yes, to the saving grace of photography itself, perhaps suspecting that they would merit neither a footnote in the pages of anybody's history book nor even a few seconds on the nightly news.

I have spent many hours looking at those empty spaces, wondering how those men lived and how they died, who they were, what their eyes might have told me if I had ever met them. The truth is that I know nothing about them. All that I really receive back from that absence is my own reflection.

In the supermarket and superspectacle that our planet is slowly becoming it is the unknown Salinas's and Aninaos of the world who pose the ultimate challenge to globalization. It is one of the great tragedies of our time that we have been unable to organize a world where men like them and their billions of brothers and sisters from all the other continents are included and finally seen, really seen. Everyone on this Earth, I believe, is a member of a vastly interconnected humanity and the terrible events of September 11, 2001 in the United States would seem to confirm that we ignore this fact at our peril.

How to imagine those who live outside the dominant forms of modernity? Is it even possible?

Strange as this may sound, I see a dreadful form of hope in the dark blizzard of photos that covered the streets of New York after September 11. It is an extraordinary recognition of our common humanity that the inhabitants of the most prosperous city in the world, when faced with the infernal dilemma of dealing with the instantaneous and violent disappearance of friends and relatives whose death could be presumed but not ascertained because of the lack of a body, spontaneously recurred to the same methods of memory and defiance that thousands upon thousands of others from the most remote and often impoverished regions of the planet have invented over the last 25 years to cope with a similar mental hell.

I am aware, of course, of the distances and differences that separate the missing of New York and their relatives, friends, and community from those who are *desaparecidos* in the rest of the world and am wary of conflating these quite distinct tragedies. It is not their own government that has concealed the bodies incinerated in the Twin Towers or mocked those who seek information about their whereabouts. And the photos themselves probably originated in a longstanding American tradition that has proliferated images of lost children over the years on milk cartons and other commercial and postal sites. And yet, the inhabitants of the most modernized society in the world may now be able to connect, in ways that would have been unthinkable before September 11, 2001, to the experience of so many hitherto inaccessible planetary others. How can they not understand, now that they know what it means to have thousands of people suddenly evaporate into nothingness with no body to prove or disprove life or death, how can they not feel closer to an old woman I know in Chile who still awakes after midnight, still awakes, even now, and listens for footsteps that could be her husband's, even if she knows that 27 years have gone by and that it would be better that he not return; who would want him to have been tortured for those many long years? How can they not empathize more, now that they

hold up their photos to search for a sliver of certainty, find a final witness to
their beloved's last moments, those words from some stranger a message
sent to us from the dead, how can their hearts not go out to the grandmothers in Argentina determined to track down the children of their sons
and daughters born in captivity and farmed out to sterile military families,
those grandmothers who want to see in the eyes of those babies now grown
up the ultimate inheritance left behind by their dead offspring? As the
operation in the smoldering ruins of the World Trade Center wearily turned
from rescue to recovery, as the expectation of one more miracle gave way to
the conviction that there can be no more survivors, how can they not share
the grief of the families of the *desaparecidos* of other lands, when there is no
more hope? If New Yorkers are discovering what the women of the missing
in Chile and Cyprus and Cambodia and Brazzaville also gradually realized,
that their flock of photographs shrouding the entire city are ultimately
destined to become a transitory burial ground where the living and the dead
can commune, a site of the collective mourning imagination, the only scattered monument immediately possible in the months to come for a city that
needs to turn itself into an extended graveyard of its missing dead if it is to
go on with life, how can these fundamental, radical experiences of death
and vulnerability not open millions of Americans up to the meaning of
disappearance in its multiple forms, how can the horror and wonder of
breathing an air filled with the oxygen of the absent dead, not help them
and us to feel linked to the deep suffering and redemption of so many of our
faraway kinsmen across the Earth?

There is, of course, no guarantee that pain and victimhood lead to
empathy, no certainty that this would allow the Salinas's of the world to
emerge from invisibility. Enormous sorrows can lead to self-absorption and
indifference.

But I would like to think that this new global tragedy draws us all closer
to the day when the most powerful members of humankind can pin to our
clothes that blank photo of the disappeared, that image of an emptiness and
absence that threatens to devour us all. Perhaps our species is getting ready
for the day when enough of us will want to wander the boundaries of this
Earth until we have brought the lost souls of modernity, like the other
missing of the world, back from death and oblivion.

Chapter 12

El Dia de los Muertos in the USA: Cultural Ritual as Political Communication

Regina Marchi

Introduction

Associated with a preindustrial past that is seemingly unrelated to the modern world, ethnic folk rituals practiced in the United States are often dismissed as apolitical activities that serve only to entertain. As a result, ritual as a medium for critiquing dominant systems of power has generally been neglected within the field of Cultural Studies in favor of analyses of mass media cultural production (Limón 1994: 11). However, cultural scholars such as Americo Paredes (1993), Olivia Cadavál (1985), José Limón (1994), and George Lipsitz (1990) suggest that folk rituals are *not* merely substitutes for politics, but communicate important messages about identity and social struggle that help to shape individual and collective practice. Much current thinking about the political importance of folk rituals is influenced by the work of Antonio Gramsci and E.P. Thompson. Gramsci discouraged the conceptual separation between modern culture and popular folk culture, believing that folk practices had the potential to challenge hegemonic beliefs and "bring about the birth of a new culture." Thompson felt that folk practices were contexts in which working class people could define and express their own values, which could be "antagonistic to the overarching system of domination and control" (Limón 1983: 42).

Working from the premise that ethnic celebrations in the United States represent a "public sphere" where conversations about identity and politics occur, this essay focuses on the communication of political messages during Day of the Dead celebrations in the United States. Using insights from E.P. Thompson's essay, "The Moral Economy of the English Crowd in the Eighteenth Century," I will discuss how U.S. Day of the Dead rituals frequently operate along a "moral economy" of social protest, encouraging moral reflection on issues of political importance and revealing dimensions of repression normally overlooked by the dominant culture. Similar to the protests of the Mothers of the Disappeared in Chile and Argentina, politicized Day of the Dead rituals in the U.S. allow what Michael Taussig has called "the tremendous moral and magical power of the unquiet dead to flow into the public sphere, empower individuals and challenge the would be guardians of the nation state" (Taussig 1994: 280).

Having participated in Day of the Dead celebrations in San Francisco's Mission district during the 1980s, I later had the opportunity while working in Central America from 1990–1994 to see how the holiday was observed in urban and rural areas of Guatemala, El Salvador, and the Chiapas and Oaxaca regions of Mexico. Over the past eight years, I have attended U.S. Day of the Dead events, workshops and exhibits in Washington DC, Boston, Los Angeles, San Diego, San Francisco, El Paso, Texas; La Mesilla, N.M.; and Tijuana, Mexico. My reflections for this paper are based on interdisciplinary readings from the fields of communication, sociology, anthropology, folklore, history, and cultural studies; a review of newspaper and Internet articles written about Day of the Dead events across the U.S.; interviews I have conducted with Day of the Dead participants both in the U.S. and Latin America[1]; and my observations of Day of the Dead activities in the United States, Mexico, and Central America.

Background on the Ritual

In many Latin American countries, the "Days of the Dead"[2] are observed on November 1 and 2, the dates of the Roman Catholic celebration of All Saints' Day and All Souls' Day. A syncretic mix of Catholic beliefs and indigenous practices of honoring the ancestors, the two days are considered as one holiday throughout Latin America (Milne 1965: 162). Rituals are celebrated in diverse ways from country to country and from region to region *within* countries, but key practices of this holiday include any of the following: sprucing up family gravesites by weeding, cleaning, and repainting them and/or refurbishing crosses; bringing flowers or other mementos to gravesites; constructing home altars to honor the departed; preparing special foods and/or beverages for the ancestral spirits traditionally believed to visit the living on these dates (or simply eating specific foods prepared only at this time of year); and attending Catholic mass to pray for the departed.

Throughout Latin America, many people visit cemeteries between October 31 and November 2 to clean and decorate family graves. Processions are sometimes held after mass on November 1, in which people walk together from the local church to the cemetery, carrying flowers, candles, and other offerings for placement on graves. The processions may include singing, praying, or musical accompaniment. In urban areas, it is customary for people to bring flowers to family graves, light candles, and pay their respects to the dead, although the visits tend to be more cursory than in rural and indigenous communities, where the festivities are often elaborate, with preparations beginning weeks or months in advance. In indigenous communities of Mexico, Central America, and South America, nocturnal vigils and serenades are held in the cemeteries to accompany the souls believed to descend to earth at this time of the year, and home altars are constructed to honor the deceased. In both Mesoamerica and South America, these altars often display a combination of candles and harvest produce (such as flowers, fruits, legumes, and gourds), specially made breads,[3] personal mementos, and favorite foods of the deceased. Photos of the departed and/or pictures of Catholic saints, Jesus, or the Virgin Mary are often in the center of family *ofrendas*, frequently surrounded by crucifixes, angels, and other Catholic iconography. Other key elements often placed on altars made by Mayan, Mixtec, Zapotec, Aymara, Quechua and other indigenous Latin American groups include incense, salt, coffee, and a glass of water (believed to quench the thirst of the traveling souls).

A major difference between the European All Saints' Day and All Souls' Day celebrations and Day of the Dead lies in the celebrants' perceived relationships between the living and the dead. In the European version, the tenets of official Catholicism are more strictly observed. The souls of children and other sexual innocents are believed to ascend directly to heaven, while those of adults are thought to suffer in purgatory, occupying a lower hierarchical position than the spirits in heaven. The role of the living, in this scenario, is to ask the saints to intercede on behalf of deceased family members in order to hasten their journey from purgatory to heaven. In the popular religion of Latin American Catholics, however, the hierarchical structure between purgatory and heaven is not emphasized (Childs and Altman 1982: 16). Most people assume that their loved ones go directly to heaven and are "free" from their earthly tribulations. Instead of asking saints to intercede on behalf of family members in purgatory, as is done in official Catholic observances, Day of the Dead celebrants in Latin America often ask the dead to intercede on their behalf in worldly affairs.

The emphasis of the celebration in southern Mexico, areas of Central America and indigenous regions of South America is on family connectedness, rather than on mournful supplications to free souls from their purgatorial incarceration. As one Guatemalan explained to me, "Day of the Dead here is similar to Thanksgiving in the U.S., because people travel across the country to be reunited with family members, living and dead."[4] The family reunion aspect of Day of the Dead has been noted by Carmichael and Sayer (1991), Garciagodoy (1998), Greenleigh and Beimler (1991), Bade (1997), and others. Thus, a Catholic holy period filled with thoughts of punishment and suffering becomes, in many Latin American countries, a celebratory time not only to remember the dead, but to actively communicate with them via shared meals, candlelight vigils, musical serenades, expressive altars, and individual and group prayer. Because the dead are felt to be particularly connected to the living at this time of the year, they are often seen as heavenly allies who can offer hope and assistance with life's tribulations.

The Day of the Dead in Latin America is most elaborately celebrated in regions with large indigenous populations, such as southern Mexico, Guatemala, Bolivia, Peru, and Ecuador, but is also observed in varying ways in countries with comparatively little overt indigenous presence, such as Argentina, El Salvador, and Nicaragua. Mexico has become internationally famous for its Day of the Dead celebrations, particularly in the areas of Oaxaca, Michoacán, Puebla, Vera Cruz, and Yucatan, where people create aesthetically intricately altars, and engage in a variety of Day of the Dead processions, vigils, popular theater, arts, and handicrafts. Less well known are the ritual practices found in other Latin American countries on November 1 and 2.

For example, the towns of Santiago, Sacatepequez and Sumpango, Guatemala, hold Day of the Dead kite flying celebrations, in which Maya villagers fly ornately designed kites (many larger in size than a house) in the cemeteries to help traveling spirits find their way back to earth.[5] Hand written notes are often attached to the kite strings, ascending into heaven as a kind of telecommunication with the dead.[6] To the delight of thousands of participants and onlookers, a festival atmosphere prevails in and around the cemeteries, with vendors selling food, flowers, candles, and the hot corn drink, *atol de maiz*. Villagers prepare special foods for the ancestors and place them by family graves as offerings for the departed. Later the food is shared with family and friends. In El Salvador, brightly colored, waxed paper flowers and chains adorn tombs, and *coronas* (wreaths) made of paper or fresh pine boughs are placed on graves. Families may leave small mementos by graves and sometimes tape letters to the tombs of loved ones.[7] In Nicaragua, on November 1 and 2, it is not uncommon for families to light candles in the home for each deceased relative and prepare *buñuelos* (fried dough pastries) and *nacatamales* (tamales) for the occasion. In rural homes, candles are sometimes arranged as an "altar" on the floor.[8]

Among the Andean regions of Bolivia and Peru, a variety of Day of the Dead festivities take place in the cemeteries, including grave adornment, vigils, singing, praying, and eating. Altars are prepared in homes, and relatives, friends, and neighbors visit each other to pray, chat, and share in consuming the specially prepared foods (Buechler 1980; Coluccio 1991; Milne 1965; Vergara 1997). Similar festivities have been documented in areas of Argentina and Colombia (Coluccio 1991: 113–118.) In both urban and rural Ecuador, a blood-like, blackberry drink called *colada morada* is prepared specifically during the Days of the Dead, along with loaves of *guaguas* (Day of the Dead bread baked in the shapes of children and animals, found throughout the Andes).[9] The indigenous Quechuas of Ecuador visit cemeteries to clean and restore grave markers, and make altars of flowers, *guaguas*, and fresh fruits (particularly bananas, oranges, and apples) on the tombs of loved ones. Like in Mexico and Guatemala, lively picnics are held in the cemeteries.[10] In all of these cases, ritual actions carried out on Day of the Dead are methods of communicating with and about the dead. They keep alive memories of the deceased in the hearts and minds of the living.

In view of these far-reaching traditions, it is not surprising that many Latinos in the United States are able to culturally and spiritually connect with the Chicano-initiated Day of the Dead celebrations held in United States. As the U.S. Latino population has become more diverse over the past 20 years, with substantial numbers of immigrants hailing from Central and South America, U.S. Day of the Dead celebrations increasingly include participation by diverse Latino populations, who incorporate a variety of their own national customs into existing festivities, or create their own celebrations. For example, in Cleveland, Ohio, Day of the Dead activities have been held by Honduran and Bolivian immigrants, featuring their traditional foods and dances.[11] In Minneapolis, Minnesota, Chilean immigrants erected Day of the Dead altars in November 2000 to remember those who disappeared during the dictatorship of Augusto Pinochet in Chile.[12] In the same year in San Rafael, California, the Guatemalan community hosted a Day of the Dead kite-flying celebration in a local cemetery.[13]

Day of the Dead in the United States

According to American folklorists, early Mexican All Saints'/All Souls' Day cemetery observances in the United States occurred in Texas and other parts of the American Southwest where, for generations, residents of Mexican heritage faithfully visited local cemeteries on November 1 and 2 to clean and decorate family gravesites (Gosnell and Gott 1989: 220; Turner and Jasper 1994: 133; West 1989: 152). In the 1970s, when Day of the Dead in Mexico experienced heightened popularity as a tourist attraction and symbol of Mexican national identity (Turner and Jasper 1994: 133; Brandes 1988: 88), Chicano activists in California were inspired to organize Day of the Dead processions and altar exhibits in the United States as a way to celebrate Mexican–American heritage (Morrison 1992: 33; Romo 2000, and personal interviews). Yet until the early 1990s, the holiday was rarely celebrated in the United Stares outside of California and the southwest. This changed with the large-scale migration of Latin Americans both *to* and *within* the United States over the past 15–20 years, and Day of the Dead has increasingly been celebrated across the country, not only in major urban areas such as Chicago, New York, or Washington DC, but in rural and urban areas with historically little or no Latino presence, such as Omaha, Nebraska; Columbus, Ohio; Seattle, Kansas City; Milwaukee, and Atlanta.[14]

While Day of the Dead in Latin America is a time specifically to honor the deceased, the holiday takes on very different purposes and meanings in the United States.[15] From a primarily family-centered celebration focusing on the ritual preparation of homes and graves in honor of the departed, the holiday is transformed in the United States into an advertised cultural "happening" celebrated primarily in public, secular locations such as community centers, schools, libraries, museums, and parks. The period of celebration, usually lasting a few days in Latin America, often lasts one to two months in the United States.[16] Advertised in newspapers and on the Internet, U.S. Day of the Dead altar exhibits, processions and vigils are performed self-consciously for audiences no longer comprised of people from the same town, region, or country, but of Latinos and non-Latinos of diverse ethnic, racial, and economic backgrounds. Rather than morally binding obligations to the deceased, U.S. celebrations are reinventions of traditions that become methods for honoring Latino cultural heritage. Alicia Gaspar de Alba refers to this as the conversion of ancient devotional expressions into "ceremonial art whose main function [is] the ritual celebration and preservation of cultural memory" (Gaspar de Alba 1998: 76). Jack Santino calls such transformations of tradition, "rituals of public presentation," that is, "rites of intensification of group unity and identity" that are also presented to outsiders to inform them about the culture (Santino 1988: 124).

Anthropologist Victor Turner notes that rituals in tribal or non-industrial contexts are observed because of "obligation, not optation," while those celebrated in modern, industrial contexts are the result of individual optation rather than social obligation (Turner 1977b: 39). These optional rituals, he asserts, are forms of "leisure activity" rather than "work," and allow participants to escape the "should" and "must" character of ritual performed in the original context. Participants are thus free to "play with ideas" and release their creativity in ways capable of either supporting or criticizing the dominant social structural values. Through these "play" frames, argues Turner, celebrants can fabricate a range of alternative possibilities of behaving, thinking, and feeling that extend beyond the confines of what is admissible in the obligatory ritual frame (Turner 1977b: 42; and 1982: 28). Such is the case with Day of the Dead celebrations, where activities considered obligatory by most practitioners in Latin America have become remarkably innovative forms of expression for practitioners in the United States. Freed from the obligatory ritual frame, these ceremonies can express both cultural faith and political skepticism, commenting on a wide range of social issues and identities.

Within the six modes[17] of ritual sensibility sketched by ritual studies scholar, Ronald Grimes, Day of the Dead in most of Latin America can be classified as *primarily* a form of ritualization, or habitual, routine, socially obligatory action, with *secondary* elements of celebration, or "expressive ritual play" (Grimes 1995: 40–56). In contrast, Day of the Dead in the United States is *primarily* a form of ceremony and celebration. As opposed to ritualization, ceremonies are "rites that are more differentiated, more intentional, and therefore more likely to be considered ritual by participants"(Grimes 1995: 47). Intentionally commemorative, ceremony "symbolizes respect for the offices, histories, and causes that are condensed into its gestures, objects and actions"(Grimes 1995: 48). Grimes notes that "celebrations" seem spontaneous, but are choreographed "happenings" arising from expressive culture, and are often linked to the arts (Grimes 1995: 54–55).

Based on a conceptual framework of Latin American celebrations, U.S. Day of the Dead activities include traditional components, such as altar construction (in which individuals or groups create altars to honor the departed); cemetery rituals (where participants adorn graves, hold vigils, pray, sing, or dance in honor of the dead); and candlelight processions (in which participants walk through town carrying candles and/or photos of the deceased).[18] Yet these events are integrated with nontraditional components such as educational workshops where participants learn to make Day of the Dead sugar skulls, masks, bread for the dead, or paper decorations (such as flowers, *coronas*, and *papel picado*). Other nontraditional practices include Day of the Dead dance and theatre performances, multimedia art installations, spoken word events (where poems or stories about the dead are recited), public lectures on Day of the Dead or the topic of death, and screenings of documentaries on Day of the Dead.

From their inception, U.S. Day of the Dead celebrations have been a hybridization of spiritual, folk, and popular elements of the holiday, reflecting an assemblage of various religious influences impacting Chicano identity. Altar installations, processions, and cemetery rituals reflect this hybrid nature, routinely including Catholic and indigenous iconography such as crucifixes, devotional candles, pictures of saints, Jesus, or the Virgin Mary, together with statues of Aztec or Mayan deities, copal incense,[19] and offerings of food, drink, and other traditional oblations. These elements have been interwoven for the purpose of creating a feeling of Mexican American cultural unity to assist in struggles for political justice (Romo 2000).

Because these commemorations were created to be public displays, rather than family religious rituals, gallery spaces, community centers, public parks, and streets became key stages for communicating messages of Latino cultural affirmation and political consciousness within mainstream U.S. culture. Influenced by the rituals and imagery of Mexico's Day of the Dead, Chicano artists reconfigured the celebration and iconography in ways that were relevant to their lives and experiences in California. Some artists transformed traditional imagery, such as *calaveras*[20] into forms that would resonate with the Chicano community, such as sardonic skeletal depictions of local political personalities, rebellious urban youth "pachucos," or feminist versions of the Virgin of Guadalupe. Others based their work on the traditional indigenous *ofrendas* found in southern Mexico. Still others utilized the holiday's focus on death and remembrance to create altar installations that would draw attention to sociopolitical issues affecting Latinos, such as pesticide-induced sickness and death among farm workers, poverty and gang-related violence in urban neighborhoods, or US-supported coups, massacres, and wars in Latin America.

Death and Political Resistance

Before discussing politicized Day of the Dead activities in the United States, it is worth observing the historical connection between Day of the Dead and popular resistance in Latin America. Much to the chagrin of Spanish missionaries in Mexico, Central America, and South America, indigenous peoples forced to convert to Catholicism resolutely retained native customs of honoring their ancestors (Ricard 1982: 269–287; Stern 1987: 161; Stern 1993: 177). While Day of the Dead rituals were considered familial, rather than political activities, on a certain level, honoring the departed invited contemplation about the myriad inequities faced by indigenous peoples living under colonialism. To remember the dead, after all, is to remember how and why they died.

In colonial times, death among the indigenous majority was, more often than not, the result of preventable phenomena such as malnutrition, poverty, or abuse by colonial authorities. Therefore, the period set aside each year to remember the dead was simultaneously a space in which the poor might express frustration toward the injustices of the existing social order responsible for so many untimely deaths. With normal inhibitions lowered during "festival time," pent-up emotions were manifested through riotous festivities and drunkenness in the cemeteries during the Days of the Dead (Carmichael and Sayer 1991: 43). Scholars such as Mikhail Bakhtin, Max Gluckman, and Peter Burke have described the place of festival in traditional societies as a time of social inversion—a privileged time when what was often thought could finally be expressed aloud with relative impunity. Day of the Dead was such a time, and historical evidence suggests that the special closeness that participants felt with departed loved ones during this holiday encouraged communal reflections about the conditions under which they lived and died.

Mexican ethnohistorian, Juan-Pedro Viqueira, argues that the observance of Day of the Dead and other popular religious festivals during colonial times represented a "resistance of the popular classes who, in order to defend their interests, entrenched themselves behind their traditions" (Viqueira 1984: 14). Writing on the resistance of Andean peasants to Spanish colonial rule, Steven J. Stern contends that a certain interplay existed between the heightened moral consciousness experienced while remembering the dead, and an increased collective consciousness of material exploitation (Stern 1987: 31). Similarly, William B. Taylor notes that by connecting communities to their past, cemeteries in colonial Latin America were frequently sites for rebellions or meeting places for the collective planning of rebellions (Taylor 1979: 118–119). So threatening to the ruling elite were the social tensions expressed during Day of the Dead in Mexico and what is now Central America, that the Royal Office of Crime passed decrees in 1766 prohibiting gatherings in cemeteries and the sale of alcohol after 9:00 p.m. during the Days of the Dead (Viqueira 1984: 13). Comparable measures to contain public manifestations during this holiday existed in Peru and other Andean countries (Stern 1987: 31) and as recently as the early twentieth century, Bolivian officials banned the sale of alcohol and fireworks and forbade musical bands from playing in and around cemeteries during All Saints' Day (Buechler 1971: 167).

During the mid-nineteenth century in Mexico, the spirit of resistance appeared in literary form during the Days of the Dead. A carry-over from the ninetienth century Spanish lampoons or *pasquines* (Carmichael and

Sayer 1991: 58), poems called *calaveras* ("skulls") were written during this time of year (Carmichael and Sayer 1991: 58). Utilizing humor to express the political dissatisfaction, which people felt privately but could not express publicly, these satiric verses were composed anonymously for publication in local newspapers. This practice continues in Mexico today, and while *calaveras* may touch on any theme, they frequently take the form of joking "obituaries" for corrupt political leaders, the wealthy, and others associated with structural inequality. The custom of writing satirical verses during the Days of the Dead is practiced on a smaller scale by university students in Guatemala and El Salvador.[21] Known as *bombas*, these anonymous poems have provided fleeting opportunities to condemn institutionalized violence and extreme disparities in wealth within a context of severe political and military repression. A late twentieth century form of political commentary to emerge during the Days of the Dead is seen in the Mexican skeletal figurines known as *calaveritas*. Crafted by working class artisans, these miniature skeletons frequently spoof the wealthy and portray cynicism toward the government, expressing the average working person's awareness of and resistance to class exploitation.[22] Thus, while Day of the Dead in Latin America is primarily about dedication to family, there has historically existed a subtext of contestation.

In recent years, urban activists in Latin America, (whose education and cosmopolitan lifestyles afford them the freedom to creatively play with traditional rituals), have sometimes drawn attention to social injustices through the creation of public Day of the Dead altars that comment on social relations of power. For example, in Mexico City, altars have been created in memory of destroyed rainforests, murdered street children, and AIDS victims (Garciagodoy 1998: 91). During the civil war in El Salvador, altars were erected near the cathedral in San Salvador to honor slain Archbishop Oscar Romero and other social justice advocates killed by government military forces.[23] In Santiago, Chile, Day of the Dead processions have been held to remember the victims of the Pinochet regime.[24] On the whole, however, politicized altars comprise a relatively small minority of the overall Day of the Dead activities occurring in Latin America, which are still overwhelmingly family and religious rituals.

In contrast, politicized altars and activities are a much greater part of Day of the Dead celebrations in the United States, largely because of the holiday's change in form from intimate, family ritual to choreographed, public "event." Freed from the traditional, religious and social constraints prevalent in Latin America, Day of the Dead in the United States becomes a reflexive expression of Latino identity that is performative and designed to communicate messages to a living audience, rather than to the dead. Advertised in newspapers, TV, radio, and the Internet, U.S. celebrations are generally viewed by many spectators and can be effective means of promoting "life and death" issues that go unreported or underreported in the mainstream media. Through community vigils, vibrant public altars and dramatic processions (that often include performative elements such as dance, music, masks, and puppetry), Latinos and others who are marginalized from formal channels of mainstream U.S. political participation and media representation, due to barriers related to educational and economic status, residency status, language fluency, or political views can put their issues on the table (or the altar, so to speak).

U.S. Day of the Dead as Political Ritual

An important part of expressing Latino identity involves acknowledging the discrimination and exploitation faced by Latinos in their lives as cultural minorities in the United States (Flores 2000; Paredes 1993; Sanchéz 1993). In expressions of Latino identity during the Days of the Dead, the deaths of local people are often used to invoke political discourses around national and global issues. Along the lines of E.P. Thompson's moral economy, deeply rooted cultural traditions provide the moral force and physical infrastructure for critiquing dominant society.

In his discussion of the moral economy, Thompson argued that the popular food riots of eighteenth century England were not merely compulsive responses to economic stimuli, but "self-conscious behavior modified by custom, culture and reason" in which people used moral indignation to defend community rights and challenge official descriptions of reality (Thompson 1991: 187). The grievances expressed by the common people, he explained, were grounded in traditional views of norms and obligations that "operated within a popular consensus as to what were legitimate and what were illegitimate practices" (Thompson 1991: 188) among various sectors of society (such as workers, consumers, business, and government). For Thompson, the moral economy was a "group, community or class response to crisis" that expressed resistance to exploitation and challenged the authorities, on moral grounds, to attend to the common weal. Tracing the origins of the highly organized eighteenth-century English working class to local traditions that emphasized decency and mutual aid, he argued that the widespread participation of common folk in traditional rituals and ceremonies sustained collectivist values that, in turn, allowed the working class to maintain solidarity under difficult political conditions. Culture, in Thompson's view, was not simply an extraneous variable, but a political necessity in the struggle for justice (Alexander 1990: 21).

Similarly, the collective Day of the Dead traditions of Latinos living in the United States help this population to create a sense of identity and solidarity in difficult political times. Grounded in Latin American traditions of moral obligation and respect toward the dead, as well as reciprocal networks of community responsibility toward the dead and toward each other, many U.S. Day of the Dead activities, "elevate the defense of the interests of the working community above those of the profits of a few" (Thompson 1991: 339). Moral arguments are advanced through colorful and dramatic rituals that attract the attention of both the media and the general public in ways that ordinary political work does not. Whether implicitly or explicitly, U.S. Day of the Dead altar exhibits and events frequently draw attention to the classism and racism in American society, that make low-income and minority people the main recipients of violence, drugs, environmental injustice, and the least desirable occupations.

Because of the novelty of this holiday for most mainstream U.S. observers and the colorful photo opportunities available to journalists, Day of the Dead activities receive significant coverage in newspapers across the United States, both in terms of promoting events beforehand and covering them afterward. This attention is particularly noteworthy in a society where 13 percent of the population is Latino but only 1 percent of national TV news focuses on Latinos[25] and only 1 percent of all characters on entertainment TV are Latinos (down from 3 percent in the 1950s).[26] While Latinos are severely underrepresented in magazine advertising[27] and often negatively portrayed on film,[28] media coverage of Day of the Dead events is positive coverage that affirms the value of Latino culture and, in the case of politicized altars and events, draws attention to political concerns affecting the Latino community.

U.S. Day of the Dead rituals create sacred spaces that serve both as sites for cultural affirmation via the enactment of ancestral customs, and sites for political expression, in which the dead become allies of the living in the condemnation of injustice. Consider, for example, a Day of the Dead altar erected by students from the Chicano Studies program at Pomona State University. To commemorate farm workers and their struggle for better working conditions, the altar displayed photos of deceased workers and union activists, along with wooden fruit crates, plastic grapes, citrus tree cuttings, real heads of lettuce, hoes, pesticides, and a section of barbed wire fence.[29] The ancient tradition of placing harvest offerings on Day of the Dead altars became politically charged, with lettuce, grapes, and wooden produce crates sardonically substituting for the fruits usually placed on altars. This altar evoked both the ancestral culture of Latino farm workers and their contemporary exploitation in the United States. Because of its artistic allure, this installation visually emphasized the dangerous labor conditions of farm workers to hundreds of passersby who might not otherwise have considered this issue.

Another example is an altar at the Mission Cultural Center for Latino Arts in San Francisco, comprised of 30,000 matches, painstakingly peeled by hand to produce "arms" and "legs," and then glued to a table to symbolize 30,000 victims of AIDS. The altar was ceremonially burned on November 2 as both a visual homage to AIDS victims, many of whom are people of color, and a political call for the need to fund more research.[30] Thompson argued that the moral economy exposes "confrontations in the market place over access (or entitlement) to necessities" (Thompson 1991: 337). Some of the most poignant Day of the Dead rituals to stir moral reflection over unfair access to necessities have been organized by the families of teens lost to violence, alcohol, drugs, and other ills besetting many inner city communities. In 1998, a Day of the Dead candlelight vigil attended by over 1,000 people in Santa Monica, California protested the rising number of gang-related deaths in Los Angeles. Organized by parishioners from St. Anne's Church, the vigil included photos and shrines honoring slain gang members. It was followed by a weekend of lengthy negotiations that resulted in the signing of a truce between warring Culver City and Santa Monica gangs.[31] With calls to "create jobs, increase educational opportunities and end a pattern of social neglect that feeds a violent gang lifestyle,"[32] community residents employed traditional rituals of honoring the dead to support moral claims about their entitlement to educational and employment opportunities, as well as the obligations of government toward tax-paying, rights-bearing citizens.

Similarly, a Day of the Dead altar dedicated to teens lost to drugs and suicide was erected in November of 2000 at the Sherman Heights Community Center in San Diego.[33] Like Latin American altars that display mementos of the deceased, the altar included photos of the teens, their personal belongings (hair clips, a folded T-shirt, and a baseball cap), their favorite foods (Pepsi, Reese's Cups, and Doritos) and handwritten notes from friends and family to the deceased teens, telling them how much they were missed and loved. Next to the altar were informational flyers about resources for depressed and drug-involved youth. Similar politicized altars have appeared across the country, dedicated to victims of social problems such as domestic violence, drugs, or drive-by shootings.[34] Because of their public nature, these altars and processions not only honor the dead, but also challenge the American-style privatization of mourning by publicly expressing the pain and anger of populations which, because of socioeconomic inequalities are disproportionately affected by an unnecessary loss of life.

A recurrent theme of U.S. Day of the Dead celebrations in the late twentieth and early twenty-first century is the issue of migration across the United States/Mexican border. In San Diego, the Interfaith Coalition for Immigrant Rights (ICIR) has held vigils on the United States/Mexico border to protest the controversial border patrol program, Operation Gatekeeper. Each November 1, a religious service is held and wooden crosses are placed along the border wall listing the names, ages and places of origin of many of the nearly 3,000 migrants[35] who have died while attempting to cross "the line" since Gatekeeper's inception in 1994. Also erected along the border are traditional Day of the Dead altars heaped with fruits, candles, flowers, and *pan de muerto* in memory of the dead migrants (see figure 12.1). Mixing the religious, the cultural, and the political, these rituals force the public to remember the desperate living conditions of millions of people south of the border, and to reflect on the U.S. government's role in maintaining a "favorable investment climate" that ensures poverty wages for the majority of people living in Latin America. By honoring migrants who die while attempting to cross the border in search of a better life, these activities emphasize the great contradictions between the rights of Latin Americans and North Americans to "life, liberty and the pursuit of happiness."

Roughly one-third of all bodies found along the border are unidentified due to the fact that Central American and other non-Mexican migrants typically travel without identification, hoping to pass for Mexican and thereby avoid deportation to their native countries, if captured by Border Patrol agents. At present, the nameless corpses are mechanically inhumed in vacant tracts of land near the border and the families of the dead have no

Figure 12.1   *Pan de Muerto* offered in memory of a dead migrant.
Photo by: Regina Marchi.

way of knowing the destiny of their absent relatives. In response to this situation, the California Rural Legal Assistance Foundation, together with St. Joseph and St. Anthony's parishes in Holtville, California, sponsored a Day of the Dead event in the Terrace Park Cemetery on November 1, 2001 (see figure 12.2). In a barren lot behind the main cemetery, the cadavers of more than 200 unidentified migrants found in the nearby desert lay buried beneath stark mounds of earth, generically marked "John Doe" or "Jane Doe." In an implicit condemnation of Operation Gatekeeper, this event combined a traditional, village-style Day of the Dead procession (from the outlying street into the cemetery) with a political call for binational efforts to identify the bodies via DNA testing.

At the entrance to the cemetery was a large sign that read, "This Day of the Dead, 600 families don't even know whether or not they have a migrant to cry for." The words "*don't even*" encouraged empathy with the migrants' families, appealing to a collective sense of right and wrong. They reminded readers that, while U.S. residents get peace of mind in mourning the loss of loved ones, families of many migrants are left to wonder, forever, about the fate of theirs. Organizers distributed buttons reading, "Would you walk across mountains and deserts for a job? 1,700 migrants did and died."[36] Once again, the message urged readers to identify with migrants and compare their differing life circumstances. The underlying discourse of the event appealed to unspoken but deeply felt concepts of basic human rights, dignity, and dedication to family—concepts that are strong in Latin American

Figure 12.2   Commemorating unidentified migrants.
Photo by: Regina Marchi.

cultures, as they were among the working-class English culture described by Thompson.

Following Latin American Day of the Dead traditions of grave adornment, nearly 100 participants proceeded to decorate the anonymous graves with flowers, candles, colored paper, incense, and *pan de muerto*, converting the lonely burial site into a vibrant commemoration of "those souls who have no one to remember them."[37] By commemorating the migrants buried in Holtville, local residents (most of whom were Latino) reenacted ancestral traditions of moral obligation to the dead. In so doing, they not only drew attention to the deaths, but simultaneously forced the public to consider the sociopolitical *reason* for them, while demanding that state and federal government address the problem. The drama, music, and color of the event drew media coverage through which community participants— working-class Latinos and social justice activists—gained access to public space from which they are usually marginalized. Each year, immigrant rights activists around the country observe Day of the Dead with processions and altars critical of U.S. border patrol policies.[38]

Yet another social justice theme frequently honored during U.S. Day of the Dead events is that of indigenous rights. On November 1999, Lakota–Sioux Indians from the Pine Ridge Reservation in South Dakota,[39] together with Maya immigrants from Guatemala[40] organized a Day of the Dead event in Washington DC. Held in downtown Lafayette Park, directly across from the White House, the event featured Guatemalan Day of the Dead kites, Mayan music, dancers, and a series of speeches.[41] Pan-indigenous themes addressed at the event included the genocide of native peoples across the Americas, solidarity with the people of Guatemala, calls to free Leonard Peltier,[42] and demands to shut down the U.S. Army's School of the Americas.[43] Participants brought photos and mementos of indigenous martyrs for placement on a community altar, which quietly underscored the U.S. government's obligation to make restitution for past and present abuses to the native peoples of both North and South America. I have seen similar altars honoring indigenous struggles at numerous Day of the Dead events, including a 2002 altar in San Diego's Chicano Park, a 2003 altar exhibit at The Mexican Cultural Institute in Los Angeles, a 2004 altar at the Fruitvale Day of the Dead Festival in Oakland, California, and a 2004 altar exhibit in the town plaza of La Mesilla, New Mexico.

Sometimes the focus of Day of the Dead events is not dead people, per se, but deadly situations. In 1994, LA CAUSA (Los Angeles Communities United for a Sustainable Environment) held a Day of the Dead community forum and art exhibit to draw attention to environmentally caused illnesses. "Revisiting the Dead: Latinos and the Environment" focused on the influx of toxins in Southeast LA caused by a high concentration of industrial plants in the area, and kicked off a community-based initiative to reduce environmental hazards. Utilizing the allure of festival and art, the event (advertised in the *LA Times* and other local newspapers) attracted a variety of residents, scholars, environmental activists, elected officials and others[44] who may not otherwise have attended a meeting about toxins in this distressed community. In a local manifestation of a global problem, residents used moral discourses about the "correct" and "incorrect" economic role of business in their community, defending working-class interests above the profits of corporations. The language used at the event embodied what Thompson calls "certain essential premises . . . [about] what humans owe to each other in time of need" (Thompson 1991: 350).

Aside from large-scale public protest events such as the above mentioned, individual Day of the Dead altars on display at museums, schools, libraries, and other community-based spaces frequently draw attention to social justice issues. For example, since 1996, the World Languages and Culture Department at California State University at Monterey Bay has erected an annual Day of the Dead altar dedicated to historical figures who have worked for social justice.[45] In November 2000, students created an altar dedicated to "Yanga," a slave from Nigeria who lived in Vera Cruz, Mexico in the 1600s. The narrative surrounding the altar explained that Yanga fought against slavery and negotiated the founding of a slave-free town in Vera Cruz. Similar altars focusing on justice leaders from Martin Luther King to Cesar Chavez[46] have been erected across the country, in cities as disparate as Fort Worth, Kansas City, Seattle, and Atlanta. Altars have also been created for the anonymous victims of global political crises such as the Holocaust, the 100 million female babies lost to infanticide around the world, and the "slow death" of homelessness.[47]

The Day of the Dead is observed in a variety of ways throughout the United States, and this paper has focused on an important subset of these celebrations—those with overtly political messages. In a country as culturally diverse as the United States, ethnic rituals are important spaces in which cultural and political minority groups may criticize and respond to hegemonic norms and values. Through personalizing public issues and infusing traditional rites with contemporary meanings, U.S. Day of the Dead events function at both the micro- and macro-political level—at times quietly inviting the public to reflect on the reality of oppressed populations, while at other times urging concrete political action toward addressing the sociopolitical causes of death. In both cases, participants employ moral arguments to open public consciousness and stir it to action on behalf of those members in society who are victimized, discarded, and forgotten.

Over time, Day of the Dead traditions have reflected the historical conditions of participants. From the initial arrival of Europeans in Latin America to the more recent experiences of Latin Americans living in the United States, the celebration has provided practitioners with an opportunity for solace and expression amidst the often-unjust realities of a globalizing world. The holiday provides a useful case study on the political character of cultural rituals that, along with grassroots community organizing and alternative media production, can be valuable resources through which marginalized populations can construct narratives of self-affirmation, solidarity, and political resistance.

Notes

1. I have interviewed people from Mexico, Guatemala, El Salvador, Nicaragua, Panama, and Ecuador concerning the various ways in which Day of the Dead is observed in these countries.
2. Throughout Latin America, November 1 and November 2 are described by a variety of names, including *Todos Santos* (All Saints') *Dia de los Muertos* (Day of the Dead); *Dia de los Difuntos* (Day of the Departed); *Dia de los Fieles Difuntos* (Day of the Faithful Departed) or *Dia de las Animas Benditas* (Day of the Blessed Souls).
3. Called "pan de muerto" in Mexico and "guaguas" in Ecuador, Bolvia, and Peru.
4. Discussion I had on November 5, 1999, with resident of Morales, Izabál, Guatemala.
5. Celso Lara, "El Origen de Todos los Santos y la Fiesta de los Difuntos," *La Hora*, October 30, 2000, 11.
6. Personal observation, Santiago, Sacatepequez, November 1, 1991.
7. Personal interviews with Salvadoran immigrants residing in San Francisco, CA, May 17, 2001.
8. Personal interview with natives of Chinandega, Nicaragua (recently relocated to San Diego, CA), June 1, 2001.
9. Personal interviews with several informants from Quito, Ecuador, April 2001.
10. Personal interviews with Ecuadorians and photos taken in November 2002, documenting these activities in a cemetery in Otavalo, Ecuador.
11. Susan Ruiz, Patton, "Day of the Dead Comes to Life," *The Plain Dealer*, November 6, 2000, 1B.
12. Maria Elena Baca, "Days of the Dead," *Star Tribune*, November 4, 2000, 5B.
13. Karen Pierce Gonzalez, [no headline] *The San Francisco Chronicle*, October 27, 2000, 6.
14. According to newspapers articles I have collected about Day of the Dead activities in these and other areas.
15. Olivia Cadavál discusses this phenomenon in "The Taking of the Renwick: The Celebration of the Day of the Dead and the Latino Community in Washington DC" *Western Folklore*, May–June 1985, 179.
16. In San Diego, for example, the 2002 Day of the Dead activities began on September 28 and continued until November 30, including art, altar, and

photography exhibits, altar "house tours," workshops in sugar skull-making, masks, *pan de muerto* and *papel picado*, film screenings, community altar-making events, poetry readings, dance and music performances, vigils, and masses. On the other side of the country in Boston in 2003 Day of the Dead events began at craft stores, community centers, and the Forest Hills Cemetery in mid-October, and ended with the closing of the annual Day of the Dead exhibit at the Peabody Museum of Harvard University on December 9. This elongated timeframe is common in cities across the United States.

17. Grimes distinguishes between Ritualization, Decorum, Ceremony, Magic, Liturgy, and Celebration.

18. Depending on the nature of the procession, participants may wear skeletal costumes and masks or carry props such as banners, signs, cardboard coffins, or giant skeletal puppets.

19. Incense made of pine resin, used by Mesoamerican religious ceremonies since pre-Columbian times.

20. Skeletal imagery in the form of figurines, engravings, paintings, wooden puppets, papier-mâché, sugar sweets, and other materials.

21. Personal conversations with students from the University of San Carlos, Guatemala, and the University of Central America, El Salvador, July 1994.

22. For detailed political analyses of these figurines, see Susan Masuoka's "Calavera Miniatures: Political Commentary in Three Dimensions," *Studies in Latin American Popular Culture*, volume 9, 1990, and Juanita Garciagodoy's, *Digging the Days of the Dead*.

23. Personal interviews with Salvadoran activist now living in the United States, May 2001, San Francisco, CA.

24. "Chile Victims Remembered," *The Toronto Star*, November 2, 1998, A12.

25. See Cecilia Alvear, "No Chicanos on TV," *Nieman Reports*, Fall 1998, 52 (3): 49.

26. Center for Media and Public Affairs' *Distorted Reality Study*, cited in Marco Portales, *Crowding Out Latinos* (Philadelphia: Temple University Press), 56.

27. Charles R. Taylor and Hae-Kyong Bang, "Portrayals of Latinos in magazine advertising," in *Journalism and Mass Communication Educator*, Summer 1997, 52 (2): 285.

28. "Combatting the network 'brownout,' " *Hispanic Business*, October 1999, 21 (10): 46.

29. Alicia Gaspar De Alba, *Chicano Art*, p. 75.

30. Denise Richards, *Calaveras*, documentary video on Day of the Dead, 1996.

31. John L. Mitchell, "1000 Hold Vigil Against Violence in Santa Monica," *The Los Angeles Times*, November 3, 1998, Metro, part B, p. 1.

32. Ibid.

33. Personal observation, Sherman Heights Community Center, San Diego, October 26, 2000.

34. Allen R. Meyerson, "Caressing Life on the Day of the Dead," *New York Times*, November 4, 1995, 9.

35. According to the California Rural Legal Assistance Foundation, November 2003. Statistics derived from immigrant deaths recorded by the Mexican

Foreign Relations Office, the Mexican consulates in San Diego and Calexico, and the INS.

36. At the time of this event the death toll was 1,700. As of the fall of 2004, nearly 3000 bodies have been found.

37. Words of Claudia Smith, California Rural Legal Assistance Foundation, in speech made at cemetery, personal observation, November 2, 2001.

38. According to newspaper articles and websites I have reviewed, such activities have occurred in at least 20 cities across the country, including Phoenix, Austin, Chicago, New York, San Francisco, Los Angeles, and Washington DC.

39. One of the poorest census tracts in the United States.

40. Members of the International Maya League, a national organization incorporated in 1990 by Guatemalans living in exile in the United States, working to raise awareness of the violent affects of U.S. foreign policy in Guatemala.

41. Retrieved November 15, 2001 from the School of the Americas Watch website <www.soaw-ne.org/daydead.html>

42. American Indian Movement (AIM) activist allegedly framed by the FBI because of his political work and imprisoned for more than 25 years on murder charges.

43. Dubbed the "School of Assassins" by international human rights activists, this U.S. facility trains Latin American military leaders in counter-insurgency tactics. Its graduates have been responsible for many of the worst human rights abuses in Latin America, including assassinations, torture, and massacres against civilian populations.

44. "Latino Event Focuses on Area's Pollution," *Los Angeles Times*, November 6, 1994, 9.

45. California State University, Monterey Bay website <http://csumb.edu/events/dead/> Also see Professor Maria Zielina's research at <http://faculty.csumb.edu/zielinamaria/yanga/yanga.html>

46. "Live Events for Day of the Dead," *The Arizona Republic*, November 2, 2000, p. 39.

47. Marcia Tanner, "Hispanic Art Risen From the Dead," *San Francisco Chronicle*, November 11, 1992, Home page 9.

Bibliography

Alexander, Jeffrey, C. 1990. *Culture and Society, Contemporary Debates.* New York: Cambridge University.

Bade, Bonnie. 1997. "The Dead Are Coming: MixTec Day of the Dead and the Cultivation of Community." In *Proceedings of the 1995 and 1996 Latin American Symposia: Death, Ritual, and the Afterlife,* ed. Alana Cordy-Collins and Grace Johnson, 7–20. San Diego, CA: San Diego Museum of Man.

Bakhtin. Mikhail. 1984. *Rabelais and his World.* Bloomington: Indiana University Press.

Baron, Robert and Nicholas Spitzer. 1992. *Public Folklore*, Washington DC: Smithsonian Institution Press.

Brandes, Stanley. 1988. *Power and Persuasion: Fiestas and Social Control in Rural Mexico*. Philadelphia: University of Pennsylvania Press.

————. 1997. "Sugar, Colonialism, and Death: On the Origins of Mexico's Day of the Dead." *Comparative Studies in Society and History*, 39 (12): 270–297.

————. 1998(a). "Iconography in Mexico's Day of the Dead: Origins and Meaning." *Ethnohistory*, 45 (2), Spring: 182–218.

————. 1998(b). "Day of the Dead, Halloween, and the Quest for Mexican National Identity," *Journal of American Folklore*, 111 (442): 359–380.

Buechler, Hans C. 1971. *The Bolivian Aymara*. New York: Holt, Rinehart and Winston, Inc.

————. 1980. The Masked Media: *Aymara Fiestas and Social Interaction in the Bolivian Highlands*. New York: Mouton Publishers.

Cadavál Olivia. 1985. "The Taking of the Renwick": The Celebration of the Day of the Dead and the Latino Community in Washington, DC. *Journal of Folklore Research*, 22 (2–3): 179–193.

————. 1998. *Creating a Latino Identity in the Nation's Capital: The Latino Festival*. New York: Garland Publishing Inc.

Carmichael, Elizabeth and Chloe Sayer. 1991. *The Skeleton At the Feast: The Day of the Dead in Mexico*. Austin: University of Texas Press.

Childs, Robert and Patricia Altman. 1982. *Vive tu Recuerdo: Living Traditions in the Mexican Day of the Dead*. Los Angels: Museum of Cultural History, UCLA.

Coluccio, Felix. 1991. *Fiestas y Costumbres de Latinoamerica*. Buenos Aires, Ediciones Corregidor.

Flores, Juan. 2000. "The Latino Imaginary: Meanings of Community and Identity," *From Bomba to Hip Hop: Puerto Rican Culture and Latino Identity*. New York: Columbia University Press.

Garciagodoy, Juanita. 1998. *Digging the Days of the Dead*. Niwot: University Press of Colorado.

Gaspar De Alba, Alicia. 1998. *Chicano Art: Inside/Outside the Master's House*. Austin: University of Texas.

Gluckman, Max. 1962. *Essays on the Ritual of Social Relations*. Manchester, England: Butler and Tanner, Ltd.

Gosnell, Lynn and Suzanne Gott. 1989. "San Fernando Cemetery: Decorations of Love and Loss in a Mexican-American Cemetery." In *Cemeteries and Gravemarkers: Voices of American Culture*, ed. Richard E. Meyer. Ann Arbor: UMI Research Press.

Greenleaf, Richard. 1971. *The Roman Catholic Church in Colonial America*. New York: Alfred Knopf, Inc.

Greenleigh, John and Rosalind Beimler. 1991. *The Days of the Dead/Los Dias de Muertos*. San Francisco: Colins Publishers.

Grimes, Ronald. 1995. *Beginnings in Ritual Studies*. Revised edition. Columbia: University of South Carolina.

Lara, Celso. 2000. "El Origin de Todos los Santos y la Fiesta de los Difuntos," *La Hora*, October 30: 11. Guatemala City, Guatemala.

Limón, José. 1983. "Western Marxism and Folklore: A Critical Introduction." *Journal of American Folklore*, 96 (379): 471–486.

———. 1994. *Dancing with the Devil: Society and Cultural Poetics in Mexican-American South Texas*. Madison: University of Wisconsin Press.

Lipsitz, George. 1990. *Time Passages: Collective Memory and American Popular Culture*. Minneapolis: University of Minnesota Press.

Masuoka, Susan. 1990. "Calavera Miniatures: Political Commentary in Three Dimensions." *Studies in Latin American Popular Culture*, 9: 263–278.

Meyer, Richard, E. 1989. *Cemeteries and Gravemarkers: Voices of American Culture*, Ann Arbor: UMI Research Press.

Milne, Jean. 1965. "November: All Saints and All Souls." In *Fiesta Time in Latin America*. Los Angeles: Ward Ritchie Press.

Moore, Sally F. and Barbara, Myerhoff. 1977. *Secular Ritual*. Assen: Van Gorcum.

Paredes, Americo. 1993. *Folklore and Culture on the Texas-Mexican Border*. Austin: University of Texas Press.

Portillo, Lourdes and Muñoz, Susana. 1990. *La Ofenda* (Day of the Dead), video. San Francisco, CA.

Ricard, Robert. 1982. *The Spiritual Conquest of Mexico*. Berkeley: University of California Press.

Richards, Denise. 1996. *Calaveras* (Documentary video on Day of the Dead).

Romo, Tere. 2000. *Chicanos en Mictlan*. San Francisco: Mexican Museum of San Francisco.

Sanchez, George. 1993. *Becoming Mexican American: Ethnicity, Culture and Identity in Chicano Los Angeles, 1900–1945*. New York: Oxford University Press.

Santino, Jack. 1988. "The Tendency to Ritualize: The Living Celebrations Series as a Model for Cultural Presentation and Validation." In *The Conservation of Culture*, ed. Burt Feintuch, Knoxville: University Press of Kentucky.

Stern, Steven, J. 1987. *Resistance, Rebellion and Consciousness in the Andean Peasant World, 18th to 20th Centuries*, Madison: University of Wisconsin Press.

———. 1993. *Peru's Indian People's and the Challenge of Spanish Conquest*. Madison: University of Wisconsin Press.

Suzanne Shumate, Morrison. 1992. *Mexico's Day of the Dead in San Francisco, California*. Unpublished doctoral dissertation, Theology Department, Berkeley: University of California.

Taussig, Michael. 1980. *The Devil and Commodity Fetishism*. Chapel Hill: University of North Carolina.

———. 1994. "Violence and Resistance in the Americas: The Legacy of Conquest." In *Violence, Resistance, and Survival in the Americas: Native Americans and the Legacy of Conquest*, ed. William B. Taylor and Franklin Pease, 269–284. Washington, DC: The Smithsonian Institute.

Taylor, William B. 1979. *Drinking, Homicide and Rebellion in Colonial Mexican Villages*. Stanford: Stanford University Press.

Thompson, Edward, P. 1991. *Customs in Common*. London: Merlin Press.

Turner, Victor. 1977a. *Ritual Process: Structure and Anti-Structure*. Ithaca, NY: Cornell University Press.

———. 1977b. "Variations on a Theme of Li. Moore and Barbara G. Myerhoff, 36–52. A

———. 1982. *Celebration: Studies in Festivity* Smithsonian Institution Press.

Turner, Kay and Pat Jasper. 1994. "Day of the Dead: *Halloween and Other Festivals of Death and Life*, ed. Knoxville: University of Tennessee.

Vergara, F. Cesar Abilio. 1997. "Tu Pallay: ritual de reciprocida muerte." In *El Cuerpo Humano y Su Tratamiento Mortuario*, e Gregory Pereira, Vera Tiesler, 51–66. Mexico City: Centro Estu y Centroamericanos.

Viqueira, Juan-Pedro. 1984. "Religion Popular e Identidad." *Cuicuilco: Rev Escuela Nacional de Antropologia e Historia*, July–December: 6–15.

West, John, O. 1988. *Mexican-American Folklore*. Little Rock: August House.

Baron, Robert and Nicholas Spitzer. 1992. *Public Folklore*, Washington DC: Smithsonian Institution Press.

Brandes, Stanley. 1988. *Power and Persuasion: Fiestas and Social Control in Rural Mexico*. Philadelphia: University of Pennsylvania Press.

——. 1997. "Sugar, Colonialism, and Death: On the Origins of Mexico's Day of the Dead." *Comparative Studies in Society and History*, 39 (12): 270–297.

——. 1998(a). "Iconography in Mexico's Day of the Dead: Origins and Meaning." *Ethnohistory*, 45 (2), Spring: 182–218.

——. 1998(b). "Day of the Dead, Halloween, and the Quest for Mexican National Identity," *Journal of American Folklore*, 111 (442): 359–380.

Buechler, Hans C. 1971. *The Bolivian Aymara*. New York: Holt, Rinehart and Winston, Inc.

——. 1980. The Masked Media: *Aymara Fiestas and Social Interaction in the Bolivian Highlands*. New York: Mouton Publishers.

Cadavál Olivia. 1985. "The Taking of the Renwick": The Celebration of the Day of the Dead and the Latino Community in Washington, DC. *Journal of Folklore Research*, 22 (2–3): 179–193.

——. 1998. *Creating a Latino Identity in the Nation's Capital: The Latino Festival*. New York: Garland Publishing Inc.

Carmichael, Elizabeth and Chloe Sayer. 1991. *The Skeleton At the Feast: The Day of the Dead in Mexico*. Austin: University of Texas Press.

Childs, Robert and Patricia Altman. 1982. *Vive tu Recuerdo: Living Traditions in the Mexican Day of the Dead*. Los Angels: Museum of Cultural History, UCLA.

Coluccio, Felix. 1991. *Fiestas y Costumbres de Latinoamerica*. Buenos Aires, Ediciones Corregidor.

Flores, Juan. 2000. "The Latino Imaginary: Meanings of Community and Identity," *From Bomba to Hip Hop: Puerto Rican Culture and Latino Identity*. New York: Columbia University Press.

Garciagodoy, Juanita. 1998. *Digging the Days of the Dead*. Niwot: University Press of Colorado.

Gaspar De Alba, Alicia. 1998. *Chicano Art: Inside/Outside the Master's House*. Austin: University of Texas.

Gluckman, Max. 1962. *Essays on the Ritual of Social Relations*. Manchester, England: Butler and Tanner, Ltd.

Gosnell, Lynn and Suzanne Gott. 1989. "San Fernando Cemetery: Decorations of Love and Loss in a Mexican-American Cemetery." In *Cemeteries and Gravemarkers: Voices of American Culture*, ed. Richard E. Meyer. Ann Arbor: UMI Research Press.

Greenleaf, Richard. 1971. *The Roman Catholic Church in Colonial America*. New York: Alfred Knopf, Inc.

Greenleigh, John and Rosalind Beimler. 1991. *The Days of the Dead/Los Dias de Muertos*. San Francisco: Colins Publishers.

Grimes, Ronald. 1995. *Beginnings in Ritual Studies*. Revised edition. Columbia: University of South Carolina.

Lara, Celso. 2000. "El Origin de Todos los Santos y la Fiesta de los Difuntos," *La Hora*, October 30: 11. Guatemala City, Guatemala.

Limón, José. 1983. "Western Marxism and Folklore: A Critical Introduction." *Journal of American Folklore*, 96 (379): 471–486.

———. 1994. *Dancing with the Devil: Society and Cultural Poetics in Mexican-American South Texas*. Madison: University of Wisconsin Press.

Lipsitz, George. 1990. *Time Passages: Collective Memory and American Popular Culture*. Minneapolis: University of Minnesota Press.

Masuoka, Susan. 1990. "Calavera Miniatures: Political Commentary in Three Dimensions." *Studies in Latin American Popular Culture*, 9: 263–278.

Meyer, Richard, E. 1989. *Cemeteries and Gravemarkers: Voices of American Culture*, Ann Arbor: UMI Research Press.

Milne, Jean. 1965. "November: All Saints and All Souls." In *Fiesta Time in Latin America*. Los Angeles: Ward Ritchie Press.

Moore, Sally F. and Barbara, Myerhoff. 1977. *Secular Ritual*. Assen: Van Gorcum.

Paredes, Americo. 1993. *Folklore and Culture on the Texas-Mexican Border*. Austin: University of Texas Press.

Portillo, Lourdes and Muñoz, Susana. 1990. *La Ofenda* (Day of the Dead), video. San Francisco, CA.

Ricard, Robert. 1982. *The Spiritual Conquest of Mexico*. Berkeley: University of California Press.

Richards, Denise. 1996. *Calaveras* (Documentary video on Day of the Dead).

Romo, Tere. 2000. *Chicanos en Mictlan*. San Francisco: Mexican Museum of San Francisco.

Sanchez, George. 1993. *Becoming Mexican American: Ethnicity, Culture and Identity in Chicano Los Angeles*, 1900–1945. New York: Oxford University Press.

Santino, Jack. 1988. "The Tendency to Ritualize: The Living Celebrations Series as a Model for Cultural Presentation and Validation." In *The Conservation of Culture*, ed. Burt Feintuch, Knoxville: University Press of Kentucky.

Stern, Steven, J. 1987. *Resistance, Rebellion and Consciousness in the Andean Peasant World, 18th to 20th Centuries*, Madison: University of Wisconsin Press.

———. 1993. *Peru's Indian People's and the Challenge of Spanish Conquest*. Madison: University of Wisconsin Press.

Suzanne Shumate, Morrison. 1992. *Mexico's Day of the Dead in San Francisco, California*. Unpublished doctoral dissertation, Theology Department, Berkeley: University of California.

Taussig, Michael. 1980. *The Devil and Commodity Fetishism*. Chapel Hill: University of North Carolina.

———. 1994. "Violence and Resistance in the Americas: The Legacy of Conquest." In *Violence, Resistance, and Survival in the Americas: Native Americans and the Legacy of Conquest*, ed. William B. Taylor and Franklin Pease, 269–284. Washington, DC: The Smithsonian Institute.

Taylor, William B. 1979. *Drinking, Homicide and Rebellion in Colonial Mexican Villages*. Stanford: Stanford University Press.

Thompson, Edward, P. 1991. *Customs in Common*. London: Merlin Press.

Turner, Victor. 1977a. *Ritual Process: Structure and Anti-Structure*. Ithaca, NY: Cornell University Press.

————. 1977b. "Variations on a Theme of Liminality." In *Secular Ritual*, ed. Sally F. Moore and Barbara G. Myerhoff, 36–52. Assen/Amsterdam: Van Gorcum.

————. 1982. *Celebration: Studies in Festivity and Ritual*, Washington, DC: Smithsonian Institution Press.

Turner, Kay and Pat Jasper. 1994. "Day of the Dead: The Tex–Mex Tradition." In *Halloween and Other Festivals of Death and Life*, ed. Jack Santino, 131–151. Knoxville: University of Tennessee.

Vergara, F. Cesar Abilio. 1997. "Tu Pallay: ritual de reciprocidad entre la vida y la muerte." In *El Cuerpo Humano y Su Tratamiento Mortuario*, ed. Elsa Malvido, Gregory Pereira, Vera Tiesler, 51–66. Mexico City: Centro Estudios Mexicanos y Centroamericanos.

Viqueira, Juan-Pedro. 1984. "Religion Popular e Identidad." *Cuicuilco: Revista de la Escuela Nacional de Antropologia e Historia*, July–December: 6–15.

West, John, O. 1988. *Mexican-American Folklore*. Little Rock: August House.

Chapter 13

Signifying Places of Atrocity

Ralph Hartley

War itself is changing. Traditional conflicts between armies of different nations have been replaced by the bloodiest internal and mixed conflicts. Where civilians are not accidental casualties, but the primary target of attacks. Where crimes against humanity and genocide are not only a means but a purpose of the conflict. Where the minimum rules that all nations had agreed would always apply, the "laws of war," are violated as a policy, not by accident.

*—Emma Bonino, former European Commissioner
of Humanitarian Affairs, May 12, 1998*

Introduction

In the last decade of the twentieth century the world has witnessed lethal conflict that resulted in genocidal behavior,[1] most notably in Rwanda and the former Yugoslavia. Military, social, and political scientists contend that the conditions that foster these behavioral phenomena will persist if not increase in the decades to come. With the intensity of lethal conflict come massacres of noncombatants, characteristics of behavior chronicled in history and visible in prehistoric contexts. Mass graves are often a result of contemporary massacres and known to be scattered throughout both the former Yugoslavia and Rwanda.

The social identities and self-images of those involved in intergroup conflict are often tied to specific places. Distinct places of violent conflict and killings are often the subject of preservation and commemoration—what

Irwin-Zarecka (1994: 50) has called "memory markers." Places that mark turning points in the sociopolitical history of a community, associated with either victory or defeat, can serve to signify ethnonationalism to a society. The preservation of battlefields often exemplifies the relationship between social identity and the history of violent conflict. This space, often loaded with monuments or memorials, becomes "sacred" to factions of the populace (Azaryahu and Kellerman 1999; Mayo 1988; Pawson 1991). Memorials of events in wars long concluded are built so as to communicate a collective grievance. Their placement on the landscape allows for assured visibility, if not direct access (Winter 1995).

The preservation and assignment of sociocultural significance to places of atrocities and mass graves associated with killing sites also exemplifies behavior that ensures the commemoration of events for generations. But the placement of shrines or memorials at these sites during active conflict is sometimes problematic since control of portions of the landscape is often contested. Nevertheless, while during or after conflict these places have the potential to support those individuals attempting to maintain power; they can serve as the foundations for promoting cultural identity and national- ism; and they can be incorporated into development programs involving cultural tourism (Farmer 1999; Winter 1995). The social sensitivity and cultural value of such places makes them worthy of investment and manipulation by individuals, political leaders, and despots. Such places can also serve as symbols of resistance that can be used in the transition of power.

Places where atrocities occur, especially those involving the mass killing of noncombatants, are subject to being assigned long-term significance in a social system such that they may: (1) function as a means of solidarity for a victimized group, (2) become the basis for accounts/stories that are pervasive and transcend generations, (3) perpetuate divisiveness in a society, alienat- ing specific groups or portions of a society's population that are spatially dis- tinct, helping to establish or reinforce "traditional" enemies, and/or (4) socially sanction revenge actions (Brown et al. 1997; Burton 1997; Chalk and Jonassohn 1990; Fein 1990; Gurr 1993; Hirsch 1985; 1995; Kressel 1996; Nagengast 1994; Peterson 1999).

Shrines erected in dedication to those killed or missing are seldom feasible in an environment of active war, if not outright dangerous. The "truth" about what happened at a place is sometimes elusive and confirma- tion of allegations of the details of atrocities is exceedingly difficult. It is the means by which these places of massacre and mass killing in the former Yugoslavia and Rwanda are confirmed and made significant that is central to this essay.

Memory, Place, and Power

The role of memory—individual and collective—is a powerful mechanism in the array of social conditions underlying violent intergroup conflict that has the potential to lead to genocidal behavior. This behavioral phenomenon is timeless and not limited to the constructs of culture. As Hirsch (1995: 3) emphasizes, "People continue to hate and to kill for the same reasons, and the memories of their attachments to ethnic, religious, racial, national, or regional identity continue as prime motivations." It is asserted here that the social imageability of those involved in intergroup conflict is often place-specific. Social imageability, as used here, is the capacity to evoke vivid and collectively held social meanings among the occupants and users of a place. A particular microenvironment can be described in terms of the imageability (or memorability) of its physical elements. Concepts of "place attachment" have found that emotion plays an important role in the meaning and significance assigned to a physical site (see Altman and Low 1992). The social meaning attributed to past experiences that are associated with a place, its "interactional past," determines the extent of place attachment to individuals in the social system. "Dependence" on a place for emotional security and identity formation is a function of the degree to which individuals perceive themselves to be strongly associated with a particular site (Milligan 1998; Stokols and Shumaker 1981: 446, 455–457, 483). Sociocultural meaning assigned to a place can be considered a bonding of individuals to a socio-physical environment defined by both material and symbolic components.

The role of myth-making in group identity is an important consideration in examining the relationship between place specific events, human memory, and interpretative social values. Descent myths provide a powerful framework for the purpose of providing a collective identity for individuals incurring social stress and/or threats to security. Distinguishing myths that rely on genealogical ancestry to "connect" individuals to ascribed status and power from those of "ideational descent" where virtuous values and distinctive qualities of a culture are attributes to emulate is a theme that Smith (1984; 1992: 440–441) finds appropriate to the process of "ethnic election" and, ultimately, ethnonationalism. He argues (1984: 96–99) that "Myths of ethnic descent are vital both for territorial claims and for national solidarity." A contemporary example is that of the former Yugoslavia where as Charles Ingrao (1998) notes, "It is commonplace for new countries to create myths about their nation, while simultaneously eradicating facts that prove inconvenient to the creation of those myths. What is so unfortunate

for central Europe is that so much of the institutionalized mythology perpetuates national tensions between peoples who still live side by side." It is important to acknowledge that myths do not necessarily require the representation or reflection of "truth" when its value is the unity of the group; "they need only be accepted" (Alexander 1989: 493).

The association of people with events or activities in the past and defined spatially underlies concepts of "homeland." To serve nationalistic goals, the collective memories of an ethnically defined group "must attach themselves to specific places and definite territories" (Smith 1992: 450; 1996: 453). Places associated with and remembered for "common suffering" can enhance national unity (Farmer 1999; Schwartz and Bayma 1999: 959–963). The assignment of significance to "sacred" sites and places contribute to the definition of ethnic landscapes—areas where the emotional memory of events or activities in the past are used by leaders of nationalistic movements to garner support. Images of place-identity are vulnerable to manipulation when the interest of power-elites is to initiate or maintain war, ethnic cleansing, or genocide (Reuber 2000: 39).[2]

The claim to a particular place is often linked to the dynamics of power relations. How identity is involved in the emotional construction of a sense of place is inextricably tied to boundaries and territoriality. The impassioned assignment of significance to a place where members of a sociocultural system were killed can become a core element of identity to a group. Hayden (1994: 172) has noted that the uncovering and acknowledgement of past massacres and other atrocities is "One of the most potent weapons for building nationalism . . . ." The place-specific dimension to these historic events help establish their potential for the preservation, if not commemoration, in the collective memory as well as in the physical environment. Collective memory, however, should be viewed as a process that is constantly subject to transformation (Zelizer 1995). The strong association between places where members of a group died and those that survived (including descendants of those contemporaneous with the place-event) is a relationship vulnerable to manipulation by individuals in power (Gross 2001; Rosenberg 2001).

The manipulation of collective memory by those in power is a contributing factor to what Pieterse (1997) has termed the "politics of polarization." Although somewhat unpredictable collective memory can be used as a tool by which to defend or promote an agenda (Zelizer 1995: 226). The orchestration of events that commemorate the past, for example, have utility in authenticating current and future social cohesion (Connerton 1989; Bodnar 1994). Political leaders, in competition for power and influence, find appeals to "ethnicity" a very useful tool. Instigating conflict among groups can sometimes further the interests of leaders; however, as Bates (1983: 161) notes, "they often behave like captives of the forces which they

helped to create." A deterrent to unification and nation-building in sub-Saharan Africa, for example, is attributed to postcolonial leaders who employ "tribalist ideology" for the purpose of fueling "ethnic animosity" and social instability (Thomas 1997: 121; cf. Mamdani 1996: 183–196).

Social psychologists argue that the structure of human memory is such that information concerning an out-group's malevolence is more easily accessed than information about benevolent actions or behavior of that group (Burnstein et al. 1993). What Willhoite (1977) has called "collective intolerance," the rejection or suppression of persons, behavior, or symbolic expressions that are not perceived as conforming to group norms, serves to describe the precursors of hate between groups.[3] Intolerance, and sometimes fear, of others not assigned to a dominant faction can also be expressed through spatial segregation. Sibley (1995) argues effectively that the mixing of "us" versus "them" spatially is resisted and that socio-spatial exclusion can be used as a form of social control by the state.

The articulation of individual experience, "in all its emotional complexity," becomes the reference point by which collective memory is compiled, sometimes resulting in controversy and struggles among power elites (Benford 1996; Irwin-Zarecka 1994: 17). Myths and hatred underlying memories, especially when associated with the places at which atrocities occurred, are vulnerable to manipulation by individuals and leaders who can motivate and direct behavior described internationally as genocide and crimes against humanity. For example, how, why, and even if genocide by the Nazi regime occurred at numerous places throughout Germany is a subject that has been highly situational in that country since 1946. The spatial and temporal variation in "official memory" of state-sponsored killing in war-time Germany is well documented by Koonz (1994). As aptly stated by Hirsch (1995: 40), "—when eyewitnesses or survivors write their memories and record what they have been able to drag from the depths of their souls or when a social scientist analyzes data and draws conclusions—they are constructing, reconstructing, or trying to explain memory, and at the same time, they are affecting the future. How the past is portrayed influences how we think."

A cogent analysis of Rwanda's "competing visions of the past" reveals the variability in Rwandan and Euro-Western interpretations of political, social history, and ethnicity (Des Forges 1995; Newbury 1998; Pottier 2002). How these interpretations are disseminated and the substance of the communication to indigenous populations has the potential to affect the relationships between power holders and the populace. "The shifting sands of politics and power are the foundations upon which the collective memory is constructed or reconstructed" (Hirsch 1995: 32). In concert with this insight is the assertion that the symbols, icons, and monuments of a society are a representation, if not an occasional manifestation, of historical memory.

Marking the Place

Places of state-sponsored mass killing, massacres, and mass graves, when known by surviving cohorts are often highly charged with emotion. The potential for these places to be marked with tangible material by surviving kin or a social group is highly situational. Acknowledging why some of these places are not marked informs our understanding of the social dynamics underlying those places that are signified with cultural material. Sites where bodies lay interred in a situation not socially sanctioned fuels a sense of injustice that transcends time yet makes the events attributed to the place vulnerable to exploitation by competing social and political entities. Places of mass killing in the former Yugoslavia and Rwanda during the 1990s serve as examples of how behavior during these events is subsequently assigned meaning in the context of competition for power and influence in the social system.

Former Yugoslavia

On the banks of the Sava River, between Croatia and Bosnia, is a site called Jasenovac. Established in 1941, Jasenovac was a complex of several concentration and extermination camps under the jurisdiction of the Croatian Security Police (Ustasha). Victims interred at Jasenovac were mostly Serbs, Jews, Gypsies, and Croats who did not support the pro-Nazi Croat regime. Estimates of those killed vary from 80,000 to 600,000, while the U.S. Justice Department, citing captured Nazi documents says at least 120,000 were victims. In the spring of 1945 the Ustasha blew up the installation and killed most of the inmates as the Yugoslav partisan army approached (Gutman 1990: 739–740; Gutman 1998).

Communist Yugoslavia constructed a museum and a towering, flower-shaped monument to the victims at Jasenovac. However the communist authorities discouraged the exhumation of bodies for reburial according to the Orthodox Church at this and numerous unmarked sites (Denich 1994: 370). Denich (1994) contends that the regime of Tito was cautious about these places becoming fuel for a resurgence of ultra-nationalist ideology in the midst of a relatively successful Yugoslav federal system.

After the death of Tito and during the atmosphere of renewed Croatian and Serbian nationalist ideology, debate about the site of Jasenovac became such a focus of discussion that a symposium was held at this place in 1989 to entertain different interpretations of what had happened there (Boban 1990; 1991; Hayden 1992; Dedijer 1992). On April 26, 1998, the 53rd anniversary of the camp's dissolution was commemorated at the site, when a crowd of World War II veterans and a few camp survivors laid wreaths at

the monument (ROMNEWS 1998). In the former Yugoslavia, accounts of World War II massacres were carried through generations by way of stories that could be repressed but not eliminated by the communist regime.

The activities at Jasenovac over 50 years ago continue to be a powerful source of emotion for political leaders. The trial of Dinko Sakic, Jasenovac's deputy camp commander (1942–1944), who was arrested in Argentina in the spring of 1998, polarized the populace of contemporary Croatia (Zadunaisky 1998; Hedges 1998; Vukic 1998). The following year Sakic was sentenced to 20 years in prison.

Places such as Jasenovac became well known to a generation of Yugoslavian soldiers and paramilitary units orchestrated by powerful elites in Belgrade when in 1991 Croatia succeeded from the Yugoslav Federation (see Mirkovic 2000). In November of that year the eastern Slovonian town of Vukovar, a city of about 50,000, fell to JNA (Yugoslav Army) forces and Serb paramilitaries after being under siege for three months. The result of this siege, the most devastating battle in Europe since 1945, was the near total destruction of the city. Thousands of inhabitants were killed, tortured, and raped—over 600 are still missing.

During this period Croatian families, especially wives and mothers of the missing, began painting names of their killed or missing relatives on clay bricks and stacking them on the streets of Zagreb, the capital of Croatia (see figure 13.1). The largest and most demonstrative of these shrines was strategically placed on the sidewalk leading to the main entrance of the

Figure 13.1   Sidewalk shrine in the business district of Zagreb.
Photo by: Ralph Hartley.

Figure 13.2 Mothers and wives of the missing mourn with bricks in front of the United Nations compound, Zagreb.

Photo by: Ralph Hartley.

United Nations compound (see figure 13.2). This medium of personal loss and especially its placement helped communicate to an international community the mourning and frustration inherent in the war, not unlike decades later, the meaning embedded in names carved in the Vietnam Veteran's Memorial in Washington, DC (cf. Melchior 2001). These stacked bricks could only be constructed in the relative safety of Zagreb, not at the location of death or the village where one disappeared. Moreover, the bricks were a means by which the populace, especially kin of those killed or whose fate was unknown, could plea for help and intervention to powers outside Croatia.

The landscape of the former Yugoslavia is littered with the sites of mass graves from both the World War II era and the 1991–1995 dissolution of the Federation. Most infamous of this later period are those resulting from the summer of 1995 when more than 7,000 Bosnian men and boys were slaughtered in the area surrounding Srebrenica and Zepa, an event deemed "the largest single war crime in Europe since the Second World War" (Honig and Both 1996: xix). Shrines or memorials near the places of killing were inconceivable in this area of Bosnia even long after active fighting due to Serb occupation of the area. As of 2003 exhumations resulted in more than 5,000 bodies. Where these bodies were to be interred was the subject of dispute between widows of the dead and missing men and Serb nationalists who control this area of Bosnia. The women wanted the bodies buried along the road leading into the village of Srebrenica to enhance the memory of the massacres, especially to those with allegiance to Serbia (Rohde 2001). It wasn't until July of 2002 that a white marble monument, signifying the massacres, was placed near the village of Potocari. And the following year 882 identified remains were buried in a nearby cemetery dedicated to those killed.

Rwanda

In the spring and summer of 1994 the first legally defined genocide since the World War II era took place in Rwanda. Within approximately four months over 800,000 people, primarily noncombatants, were slaughtered. The genocide was, by all subsequent analyses, an effectively organized and administered system of exterminating Tutsi and politically moderate Hutus. More were killed in some places than others, but as Maurice Nearuhirira, a law student at Butare University, notes, "If you put a cross in every place that someone was killed—the whole country would be a memorial" (Stockman 1999).

In late April of 1994 approximately 25,000 Tutsi men, women, and children from 13 districts surrounding Gikangaro in the southwest region of Rwanda, were told to go to a school for protection from marauding Hutu bands. Thousands were massacred at the school, in church compounds, and markets. Since that time many bodies have been exhumed by the Rwandan government for preservation and display in former classrooms. Near the Tanzanian border, at the parish Church at Nyarubuye nearly 3,000 people were slaughtered by the Interahamwe (Santoro 1997). The remains of many of the victims have been left where they died, a phenomenon not universally supported by Rwanda's Catholic clergy (Sibomana 1999: 114).

In mid-April in the town of Kibuye over 6,000 people were herded into the stadium and over 3,000 took refuge at the Home St. Jean, the Catholic Church complex. On the 16th and 17th massacres took place at the church and three days later at the stadium. Thousands were killed with grenades, machetes, pangas, and hoes. Of the approximately 500 bodies exhumed from a mass grave at the rear of the church, half were infants, children, and young people under the age of 18. A mountainous ridge in the prefecture of Kibuye called Bisesero was the scene of massive massacres of Tutsi in May and June. Several thousand men, women and children were killed on this hill (African Rights 1995: 662–670; Des Forges 1999: 216–220). Today many of the remains of more than a 1,000 of these victims lie in canvas bags as a memorial. A survivor of the massacre, Simon Ngamije stated, "It is [the leaders of the prefecture] who [are] responsible for this. So many people died here and everybody should know that they were the ones who did this" (Metcalfe 1999). Not only was the erection of a shrine at such places not feasible, there was no audience—all potential sympathizers were either dead or had fled the region. Unlike the painted bricks in Zagreb there was no place of safety in Rwanda and almost no means by which to communicate through cultural material the horror, loss, and fear to an affluent Western world. The Kibuye church, however, has since become symbolic as one of scores of churches where people took refuge or were deceived to believe they were safe, only to be killed.

Those commemorations to the genocide that exist are sponsored by the ruling elite of Rwanda. General Paul Kagame, president of Rwanda, states, "We need to preserve the remains of genocide so that people would not forget. It is fair to those who died and to those who remain." Asked whether the exhumations and display were conducive to the country's reconciliation, Kagame stated, "We have to prevent this from happening again in the future. We want to teach a lesson explaining that what happened was not an accident of history; it was a premeditated, deliberate attempt at genocide" (IRINWIRE July 27, 1997).

Confirming the Message

Temporary shrines at the place of mass killing and as a means of communicating loss and fear is rare, if not impossible, in an environment of active lethal conflict. Where these shrines can have value is only in an environment of relative safety, usually far from the place of atrocity, where a potential recipient of the message embedded in the shrine is presumed to be a powerful ally in the cause to acknowledge injustice. The use of material or imagery to communicate a message about loss and injustice is, of course, vulnerable to manipulation in order to deceive. Confirmation of the visual information inherent in a shrine signifying an alleged mass killing or episode of atrocities is greatly aided by physical evidence. As unimaginable as the horror of the 1990s in Rwanda and former Yugoslavia was, confirmation of places, numbers, and means of killing are needed to buffer those who might benefit from misrepresenting reality.

Reconstructing the "truth" about events or atrocities at a place even in the recent past can be extraordinarily difficult. Nevertheless, recording the statements of witnesses and survivors, the exhumation of mass graves, and the compilation of diverse physical and documentary evidence constitute some of our most effective means of constructing an interpretation of activities and behavior. Unfortunately, it is "interpretation" that makes attempts at documentation vulnerable to manipulation. Unlike positivist science in the Western tradition, interpretation allows for empirical data or "evidence" to be deleted, reconstructed, or re-construed. There exists no level playing field—no common, agreed upon units of analysis. The only effective judge of an interpretation is the effect such a conclusion may have on those living in the present and those of the immediate future.

Place-specific atrocities, incompletely documented and/or biased in description, serve as fuel when the resurrection of violence between long-term competing groups is in the interest of those in power. The complimentary action of reality and myth is subject to manipulation when the goal is to require sacrifice. Interpretations of "memory" can be used to stoke revenge. Adolescents and young adults are particularly susceptible to interpretations of atrocities by power elites (Olick and Robbins 1998: 123). Contemporary textbooks for Bosnia history courses, for example, may vary with respect to targeted high school students. Photographs and descriptions of cruel death and suffering of Serbs is, for example, a component of the Bosnian Serb version only, to be consumed and interpreted by the adolescent teenage population of what is currently Serb Bosnia (Republika Srpska) (Holley 2001; Stephen 1997; cf. Hayden 1994: 181).

Revenge for current oppression and past killings and torture is an extremely powerful motive for action, all within the frame of power over the opposition (Burton 1997: 52–55). It is worth noting that the role of "revenge" in the former Yugoslavia and Rwanda is often invoked by journalists and other writers as a communal motive for a myriad of atrocities that became valued news-copy. A politically and socially sanctioned rationale for extreme Serb actions against noncombatants in the former Yugoslavia during the 1991–1995 conflict was vengeance for World War II-era atrocities committed by Croatian Ustasha, such as those at Jasenovac. Hundreds of thousands were likely killed in the 1940s, but it is the emotional memories and stories of individual experience that can motivate behavior that transcends generations, as revealed in Crnobrnja's (1994: 66) statement concerning this period in Yugoslav history, ". . . the bestiality of these mass murders is perhaps more important than the numbers killed."

The desire for vengeance in contemporary environments of violent conflict is most often of a local nature, focusing on activities at a particular place. For example, the remaining Muslim population of Gorazde in Bosnia wants punished the 30-year-old Bosnian Serb militia commander (Milan Lukic), accused of killing about 3,000 noncombatants in the area during the early summer of 1992. When asked who would organize and participate in the revenge killing of Lukic, an informant replied, "Probably people whose relatives were killed by Lukic and his gang, whose fathers were forced to rape their daughters, whose brothers were forced to kill their own brothers, the people obliged to torch houses with entire families inside" (Randal 1997).

The 1996–1997 massacres of Hutu by soldiers associated with Laurent Kabila's forces in refugee camps and villages in the Democratic Republic of Congo (former Zaire) is an excellent example of what Daly and Wilson (1994: 276) term "deterrent vengeance." Rwandan Vice President Paul Kagame was quoted as saying "The only thing we plan is to kill more of those who cause problems. They have arms they use to kill our people" (IRINWIRE, June 18, 1997).

Sensitivity of power holders to the ease with which verbal, written, and visual information is now transferred was demonstrated when Kabila's Alliance of Democratic Forces for the Liberation of the Congo were attempting to eliminate or destroy human remains and other physical evidence at the sites of massacres of noncombatants in eastern Congo prior to United Nations proposed field investigations in 1997. The disappearance of as many as 180,000 Rwandan refugees in the Congo testifies to the extent to which power holders must manipulate how, when, or if material evidence is collected that can be translated into data and ultimately information to potentially threaten their control (Crossette 1998; French 1998; McNeill 1997; Pomfret 1997; Russell 1997; Winfield 1998). As emphasized by

Harff (1992: 41) long before the Congo massacres, "Today's perpetrators are more likely to burn or bury the dead. Is it because they realize that they have committed a crime against humanity?"

In recent years intensive forensic investigations have taken place at killing sites and mass graves in the former Yugoslavia and Rwanda, most notably under the umbrella of the two United Nations tribunals (the International Criminal Tribunal of the Former Yugoslavia and the International Criminal Tribunal for Rwanda). This was done with the intention of acquiring evidence in order to facilitate the prosecution of those individuals responsible. These investigations, in conjunction with witness and survivor accounts, help in the reconstruction of the activities that occurred at these places.[4] The detailed accounting of the behavior that occurred in relatively brief episodes makes interpretations of those activities that do not take into account material evidence relating to the perpetrators and victims far less compelling. Interpretative scenarios, not accountable to the evidence, will nevertheless be made, albeit with presumably fewer subscribers.

These kinds of investigations and the "hard" data collected are an extremely sensitive issue with political and military leaders, warlords, and despots. Avoidance of United Nations or other nonpolitically assigned forensic investigations of places where atrocities occurred and where material evidence exists is increasingly prevalent, due especially to the visual communication inherent at places of atrocities and associated victims, both living and dead.

It is assumed that clear verbal, written, visual and/or material evidence of atrocities makes "revisionist" history more difficult, accepting, however, that products of this documentation do not inhibit its potential and concomitant social affect. Interpretations of past atrocities at particular places is open to selective exploitation. When stories or interpretations are not fully regarded as factual they still may be used through various means of communicative media, and possibly elaborated upon, to unify and/or direct the behavior of a target group or cohort. Deception of others, even when grounded in self-deception, is a relatively low-cost strategy in the attempt to manipulate others to take extreme risks.

Memory, both emotional and collective, is influenced strongly by meaning assigned to a place. Shrines, temporary as they may be, help crystallize that memory by establishing a visual marker for those not present during an event. When that place is the site of atrocities performed by one group on another, future social interaction between those groups requires transcending the memories associated with that place. When political and military leaders find it advantageous to enhance these places by erecting a memorial and thereby changing the built environment, the emotional linkage formed between individuals (constituents) and the site are perpetuated, and made vulnerable to manipulation in future generations.

Notes

1. The term "genocide" is used in many contexts; however, I concur with Simon (1996) that the ingredients of genocidal behavior are "a negative group identity, an intentionality, and acts of killing." Often the term genocide is used with ". . . and related acts" (see Simon 1996: 245; cf. Hayden 1996). The *International Law Commission Draft Code of Crimes Against the Peace and Security of Mankind, 1996* differentiates by definition the crime of aggression (Article 16), the crime of genocide (Article 17), crimes against humanity (Article 18), and War Crimes (Article 20) (Ratner and Abrams 1997: 338–340).

2. In most social systems political and military leaders tend to be males that are the most prosperous (i.e. those that control material resources, directly, control access to resources, and labor) (Low 1993). In the former Yugoslavia, for example, several warlords and gunmen who gained power during the active fighting of 1991–1995 have been voted into positions of political leadership especially at the local and municipal level. To their constituents they have, in effect, legitimized what journalists have called "ethnic cleansing." With their militias these men have gained power and immense wealth by forcefully eliminating most competitors, taking all their valuable resources—houses, land, and money. These "competitors" can include members of their own "ethnic" constituency (Stojanovic 1997).

3. The use of terms that demean or assign dehumanizing characteristics to a group suggests a lack of tolerance that has the potential to incite genocidal behavior (see Gilliland 1995: 215; Hinton 1997: 824–825; Hirsch 1985: 45–47; Jackson 1989: 96; Kressel 1996: 250; Markusen and Kopf 1995: 183–195). For example, use of the term "inyenzi" or "cockroach" by Hutu extremists for Tutsi was used in both 1963–1964 and 1994 in Rwanda to manipulate emotions that led to the massacres there. The term initially was used to describe guerilla bands of Tutsi exiles in the early 1960s. Likewise to "hunt down python in the grass" served as common phrase to encourage the killing of all educated Hutu in Burundi in 1972 (African Rights 1995: 6–80; Chalk and Jonassohn 1990: 28; Fein 1990: 43; Greenland 1976: 113,120).

4. In the fall of 1993 the secretary-general of the United Nations instructed the Legal Counsel of the United Nations to prepare a document constituting "guidelines" as a frame of reference for future investigations undertaken by the United Nations (United Nations 1997). The U.N.'s Special Rapporteur for Extrajudicial, Summary, and Arbitrary Executions retains a standing mandate from the Commission on Human Rights to investigate allegations of massacres and other violations of the right to life.

References Cited

African Rights. 1995. *Rwanda—Death, Despair, and Defiance.* London: African Rights.

Alexander, R. D. 1989. "Evolution of the Human Psyche." In *The Human Revolution: Behavioral and Biological Perspectives on the Origins of Modern Humans*, ed. P. Mellars and C. Stringer, 455–513. Princeton: Princeton University Press.

Altman, I. and S. M. Low (eds.). 1992. *Place Attachment.* New York: Plenum Press

Azaryahu, M. and A. Kellerman. 1999. Symbolic Places of National History and Revival: A Study in Zionist Mythical Geography. *Transactions of the Institute of British Geographers* 24: 109–123.

Bates, R. H. 1983. "Modernization, Ethnic Competition, and the Rationality of Politics in Contemporary Africa." In *State versus Ethnic Claims: African Policy Dilemmas*, ed. D. Rothchild and V. A. Olorunsola, 152–171.

Benford, R. D. 1996. Whose War Memories Shall Be Preserved? *Peace Review* 8: 189–194.

Boban, L. 1990. Jasenovac and the Manipulation of History. *East European Politics and Societies* 4: 580–592.

————1991. Still More Balance on Jasenovac and the Manipulation of History. *East European Politics and Societies* 6: 213–217.

Bodnar, J. 1994. "Public memory in an American City: Commemoration in Cleveland." In *Commemoration—the Politics of National Identity*, ed. J. R. Gillis, 74–89. Princeton, NJ: Princeton University Press.

Bonino, E. 1998. Address to the Congressional Human Rights Caucus, Washington DC, May 12, 1998.

Brown, M. E., O. R. Cote, Jr., S. M. Lynn-Jones, and S. E. Miller (eds.). 1997. *Nationalism and Ethnic Conflict.* Cambridge: The MIT Press.

Burnstein, E., M. Abboushi, and S. Kitayama. 1993. "How the Mind Preserves the Image of the Enemy: The Mnemonics of Soviet-American Relations." In *Behavior, Culture, and Conflict in World Politics*, ed. W. Zimmerman and H. K. Jacobson, 197–229. Ann Arbor: The University of Michigan Press.

Burton, J. W. 1997. *Violence Explained—The Sources of Conflict, Violence and Crime and their Prevention.* Manchester: Manchester University Press.

Chalk, F. and K. Jonassohn. 1990. *The History and Sociology of Genocide: Analyses and Case Studies.* New Haven: Yale University Press.

Connerton, P. 1989. *How Societies Remember.* Cambridge: Cambridge University Press.

Crnobrnja, M. 1994. *The Yugoslav Drama.* Montreal: McGill-Queens University Press.

Crossette, B. 1998. "U.N. stymied by Congo Leader—Halts Inquiry on Rwanda Killings." *The New York Times*, April 10, 1998: Sec. A, 1.

Daly, M. and M. Wilson. 1994. "Evolutionary Psychology of Male Violence." In *Male Violence*, ed. J. Archer, 253–288. London: Routledge.

Dedijer, V. 1992. *The Yugoslav Auschwitz and the Vatican: The Croatian Massacre of the Serbs during World War II.* Translated by H. L. Kendall. Buffalo, NY: Prometheus Books.

Denich, B. 1994. Dismembering Yugoslavia: Nationalist Ideologies and the Symbolic Revival of Genocide. *American Ethnologist* 21: 367–390.

Des Forges, A. 1995. The Ideology of Genocide. *Issue: A Journal of Opinion* 23: 44–47.

———. 1999. *Leave None to Tell the Story—Genocide in Rwanda.* New York: Human Rights Watch.

Farmer, S. 1999. *Martyred Village—Commemorating the 1944 Massacre at Oradour-sur-Glane.* Berkeley: University of California Press.

Fein, H. 1990. Genocide: A Sociological Perspective. *Current Sociology* 38: 1–126.

French, H. W. 1998. "Cold Trail: A Special Report—Congo Not Alone in Ending Massacre Inquiry." *The New York Times*, May 7, 1998: Sec A, 1.

Gilliland, M.K. 1995. "Nationalism and Ethnogenesis in the Former Yugoslavia." In *Ethnic Identity: Creation, Conflict, and Accommodation*, ed. L. Romanuccci-Ross and G. A. DeVos, 197–221. Walnut Creek, California: AltaMira Press.

Greenland, J. 1976. "Ethnic Discrimination in Rwanda and Burundi." In *Case Studies on Human Rights and Fundamental Freedoms: A World Survey*, ed. W. A. Veenhoven, 95–134. The Hague: Mautinus Nijhoff.

Gross, J. T. 2001. *Neighbors: The Destruction of the Jewish Community in Jedwabne, Poland.* Princeton: Princeton University Press.

Gurr, T.R. 1993. *Minorities at Risk: A Global View of Ethnopolitical Conflicts.* Washington, DC: United States Institute of Peace Press.

Gutman, I. (ed.) 1990. *Encyclopedia of the Holocaust.* Vol. 2. New York: Macmillan Pub. Co.

Gutman, R. 1998. Details of Death Camp in Document. *Newsday*, May 2: A07.

Harff, B. 1992. "Recognizing Genocides and Politicides." In *Genocide Watch*, ed. H. Fein, 27–41. New Haven: Yale University Press.

Hayden, R. M. 1992. Balancing Discussion of Jasenovac and the Manipulation of History. *East European Politics and Societies* 6: 207–212.

———. 1994. "Recounting the Dead: The Rediscovery and Reinterpretation of Wartime Massacres in Late- and Post-Communist Yugoslavia." In *Memory and Opposition under State Socialism*, ed. R. S. Watson, 167–184. Santa Fe, NM: School of American Research.

———. 1996. Schindler's Fate: Genocide, Ethnic Cleansing and Population Transfers. *Slavic Review*: 727–748.

Hedges, C. 1998. Sakic—Major Jasenovac Trial Looks Likely. *The New York Times*, 2 May.

Hinton, A. L. 1997. Agents of Death: Explaining the Cambodian Genocide in Terms of Psychosocial Dissonance. *American Anthropologist* 98: 818–831.

Hirsch, H. 1985. Why People Kill: Conditions for Participation in Mass Murder. *International Journal of Group Tensions* 15: 41–57.

———. 1995. *Genocide and the Politics of Memory.* Chapel Hill: University of North Carolina Press.

Holley, D. 2001. Serbs Face their Past, Dose of Truth at a Time. *The Los Angeles Times*, April 17.

Honig, J. W. and N. Both. 1996. *Srebrenica—Record of a War Crime.* New York: Penguin Books.

Ingrao, C. 1998. Available from listserv@ TWATCH-L. April 3.

IRINWIRE. 1997. *Integrated Regional Information Network for the Great Lakes.* United Nations, Department of Humanitarian Affairs.

Irwin-Zarecka, I. 1994. *Frames of Remembrance: the Dynamics of Collective Memory.* New Brunswick: Transaction Pub.

Jackson, W. D. 1989. The Construction of Conflicts. *Conflict* 9: 89–100.

Koonz, C. 1994. "Between Memory and Oblivion: Concentration Camps in German Memory." In *Commemorations—the Politics of National Identity*, ed. J. R. Gillis, 258–280. Princeton, NJ: Princeton University Press.

Kressel, N. J. 1996. *Mass Hate—the Global Rise of Genocide and Terror.* New York, NY: Plenum Press.

Low, B. S. 1993. "An Evolutionary Perspective on War." In *Behavior, Culture, and Conflict in World Politics*, ed. W. Zimmerman and H. K. Jacobson, 13–55. Ann Arbor: University of Michigan Press.

Mamdani, M. 1996. *Citizen and Subject—Contemporary Africa and the Legacy of Late Colonialism.* Princeton, NJ: Princeton University Press.

Markusen, E. and D. Kopf. 1995. *The Holocaust and Strategic Bombing—Genocide and Total War in the Twentieth Century.* Boulder, Colorado: Westview Press.

Mayo, J. M. 1988. War Memorials and Political Memory. *Geographical Review* 78: 62–75.

McNeil, D. G., Jr. 1997. Reports Point to Mass Killings of Refugees in Congo. *The New York Times*, May 28.

Melchior, M. B. 2001. The Art of Public Mourning: The Wall and the Continuing American Failure to Come to Terms with the Loss of the Vietnam Wall. *Humanity and Society* 25: 263–288.

Metcalfe, J. C. 1999. Genocide Suspect Arrested in Tanzania. *INTERNEWS.* International Criminal Tribunal for Rwanda. November 9.

Milligan, M. J. 1998. Interactional Past and Potential: the Social Construction of Place Attachment. *Symbolic Interaction* 21: 1–33.

Mirkovic, D. 2000. The Historical Link between the Ustasha Genocide and the Croato-Serb Civil War: 1991–1995. *Journal of Genocide Research* 2: 363–373.

Nagengast, C. 1994. Violence, Terror, and the Crisis of the State. *Annual Review of Anthropology* 23: 109–136.

Newbury, C. 1998. Ethnicity and the Politics of History in Rwanda. *Africa Today* 45: 7–24.

Olick, J. K. and J. Robbins. 1998. Social Memory Studies: From "Collective Memory" to the Historical Sociology of Mnemonic Practices. *Annual Review of Sociology* 24: 105–140.

Pawson, E. J. 1991. Monuments, Memorials and Cemeteries: Icons in the Landscape. *New Zealand Journal of Geography* 92: 26–27.

Peterson, H. 1999. East Timor Commemorates 1991 Massacre. *Associated Press*, November 12.

Pieterse, J. N. 1997. Sociology of Humanitarian Intervention: Bosnia, Rwanda and Somalia Compared. *International Political Science Review* 18: 71–93.

Pomfret, J. 1997. Massacres were a Weapon in Congo's Civil War—Evidence Mounts of Atrocities by Kabila's Forces. *The Washington Post*, June 11: A01.

Pottier, J. 2002. *Re-Imagining Rwanda—Conflict, Survival and Disinformation in the Late Twentieth Century.* Cambridge: Cambridge University Press.

Randal, J. C. 1997. In Gorazade, Thirst Rises for Revenge. *The Washington Post,* May 8: A20.

Ratner, S. R. and J. S. Abrams. 1997. *Accountability for Human Rights Atrocities in International Law—Beyond the Nuremberg Legacy.* Oxford: Clarendon Press.

Reuber, P. 2000. Conflict Studies and Critical Geopolitics—Theoretical Concepts and Recent Research in Political Geography. *Geojournal* 50: 37–43.

Rohde, D. 2001. In Bosnia, Massacre Victims Lie While the Living Bicker. *New York Times Magazine,* March 11.

ROMNEWS. 1998. Croatia Commemorates Victims of World War II Fascist Camp. *Roma National Congress of Europe.* May 2.

Rosenberg, T. 2001. Poland Faces an Ugly Truth, and Doesn't Blink. *The New York Times,* April 8.

Russell, A. 1997. Kabila Faces UN Inquiry into Hutu Massacre. *International News Electronic Telegraph,* June 21.

Santoro, L. 1997. Rwanda Massacre Sites Now Grim Memorials. *The Christian Science Monitor,* August 8.

Schwartz, B. and T. Bayma. 1999. Commemoration and the Politics of Recognition: The Korean War Veterans Memorial. *American Behavioral Scientist* 42: 946–967.

Sibley, D. 1995. *Geographies of Exclusion—Society and Difference in the West.* London: Routledge.

Sibomana, Andre. 1999. *Hope for Rwanda—Conversations with Laure Guilbert and Herve Deguine.* London: Pluto Press.

Simon, T. W. 1996. Defining Genocide. *Wisconsin International Law Journal* 15: 243–256.

Smith, A. D. 1984. National Identity and Myths of Ethnic Descent. *Research in Social Movements, Conflict and Change* 7: 95–130.

———. 1992. Chosen Peoples: Why Ethnic Groups Survive. *Ethnic and Racial Studies* 15: 436–456.

———. 1996. Culture, Community and Territory: The Politics of Ethnicity and Nationalism. *International Affairs* 72: 445–458.

Stephen, C. 1997. Education in Bosnia. *Agence France Presse,* November 5.

Stockman, F. 1999. Special Internews Report from Rwanda: Coping with Genocide Five Years Later. *Internews Network,* April 7.

Stojanovic, D. 1997. Bosnia-Beleagured Serbs. *Associated Press,* July 31.

Stokols, D. and S.A. Shumaker. 1981. "People in Places: A Transactional View of Settings." In *Cognition, Social Behavior, and the Environment,* ed. J. H. Harvey, 441–488. Hillsdale, NJ: Lawrence Erlbaum Ass.

Thomas, D. 1997. "Constructing National and Cultural Identities in Sub-Saharan Francophone Africa." In *Not on Any Map—Essays on Postcoloniality and Cultural Nationalism,* ed. S. Murray, 115–134. Exeter: University of Exeter Press.

United Nations. 1997. *Guidelines for the Conduct of United Nations Inquiries into Allegations of Massacres.* New York: United Nations, Office of Legal Affairs.

Vukic, S. 1998. World War II Crimes Suspect Arrives Home for Trial. *Associated Press*, June 18.

Willhoite, F. H. 1977. Evolution and Collective Intolerance. *Journal of Politics* 39: 667–684.

Winfield, N. 1998. U.N. Calls for Human Rights Tribunal. *The Associated Press*, June 30.

Winter, J. 1995. *Sites of Memory, Sites of Mourning*. Cambridge: Cambridge University Press.

Zadunaisky, D. 1998. Argentina Arrests Croatian Suspect. *The Associated Press*, May 1.

Zelizer, B. 1995. Reading the Past Against the Grain: The Shape of Memory Studies. *Critical Studies in Mass Communication* 12: 214–239.

Chapter 14

Forty Years of Conflict: State, Church, and Spontaneous Representation of Massacres and Murder in Guatemala

Matthew J. Taylor and Michael K. Steinberg

Images of Guatemala

Guatemala, 1962–present: Two hundred thousand murdered and disappeared Guatemalans, one hundred and fifty thousand Guatemalans seek refuge outside of their patria (homeland), one and a half million internally displaced Guatemalans escape violence, countless orphans and widows, indelible scars of horror deeply ingrained in the minds of victims and perpetrators alike, and counting . . .

—CEH 1999

No doubt, Guatemala's hidden war exacted an onerous toll on both indigenous and Ladino (non-indigenous) minds and hearts.[1] The publication of the United Nations sponsored *Guatemala: Memoria del Silencio* (CEH 1999) and the Guatemalan Office of the Archbishop's *Guatemala: Nunca Más* (REMHI 1998) reveal to the outside world, in horrific detail, the acts and impacts of almost 40 years of violence. These grisly tomes documenting death and destruction in Guatemala's towns and countryside permit, in the words of a witness,

Que la historia que pasamos
quede en las escuelas,
para que no se olvide,
para que nuestros hijos la conozcan.
(So that the history we experienced
stays in schools,
so that it is not forgotten,
so that our children know what happened).
(CEH 1999, vol. 5: 9).

The printed page provides a permanent place for the victims of Guatemala's genocide.[2] Most Guatemalans, however, cannot read or write. How then, do these Guatemalans externalize their memory?

Mention of Guatemala conjures up many exotic images. These images include past and present Maya cultures; majestic Maya temples surrounded by tropical forest, smoking volcanoes, military dictators behind dark sunglasses, and grave human rights violations.[3] Guatemala's natural and cultural diversity at first attracts researchers and travelers. Yet these tourists and academic voyeurs often, upon delving deeper into Guatemala's realities, feel compelled to reveal the other side of this small nation's beauty. This contradictory facet of Guatemala is reflected in writings about Guatemala. Recent titles include: George Lovell's *A Beauty that Hurts: Life and Death in Guatemala*, Richard Adams' *Crucifixion by Power*, Jim Handy's *Gift of the Devil: A History of Guatemala, Shattered Hope* by Piero Gleijeses, Robert Carmack's *Harvest of Violence: Maya Indians and the Guatemalan Crisis*, Jean-Marie Simon's *Guatemala: Eternal Spring, Eternal Tyranny*, and Jennifer Schirmer's *The Guatemalan Military Project: A Violence Called Democracy*. These titles suggest the conflicting relationship these scholars have with their field locations. Guatemalan landscapes exude beauty, but hidden within that beauty lies pain and a history of extreme inequalities and continued repression. When we read the landscape more closely, the beauty appears tarnished or obliterated, just like many Guatemalan families and villages during the "problematic time." We explore these contradictions by presenting images of contrasting landmarks, memorials, and other landscape features associated with the Guatemalan civil war that ended in 1996 with an internationally brokered peace accord between guerilla groups and the state.

How to Read Guatemalan Landscapes

We examined Guatemala's landscape for the presence of memorials and less intentional landmarks related to the recently concluded armed conflict. We did this while journeying through mountainous rural areas in the Department of Huehuetenango and Ixíl country in the Department of Quiché. We also slogged through tropical lowlands of Ixcán area in the extreme north of Quiché and Huehuetenango. We spoke to locals about how they remember thousands of massacre victims. Upon entering a town or village, for example, we often approached officials in municipal buildings that surround the central plaza of most Guatemalan communities. Enquiries to local police officers and other municipal employees about the existence of memorials (or other ways in which the dead are remembered) that com-memorate "the conflict" were received with incredulous stares. Officials often denied the existence of any monuments even if their office sat a mere 50 meters from the Catholic cathedral containing hundreds of crosses that record the name and date of each massacred or disappeared person. We often had to ask long and hard before being pointed to any monuments that commemorate victims because locals still fear talking about the past.

We focused on these rural areas of Guatemala because at the height of conflict in the early 1980s this region bore the brunt of insurgency and counter-insurgency campaigns and thus earned the "red" label from gov-ernment security forces. Red zones consisted of enemy territories, where "no distinction was made between *guerilleros* (anti-state insurgency forces) and their peasant supporters. Both were to be attacked and obliterated" (Schirmer 1998, 42).[4] These areas received military "attention" during the civil war because, for a short time at least, they were strongholds for the rebel forces, especially the Guerrilla Army of the Poor (EGP) (Ball et al. 1999; Falla 1992; Lovell 1990; Manz 1988; Montejo 1992; Moreno 1998; Payeras 1998; Stoll 1993). We also crossed Lake Atitlán to Santiago Atitlán to investigate how this town remembers the recent violence and the murder of a U.S. priest. The search for monuments also led to Guatemala City. Intense violence wracked the city in the early 1980s and formed the point from which generals and government officials planned counter-insurgency campaigns and subsequent peace negotiations (Payeras 1987).

We became intrigued by what we saw and, just as importantly, what we did not see regarding public memory and commemoration of the civil war. Driving through the poorly maintained back roads and living with residents of former conflict zones, we found it hard to believe that this area formed the focus of state orchestrated murder, massacre, disappearances, and refuge

(Green 1999; Zur 1998). Jean-Marie Simon (1987, 16) warns that "many of those who now travel there will be hard pressed to imagine the enormity of its tragedy." An uninformed traveler, tourist, or aid worker not versed in Guatemala's recent violent history and not specifically looking for landmarks, might easily continue unaware of clandestine graves and thousands of wooden crosses, one for each victim, nailed to the walls of village churches. In Ixcán for instance, we stayed in villages "wiped off the map" by military actions in the early 1980s that show no signs of past conflict—in fact the military often built model villages on the ashes of destroyed community centers (CEIDEC 1990; Nelson 1999). It is in these very villages, as González (1998, 13–14) bluntly relates,

> in every corner of Yichkan [Ixcán], every turn of the roads of Yichkan, every corner of the bleeding fatherland, every spot was a silent witness to massacres and tortures. The land, the face of the earth, was splattered with the blood of her children. The rivers became the veins of the community in which the blood of the people flowed . . . it was like cutting down a great forest . . . more than four hundred villages were wiped off the face of the earth.

In fact, little evidence of any type of conflict remained after a few months. Simon (1987, 8) poignantly recalls: "scorched earth was overgrown with corn six months later; refugee camps where helicopters dumped grieving widows and children were renamed and reconstructed over razed huts; and model villages were built on top of these camps, often over the ashes of the dead."[5] It is on this landscape that rural survivors must remember. Often, their remembering is an inconspicuous everyday act; simply by living in a humble house that sits on the foundations of a former house, people are remembering. The site of the massacre becomes the monument. These are, intangibly yet palpably, memories of the mind, memories that leave no obvious permanent mark on the visible landscape.

State versus Spontaneous Memories and Memorials

Although few in number, landmarks in post-conflict Guatemala point to a continuing struggle as to how two opposing sides—the state and victims of the state—represent the years of *problemas*. The paucity of overtly public landmarks in many villages and towns severely affected by the war illustrates how residents continue to negotiate and struggle with the aftermath and realities of postwar life and indicates little closure for victims and survivors of violence. Alternatively, the absence of monuments may reflect how people choose to internalize their experiences and use their own bodies as sites of resistance and as a way to continue the daily struggle of survival. Internalizing grief may be the only strategy for survival in a country where, in the words of Linda Green (1999), "fear is a way of life." Many rural folk do not see the new government as a significant departure from previous regimes. In fact, under the Portillo government (2000–2004) the tenuous strings of peace are stretched to a maximum as politically motivated murders, land conflicts, and mob lynching continue.[6] Although some Guatemalans feel slightly more inclined to reveal their political leanings and feelings surrounding the war, many remain guarded for fear of future reprisals.

How can villagers build monuments to the dead when many members of civil patrols (government created militias called *Patrulleros de Autodefensa Civil*—PAC), who often participated in military-sanctioned violence directed at other villagers accused of supporting guerillas, continue to live among relatives of the victims?[7] Thus, many survivors of the war receive little or no closure because they must constantly interact with those who abducted, tortured, or killed their loved ones. Given that both perpetrators and victims continue to live side-by-side, and that communal graves are only now being excavated to provide some sort of closure for relatives (e.g., Prensa Libre 2001b), the momentum to construct public memorials is delayed or muted. Eduardo Galeano attributes such apprehension to the fact that,

Guatemala sufre de una historia official mutilada . . . como que si recordar fuera peligrosa, porque recordar es repetir el pasado como una pesadilla
(Guatemala suffers from an official history that is mutilated . . . as though it is dangerous to remember, because to remember is to repeat the past like a nightmare.) (cited in Wilson 1998)

Certainly, much written work document the last 40 years of "unrest" in Guatemala—this in itself is a memory. Detailed accounts of death and destruction (Ball, Kobrack, and Spirer 1999; CEH 1999; REHMI 1998) and personal testimonies (e.g., Diocesis del Quiché 1994; González 1998; Menchú 1984; Montejo 1987 and 1992), rapidly multiply in the "safer to speak" climate of the late 1990s and early years of the twenty-first century.[8] Despite the proliferation of printed memories, the words remain unknown to Guatemala's illiterate population. Moreover, only a small portion of the literate population can access the "published memories" that appear to satisfy an international and academic demand for accountability.[9] For example, the exhaustive details found in *Guatemala: Memoria del Silencio*

(CEH 1999) cover 12 volumes and cost over U.S. $100. The text and figures now also reside on compact disk, making the information even less accessible to most Guatemalans. The REMHI (1998) publication totals four volumes and sells for U.S. $70, and a summary of the four volumes sells for about U.S. $40.

The memory of those most affected by the war—those who will never access the documents produced by national and international truth commissions, which present a very official, impersonal memory—lies in the hands of the church and the state.

The Catholic Church

Most landmarks commemorating the victims of Guatemala's turmoil fall under the auspices of the Catholic Church. Small crosses inside Catholic Churches bearing the names and dates of murder or disappearance form the only tangible memorial in many villages and towns impacted by the violence (figure 14.1). The Catholic Church consistently plays the role of unofficial "moral conscience" because its members and clergy were (and continue to be) persecuted during the conflict. The military targeted members of the Catholic

Figure 14.1   Inside the Catholic Church in San Juan Cotzal, Quiché.
Photo by: Michael Steinberg.

clergy who embraced Liberation Theology, labeling them as dissenters and guerilla collaborators—these men and women did not last long in the Guatemalan countryside (Diocesis del Quiché 1994; Falla 1992 and 1993). Harassment and assassinations of Catholic Church members continues even after the signing of the peace treaty in 1996. Most infamously, Bishop Juan Gerardi, chair of the Catholic Church's Recovery of Historical Memory project (REMHI), was murdered two days after presenting REMHI's findings to the public on 26 April 1998. More recently, on May 8, 2001, another member of the Church, Sister Barbara Ford, was murdered, in part (according to some of our sources in Guatemala) for assisting in the development of the REMHI project. The REMHI project recorded over 6,500 testimonials that detailed over 55,000 humans rights violations, including 25,000 deaths. Strangely, although no large public monument in Guatemala City honors the hundreds of thousands of deaths and disappearances, a large monument, uncovered on April 26, 2000, at a ceremony commemorating the second anniversary of his assassination, commemorates Bishop Gerardi (Nunca Más 2000). Does this monument to Gerardi vicariously represent the victims of 440 village massacres with the words "*Guatemala Nunca Más*" (Guatemala Never Again) replacing the names of the dead?

The Church, through landmarks and memorials to the dead and disappeared, reminds parishioners and the military of human suffering caused by military actions. The large mural (figure 14.2) painted on the wall of the Catholic Church grounds in Cantabal, Ixcán, and the placement of hundreds of individual crosses inside the Catholic Churches in Nebaj, San Juan Cotzal, and Santiago Atitlán attempt to formalize the past and educate

Figure 14.2   This 15-meter-wide mural is painted on the perimeter wall of the Catholic Church in Cantabal, Ixcán. This full-color mural was painted in January 2001, a full four years after signing the peace treaty in December 1996.

Photo by: Matthew Taylor.

new generations about past atrocities.[10] The Catholic Church in Chajul contains a powerful mural that depicts dead community members and a woman bent in mourning over the prostrate bodies. The mural is entitled "In memory of our martyrs" (Diocesis del Quiché 1994, p. 200).

The Catholic Church in Santiago Atitlán also contains a memorial to Father Stanley Rother, and American priest who was killed on church grounds on July 28, 1981 and whose remains are interred there. As one arrives by boat to Santiago Atitlán visitors see no obvious, open memorials to the town's troubled past, or of the public outcry that military occupation and repression sparked—again memories remain deep in the folds of the Church. In Santiago Atitlán no overt landmarks in tourist areas indicate the confrontation between the townsfolk and the military that left 19 people dead and which eventually led to popular resistance and the forced abandonment of the town by the military in 1990—the first successful ousting of the military in Guatemala (Carlsen 1997). If tourists do trek up to the town center, up the steep streets laden with arts and crafts, and make their way into the dimly lit church, they finally reach the memorials. But, is the significance of the tiny brass crosses on a side wall lost on people who come to experience Guatemala's indigenous cultures and natural beauty? Tourists do not make the journey to Santiago to relive a violent past. The crosses on the church wall maybe then, if we think of their intent, serve their purpose—they commemorate the dead for friends and family who frequent the church.

The Catholic Church provides refuge for public commemoration and protest against the actions of the military. The construction of monuments inside churches or on church grounds is the first step toward construction of more public monuments. Foote, Tóth, and Arvay (2000) observed a similar scenario in Hungary, where monuments banned by the communist regimes first appeared in churchyards and cemeteries before the fall of communism.

Not all monuments in Guatemala commemorate civilian victims of the civil war. The military also suffered losses. We now turn to examine how the military represent their soldiers who died on the line of duty.

State Sponsored Monuments

The Military

When interpreting the conflict, the Guatemalan military, plays the role of state "savior," without whom a leftist takeover was imminent. The military's portrayal of the war is vastly different than that of the Catholic Church.

Their landmarks and memorials often stress sacrifice, unity, national service, and power. In contrast to monuments created by the Catholic Church, military and government landmarks figure prominently in public spaces and take on official tones in both form and content.

After announcing our arrival to Ixcán by thundering across the metal sheets of the bridge spanning the turbulent waters of the Chixoy River, we hit the brakes of the pickup truck to ease over speed bumps, which, at the same time, allows the soldier in an elevated guard post to give us the once over. Next, signs on the massive block wall of the military base at Playa Grande (near Cantabal) flood our vision. The signs invite locals and travelers to visit the military museum inside the walls—the only regional military museum in the country. Paradoxically, or maybe intentionally, this museum sits in the heart of the zone that experienced the most intense conflict in the 1980s and 1990s.

The displays in the museum reinforce the portrayal of sacrifice and salvation of the people from insurgents by the military. For example, a display describes the role of the air force in the counter-insurgency campaign as the *guardian del Ixcán* (guardian of Ixcán). Museum displays include photographs of captured weapons, captured rebels, and battleground scenes—features that emphasize military victory and power. Other displays include tributes to military losses such as photographs, examples of field accommodations, and lists of officers killed in the Ixcán, all which emphasize sacrifice to the state. The military depiction of the guerillas is far from objective. Every verbal and written mention of the guerrillas or insurgents presented to visitors to the museum is prefaced by the word "delinquents."[11] An inspection of the visitor's logbook reveals that most visitors to the museum are local. Locals, who once feared the military, can now openly visit the site of their own torture, pain, and imprisonment.[12]

The Guatemalan armed forces in the Ixcán also constructed roadside memorials in honor of their casualties. Two of the monuments sit on the side of the *Transveral del Norte* (the Northern Transversal route), a road network constructed in the late 1960s and early 1970s by the state to gain access to oil deposits, large tracts of land, and nascent guerilla camps (Kading 1999; Le Bot 1995). One of the roads cuts east to west though the *Franja Transversal del Norte* (Northern Transversal Strip), parts of which are known as "the land of the generals" because members of the military elite appropriated large tracts of land for cattle ranches and for the promise of oil wealth.

One roadside monument sits at the entrance to the village of San Lucas in the Ixcán. Guatemalan troops occupied this village and created a temporary outpost here for further forays into the rainforests of the Ixcán. Although the monument is slightly defaced, soldiers from the base in Playa Grande saw fit to give the monument a bright yellow coat of paint early in

2001. This new coat of paint represents the new self-proclaimed relationship of the Guatemalan military with Ixcán residents, a relationship in which the military "defends and protects the communities to maintain a peaceful atmosphere in which integral development can occur" (Girón 2000, 3). Yellow is the color associated with the large road building machines that the military now uses; yellow, then, renders a positive air of prosperity and development. Previously, all monuments and machinery bore military olive green paint. With time, though, the yellow coat chips and fades to reveal true military origins—drab olive green.

The monument serves several purposes. In the rainy season, before construction of a shelter, locals sat on the dry concrete base while they wait for transport to nearby Cantabal, or, now that a bridge crosses the formidable Ixcán River, to Barillas in Huehuetenango. The monument lists the names of army engineers killed by guerrillas while they built the road. In this sense, the monument serves its intended purpose—to commemorate the road builders killed by "delinquent" guerrillas. This monument also served its (un) intended purpose by triggering the memory of an Ixcán resident who told me of his experiences as a PAC member, his relationships with military commanders in Playa Grande, and the orders from above that he and other PAC members received to search and destroy suspected guerrilla sympathizers.

The other bright yellow roadside monument is in the form of a castle found on the Army Corps of Engineers emblem. The bright yellow castle also commemorates the death of army road builders. It was barely noticeable until the recent painting campaign brought attention to the diminutive structure by clearing away encroaching secondary growth and by carving a stairway through the red lateritic rainforest soils from the road to the monument itself.

The Government

On December 26, 1996, PAN (National Party for Advancement) and URNG (Guatemalan National Revolutionary Unit) signed an internationally negotiated peace agreement that ended almost 40 years of internal conflict. The government erected several monuments that commemorate the peace treaty and victims of the conflict. These monuments always include a dove and the following phrase: "firm and lasting peace." Although these structures represent significant events in Guatemala's history, they are not significant structures themselves. The diminutive nature of the peace monuments is clearly illustrated by the eternal flame and plaque set in the ground in Guatemala City's national plaza. This monument—one-meter high in glory—fades into insignificance against the backdrop of the National Palace, which is still guarded by troops in combat fatigues carrying automatic weapons.

When we visited the peace memorial in mid-2001, the "eternal" flame did not burn, orange peels and trash cluttered the glass case, which sits atop a small stone block. To top off this poor appearance, graffiti adorned the glass casing. When ignited, "the flame is the size of a Bunsen burner" (Smith 2001). Given the length of the civil war (36 years), and associated human suffering, we must question why the state constructed such a small monument. All the same, it is surprising that the state *did* acquiesce to build a monument in Guatemala's most public space. Perhaps answers to our questioning and doubts surface upon examination of the vague and noncommittal words inscribed on the side of the monument, "*A los heroes anónimos de la paz*" (to the anonymous heroes of the peace).

Another diminutive monument to war and peace competes with food vendors and video games in Nebaj, Quiché, the southernmost town in hard-hit Ixíl country. Curiously, the barbed wire bounded memorial stands in a hidden corner of the town square. The unstable appearance of the white dove instills little sense of celebration, or even solemn remembrance. Instead, the monument resembles military-controlled model villages during the 1980s, some of which the military encircled with barbed wire to maintain direct control of residents' movements (CEIDEC 1990; Falla 1992). The paint-spattered plaque below the white dove repeats vague nationalistic apologies for the war. The text informs us that this monument honors

> our brothers who perished in the armed conflict, hoping that this event will never occur again. The people of Nebaj and the municipality offer this monument as a symbol of the new democratic cohabitation and culture of firm and lasting peace.

In Nebaj the real homage to rural Guatemalans resides a mere 20 meters away inside the nearby Catholic Church in the form of hundreds of wooden crosses, which bear the details of each victim of terror (figure 14.3). The crosses come from the people and are personal in regard to their message or content (i.e., someone important to me died). The official memorials, in contrast, are vague and platitudinous, and ignored. On the other hand, the military memorials tout their position, power, and achievements, and are imposed on the landscape.

The lack of investment in public monuments speaks of the current political and cultural climate in Guatemala and how the military and social elite struggle to acknowledge their role in the violence of the past. Despite wide publication and recognition of Guatemala's atrocious human rights record, many upper- and middle-class Guatemalans retort that academics and international agencies side with the Indians and the left. Further, because the elite were physically, as much as geographically, removed from

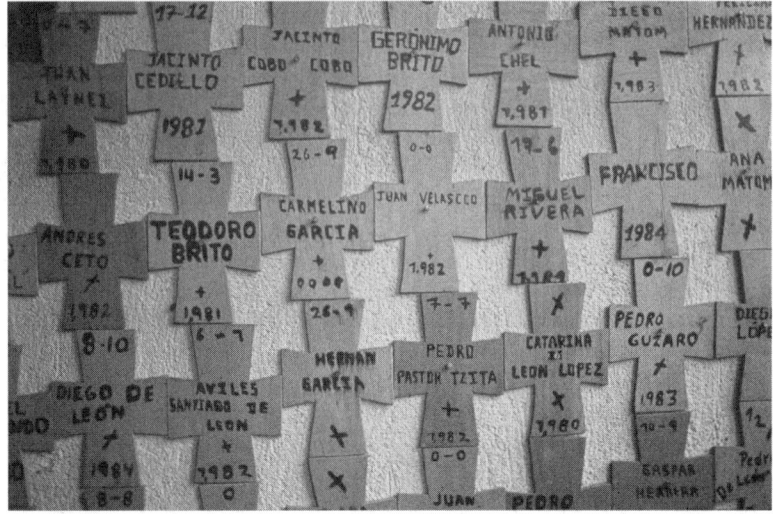

Figure 14.3   Small wooden crosses on the inside wall of the Catholic Church in Nebaj, Quiché record the name and date of death of victims.
Photo by: Michael Steinberg.

the worst violence in the countryside, they refuse to recognize the magnitude of massacres in rural Guatemala. For example, the minister of defense in 2001, Eduardo Arévalo Lacs, when referring to rapes and land seizures by ex-PAC members in Quiché in July 2001, simply stated that *"ex patrulleros civiles ya no hay, porque fueron disueltos hace años"* (there are no longer any ex-civil patrollers because they were dissolved years ago). In this statement he absolves the military of all responsibility in this case (Prensa Libre 2001c).

The static nature of Guatemala's power structure and class relations means that the state will probably not fund more meaningful monuments representing the violence and victims of almost four decades of war. The act of remembering will remain in the hands of the church and communities that fund their own projects. The highly centralized Guatemalan state and life in the capital city bear little relation to the countryside, so in some respect, rural folk (about 60 percent of the population) increasingly follow their own plans for transforming spaces into places of mourning.

Spontaneous Monuments

Some rural communities in Guatemala, in the face of institutional neglect, construct their own monuments to victims and conduct yearly memorial services on the anniversary dates of village massacres (Noack 2001). For example, a large monument commemorates the massacre in Cuarto Pueblo, Ixcán (figure 14.4). This twenty-foot high, blue and white concrete structure bears brass plaques listing about 470 residents of Cuarto Pueblo, Xalbal, Zunil, Los Angeles, and Ixtahuacan Chiquito murdered in military massacres in March and April, 1982.[13] A small plaque on the front of the memorial commemorates Father Guillermo Woods, a Maryknoll missionary involved in the early stages of Ixcán colonization in the late 1960s and early 1970s (Morrissey 1978). Father Woods died when the plane he piloted from Guatemala City to Ixcán mysteriously crashed. Many Guatemalans believe the military "downed" the plane (Falla 1992). Candle wax stains the concrete steps around the monument, testament to the active—and ritualistic—use of this site.

González (1998) depicts another spontaneous site and relays plans to build a memorial in the shape of a pyramid in Nueva Esparanza, Huehuetenango.[14] And, in Dos Erres, Petén, where 180 members of the community were massacred and thrown into a well in 1982, the community plans to construct a monument at the site of the well and in the center of the village (Rosales 2000). Residents of Nimlaha'kok in Alta Verapaz and

Figure 14.4   The large monument in Cuarto Pueblo, Ixcán. Built by local residents, this white and blue monument records the names of over 470 residents murdered in Cuarto Pueblo, Xalbal, Zunil, Los Angeles, and Ixtahuacan Chiquito by the Guatemalan military in March in April 1982.

Photo by: Matthew Taylor.

Río Negro outside Rabinal remember massacres and victims by inscribing their names in monuments (Wilson 1997).

A statue of an indigenous woman breaking an M-16 rifle over her head is perhaps the most public and overt memorial in Guatemala (figure 14.5).

Figure 14.5   Monument of an indigenous women in the plaza of Chimaltenango. An indigenous woman breaks an M-16 rifle symbolizing the end of 40 years of civil war. This monument occupies a prominent place in the plaza of Chimaltenango. *Photo by*: Matthew Taylor.

The three meter-high base and statue stand in the busy town square of Chimaltenango, a majority Indigenous town 80 kilometers west of Guatemala City. This memorial occupies a prominent place in the central plaza, which still forms an integral part of social life in many Latin American towns and cities (Low 2000). The plaque tells us about the

> thousands and thousands of martyrs who fought for peace with social justice of the Maya Kaqchikel people and non-indigenous people who were: kidnapped, disappeared, tortured, massacred, and murdered by the repressive forces of the last thirty-six years. (My translation of a section of the inscription from the statue's base.)

Residents of Chimaltenango meet, eat, polish shoes, chat, read, gossip, flirt, and simply stroll around the plaza. Erected in January 1997, a mere few weeks after the beginning of "official" peace in Guatemala, the statue makes a bold statement in a time of tender peace. We must note, however, the restrained and vague language used in the memorial. Placing the blame for the violence on "repressive forces" perhaps allows the statue to stand— no specifics about "responsible" forces surface in the text. Even if locals far from the capital decide to "finger" the government and openly blame the masterminds and perpetrators of massacres, they remain immune to justice because the June 1994 accord that established the UN-administered Clarification Commission (CEH 1999) stipulates that the information pro-duced "will not individualize responsibility, nor have any legal implications" (Wilson 1997).

Unintended markers of the past

Unplanned markers of past strife riddle Guatemale's countryside. These features provide subtle but important insights into Guatemala's post-conflict environment, and, although unplanned, provide residents with a permanent memory of past events. Driving east from Huehuetenango to Cobán by a back road that hugs the foothills of the rugged Cuchumatán Mountains, we encountered the official road sign that announces the entry into the Ixíl Triangle, Quiché. The sign—a leftover from "those times of the guerillas"—is riddled with bullet holes. It is a constant reminder of Guatemala's worst massacres and remains standing despite the complete inundation of rural Guatemala with new signs advertising banks, money transfer services, fuel stations, development projects, and motels. What is the intent of leaving such a sign in Ixíl country?

Another public sign of the past, sadly common in many postwar countries warns residents of unexploded munitions. These posters dot the sides of wooden houses in both Ixcán and Ixíl country. Adding further insult to injury, farmers who were denied access to their fields during the height of the conflict so that the military could better control them, now cannot farm those same mine-strewn fields and forests.

These signs contrast with the stunning physical and cultural landscape of the Ixíl area, which includes mountainscapes, picturesque wheat and maize fields, and seemingly idyllic villages. Travelers and tourists admire the remote beauty of Nebaj and surrounding villages, but without cues to the violent past, visitors often succumb to the scenery and the beautiful geometric designs unique to the cloth weavings of the area. Visitors seldom realize that they stand in the middle of former "red" zones of death and destruction. The clues to the past lie deep in the recesses of the Catholic Church in the form of thousands of individually carved crosses bearing the name, age, and date of death of each victim. Other clues lie in the military base a few kilometers outside Nebaj (here no signs invite visitors to inspect the military interpretation of recent events), and an abandoned landing strip (formerly known as "Camp New Life") used in the past to launch bombing missions on isolated Ixíl villages and suspected guerilla camps.

Other public landmarks of the conflict include military outposts at certain strategic geographic locations, such as bridges crossing the Chixoy and Xaclbal rivers in the Ixcán. Over the months of living in Ixcán and traversing its muddy roads with residents, we noted that each time we passed a military checkpoint (current or past) the locals we accompanied broke into stories related to that point in the road. Soldiers carrying automatic weapons still occupy some outposts. We were not allowed to photograph any of the outposts or the soldiers. Again, one wonders about the purpose or message of soldiers guarding river crossings in a "peaceful" country? Because these military installations continue to stand ground in Ixcán and Ixíl country, centers of past guerilla and military activity, the message does not lie too deep beneath the surface. Their presence reminds locals of past and present power relations (e.g., Flores 2003). Military displays of power are especially relevant in the Ixcán, where, according to the soldier who led our tour of the military museum, two local villages continue to reject all government regulations and military control of the region. These villages are made up of residents from former Communities of Population in Resistance (CPR), and returning refugees who fled to Mexico in the 1980s.[15] These villages now enjoy protection because of the presence of international accompaniers and United Nation's officials, headquartered in Cantabal, who monitor the postwar activities of the military and verify social reforms promised in the 1996 peace treaty.[16]

Apart from the scars that remain on the minds and bodies of thousands of rural residents in highland towns, the military also left less obvious markers of their years of occupation. In many towns, such as Santa Ana Huista, Huehuetenango, motorists pass guard towers (albeit in ruins) at the entrance to towns where all travelers were stopped, questioned, and checked. These checkpoints stand firm in the memory of residents, who recount hardships endured when revision points functioned.

In the heart of Guatemala City, the military academy (Escuela Politécnica) also conveys a message of continued military power and presence to pedestrians and motorist transiting one of the capitals' busiest boulevards. This imposing building, paradoxically located adjacent to the trendy nightclub and restaurant-infested "Zona Viva," resembles a medieval castle and remains a dominant feature in the City, another reminder of the past to the thousands of buses and cars that pass every day. Memories pop into the minds of motorists when traffic slows to permit passage of armored Jeep Cherokees and Mercedes sedans emerging from the recesses of this formidable building. The armed soldiers who patrol the *La Politécnicas* walls send an intimidating image to pedestrians and motorists. The continued presence of armed, ready-for-combat military personnel in the heart of the capital city indicates Guatemala's incomplete transition to a civilian-controlled democracy.

Certainly, military checkpoints and soldiers patrolling in public spaces appear less commonplace today than in the 1980s and early 1990s. Automatic-weapon toting soldiers riding in the back of unmarked pick-up trucks, however, remain fixtures in Guatemala. Today, like the past, the military forms an integral part of the Guatemalan life. This comes as no surprise. Eduardo Galeano, a celebrated Latin American author who writes extensively about the permanent links between politics and the military in Guatemala, writes,

> The president of Guatemala does not wear a prison uniform, but he is a prisoner. The military, his gaolers, have given him permission to enter the National Palace. He has given them a promise of impunity for their killings and has assured them that he will not commit agrarian reform or any other sin. (Galeano 1967)

Given the recent history and influence of the military in most facets of Guatemalan daily life we cannot expect a radical transition from the past.

In contrast to the imposing presence of the Escuela Politécnica, Jean Marie Simon (1988, 95) points to small plaques and crosses remembering the dead (nonmilitary) scattered throughout Guatemala City. Simon provides examples of these more personal memoirs imprinted in city curbs and traffic islands. These spontaneous shrines constructed by families of assassinated students and politicians do not receive any form of public funding or sanction.

Back out in the countryside, evangelical churches make up another powerful feature of the postwar landscape. Guatemala boasts the highest percentage of Protestant members for any Latin American country (although recent conversion rates appear slower with the ending of the war) (Green 1993; Stoll 1993). Although various factors explain the massive conversion to Protestantism, one common theory involves Efraín Ríos Montt, the general who governed Guatemala at the height of military-led massacres in the early 1980s. Ríos Montt, a member and vocal proponent of the "new" religion, claimed that Guatemalans represented the new Israelites. He aimed to create the first Evangelical, anticommunist state in Central America. Many Indian villagers joined Evangelical churches in part to prove allegiance to the state and to avoid persecution by the military (Green 1993; Le Bot 1995). Today Evangelical churches of various sects squeeze into even the smallest hamlets in the Guatemalan countryside. Their loud "broadcast style" of preaching and singing besieges the homes of both Catholics and Evangelicals. Stoll (1993, 5) states that, "the Catholic Church, driven underground after the army killed three Spanish priests and hundreds of local leaders, reported that parishioners were turning Protestant to save their lives." Catholicism was considered tantamount to communism and guerrilla insurgency because of its involvement with liberation theology, church supported cooperatives, and literacy programs, especially in the conflict zones (Green 1993).

Unlike their Catholic counterparts, Evangelical churches do not contain memorials to war victims simply because evangelists avoided some of the direct military persecution (Green 1993). Thus, places where evangelicals worship now symbolize the breakdown of the close-knit corporate, Catholic community that characterized many Maya villages before the war. This developed not only because villages split along denominational lines, but also because the civil patrols and the conflict in general allowed some individuals to violently seek retribution for past personal rivalries and vendettas (Green 1993; Falla 1992; Stoll 1993).

A final, unintended, trigger for memories lies in dead and rotting trees along RN9 (National Road 9) as one approaches the town San Mateo Ixtatán from the south. When we traveled through the foggy, cold, and remote reaches of the 3000 meter high Cuchumatán Mountain ranges, we wondered aloud why so many trees where left to rot in an area where wood is the most important source of fuel. We speculated that perhaps the trees succumbed to disease. Later, we discovered that the military forced local people to cut trees on either side of the road (30–40 meters) to guard against rebel ambushes (Castañeda Salguero 1998; Manz 1988).[17] Today, residents of the area refuse to collect or remove the rotting wood. Residents of the area told Castañeda Salguero, "to leave the trees as they lie is like leaving the skeleton of somebody we did not kill. For that reason we do not collect the wood. And they will be there until they turn to dust" (my translation from the original Spanish, 109). Therefore, locals participate now in a subtle form of protest—they leave the tree trunks in place as testament to past atrocities.

Discussing Unsettled Landscapes in Post-Conflict Regions

Landmarks and memorials in a landscape, overt or discreet, play a powerful role in telling us about a people's values, history, struggles, and successes. Traditionally, landscape studies in the discipline of geography focused on material features expressive of folk, indigenous, and ethnic cultures, such as vernacular architecture, religious icons, settlements forms, and agricultural landforms (Domosh 1989; Hobbs 1995; Jordan 1982, 1985; Kniffen 1990; Mathewson 1984; Sauer 1925). More recently, socially and politically oriented landscape studies have started to examine the messages communicated in buildings, landmarks, and memorials (Atkinson and Cosgrove 1998; Cosgrove 1984; Gillis 1994; Lowenthal 1985; Till 1999, 2003). Most, if not all of these studies focus on landscapes in developed nations and within the context of contestation, but not open insurgency or full-scale warfare. The postcolonial world beyond the North Atlantic realm's of relatively tame symbolic and actual political terrains, offers rich, if horrific, material for interpretation and analysis. For example, post-revolutionary landscapes, including Cambodia, Sierra Leone, Afghanistan, and Guatemala have received little, if any, attention from geographers. A partial exception is the work of Foote, Tóth, and Arvay (2000) in Hungary. Foote and his colleagues analyze the change in political monuments and historical shrines in Hungary after the fall of the Communist government in 1989.

Perhaps the absence of post-conflict landscape analyses is not surprising given the paucity of monuments in areas of recent conflict. Many post-conflict regions still grapple with new regimes and power relations remain unsteady, thus no one side can claim public space in which to construct obvious landmarks. In other words, states and their citizens do not agree on what or how events should be remembered, thereby delaying construction of memorials or other landmarks (Till 1999). Moreover, many people, just like those in Guatemala, inhibit the desire to build spontaneous shrines for fear of reprisal. Also, post-conflict landscapes present problems of access to outsiders asking questions about past violence (see Santino 2001). Indeed, many of the villages we visited in Guatemala witnessed brutal massacres, making some residents tentative to talk about past violence and how they plan to commemorate past events (Montejo 1987; REMHI 1998). In short, the absence of overt public landmarks and memorials makes the interpretation of post-conflict landscapes more challenging.

However subtle or limited in scale and number, examination of landmarks that do exist in post-conflict landscapes can provide important indicators of past and present political and social relationships. The presence, placement, and prominence of landmarks in post-conflict landscapes can tell the observer about who "won," or, if there are no clear victors, the continuing struggle for power. In the case of Guatemala, although the state successfully destroyed the armed opposition (and anyone remotely associated with it), the government of Alvaro Arzu signed a United Nations' monitored peace agreement in 1996 that mandated a reduction in numbers of armed personnel and the state military budget (Jonas 2000).[18] The state "victory" remains tainted among much of the Guatemalan citizenry because of the egregious human rights violations (especially against rural residents). Many Guatemalans, especially in rural areas, see the conflict solely as a ploy by the elite to protect economic and social interests. This ploy eliminated those individuals and groups who questioned the power structure within Guatemalan society (Diocesis de Quiché 1994; Kading 1999; Le Bot 1995). Power within Guatemala's post-conflict landscape—as reflected and captured in the landmarks—continues to settle along the dualities of rural and urban, rich and poor, Catholic and Protestant, and military and civilian.

In Guatemala power and social relations continue in a fashion similar to the years prior to the civil war. Ladino elites control politics, land, and capital. Unlike the power shift that Foote, Tóth, and Arvay (2000) document in postcommunist Hungary, Guatemala did not experience a major power shift. Therefore, the construction of new monuments and historical shrines that reflect the ideology of a new regime remains limited. Individuals in Guatemala who desire to construct memorials that contrast with the policies of the military and social elites often do so at great personal risk. In other parts of the world (e.g., Hungary) the radical change from one form of government to another distinct form allows the new government and the people it represents to decide which events and martyrs they wish to memorialize (Foote et al. 2000).

Conclusion

Geographer Steven Hoelscher (1998) writes, "what we see on the landscape . . . stems from the social, economic, and political ideologies of their creators and from their creative exigencies" (p. 390). In the case of Guatemala, the "creators" of the landscape continue to struggle and compete with one another regarding what is presented to the public. These presentations (both subtle and obvious landmarks and memorials) by groups of citizens, the Catholic Church, and the military/government offer radically different memories of the recently concluded civil war. The Catholic Church commemorates victims. The Guatemalan military emphasizes victory and power.

Sadly, for the people of Guatemala, a long-standing military desire to control the text of the landscape ensures continued tension and violence (e.g., Flores 2003). The military no longer drops bombs on indigenous villages in Ixíl country, but military forces and their allies continue to target individuals who seek to portray opposing landmarks and memories of the war (e.g., Nash 2002). The military (i.e., the state) eliminates anyone trying to create a different, victim-oriented post-conflict landscape. For example, Sister Barbara Ford was murdered for her role in the REMHI project. In a separate incident, ex-PAC members raped women, burned several houses, and forced villages off their plots of land in a Quiché village (Prensa Libre 2001a). The violence in Quiché was attributed to a long-running land dispute between returned refugees and members of the PAC who occupied the land in the absence of the refugees.

Monuments in contemporary Guatemalan landscapes reflect the torturous and tentative path to political and social reform. Competing markers in the landscape send contradictory messages to the Guatemalan public and the world. Memorials and landscape features commemorating victims slowly spread from books to inside churches, to exterior walls of churches and beyond. What will be the next step? Will monuments that provide details of massacres and murders find their way from isolated villages to Guatemala's most public places for all to see? Will the government and church openly sanctify spontaneous monuments and permit memories unfettered by fear? Or, will powerful segments within Guatemalan society continue to control the past?

Notes

1. The thousands of dead, disappeared, tortured, and displaced, and the hundreds of Mayan communities wiped off the map during the armed conflict all left indelible scars on the minds and hearts of Guatemalans. The impacts of the violence differ according to ethnicity, social class, economic status, gender, age, place of residence, political, and religious affiliation of individuals and social groups. Fear, fright, sadness, depression, sleeping disorders, lack of trust . . . are some of the symptoms frequently shown by people interviewed by CEH" (CEH 1999, Vol. 4, pp. 14–15).

2. The 12 volumes of CEH also reside on compact discs and on a searchable Web site hosted by the American Association for the Advancement of Science: <http://shr.aaas.org/guatemala/ceh/>

3. Many Mayan activists within and outside of Guatemala adopted the term "Maya," however, based on discussions with Guatemala's indigenous folk (i.e., nonacademic or activist) in the rural areas of Guatemala. We elect to use the term "indigenous" and "Indian" because most rural indigenous people self-identify using the terms "natural" or "indigena." They use the term "Maya" when referring to "nuestros antepasados" (our ancestors). We use the term "indigenous" not because we negate the relationship between the splendor of the classical Maya culture with their descendents, but because we prefer to use terms that the people themselves employ (some academics claim that the Guatemalan elite refuse to recognize the term "Maya" in their effort to continually belittle the indigenous segment of the population (see Arias 1997; Secaira 2000).

4. David Stoll (1993) reports that many rural Guatemalans existed in a limbo between two armies. Guatemalans we interviewed expressed similar feeling about their lives "between two fires." We must note, however, that many North American and Guatemalan scholars contest David Stoll's research in Quiché and his reports about how indigenous people coped with the war (e.g., Arias 2003; Hale 1997; Stoll 2003).

5. Nelson (1999, p. 10) also notes how Guatemalans "live among the eloquent ruins left by the war: model villages built on the charred remains of burned houses, clandestine cemeteries, holding cells for the disappeared built into houses, and military and civil patrol institutions throughout the countryside."

6. Lack of trust in the Portillo regime for many Guatemalans lies in the simple fact that Ríos Montt heads up Guatemala's Congress—Montt was President of Guatemala for 18 months in 1982 and 1983 and, some claim, the mastermind of the worst military massacres and maneuvers in Guatemala.

7. See Prensa Libre 2001a, for an example of strained relationships between ex-PAC members and residents of one community.

8. Although foreign nationals can speak with near impunity, Guatemalan social science researchers, academics, and human rights activists work under renewed death threats and intimidations from "unknown" quarters (Nash 2002).

9. We cannot deny, however, the importance of empirical documentation of massacre victims. Indeed, the type of documentation represented by Falla's *Massacres in the Jungle* (1992) and the CEH and REMHI publications where details surrounding death and destruction surface, in Richard Wilson's words, form "the first act of both remembering and rupturing the silence around violations. Faithfully recording the names of the victims is an attempt to tell the 'public secrets' of a community in order to initiate a break with the official regime of denial. The first statement on the past by Guatemalan society must be a credible and a defensible account of what exactly happened when and to whom, without which other discussions (such as what agents were thinking at the time) cannot begin" (1997, 833).

10. The government carved Cantabal out of the rainforest in 1985 to serve as the administrative center for the newly created *municipio* of Ixcán. Cantabal

formed part of the "Playa Grande" development pole that consisted of at least 100 villages under army control (CEIDEC 1990). The structure of the villages and towns facilitated military control of rural residents by concentrating residents in geographic areas easily observed by the army in an effort to eradicate the "sea" (rural farmers) from which the "fish" (guerillas) drew sustenance.

11. Visitors to the museum cannot browse the artifacts at their leisure. A civil affairs officer interprets displays for visitors.

12. See the testimonies about imprisonment, torture, and mass graves inside the military base at Playa Grande in Falla (1992, 192–197).

13. Guatemala's national flag is blue and white.

14. "On this day . . . we will be beginning construction of a great monument to the memory of all the men and women, victims of these thirty-six years of violence. As we raise the monument, we will be embedding into it various objects that we have saved as mementos of our dead: crosses with names, personal objects, or other things that remind us of their existence. I will place at the top of this pyramid . . . the 'deer-eye' seed that I have been wearing around my neck ever since that old lady who gave me her blessing in the darkness placed it in my hand" (González 1998, 157, when referring to reconstruction of lives in Nueva Esparanza, Yichkan [Ixcán]).

15. The Communities of Populations in Resistance resisted military rule during the 1980s and 1990s and eked out a livelihood in the forests of the Ixcán, the Petén, and the mountains of northern Quiché (Falla 1993). They only emerged from hiding after promises from the Guatemalan government to recognize these communities as civilian populations (Primavera del Ixcán 1999; REHMI 1998).

16. Much controversy surrounds the MINUGUA (United Nations Verification Mission in Guatemala) presence in Guatemala. Because MINUGUA protects human rights in Guatemala, many people believe that criminals call in MINUGUA when their rights are in jeopardy. For example, in highland villages around Totonicapán, villagers often deal with their own criminals by cutting off water or electricity rights to offenders of community norms. However, these criminals now call in MINUGUA to illustrate how their rights are in danger. This leads many to believe that MINUGUA is overstepping its bounds and call for its withdrawal. Despite controversy about its presence, Guatemalans voted to keep MINUGUA in country for another four years after their stay expired in 2001.

17. Castañeda Salguero (1998) relates that in "August 1982 the Guatemalan Army gathered the people from various villages of San Mateo Ixtatán to help them cut the trees on either side of the road. En San Mateo Ixtatán, 30 to 40 meters either side of the road were cleared for a distance of 18 kilometers (this includes the road from Santa Eulalia to San Mateo and the road to the east to Yolcultac). This represents about 126 hectares of cleared forest and about 113,400 trees. The rotten trunks still lie on the side of the road as evidence, and none of the locals use them" (108).

18. Hale (1997) draws on the work of Falla (1992), Stoll (1993), and McCreery (1994) to show how the counterinsurgency campaign of the Guatemalan military mimicked strategies developed during the Vietnam War—security, control, and development. However, Hale goes on to state, that the main difference

between Vietnam and Guatemala is that "the Guatemalan army carried the euphemistically defined objective of the first phase, 'eliminate enemy infrastructure' (read noncombatant population) to its beastly logical extreme" (818).

Bibliography

Adams, Richard. 1970. *Crucifixion by Power: Essays on Guatemalan National Social Structure, 1944–1960.* Austin: University of Texas Press.

Arias, A. 1997. Comments on Hale's Consciousness, Violence, and the Politics of Memory in Guatemala. *Current Anthropology* 38 (5): 824–826.

Arias, A. 2003. Response to David Stoll. *Lasa Forum* 33 (4): 22–23.

Atkinson, D. and D. Cosgrove. 1998. Urban Rhetoric and Embodied Identities: City, Nation, and Empire at the Vittorio Emanuele II Monument in Rome, 1870–1945. *Annals of the Association of American Geographers* 88 (1): 28–49.

Ball, P., P. Kobrack, and H. F. Spirer. 1999. *State Violence in Guatemala, 1960–1996: A Quantitative Reflection.* New York: American Association for the Advancement of Science.

Blake, K. S. and J. S. Smith. 2000. Pueblo Mission Churches as Symbols of Permanence and Identity. *The Geographical Review* 90 (3): 359–380.

Carlsen, R. 1997. *The War for the Heart and Soul of a Highland Maya Town.* Austin: University of Texas Press.

Castañeda Salguero, C. 1998. *Lucha por la Tierra, Retornados y Medio Ambiente en Huehuetenango.* Guatemala City: FLACSO.

Casaús Arzú, M.E. 1998. *La Metamorfosis del Racismo en Guatemala.* Guatemala City: Editorial Cholsamaj.

CEH (Commission for Historical Clarification). 1999. *Guatemala, Memory of Silence / Tz'inil Na' Tab'al*, Report of the Commission for Historical Clarification. Guatemala City: United Nations.

CEIDEC (Centro de Estudios Integrados de Desarrollo Comunal), 1990. *Guatemala: Polos de Desarrollo. El Caso de la Desestructuración de las Comunidades Indígenas.* Mexico, D.F.: Editorial Praxis, 257.

Cosgrove, D. E. 1984. *Social Formations and Symbolic Landscape.* London: Croom Helm.

Craig, L. 1978. *The Federal Presence: Architecture, Politics, and Symbols in the United States Government Buildings.* Cambridge, MA: MIT Press.

Diocesis del Quiché, 1994. *El Quiché: El Pueblo y su Iglesia, 1960–1980.* Santa Cruz del Quiché, Guatemala.

Domosh, M. 1989. A Method for Interpreting Landscape: A Case Study of the New York World Building. *Area* 21: 347–355.

Falla, R. 1992. *Masacres de la Selva: Ixcán, Guatemala (1975–1982).* Universidad de San Carlos, Guatemala: Editorial Universitaria, 253.

Falla, R. 1993. *Historia de un Gran Amor.* Guatemala.

Flores, O. 2003. Ixcán, un pueblo Olvidado. *Siglo Veintiuno*, February 9.

Foote, K. E. *Shadowed Ground: America's Landscapes of Violence and Tragedy*. Austin: University of Texas Press.

Foote, Kenneth E., A. Tóth, and A. Arvay. 2000. Hungary after 1989: Inscribing a New Past on Place. *Geographical Review* 90 (3): 301–334.

Galeano, E. 1967. *Guatemala: Pais Occupado*. Mexico City: Editoria Nuestra Tiempo.

Gillis, J. R. ed. 1994. *Commemorations: The Politics of National Identity*. Princeton, NJ: Princeton University Press.

Girón, F. R. R. 2000. Coronel de Infantería y Comandante de Zona Militar No. 22, Playa Grande, Ixcán. In *Mensaje de la Comandancia*. Ixcán: Puerta abierta al desarollo. Magazine published by the division of Civil Affairs, Zona Militar 22, Playa Grande, Ixcán, Quiché, Guatemala.

Gleijeses, Piero. 1998. *Shattered Hope: The Guatemalan Revolution and the United States, 1944–1954*. Princeton, NJ: Princeton University Press.

González, G. P. 1998. *Return of the Maya*. Yax Te' Foundation, Rancho Palos Verdes: California.

Green, L. 1993. Shifting affiliations: Mayan widows and Evangélicos in Guatemala. In *Rethinking Protestantism in Latin America*, ed. Virginia Garrard-Burnett and David Stoll, Philadelphia: Temple University Press.

Green, L. 1999. *Fear as a Way of Life: Mayan Widows in Rural Guatemala*. New York: Columbia University Press.

Hale, C. R. 1997. Consciousness, Violence, and the Politics of Memory in Guatemala. *Current Anthropology*, 38 (5): 817–838.

Handy, J. 1994. *Revolution in the Countryside: Rural Conflict and Agrarian Reform in Guatemala, 1944–1954*. Chapel Hill, NC: The University of North Carolina Press.

Hobbs, J. J. 1995. *Mount Sinai*. Austin: University of Texas Press.

Hoelscher, S. D. 1998. Tourism, Ethnic Memory and the Other-Directed Place. *Ecumene* 5 (4): 369–398.

Jonas, S. 2000. *Of Centaurs and Doves, Guatemala's Peace Process*. Boulder, CO: Westview Press.

Jordan, T. G. 1982. *Texas Graveyards: A Cultural Legacy*. Austin: University of Texas Press.

Jordan, T. G. 1985. *American Log Buildings: An Old World Heritage*. Chapel Hill, NC: University of North Carolina Press.

Kading, T. W. 1999. The Guatemalan Military and the Economics of La Violencia. *Canadian Journal of Latin American and Caribbean Studies* 24 (47): 57–91.

Kniffen, F. B. 1990. Cultural Diffusion and Landscape: Selections From Fred. B. Kniffen. *Geoscience and Man* 27: 1–77.

Le Bot, Y. 1995. *La Guerra en Tierras Mayas: Comunidad, Violencia y Modernidad en Guatemala (1970–1992)*. México: Fondo de Cultura Económica.

Lewis, P. 1983. Learing From Looking: Geographic and Other Writing about the American Cultural Landscape. *American Quarterly* 35: 242–261.

Lovell, W. G. 1990. Maya Survival in Ixíl Country, Guatemala. *Cultural Survival Quarterly* 14 (4): 10–12.

330 Matthew J. Taylor and Michael K. Steinberg

Lovell, W. G. 1995. *A Beauty That Hurts: Life and Death in Guatemala*. Toronto: Between the Lines.
Low, Setha M. 2000. *On the Plaza: The Politics of Public Space and Culture*. Austin: University of Texas Press.
Lowenthal, D. 1985. *The Past is a Foreign Country*. Cambridge, UK: Cambridge University Press.
Manz, B. 1988. *Refugees of a Hidden War: The Aftermath of Counterinsurgency in Guatemala*. Albany, NY: State University of New York Press.
Mathewson, K. M. 1984. *Irrigation Horticulture in Highland Guatemala: The Tablon System of Panajachel*. Boulder, CO.: Westview Press.
Montejo, V. 1987. *Testimony: Death of a Guatemalan Village*. Translated by Victor Perera. Willimantic, CN: Curbstone Press.
Montejo, V. 1992. *Brevisima Relación de la Continua Destruccíon del Mayab' (Guatemala)*. Providence, Rhode Island: Guatemala Scholars Network.
Moreno, G. S. 1998. *Guatemala: Contreinsurgencia o Contra el Pueblo?* Colección Gnarus, Spain.
Morrissey, J. A. 1978. *A Missionary Directed Resettlement Project Among the Highland Maya of Western Guatemala*. Ph.D. dissertation. Stanford University.
Nash, June. 2002. AAA delegate to Guatemala urges security for anthropologists. *Anthropology News, Newsletter of the American Anthropological Association* 43 (9): 22–23.
Nelson, D. M. 1999. *A Finger in the Wound: Body Politics in Quincentennial Guatemala*. Berkeley, CA: University of California Press.
Noack, C. 2001. Conmemoración de una massacre. *Debate* 10 (abril 2001): 14–15.
Nunca Más, 2000, Conmemoran segundo aniversario del asesinato de Monseñor Juan Gerardi. *Nunca Más: Asociación Familiares de Detenidos–Desaparecidos de Guatemala (FAMDEGUA)* 42: 10–14.
Payeras, M. 1996. *Asedio a la Utopía: Ensayos Políicos 1989–1994*. Guatemala: Luna y Sol.
Payeras, M. 1998. *Los Dias de la Selva*. Guatemala City: Editorial Piedra Santa.
Prensa Libre, 2001a. Chajul: Tierra de Nadie en Confrontación. July 2, Guatemala City, Guatemala: 1–3.
Prensa Libre, 2001b. Contra Genocidio. June 15, Guatemala City, Guatemala: 6.
Prensa Libre, 2001c. Las PAC Siguen Activas. June 30, Guatemala City, Guatemala: 8.
Primavera del Ixcán, 1999. *El Derecho Indigena de la Comunidad Primavera del Ixcán, Region Multiétnica de Ixcán*. Comunidad Primavera del Ixcán y Santa Maria Tzejá, Quiché, Guatemala.
REMHI (Recuperación de la Memoria Historica). 1998. *Nunca Mas*. Volume 1: Impactos de la Violencia. Oficina de Derechos Humanos del Arzobispado de Guatemala (ODHAG). Guatemala City, Guatemala.
Rosales, E. 2000. Erigirán monumentos a víctimas de massacre. *Siglo Veintiuno* 4 (December): 12.
Santino, Jack. 2001. *Signs of War and Peace: Social Conflict and the Use of Public Symbols in Northern Ireland*. New York: Palgrave.
Sauer, C. O. 1925. Morphology of Landscape. *University of California Publications in Geography* 2: 19–54.

Schirmer, J. 1998. *The Guatemalan Military Project: A Violence Called Democracy.* Philadelphia: University of Pennsylvania Press.

Secaira, E. 2000. *La Conservación de la Naturaleza, El Pueblo y Movimiento Maya, y la Espiritualidad en Guatemala: Implicaciones para Conservacionistas.* Guatemala.

Simon, J. M. 1988. *Guatemala: Eternal Spring, Eternal Tyranny.* New York: W.W. Norton and Co.

Smith, P. 2001. Memory Without History: Who Owns Guatemala's Past? *The Washington Quarterly* 24 (2): 59–72.

Stoll, D. 1993. *Between Two Armies in the Ixíl Towns of Guatemala.* New York: Columbia University Press.

Stoll, D. 2003. On the LASA President. *Lasa Forum* 33 (4): 20–22.

Till, K. E. 2003. Places of Memory, In *Companion to Political Geography*, ed. John Agnew, Kathyrne Mitchell, and Georid O'Tuathail. New York: Blackwell.

Till, K. E. 1999. Staging the Past: Landscape Designs, Cultural Identity, and Erinnerungspolitika at Berlin's Neue Wache. *Ecumene* 6 (3): 251–283.

Wilson, R. 1997. Comments on Hale's Consciousness, Violence, and the Politics of Memory in Guatemala. *Current Anthropology* 38 (5): 832–835.

Wilson R. 1998. *Verdades Violentas: las Politicas de Recordar el Pasado en Guatemala, in Guatemala 1983–1997 Hacia Dónde Va la Transición?* FLACSO, Guatemala, Debate 38.

Zur, J. 1998. *Violent Memories: Mayan War Widows in Guatemala.* Boulder, CO.: Westview Press.

Chapter 15

Trains of Workers, Trains of Death: Some Reflections after the March 11 Attacks in Madrid*

Cristina Sánchez-Carretero

"Dreams about nations produce monsters, why?
Trains of workers, trains of death,
We, Rumanians are close to Madridians, to Spaniards in these days of pain"

—Anonymous note placed in a column at Atocha
train station (3/18/04)

Madrid was transformed after March 11, 2004. The following day the streets were filled with massive numbers of mourning demonstrators. Since the day of the attack, spontaneous shrines had appeared in the train stations and other emblematic sites in Madrid. They blanketed sidewalks, platforms, squares, and subway corridors. Spontaneous gatherings and shrines flowered not only in Madrid but also in many cities throughout Spain as people mourned, memorialized, and prayed for the missing; and they also confronted the conservative Government headed by José María Aznar from the Partido Popular (PP). The Government had immediately blamed the Basque terrorist group ETA (Euskadi Ta Askatasuna ["Basque Homeland and Liberty"]) for the attacks. Finally, after two and a half days of evidence to the contrary, the government confirmed what had already been stated in international and nongovernmental by controlled media: the attack was perpetrated by Islamist terrorists. The voting public punished the government's apparently deliberate omission, manipulation, and distortion of information at the polling booths the following Sunday and, contrary to all predictions, the PP was not reelected. Civil society had confronted, reclaimed, and affirmed its right to accurate information from its elected officials.

The popular responses—the reactions of the people—after the attacks produced results that depended upon the use of powerful tools and the strategic mechanisms available as arts of resistance: e-mails and cellular text messages (SMS) were sent across Spain calling for a demonstration on Saturday, March 13, the day before the elections, in front of PP Headquarters.[1] These were reinforced by the writings at the shrines, and by slogans shouted at the demonstrations such as *"con los muertos no se juega"* (you cannot play with our dead people) *"con los muertos no se manipula"* (don't manipulate our deceased), *"antes de votar, queremos la verdad"* (before voting, we want the truth), *"¿quién ha sido? Europa ya lo sabe"* (who did this? Europe already knows it), *"mentirosos, mentirosos"* (liars, liars).

The spaces of civil sacralization[2] created after the attacks in Madrid follow the pattern of collective mourning after massacres, such as September 11, and deaths of emblematic personalities, such as Princess Diana,[3] but with their own particularities due to the political effects in terms of popular agency. The spontaneous shrines in Madrid are part of the political sphere developed after the attacks and cannot be understood outside the context of the general elections held three days after the train massacres (see figure 15.1).

On Friday, March 12, men and women took to the streets and cried together after the attacks in the train stations of Atocha, El Pozo, and Santa Eugenia (Madrid). Instead of staying at home, people used public spaces to express nation-wide solidarity with the victims. What does a folklorist do when a whole country steps out of its homes to voice its anger and express its grief via a morning parade of 11 million people? What is the role of the ethnologist—and scholars in general—in times of crisis? In a sense, this article is a modest answer to this question. I am presenting here an early work-in-progress on the spontaneous shrines built after the attacks at Madrid that took place on March 11. In particular, I will concentrate on the representation of various nationalities in the shrines, while presenting the research project developed at the Department of Anthropology at the Spanish Council for Scientific Research (CSIC) to document those shrines and the collective mourning after the attacks. After March 11, hundreds of shrines were placed at the train stations where the bombings took place. The following week a group of researchers from the CSIC sent out e-mails to anthropologists, folklorists, sociologists, and community-based workers asking for help in collecting various materials from the shrines, testimonies, e-mails related to the attack, and any other mourning-related materials.

Figure 15.1   A family lighting candles at the shrines in Atocha next to a banner used in the demonstration on Friday, March 12.[4]

Photo by: Cristina Sánchez-Carretero.

Of the three steps that are included in the formation of an archive (compiling, cataloguing and making it accessible to the public) we at CSIC are in the first one. At the time of this writing, May 2004, various collaborators have donated more than 2000 stills of the shrines (including poems, letters, candles, and various kinds of displays at the train stations) along with other artifacts: t-shirts sold at the shrines to collect money for the victims, stamps with black ribbons, and a collection of e-mails that were sent as mourning messages. Each photograph, tape, or artifact is accompanied by logs that document the context, content, and technical data (following the model used by the Folklife Center at the Library of Congress in Washington, DC). Barbara Kirshenblatt-Gimblett asks in her piece on September 11, "How do you collect a present that is already historical?" (2003: 17). Collecting and archiving pieces of the present that are ephemeral and, at the same time, are everywhere and are part of a consciousness that one is in a historic moment raises many difficulties that we are just starting to face: Which testimonies should be recorded? Which rumors? Should the political e-mails and SMSs that people sent and blocked computers and cellular phones on March 13, a day prior to the general elections in Madrid, be included in an archive of mourning?

The attacks on March 11 in Madrid consisted of a series of bombs that were placed on commuter trains: four bombs and four trains, all of them on the Alcalá-Madrid line. The first train left Alcalá at 7:00 in the morning, followed by the others at 7:05, 7:10 and 7:15 AM, during rush hour for commuters. The bombings took place between 7:36 and 7:39 AM in Santa Eugenia, El Pozo, and Atocha. In each train there were numerous explosions that killed a total of 191 people and injured more than 1900, one third of whom were foreigners. A police officer died a few days later.

Both the "when" of this attack (at 7 AM on a weekday) and the "where" (working-class residential areas outside Madrid) indicate that most of the people who traveled in those trains were workers: construction workers, waiters and waitresses, domestic workers, and some students. Fortunately, a university strike was held that day and the number of students traveling was much lower than on other days.

The shrines at the four epicenters (Atocha, El Pozo, Santa Eugenia, and Alcalá) displayed different characteristics regarding their structure. Atocha is one of the main train stations in Madrid and it had more and longer-standing shrines. Atocha is in fact a cosmopolitan train station. While Atocha's shrines can be considered ecumenical representations of a combination of tourists and daily commuters, the shrines in El Pozo, Santa Eugenia, and other train stations of the line, such as Alcalá, showed more personal links to the victims (see figure 15.2).

El Pozo, for instance, is a local neighborhood. The name "El Pozo" is synonymous with revolutionary uprisings and riots during Franco's dictatorship, poverty that nurtured communist and labor movements, and unpaved streets until the 1980s. At the beginning of the twenty-first century, it has a high number of housing projects with almost 10 percent of the residents immigrants primarily from Latin America and Eastern Europe (Madrid Datos 2004: 2)[5] (see figure 15.3).

Due to the different locations of the bombings, pilgrimage was one element of the mourning process. In the first weeks, visitors to the shrines went from one train station to another, producing a certain kind of pilgrimage. At the same time, there was an institutional pilgrimage by political representatives, religious figures, and other famous people, such as soccer teams. For instance, after the royal wedding between Prince Felipe and Letizia Ortiz, many international political figures stopped by the shrines to pay their respects. In addition to the spontaneous shrines, various institutionalized memorials are being constructed ("*El bosque de los ausentes*" in Atocha, a plaque in Sol dedicated to the public services that

337

Figure 15.2   Shrines at Atocha train station.
Photo by: Cristina Sánchez-Carretero.

Figure 15.3   Shrines at El Pozo train station.
Photo by: Cristina Sánchez-Carretero.

helped during those days, and a sculpture commissioned in memory of Antonio López to be placed in Atocha).[6]

However, those institutionalized memorials are different from the spontaneous shrines. I use the word "spontaneous," following Santino, "to indicate its unofficial nature and the word 'shrine' because these are more than memorials. They are places of communion between the dead and the living" (Santino, this volume). Some of the graffiti written at the train stations was, indeed, addressed directly to the deceased. In addition, there was also a spontaneous organization to keep the candles lit and the sites clean. For example, in El Pozo a group of women in their late fifties were taking care of the shrines. In Atocha, there were candles lit all night during the first few weeks. After a month, the cleaning services of the station took on the role of cleaning the empty containers of the candles.[7]

The shrines are used as a means for performing and initiating changes. They are mechanisms of agency. This last aspect is especially relevant in the case of the Madrid attacks because the aftermath of "11M" provoked radical political consequences. Participation, interpretation, and the possibility of opening up a space for a certain degree of agency point to the political nature of the spontaneous shrines. The shrines are, indeed, performative acts, that can cause or imply an action (see introduction to this volume by Jack Santino). The performance of agency via the shrines—and other communication devices such as SMSs and e-mails—enabled actual political change at the level of government and demonstrate the potential of noninstitutionalized or unofficial—but popular—cultural practices.

In addition to personal memorabilia, the banners used in the demonstrations against terrorism, and against the government for its deceptions, were also attached to the shrines (see figure 15.1). The demonstration against terrorism on Friday 12 had a general meaning of honoring the deceased in public (11 million people, out of a population of 40 million, participated in these demonstrations). The traditional moment of silence was interrupted by groups yelling: "*Ibamos todos en ese tren*" ("We all were in that train"). Other calls addressed the president of Spain, Aznar, asking for an explanation before the general election: "*Antes de votar, queremos la verdad*" ("Before we vote, we want the truth"). Along with the demonstrations, the shrines were also used as a political arena with clear effects on the elections of March 14, in which Aznar's party was not reelected. The walls of the train stations were used to voice ideas or reject those expressed by others. The capacity to invite participation and interpretation is due to the polysemy inherent in these assemblages (Santino 1986) and the multivocality over time, because the postings are responded to, adding—in a dialogic way—new meanings. Interestingly, the shrines, the demonstrations, and the writings all were parts of a popular response to the bombings. They registered sympathy and identification with the victims; outrage at the perpetrators; and outrage, also, at the Government, which had attempted to deceive the people.

One third of the 192 people murdered in the train bombings were immigrants and the shrines included a wide variety of offerings from people who identified themselves with their country of origin. Solidarity was constructed supporting Madrid and Spain. At the city level, it is possible to say, and imagine, "We are all Madrid" or "We were all in those trains." However, the level of the nation state is different and solidarity with "Spain" as a concept requires the conception of other nation states producing a separate but equal relationship. On the other hand, "Madrid" (representing the concrete locality) allows a total, mutual self-identification: "we all experience the same things, we all were subject of the same threats," "we are you," and, therefore, "We are all Madrid." The "We all were in those trains"—yelled at the demonstrations and repeated at the shrines—is also represented by the various nationalities that express their grieving in the shrines: for example, *Brasil es Madrileño* (Brazil is Madridian). While the nation states and different regions in Spain appear identified with Madrid, interestingly enough I couldn't find equivalent notes referring to Spain such as "We all are Spanish" but rather "We are *WITH* Spain," "We love Spain," or "We cry *FOR* Spain" (see figure 15.4).

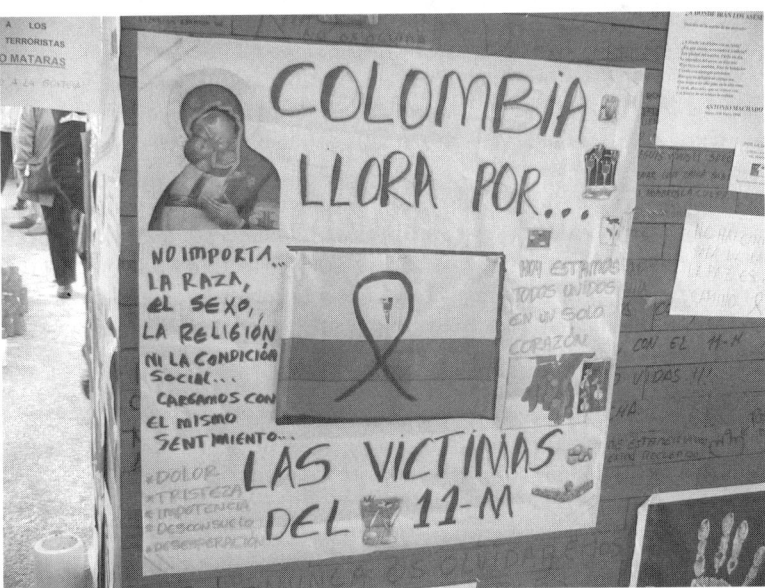

Figure 15.4   Colombia cries for the 11M victims.

Photo by: Cristina Sánchez-Carretero.

My thesis is that the conception of the nation state necessitates a solidarity that, in part, constructs the opposition to other nation states, reaffirming one's own national identity. Therefore, at the international level, identification is never complete because it entails its own opposition. The city, however, is an inclusive, experiential paradigm, allowing inhabitants to identify with others of different national background in terms of everyday life and experience: all the residents of Madrid, regardless of their backgrounds, ride the same trains.

In some of these notes, the nation is personified and the writer assumes the role of representing the nation state of origin: "Spain, Colombia cries with you," "Spain, Morocco is with your suffering, we're all victims of terrorism," "Chile is with you," "Spain, Ecuador cries with you," "Venezuela accompanies you in your crying," "Venezuela is with Spain, Peace in the World." Once again, the nation-to-nation relationship allows for a solidarity that, at the same time, acknowledges the difference. The construction of smaller-scale relationships (Madrid or the train itself) permits a communitas-relationship, a sense of feeling together because "we *ARE* you." However, the level of the nation state is different and the solidarity with "Spain" is expressed in terms of nation to nation. "Chile and Spain united for ever" says one of the drawings, which includes a Chilean flag that melts into the Spanish flag. "United forever" expresses the solidarity of Chileans and at the same time marks the difference in terms of equality: we are united as far as we continue being two different entities.

Some of the writings include an explanation of the solidarity: "Spain: Cubans are with you because your blood is our blood and your pain is also our pain." Other times, even the signature is the nation itself: "We cry with you, [signed] Hungary." On a very few cases, the writer of the note gives a detailed account of the group he or she decides to represent: "Cubans living in Madrid." A person addresses Spain as an individual: "Train me, give me a weapon and I'll give you my life, Spain, My dear country, where I saw my daughter being born. God save Spain! An Ecuadorian."

In some of the letters written by migrants, the narrator represents the entire collectivity of migrants:

> Ecuador. I'm an immigrant searching for a better future; just like many other immigrants who search for a better future and didn't get it, because there're men who don't know the meaning of peace. From this note I send my greetings to those affected [by the attack]

In other examples, the writer represents the "undocumented migrants":

> I'm an undocumented migrant but the pain has united all of us (. . .) sometimes I think, why is that I wasn't there [in the train] so my family could work

fearless, non-exploited, even if it's without me. Should we wait for another terrorist attack? Shameless! I will not write more. An Ecuadorian. Ana María.

A letter complaining about the policy regarding migration. The writer of this note complains to the government about their policy to give Spanish citizenship to those injured and the families of those who were killed. This measure tried to solve the difficult position of some of the families who were afraid of reclaiming the bodies of some of the victims due to their irregular situation concerning their visas.

Another note almost yells "Immigrants are NOT guilty" and somebody (a nonimmigrant) adds with a pen "they were also victims". A person from Morocco writes:

> All Moroccans are with the victims and their families. All of us are not the same. They are radical murderers, terrorists. We are a community of Muslim immigrants with big reasons against wars, against all kinds of terrorism, against absurd revenge. We are pacifists. We wish there were no borders, or colors, or languages or religions so the world can live in peace. I ask Madridians not to mistake us with them "the terrorists" and united we'll win. And no more death either in Madrid or in Iraq or in the Basque country . . . or in any other place in the earth. Say yes to Peace, no to war, kill terror.

The genres represented in the shrines include letters, poems, personal narratives, and drawings among others. Nevertheless, the most common one is the assemblage: mixtures of photographs, drawings, writings, and other artifacts such as toys, candles, and religious images. In addition, a variety of languages are employed (among others, Spanish, Arabic, Rumanian, Polish, Catalan, and Basque). El Pozo and Alcalá include more memorabilia to particular victims by their families and friends, with messages addressed to the victims, and, in some cases, to the murderers of the victims. I did not find differences in terms of how the grief is expressed depending on the country of origin, but there are some aesthetic differences between artifacts by people who knew the victims and general writings of condolences, and, therefore between the shrines in Atocha and the smaller train stations. Black ribbons and white palms are two common elements repeated in all the shrines and the demonstrations. The white palms stand for fighting terrorism with peace. It has become a national symbol in Spain in the fight against terrorism. A group of law students at the *Universidad Autónoma de Madrid* first adopted the gesture of painting the palms of their hands white or wearing white gloves to signify the hands of people who want peace, as opposed to the bloody hands of terrorists. The symbol started when Francisco Tomás y Valiente, a law professor, was murdered in 1992 by the ETA. In the demonstrations, everybody raised their palms painted in white as a way of saying "our hands are clean and will continue being clean because we fight without violence" (see figures 15.5 and 15.6).

Figure 15.5   White palms in Atocha.
Photo by: Cristina Sánchez-Carretero.

Figure 15.6   Black ribbon: "Sergio, 17 year old, why?"
Photo by: Cristina Sánchez-Carretero.

In those assemblages, snapshots are the elements that clearly differenti-
ate the offerings made by the people who knew personally the victims.
Photographs are umbilical cords—using Roland Barthes expression (1981:
80)—that link the body of the missing being to the gaze of the viewer. The
sensorial experience and the indexical quality of photographs make them
part of the collage of closeness and remembrance to those who had personal
ties with the deceased. At El Pozo, 10 days after the attacks, a woman was
rubbing a picture of her deceased relative against the walls carpeted with
notes, poems, and drawings, as if the physical contact of the picture with the
materiality of the shrines would penetrate into the photograph and touch
the loved being. At the same time, by mourning at the shrines we are
touched by the pieces of incomplete grief to make sense of our own suffering. The act of reading, gazing, or breathing the smoke of the candles makes
us incorporate into our bodies the shrines themselves.

Not only does the materiality of the shrines permit a corporeal response,
but so also do other media less tangible. In addition to spontaneous shrines
at the train stations, the Internet provided another medium for the production, participation, and dialogic interpretation of shrines. Many cybershrines take the shape of chats and forum[8]; others are built as memorial
sites[9] where visitors can contribute poems, photographs,[10] songs,[11]
comics,[12] or light their own virtual candles.[13]

Civil society appropriates new technologies to communicate, call a
demonstration, or mobilize. The flash-mob mobilization that took place via
SMSs, telephone calls, and e-mails on the evening of the general election
has been seen to play an essential role in the Spanish national election.[14]
The PP claimed that there was a conspiracy performed via SMSs; however,
more than 2,000,000 changed their votes unpredictably and only a few
thousands met that evening. Those in power forgot about the strategic,
peaceful weapons of resistance from below employed in Madrid (Scott
1990). SMSs were one more of the various ingredients of the collective
mourning after the attacks in Madrid that provoked this drastic change in
Spanish politics.

Another element in the performance of civil society that took place in
Madrid was poetry; an essential component of these shrines that sometimes are
signed, other times anonymous, and in many cases copied from well-known
poets (Antonio Machado, Miguel Hernández) and from singers (Joaquín
Sabina, Joan Manuel Serrat). Poetry becomes a portal "where the living and the
dead touch one another" (Zeitlin, this volume).[15]

I conclude with a poem by a resident of El Pozo—one of the few messages written in English—in which he expresses the new construction of a

Figure 15.7   Child's drawing.
Photo by: Cristina Sánchez-Carretero.

locality after the attacks; in particular, the locality is linked to the train station:

> How can someone feel an emotional
> connection with a commuter train
> station?
> The place where I get off the train and
> shuffle along on my way home with
> nameless other commuters.
> Today I feel no emotion with the grocery
> store I shop in, nor the news stand, nor
> any other place I pass by to and from
> work each day.
> But the train station is where I am
> going to, now on a Saturday to take a
> candle. Those people now have names I
> can look at on a list of the 67 who died
> here two days ago. People
> passing through our humble
> neighbourhood. Spanish and immigrant,
> young people, men, women, and children

on their way to work or school.
And that is how I have come to feel an
emotional attachment with a building of
steel and concrete. My train station in
My neighbourhood, is now a reminder of
the pain and suffering that terrorism
creates.

Notes

* I want to thank Jack Santino for his feedback on this paper. Jack Santino and Margaret Kruesi (Library of Congress) encouraged our research group to start an ethnographic archive after the attacks in Madrid and I want to thank them for their unconditional support.

1. Any kind of political demonstration is forbidden the day prior to the election. It's called "*Jornada de Reflexión*" (Reflection Day). It is against the law to show on TV—or any other media—any piece of information that might be considered a political campaign in order to allow individuals make their own decisions. Therefore, the demonstrations on Saturday 13 were considered illegal by the PP and by the "Junta Electoral Central."
2. Luis Miguel García Mora suggested to me that I use the Spanish expression "*espacios de la sacralidad civil.*"
3. Regarding the mourning of Diana see Walter (1999) and Kear and Steinberg (1999).
4. All the photographs included in this article were taken by Cristina Sánchez-Carretero and are part of the Archive of Mourning, Spanish Council for Scientific Research (CSIC). Research project funded by the Spanish Ministry of Science and Education (MEC: HUM 2005. 03496/ HIST) and the CSIC.
5. This percentage is taken from the municipal census, which includes both regularized and nonregularized population.
6. Regarding the immediacy to memorialize in these tragedies, Marita Sturken argues that in the face of absence, "especially an absence so violently and tragically wrought at the cost of so many lives, people feel a need to create a presence of some kind, and it may be for this reason that questions of memorialization have so quickly followed this event." The author asks herself: "What, we might ask, is behind this rush to memorialize and to speak of memorials? Could we imagine people talking of memorialization after the destruction of the Warsaw Ghetto, or the bombing of Hiroshima? Or, for that matter, that the people of Rwanda talked of memorialization after the massacres that killed hundreds of thousands there? Throughout history, collective and public memorialization has most commonly taken place with the distance of time. After wars have been declared over, towns, cities, and nations have built memorials to name the dead and those sacrificed" (Sturken 2004).
7. At the moment of writing this essay, representatives of the cleaning services asked the Atocha station officials to take the shrines out of the station for a double reason: with the beginning of the summer the heat and smell of the candles is

unbearable; and, second, they argue that the shrines make them think constantly of that day and they cannot perform their duties properly. The Spanish train service (RENFE) is preparing an online shrine to substitute the physical one: http://www.mascercanos.com

8. See for instance, http://www.elmundo.es/documentos/2004/03/espana/atentados11m/foros.html http://11m.cjb.net/;http://www.paz-digital.com/portal/modules.php?name=Sections&op=listarticles&secid=48 http://www.todo-linux.com/modules.php?name=News&file =article&sid=1676; http:// www.es.amnesty.org/11demarzo/index.php; http://foros.abc.es/cgi-local/forosabc/ultimatebb.cgi?ubb=get_topic;f=5;t=000432

9. See, for instance, http://www.madrid11demarzo.org; http://www.madrid11m.com; http://www.manosblancas.org/es/index.html; http://www.bastaya.org/actualidad/Atentado%20Atocha/Enlaces.htm. In addition, the sites produced by different newspapers include their own cybershrines: El País, Cadena Ser, and Canal +: http://www.cadenaser.com/comunes/2004/11m; El Mundo: http://www.elmundo.es/documentos/2004/03/espana/atentados11ml; Bitácoras: http://11demarzo.bitacoras.com/; Noticiasdot.com: http://www.noticiasdot.com/publicaciones/2004/especiales2004/0304/atentado.htm.

10. http://www.madridinmemoriam.com.

11. http://www.lacabramecanica.com/musica/silencio/silencio.htm.

12. http://dreamers.com/noviolencia; http://www.imakinarium.net/comic/11.3.4/index.htm.

13. http://enciendeunavela.wad-net.com.

14. The strategies of misinformation developed in those days have been the focus of various books speedily written. See, for instance Artal (2004) and Rodríguez (2004). Rodríguez includes copies of all the official documentation communicated to the press. See also Cardeñosa (2004).

15. The "Asociación de Vecinos del Pozo del Tío Raimundo" edited a collection of poems, letters, and drawings by children from El Pozo neighborhood (Asociación de Vecinos 2004). In addition, al least two collections of poems have been published (Jordá y Mateos 2004; VVAA 2004).

Bibliography

Artal, Rosa María. 2004. *11-M-14-M. Onda expansiva*. Madrid: Espejo de Tinta.

Asociación de Vecinos y Amigos del Pozo del Tío Raimundo. 2004. *Palabras para el recuerdo*. Madrid: Punto de Lectura.

Barthes, Roland. 1981. *Camera Lucida: Reflections on Photography*. New York: Hill and Wang.

Cardeñosa, Bruno. 2004. *11-M: Claves de una conspiración*. Espejo de Tinta.

Jordá, Eduardo y José Mateos (eds). 2004. *Madrid, once de marzo. Poemas para el recuerdo*. Madrid: Pre-Textos.

Kear, Adrian and Deborah Lynn Steinberg (eds). 1999. *Mourning Diana: Nation, Culture, and the Performance of Grief*. London: Routledge.

Kirshenblatt-Gimblett, Barbara. 2003. *Kodak Moments, Flashbulb Memories: Reflections on 9/11* [cited April 5, 2004]. Available from http://www.nyu. edu/classes/bkg/web

Madrid Datos. 2004. *Madrid Datos*. Madrid: Dirección General de Estadística. (cited June 3, 2004). Available from http://www.munimadrid.es/estadistica/ poblacion/ documentos/ext0401bol.pdf

Pablo, Francisco Minaya Ropero y Pilar Benito Sacristán. 2004. *11M: Homenaje a las víctimas*. Barcelona: Ediciones Martínez Roca.

Rodríguez, Pepe. 2004. *11-M. Mentira de Estado. Los tres días que acabaron con Aznar*. Barcelona: Ediciones B.

Santino, Jack. 1986. The Folk Assemblage of Autumn: Tradition and Creativity in Halloween Folk Art. In *Folk Art and Art Works*, ed. Vlach and Bronner, Logan, Utah: Utah State University Press, 151–169.

Scott, James C. 1990. *Domination and the Arts of Resistance: Hidden Transcripts*. New Haven: Yale University Press.

Sturken, Marita. 2004. *Memorializing Absence* (cited May 29, 2004). Available from http://www.ssrc.org/sept11/essays/sturken.htm.Torres

VVAA. 2004. *11-M: Poemas contra el olvido*. Madrid: Bartleby Editores.

Walter, Tony (ed.). 1999. *The Mourning for Diana*. New York: Oxford University Press.

Contributors

Ariel Dorfman is a writer whose imagination has been engaged with the great moral and political issues of our time, he is a Chilean expatriate who holds the Walter Hines Page Chair of Literature and Latin American Studies at Duke University. He has received numerous international awards, including the Sudamericana Award for a novel, the Laurence Olivier Award for Best Play ("Death and the Maiden," which has been made into a feature film by Roman Polanski), and two awards from the Kennedy Center. His books, written both in Spanish and English, have been translated into more than 30 languages and his plays staged in more than 100 countries. His novels include a reissued edition of *Widows, Konfidenz, The Nanny and the Iceberg, and Blake's Therapy*. Among his non-fiction works are *Exorcising Terror: The Incredible Unending Trial of General Augusto Pinochet, The Empire's Old Clothes* and his memoir, *Heading South, Looking North: A Bilingual Journey*. He has written a bilingual book of poetry, *In Case of Fire in a Foreign Land*, and a novel with his son, Joaquin Dorfman, *The Burning City*. His latest works are a Lowell Thomas Award-winning travel book, *Desert Memories: Journeys through the Chilean North* from National Geographic Directions, and a new book of essays, *Other Septembers, Many Americas: Selected Provocations, 1980–2004* from Seven Stories Press. His newest play "The Other Side" had its world premiere at the New National Theater in Tokyo, Japan in April 2004 and will open in New York in 2005 and London in 2006 with Sir Peter Hall directing. He also contributes regularly to the major newspapers of the world and is a member of L' Académie Universelle des Cultures in Paris and the American Academy of Arts & Sciences.

Cristina Sánchez-Carretero holds a Ph.D. in Folklore and Folklife from the University of Pennsylvania and is currently a researcher at the Spanish Council for Scientific Research (CSIC), Department of Anthropology (Madrid). She conducted fieldwork in the Dominican Republic and Spain, studying the role of narrating in the creation of locality and agency in the diaspora. She has coedited various books: together with Dorothy Noyes,

Performance, arte verbal y communicacón. Nuevas perspectivas en los estudios de folklore y cultura popular en USA (2000); with Luis Díaz et al., *Palabras para el pueblo.* Vols I and II. (2001); and with Jack Santino, *Holidays, Ritual, Festival, Celebration, and Public Display* (2003). She is currently conducting research on Afro-Dominican Religious Centers in Madrid and their function maintaining transnational families. Cristina Sánchez-Carretero is also the coordinator of an ethnographic archive that documents the spontaneous shrines and the collective mourning after the March 11 attacks in Madrid.

Diane E. Goldstein is Associate Professor of Folklore at Memorial University of Newfoundland and is cross-appointed to Memorial University's Faculty of Medicine. Her books include *Talking AIDS: Interdisciplinary Perspectives on Acquired Immune Deficiency Syndrome* (ISER Press, 1991) and *Once Upon A Virus: AIDS Legends and Vernacular Risk Perception* (Utah State University Press, 2004). She has published widely on cultural issues in health care, folk religion, supernatural folklore, narrative, and applied folklore. The piece in this volume is part of a larger collaboration with Diane Tye on topics related to expressions of grief in the landscape.

Diane Tye is an Associate Professor in the Department of Folklore, Memorial University, who works in a number of areas, including everyday autobiography, custom, and material culture. She specializes in forms of women's traditional culture and is coeditor with Pauline Greenhill of *Undisciplined Women: Tradition and Culture in Canada* (McGill-Queen's, 1997).

Harriet F. Senie has been director of museum studies and professor of art history at City College since 1986. She also teaches art history at the Graduate Center, City University of New York. In Fall 2000 she was visiting distinguished professor at Carnegie Mellon University. Prior to that (1982–1985) she was associate director of the Art Museum, Princeton University; and from 1978–1982, director of the Amelie Wallace Gallery and Assistant Professor of Art History at State University of New York, Old Westbury. She is the author of *The 'Tilted Arc' Controversy: Dangerous Precedent?* (2002), *Contemporary Public Sculpture* (1992), and coeditor of *Critical Issues in Public Art* (1992; 1998), as well as numerous articles and essays on public art, memorials, and audience response, including most recently "Reframing Public Art: Audience Use, Interpretation, and Appreciation," in Andrew McClellan, ed. *Art and Its Publics: Museum Studies at the Millennium.* She received her doctorate in art history from the Institute of Fine Arts in 1981; an MA in art history from Hunter College in 1978; and a BA in English and American Literature from Brandeis University in 1964.

Hege Westgaard has a post graduate degree in folklore from the University of Bergen, Norway, where she has worked as a lecturer. She has also worked in the drugs field as a consultant for the Bergen Clinics Foundation. In 2005 she returned to the University of Bergen on a Ph.D. scholarship.

Jack Santino is a professor of folklore and popular culture at Bowling Green State University. He has been President of the American Folklore Society and Editor of the Journal of American Folklore. He has published extensively in occupational folklore and more recently in rituals, festivals, and celebrations. He is the author of several scholarly articles, ethnographic films, and books, including *Signs of War and Peace: Social Conflict and the Public Use of Symbols in Northern Ireland* (Palgrave, 2001).

Jeannie B. Thomas is Associate Professor of English and Director of the Folklore Program at Utah State University. A former editor of Midwestern Folklore, Thomas is the author of *Naked Barbies, Warrior Joes, and Other Forms of Visible Gender* (University of Illinois Press, 2003) and *Featherless Chickens, Laughing Women and Serious Stories* (University Press of Virginia, 1997), which won the Elli Kongas-Maranda award for its contribution to gender studies. She researches and publishes articles on gender, legend, and humor.

Jonathan Lohman is the Director of the Virginia Folklife program, a public program of the Virginia Foundation for the Humanities. He earned an M.A. degree in Social Sciences from the University of Chicago and a Ph.D. in Folkore in Folklife from the University of Pennsylvaina. Dr. Lohman's academic work focuses on the public reception of murals and other forms of public art, and on the transatlantic celebration of Mardi Gras, of which he is dedicated participant. Dr. Lohman first became enamored with the latter topic as an elementary school teacher in New Orleans, Louisiana.

Maida Owens has been Director of the Folklife Program and the Crafts Marketing Program at the Louisiana Division of the Arts since 1986. She is a cultural anthropologist who has produced two video documentaries, edited the publication *Swapping Stories: Folktales from Louisiana*, directs the *Louisiana Voices* Folklife in Education Project, and produced the louisianafolklife.org and louisianavoices.org websites.

Margaret R. Yocom (Ph.D., English, University of Massachusetts, Amherst: 1980), a folklorist who specializes in family folklore, oral narrative, material culture, and gender studies, is an Associate Professor of English at George Mason University, Fairfax, Virginia. She has conducted fieldwork in her home Pennsylvania German culture as well as with the Inuit of northwestern Alaska and several Northern Virginia communities. Her major fieldsite is a

North Appalachian mountain community in Maine. She has published articles and photographs on ethnographic fieldwork, regional study, ethnopoetics, family folklore, gender, and material culture. Her most recent work includes " 'Awful Real': Dolls and Development in Rangeley, Maine" (1993), "The Yellow Ribboning of the USA: Contested Meanings in the Construction of a Political Symbol" (1996), and "Exuberance in Control: The Dialogue of Ideas in the Tales and Fan Towers of Woodsman William Richard of Phillips, Maine" in *Northeast Folklore: Essays in Honor of Edward D. Ives* (2000). She is the assistant editor of Ugiuvangmiut Quliapyuit: King Island Tales (1988); and in 1994, she edited and wrote *Logging in the Maine Woods: The Paintings of Alden Grant*. Her current project is a book on the traditional arts of the Richard family of Rangeley, Maine. Active in public sector folklore, she serves as folkorist at the Rangeley Lakes Region Logging Museum as well as consultant to various projects at the Smithsonian Institution, the NEA, and the Maine Arts Commission. She also serves on the boards of the American Folklore Society and the National Council for the Traditional Arts.

Matthew J. Taylor is an Assistant Professor of Geography at the University of Denver. He has conducted research in Guatemala for the last 10 years. During that time he has studied testimonial literature, the lives of returnes and residents who stayed in Guatemala and endured military rule, the impacts of international migration on rural Guatemalan lives and landscapes, and energy development in rural Guatemala. He continues to work among rural Guatemalans to better understand their survival strategies.

Michael K. Steinberg is currently an Adjunct Assistant Professor of geography at Louisiana State University and a cultural biogeographer with the USDA's National Plant Data Center. His research examines questions pertaining to agro-ecological diversity and genetic conservation; human impacts on forests; indigenous and ethnic minority cultures; endangered species; and political conflict and the environment.

Ralph Hartley, Ph.D., is an Archaeologist with the National Park Service, Department of the Interior. He assisted Physicians for Human Rights (United States) and the United Nations with forensic investigations in Rwanda and the former Yugoslavia during the 1990s.

Regina Marchi has the Ph.D. from the Department of Communication, University of California, San Diego. She researches and teaches in the areas of cultural studies and media studies, specializing in communication and culture, globalization, social movements and media, and communication strategies of marginalized groups. Her dissertation examined Day of the Dead celebrations in the United States is a form of vernacular media that communicate about Latino identity, contemporary political issues, and modernity.

Steve Zeitlin received his Ph.D. in Folklore from the University of Pennsylvania, and an M.A. in Literature from Bucknell University. He is the Director and cofounder of City Lore, an organization dedicated to the preservation of New York City's—and America's—living cultural heritage. Prior to arriving in New York, Steve Zeitlin served for eight years as a folklorist at the Smithsonian Institution in Washington, D.C. He has taught at George Washington University, American University, NYU, and Cooper Union. Steve Zeitlin has served as a regular commentator for the nationally syndicated radio shows, *Crossroads* and *Artbeat,* and currently develops segments on "The Poetry of Everyday Life" for *The Next Big Thing,* heard on National Public Radio. His commentaries have appeared on the Op Ed pages of the *New York Times* and *Newsday.* He also coproduces the storytelling series "American Talkers" for NPR's *Weekend Edition Sunday* and *Morning Edition.* He is the author and coauthor of a number of award winning books on America's folk culture including *A Celebration of American Family Folklore* (Pantheon Books, 1982); *The Grand Generation: Memory Mastery and Legacy* (University of Washington Press, 1987); *City Play* (Rutgers University Press, 1990); *Because God Loves Stories: An Anthology of Jewish Storytelling* (Simon & Schuster, 1997); and *Giving a Voice to Sorrow: Personal Responses to Death and Mourning* (Penguin-Putnam, 2001). His children's books include *While Standing One One Foot: Puzzle Stories and Wisdom Tales from Jewish Tradition* (Henry Holt, 1996); *Cow of No Color: Riddle Stories and Justice Tales from World Traditions* (Henry Holt, 1998); and a book on world cosmologies, *The Four Corners of the Sky* (Henry Holt, 2000). He is the author of a new volume of poetry, *I Hear America Singing in the Rain* (First Street Press, 2003).

Sylvia Grider is Associate Professor of Anthropology at Texas A&M University, where she teaches courses in material culture, folklore method and theory, anthropological ethics, and Texas cultural history. Following the fatal collapse of the student spirit bonfire at Texas A&M University in 1999, she organized and directed the Bonfire Memorabilia Project in order to collect and archive all of the artifacts that were left at the various spontaneous shrines that developed on campus. She has published scholarly articles about numerous folklore topics, including spontaneous shrines, as well as coediting two books on Texas literature, *Texas Women Writers: A Tradition of Their Own* (1997) and *Let's Hear It: Stories by Texas Women Writers* (2003).

Index

Abrahams, Roger, 9
AIDS, 1–2, 7, 207, 270, 273
Åkesson, Lynn, 150
Alfred P. Murrah Federal Building, *see*
    Oklahoma City Bombing
altars, 31, 263–5, 270–2, 276, 277
    see also Day of the Dead
Ariès, Philippe, 149–50, 171
Arlington National Cemetery, 44, 59,
    62, 69, 81, 85
    see also graves
art, 83, 193
    see also poetry, murals, grafitti
Austin, J. L., 1, 11
automobile accidents, *see* roadside
    memorials

Beau Geste, 241
    see also funerals
bonfire, *see* Texas A&M Bonfire
    Collapse
buildings as memorial symbols, 37, 42,
    50–1, 77–9, 110–12, 114

Catholicism, 13, 46, 184, 236, 239,
    262–263, 307, 310–12
cemeteries, *see* graves
children, 62–3, 223–4
Chile, 256–60
City Lore, *see* poetry
Columbine High School, 42
commemoration, 1, 7
consumerism, 36–8

crosses
    as generalized death symbol, 120
    at shrines, 11, 42, 60, 119, 121,
        123–38, 224, 242, 274,
        307–8, 311–12, 315–16

Day of the Dead, 31, 261–78
death, sudden, *see* drowning, genocide,
    roadside memorials, spontaneous
    shrines
definitional ceremonies, 9–10
Dewey, John, 85–6
Diana, *see* Princess Diana
Dissanayake, Ellen, 64
domestic violence, 8, 187–9
drowning, 233–52

evangelism, 322
Evans, Richard Paul, 32

Families are Victims Too, *see* murals
Featherstone, Mike, 169
fences as memorial sites, 34, 42, 48–9,
    50–1, 59, 61–4, 72–73, 81, 104,
    112, 219–22, 235
flower revolution, *see* Princess
    Diana
Foote, Kenneth, 48
fragments of meaning, 82–5
Freud, Sigmund, 205,
funerals, 8, 151–5, 157, 199
    and resistance, 239–40
    see also graves

genocide, 255–60, 276, 285–98, 316–19
Glassie, Henry, 208
globalization, 255, 259–60
Gorer, Geoffrey, 204
graffiti, 18, 23–25, 50, 180, 183–186, 315, 338
Gramsci, Antonio, 261
graves, 155, 229, 240–4, 262–3, 269–70, 276, 286, 309
   and African American tradition, 199–200
   for pets, 33–6
   relation to shrines, 138
   as shrines, 17–36
grief, 148
   as cultural expression, 148–72
   and protest, 51
   and regional differences, 120
   as secular memorials, 17–26
   and tourism, 36–7
Green, Malice, 41
greeting cards, 28–30
Grimes, Ronald, 9, 267
Ground Zero, see September 11
Guatemala, 305–25
Gullestad, Marianne, 164

Habermas, Jurgen, 13
Handeleman, Don, 9
Hass, Kristin, 200
hate crimes, 67
history texts as memorials, 309–10
   see also official memorials
Hodne, Bjarne, 163, 165
Homans, Peter, 205–6

illiteracy and printed memorials, 309–10
immigration, 273–6
Ireland, see Northern Ireland

Jones, Michael Owen, 64

King Olav, 147
Kinser, Samuel, 8–9

Kirshenblatt-Gimblett, Barbara, 335
Krepps, Karen, 199

Lyn, Maya, 46
   see also Vietnam Veterans Memorial

Madrid, see March 11 Attacks in Madrid
March 11 Attacks in Madrid, 333–45
Margalit, Avisha, 79–80
massacre, see genocide
media and spread of tradition, 12, 37, 47, 120, 151, 162, 236, 239, 242, 247, 272, 276
   see also technology and protest
memorials, see altars, graves, history texts as memorials, official memorials, roadside memorials, spontaneous shrines
metaphysically performative, 25, 36
Mexico, see Day of the Dead
Morrison, Jim, 17–22
Mourning Wall, see Oklahoma City Bombing
murals, 311–312
   as art, 186, 192–3
   as contested spaces, 194
   and domestic violence, 187–9
   and innocence, 182–3
   and intention of creators, 208–9
   as landscapes, 178, 196
   as objects of transition, 205–6
   and police violence, 41
   as preferred to gravesites, 197
   as warnings, 183–4
   see also art, graffiti, spontaneous shrines
murder, see domestic violence, genocide, murals, September 11
Myerhoff, Barbara, 9–10, 148

NAMES Quilt, see AIDS
NASA, 215
Newfoundland, 233–52

Northern Ireland, 13–14, 19, 22, 242
   see also ragwells
Norway, 147

official memorials, 26, 45–7, 60, 88,
   147, 312–14
Oklahoma City Bombing, 1, 12,
   32–3, 104

Palme, Olof, 147
Paris, memorials in, 17–26
Pentagon, 57–93
   see also September 11
performative commemoratives, 1,
   11–13, 16, 24, 36
performative utterances, 11
performativity, 1, 7
   see also commemoration
Philadelphia Mural Arts Program,
   see murals,
photographs
   as part of memorial, 48–9, 71–3, 343
   and protest, 255–260
pilgrimage, 14, 42, 60, 106, 336
plaques, 26–28
poetry, 34, 99–115
police brutality, 41, 45, 257
   see also genocide
politics, 13–15, 24–5, 28, 45, 51,
   75–6, 188, 209, 261–78,
   335–6
priests, murdered, 310–2
   see also Catholicism
Princess Diana, 7, 22–6, 41
   see also spontaneous shrines
protest, see politics
public ritual, 9

ragwells, 10–11; 13
rites
   of passage, 154–5, 168
   of public presentation, 9
rituals, 161–2
   the Church and, 157
   politics of, 271–8

shrines as, 148–52
   see also funerals, Day of the Dead
roadside memorials, 27, 150, 313
   composition of, 124–7, 152
   construction of, 121, 123–4
   geographic distribution of, 129–34
   longevity of, 134
   media influence on, 130–4
   negotiating space for, 121, 123–4,
      125, 136–7, 165
   relationship of graves to,
      119–20, 138
   see also crosses, spontaneous shrines
Rwanda, 289, 293–4
   see also genocide

Santino, Jack, 19, 21, 22, 24, 242–3,
   266, 338
September 11, 30, 47–51, 99–115,
   259
   see also World Trade Center,
      Pentagon, spontaneous shrines
Shaken Baby Syndrome, 32
South America, see Day of the Dead
Spain, see March 11 Attacks in Madrid
spontaneous shrines
   as communal altars, 31
   and communion with the dead, 14,
      23, 31, 57–93, 112, 154
   compared with state sponsored
      memorials, 308–19, 338
   as contested spaces, 80–1, 188–9,
      239–41
   and contributions by children,
      62–3, 223–4
   and contributions by non-nationals,
      78, 334, 339–45
   and generational differences of
      mourners, 158–9, 170
   as a genre of mourning, 2,
      148, 155–7
   as landscapes, 196, 208
   as memorials to innocence, 182–3
   for migrants, 274–6
   and negotiating placement, 234

spontaneous shrines—*continued*
and objects left at, 43, 57–93, 222,
224–9, 236–7, 341–3; *see also*
crosses
as pilgrimage sites, 14, 42, 60,
106, 336
as political, 13–15, 24–5, 28, 45,
51, 75–6, 188, 209, 261–78,
335–6
as "popular" or "folk" acts, 14
in post-conflict landscapes, 323–4
as public and private spaces, 25, 33
as related to gravesites, 27,
199–200, 240
as a response to sudden death, 7,11
as ritual, 3, 148
as shaped by media, 12, 37, 47, 120,
130–134, 151, 162, 236, 239,
242, 247, 272, 276
as transformed spaces, 27, 86–7,
161–2
as unique spaces, 215
from unintended markers, 319–23
for victims of genocide, 285–9,
290–8, 316–19; *see also*
genocide
as warnings to living, 14, 27, 183–4;
see also altars, graves, roadside
memorials
state memorials, *see* official memorials
Stewart, Susan, 84

technology and protest, 335–6
see also politics
terrorism, *see* September 11, March 11
Attacks in Madrid
Texas A&M Bonfire Collapse, 215–230
The Christmas Box (book), 32
Thompson, E.P., 261–2, 271
train bombings, *see* March 11 Attacks
in Madrid
Turner, Victor, 154
Twin Towers, *see* World Trade Center,
September 11

van Gennep, Arnold, 154
see also rites of passage
Vietnam Veterans Memorial, 43, 46–7,
200, 207, 229

Walls, Robert, 64
World Trade Center, 37, 47–51, 111–12
as symbol, 50, 76–9, 215–16
see also September 11
World War II, 22, 26–8, 46, 290–1,
293, 296

youth violence, 180
see also Columbine High School
Yugoslavia, 290–3
see also genocide

Ziehe, Thomas, 159–60